U.S. FOREIGN POLICY
AFTER THE
COLD WAR

A WASHINGTON QUARTERLY READER

U.S. FOREIGN POLICY
AFTER THE COLD WAR

Edited by
Brad Roberts

MIT Press
Cambridge, Massachusetts
London, England

With one exception, the contents of this book were first published in *The Washington Quarterly* (ISSN 0163–660X), a publication of The MIT Press under the sponsorship of The Center for Strategic and International Studies (CSIS). Except as otherwise noted, copyright in each article is owned jointly by the Massachusetts Institute of Technology and CSIS. No article may be reproduced in whole or in part except with the express written permission of The MIT Press.

Robert E. Hunter, "Starting at Zero: U.S. Foreign Policy for the 1990s," *TWQ* 15, No. 1 (Winter 1992); Robert A. Scalapino, "The Crisis of Leninism and the U.S. Response," *TWQ* 13, No. 4 (Autumn 1990); Hans Binnendijk, "The Emerging European Security Order," *TWQ* 14, No. 4 (Autumn 1991); Daniel Hamilton and James Clad, "Germany, Japan, and the False Glare of War," *TWQ* 14, No. 4 (Autumn 1991); Raymond Vernon, "The Japan–U.S. Bilateral Relationship: Its Role in the Global Economy," *TWQ* 13, No. 3 (Summer 1990); Jan Zielonka, "East Central Europe: Democracy in Retreat?" *TWQ* 14, No. 3 (Summer 1991); Richard E. Bissell, "Who Killed the Third World?" *TWQ* 13, No. 4 (Autumn 1990); Richard N. Haass, "Regional Order in the 1990s: The Challenge of the Middle East," *TWQ* 14, No. 1 (Winter 1991); Rodney W. Jones, "Old Quarrels and New Realities: Security in Southern Asia After the Cold War," *TWQ* 15, No. 1 (Winter 1992); William Perry, "In Search of a Latin America Policy: The Elusive Quest," *TWQ* 13, No. 2 (Spring 1990); David D. Newsom, "After the Cold War: U.S. Interest in Sub-Saharan Africa," *TWQ* 13, No. 1 (Winter 1990); James E. Goodby, "Can Arms Control Survive Peace?" *TWQ* 13, No. 4 (Autumn 1990); Paula L. Scalingi, "U.S. Intelligence in an Age of Uncertainty: Refocusing to Meet the Challenge," *TWQ* 15, No. 1 (Winter 1992); John W. Sewell, "Foreign Aid for a New World Order," *TWQ* 14, No. 3 (Summer 1991); Paul P. Blackburn, "The Post–Cold War Public Diplomacy of the United States," *TWQ* 15, No. 1 (Winter 1992); Ian Rowlands, "The Security Challenges of Global Environmental Change," *TWQ* 14, No. 1 (Winter 1991); Peter M. Ludlow, "The Future of the International Trading System," *TWQ* 12, No. 4 (Autumn 1989); Penelope Hartland-Thunberg, "A Capital-Starved New World Order: Geopolitical Implications of a Global Capital Shortage in the 1990s," *TWQ* 14, No. 4 (Autumn 1991); Gregory D. Foster et al., "Global Demographic Trends to the Year 2010: Implications for U.S. Security," *TWQ* 12, No. 2 (Spring 1989); Robert L. Rothstein, "Democracy, Conflict, and Development in the Third World," *TWQ* 14, No. 2 (Spring 1991); Brad Roberts, "Democracy and World Order," printed with permission from the *Fletcher Forum of World Affairs* 15, No. 2 (Summer 1991); Jay Winik, "The Quest for Bipartisanship: A New Beginning for a New World Order," *TWQ* 14, No. 4 (Autumn 1991); Robert A. Pastor, "Congress and U.S. Foreign Policy: Comparative Advantage or Disadvantage?" *TWQ* 14, No. 4 (Autumn 1991); George Weigel, "Exorcising Wilson's Ghost: Morality and Foreign Policy in America's Third Century," *TWQ* 10, No. 4 (Autumn 1987); Richard N. Gardner, "The Comeback of Liberal Internationalism," *TWQ* 13, No. 3 (Summer 1990).

Selection and introduction, copyright © 1992 by The Center for Strategic and International Studies and the Massachusetts Institute of Technology.

All rights reserved. No part of this book may be reproduced in any form or by any means, electronic or mechanical, including photocopying, recording, or by any information storage and retrieval system, without permission in writing from The MIT Press. For information, please address The MIT Press, Journals Department, 55 Hayward Street, Cambridge, MA 02142.

Library of Congress Cataloging-in-Publication Data

U.S. foreign policy after the Cold War / edited by Brad Roberts.
    p. cm.
  "A Washington quarterly reader."
  Includes bibliographical references.
  ISBN 0-262-18148-7. —ISBN 0-262-68074-2 (pbk.)
  1. United States—Foreign relations—1989– I. Roberts, Brad.
II. Washington quarterly.
JX1417.U17 1992
327.73′009′049—dc20   91-45374
                                                                                  CIP

Contents

vii Introduction
Brad Roberts

I. The United States in a New Era

3   Starting at Zero: U.S. Foreign Policy for the 1990s
Robert E. Hunter

19 The Crisis of Leninism and the U.S. Response
Robert A. Scalapino

II. Alliances Transformed

35 The Emerging European Security Order
Hans Binnendijk

51 Germany, Japan, and the False Glare of War
Daniel Hamilton and James Clad

63 The Japan–U.S. Bilateral Relationship: Its Role in the Global Economy
Raymond Vernon

III. Regional Policies

77 East Central Europe: Democracy in Retreat?
Jan Zielonka

91 Who Killed the Third World?
Richard E. Bissell

101 Regional Order in the 1990s: The Challenge of the Middle East
Richard N. Haass

109 Old Quarrels and New Realities: Security in Southern Asia After the Cold War
Rodney W. Jones

133 In Search of a Latin America Policy: The Elusive Quest
William Perry

143 After the Cold War: U.S. Interest in Sub-Saharan Africa
David D. Newsom

IV. Updating Policy Instruments

161 Can Arms Control Survive Peace?
James E. Goodby

171 U.S. Intelligence in an Age of Uncertainty: Refocusing to Meet the Challenge
Paula L. Scalingi

181 Foreign Aid for a New World Order
John W. Sewell

193 The Post–Cold War Public Diplomacy of the United States
Paul P. Blackburn

V. A More Complex Agenda

207 The Security Challenges of Global Environmental Change
Ian Rowlands

223 The Future of the International Trading System
Peter M. Ludlow

237 A Capital-Starved New World Order: Geopolitical Implications of a Global Capital Shortage in the 1990s
Penelope Hartland-Thunberg

251 Global Demographic Trends to the Year 2010: Implications for U.S. Security
Gregory D. Foster et al.

271 Democracy, Conflict, and Development in the Third World
Robert L. Rothstein

293 Democracy and World Order
Brad Roberts

VI. Domestic Politics and U.S. Leadership

311 The Quest for Bipartisanship: A New Beginning for a New World Order
Jay Winik

327 Congress and U.S. Foreign Policy: Comparative Advantage or Disadvantage?
Robert A. Pastor

341 Exorcising Wilson's Ghost: Morality and Foreign Policy in America's Third Century
George Weigel

351 The Comeback of Liberal Internationalism
Richard N. Gardner

Introduction

PROFOUND IS ARGUABLY the one word best suited to capture the significance of international events of recent years. The word conveys a sense of both their intense drama and the far-reaching, absolute character of the changes they have wrought. Between the breaching of the Berlin Wall in November 1989 and Iraq's expulsion from Kuwait in February 1991, a global era ended. The collapse of the central Soviet state, the disappearance of the Warsaw Pact, and the end of the Cold War are milestones in this historic shift. They represent the triumphant culmination of decades of consistent effort by the United States and its allies. As such, they are endings, not beginnings. It is too simple, of course, to suggest that the U.S. world role has been defined solely by bipolar confrontation—indeed, the United States has had many political, economic, and security concerns abroad related only tangentially to competition with the Soviet Union of which the 1991 war in the Persian Gulf is but one example. But they have been largely secondary to the East–West conflict. An era has ended, and decisively so.

Not only has an era passed but also a way of thinking. Profound international events have raised questions at the very heart of our understanding of international politics. America's place in the world is no longer clear. Old thinking will not suffice. The United States cannot simply carry forward the strategies, policies, and concepts of the past into a quite different future. It must find some new thinking of its own (as a kind of parallel to the "new thinking" of Mikhail Gorbachev) if it is going to use its resources wisely on the world scene in the years ahead for its own benefit and the greater good.

The specific intellectual agenda within the debate about U.S. foreign policy after the Cold War is defined by three challenges. The first is to evaluate how long-standing policy priorities and instruments carry over into the new era. The second is to identify new foreign policy issues that have emerged in the shadow or wake of the Cold War. The third is to pose the larger, transcendental questions about what the United States stands for in the world and what we want to accomplish as a nation. Without answers to these questions, the evaluation of priorities and policies is sterile and impractical. Not since the late 1940s has the policy research community faced so all-encompassing a task.

The student of international affairs and the policy practitioner do not have many tools available to them with which to meet these challenges. The daily media provide an abundant, indeed perhaps overwhelming, flow of information and opinion about events but very little analysis. Books, on the other hand, which digest events and put them in long-term perspective, are necessarily slow to appear. In between

Introduction

are journals. Especially in this time of rapid change, they have become the premier medium for the presentation of serious analysis and discourse about it. More than any other medium, they have stimulated debates about contemporary events and their implications for policy. They enjoy an additional advantage over books in that they keep their readers abreast of intellectual developments in a variety of issues and disciplines.

As the contents of this volume demonstrate, *The Washington Quarterly* has tackled the three challenges directly. Founded in 1977 as *The Washington Quarterly Review of Strategic and International Studies*, the journal quickly adopted a shorter name, although one less indicative of its contents. Published by the press of the Massachusetts Institute of Technology for the Center for Strategic and International Studies, it has emerged as one of the world's top periodicals in the international affairs field. Its purview is broad, ranging across the full set of political, economic, and security topics related to the international engagement of the United States. But its focus is policy and the way in which analysis of international events must be translated into policy choices and actions. Free of the need to sustain any particular worldview, it has enjoyed the latitude to take risks on new authors, many from overseas, and new ideas, many not accepted within the "establishment" or by its liberal critics, in the name of intellectual curiosity and policy creativity. Its contributors are professionally, politically, and geographically diverse. This volume, for example, includes contributors from both major political parties, both the executive and legislative branches of government, a variety of research institutions in Washington and elsewhere, including overseas institutes, and a number of the nation's leading universities.

The importance of generating new thinking in the research community is testified to by the difficulty of doing so. Unsolicited manuscript submissions usually stream into most editorial offices, but with the accelerating events of late 1989, they tapered off dramatically. The rapid pace of change was the culprit at first, but then the increasing scope of change simply eclipsed the expertise of a broad cross section of academics, policymakers, and others interested in world affairs. The ability of the research community to respond with innovative thinking and fresh policy prescriptions has proven to be significantly impaired by professional specialization and institutional compartmentalization. Only a few authors have been able to broaden their expertise, experiment with new methodologies, tackle new issues with authority, or see that thing most prized by editors but impossible to define— the big picture. Hence a strong emphasis in the editorial policies of *The Washington Quarterly* on the commissioning of essays, in order to draw in these authors and their rigorous, provocative analyses.

This volume represents a selection of *TWQ* articles most closely related to the debate about U.S. foreign policy after the Cold War. A companion volume, entitled *The United States in an Uncertain World*, will be available later in 1992 on the defense and security policy agenda after the Cold War. Articles have been selected for their salience in the continuing debate, even if some part of their argument may have been overtaken by events. This is most obvious in places where there is a discussion of the now apparently defunct Soviet Union or of the Middle East prior to the Persian Gulf War. This is of course an unavoidable dilemma in these rapidly changing times, but the core arguments and basic contextual references in each article endure beyond these vagaries. The editor recognizes that a generous new crop of intellectual capital does not spring forth without some reaping of early crops, sowing of new ones, and continuous tilling of the soil. If articles turn out in hindsight not to be definitive pronouncements on given subjects, each certainly sets down important markers for the debate ahead. Authors have not been asked to update their arguments. Biographical data on each author are current to late autumn 1991 and may have changed from the time of original publication. The views expressed in each article are those of the authors and should not be attributed to any institutions with which they may be or have been affiliated.

Chapter I includes two essays that define the new era and the United States role in it. The opening essay, the most recent in the volume and written after the failed August 1991 putsch in Moscow, sets aside traditional arguments about U.S. interests overseas and defines a new foreign policy by "starting at zero." The other article is a bit dated but offers a thorough review of the global fate of communism and of the implications for the United States.

Chapter II addresses questions related to the future of U.S. alliances with Europe and Japan, with full attention to the economic and political as well as the security dimensions. The importance of the Persian Gulf War of 1991 in framing the different leadership capacities and interests of the allies is also discussed.

Chapter III focuses on regional issues in U.S. foreign policy. The first two essays examine respectively the fate of democracy in formerly Communist Eastern Europe and the fate of the erstwhile Third World in a post–cold war era. The article on the Middle East appeared before the Persian Gulf War, but its basic arguments about the perils of proliferation and the challenges to U.S. leadership remain unchanged. Remaining articles focus on South Asia, Latin America, and Africa; each evaluates the implications of the end of the Cold War for U.S. interests in the region, including especially the ability of the United States to sustain commitments there.

Chapter IV reviews key foreign policy instruments in the light of changing needs. What are the continuing roles of arms-control agreements, the intelligence community, foreign aid, and public diplomacy mechanisms in a post–cold war era?

Chapter V assesses new elements of the more complex foreign policy agenda of the 1990s. Two essays examine the implications of global environmental change and demographics for U.S. interests. Two essays on trade and finance represent an attempt to introduce to the foreign policy community key problems of economics, which are emerging in the 1990s as more relevant to traditional national interests than formerly. Two essays, including one by the editor that appeared in another journal, evaluate the movement toward democracy in world politics and the outlines of a U.S. foreign policy designed to promote democracy.

The final, closing chapter returns to some of the oldest themes in the debate about the world role of the United States. One is divided government and the question of whether it is a strength or weakness in the pursuit of effective U.S. leadership, especially in pursuit of a new world order. Another is the moral underpinnings of the U.S. foreign policy debate and the nation's capacity to articulate a new world role at a time of declining domestic consensus. The volume closes with an essay about liberal internationalism and the domestic politics of the nation's world role.

The editor wishes to express his gratitude to his colleagues at CSIS and MIT for their partnership in producing the journal, with special thanks to those whose labors have been especially critical to the final products—managing editors Yoma Ullman, Linda Crowl, and Teresa Smith, assistant editors Lynn Northcutt de Vega and Melinda Amberg, and cochairmen of the editorial board Stanton Burnett and Walter Laqueur. A final word of thanks is due the authors, whose work we have only helped to stimulate, focus, or collect. To them goes the credit of putting in place the foundations of a new debate about U.S. foreign policy after the Cold War.

Brad Roberts
Washington, D.C.
November 15, 1991

I. The United States in a New Era

Starting at Zero: U.S. Foreign Policy for the 1990s

Robert E. Hunter

FOR THE FIRST time in more than four decades, the United States is faced with basic choices and decisions in foreign policy. It cannot escape a root-and-branch reassessment of its role and purpose, both at home and abroad. Following nearly half a century during which habits of acting in the world have become firmly set, the tools of critical analysis have tended to atrophy. The willingness and ability of the nation to make major readjustments have not been tested since the end of World War II and the onset of the Cold War. Factors are coming into play that have not been evident before. New circumstances will confront the nation. And foreign and domestic interests and policies are beginning to interact in novel ways.

In late 1991, the United States is engaged in a significant psychological withdrawal from the outside world of unclear dimensions and duration. A war in the Persian Gulf produces an astounding victory, but within days of cease-fire the American people set aside concerns about the region and let it return to obscurity. Yugoslavia dissolves in civil war without a major intervention by the United States, not even as peacemaker, as U.S. leaders see the Yugoslav future to be basically an "internal matter." U.S. troops in Europe are reduced substantially with little remark in the media, and once-vital issues relating to nuclear weapons are passed over with scant comment or attention. In the Philippines, the U.S. Clark air base is removed by an act of God and the Subic Bay naval base is removed by an act of the Philippine Senate, yet there is no wringing of hands in the Pentagon or on Capitol Hill. Meanwhile, the American people are mesmerized as the Soviet Union, for so long the vaunted rival of the United States, falls apart; but they soon turn their attention to the next drama being played out elsewhere.

There are calls for the United States to withdraw from the outside world, for America to fold its tents and steal silently away, to celebrate victory—in the Cold War, in the Persian Gulf—then, like Cincinnatus two millennia ago, to return metaphorically to the plow. These calls come amid rediscovery of a pressing agenda in the United States and of efforts deferred: in health and education, infrastructure and investment, drugs and crime, the inner cities and the environment. This agenda must now come first, it is argued, while the rest of the world takes care of itself, without benefit of U.S. leadership, intervention, and, in some cases, even interest.

Robert E. Hunter is vice president for regional programs and director of European Studies at the Center for Strategic and International Studies.

Except for challenges from a handful of observers who have little understanding either of the United States or of the outside world, calls for U.S. withdrawal are not harbingers of a new isolationism, like that which ultimately was so threatening to U.S. interests between World War I and World War II. That earlier turning away from the world was an active policy that flew in the face of the facts about America's situation; this one is more passive and, up to a point, is a valid response to recent events.

The twin ideas of withdrawal and turning inward are not unnatural to the American experience. In a profound sense the era just concluded has been the aberration. The classic American way of making war has been to see the threat, engage the enemy, enter the breach, win the victory, and then return to business as usual. The Persian Gulf victory demonstrated that the Korean and Vietnam wars represented exceptions, not the rule: Indeed, two wars ended on February 28, 1991, the one then in progress and the other that had tortured the nation since the August 1964 episode in the Tonkin Gulf. The Cold War itself was part of this pattern of irregular U.S. experience, unlike the great world wars of this century that yielded to clear-cut victories in periods of less than half a decade each. Yet the Cold War, too, has now followed the classic pattern, resulting, like its predecessors, in victory for the United States.

On the morrow of this triumph, it is already possible to assess many of the most salient results of an era's passing. During the last few years, the Soviet Union has been engaged in nothing less than a strategic retreat as profound as any carried out in peacetime history. It has disgorged all the physical fruits in Europe of its success in the Great Patriotic War. It has dismantled all but a handful of outposts of its external empire and even aided the United States (and allies) in mounting a military venture against a former Soviet client state, Iraq. That venture not only led to Iraq's crushing defeat but also seemed to demonstrate to the world that the United States towered over the Soviet Union in a principal, classic coin of national power—the ability to produce weapons that work.

Even more stunning has been the progressive dissolution of the Soviet Union and, in the process, of the capacity either of the center or of key republics to mobilize military power (still in being) for purposes of intimidating or attacking other countries. Thus the Soviet Union has given up not just external position but also much if not most of its internal capacity to deviate from its new course, at least for many years to come. Soviet retreat is proving to be not just tactical or strategic, but also elemental, removing the Soviet Union and all of its republics from the ranks of major powers for the foreseeable future.

Nor is change in the basic constituents of global power limited to geostrategic factors and concerns. What has happened in the Soviet Union and its external empire is also being widely read as a triumph for two basic tenets of Western power and position: the market economy and the pluralistic society. The Cold War, in fact, was a three-part struggle, only one element of which was a classic confrontation between two opposing great powers. Ideology also played a critical role, in two broad dimensions, economic and political. Here, too, the West is acknowledged to have prevailed, at least for the foreseeable future and in those countries in the Northern Hemisphere that were the primary focus of the most intense aspects of cold war competition in its many guises.

New Thinking

The aftermath of the Cold War is thus different from and more profound than the aftermath of the two world wars. Gone, in particular, is a set of paradigms or unifying themes that extended far beyond U.S.–Soviet relations to shape U.S. thinking about virtually everything happening abroad and about much U.S. policy at home. Of course, some parts of the globe were insulated from concerns about the Cold War, and most domestic debate made no reference to it. But the basic framework of foreign policy was still set by this overall paradigm—countries and regions might be excepted, but that was a conscious act. Whether directly or indirectly, domestic matters were also often swept up in cold war concerns; this was certainly true whenever the allocation of national resources was at issue. Even the great national trauma of Vietnam was, from the standpoint of strategy and U.S. commitment, a tactical matter—that is, whether the prosecution of the war contributed to or detracted from the central purpose of containing the Soviet Union. Few critics of the war, arguing from strategic grounds, also challenged the existence of the Cold War or the settled question of containing the Soviet Union; at most, they argued either that the conduct of the war detracted from that central purpose, that it might provoke cold war–related losses elsewhere, or that it was simply irrelevant and thus should be judged by non–cold war criteria.

There were, in fact, three paradigms—and three paradigms only—for U.S. policy during the Cold War, one of which has been alluded to in the preceding paragraph: containing the Soviet Union. The other two were as simply stated—containing the spread of communism (whether or not directly related to the increase of Soviet power and position), and promoting a growing, global economy under U.S. leadership. During the Cold War, the great bulk of U.S. concerns and attitudes about the outside world and America's place in it could be organized and explained in terms of these three paradigms. They made for as close to a unified field theory of foreign policy (including domestic components) as any nation has ever had.

One of these three paradigms, containing the Soviet Union, has now become irrelevant; a second, containing the spread of communism, has so diminished in significance as to be important only to the extent that communism still motivates China's and North Korea's behavior; and even the third, a growing, global economy under U.S. leadership, has altered in significance. This is not to say that key elements of the paradigms can be dismissed altogether. The Russian Republic and whatever replaces the Soviet Union can be expected to play major roles on the global scene at some point in the future. For all practical purposes, communism may be dead, certainly as a rallying point for discontents in different parts of the world, but the historic struggle between competitive visions of production versus distribution is far from resolved; indeed, it is likely to intensify in what we have called the Third World. And management of a growing, global economy is still critical, not just for the United States but also for other states, although questions of U.S. leadership and the degree of U.S. engagement in that economy are subject to debate and revision.

Deriving from this experience is the first cardinal lesson for the United States in the post–cold war era: There will be no encompassing paradigm of thought and action to rival those that dominated the past 40 years. This is not a trivial point. Even if new threats or unifying opportunities emerge—from rising tensions with either Japan or the Islamic world on the one hand to global concerns about the future of the environment on the other—none is likely to offer the simplicities of explanation or spurs to action in so many areas of U.S. activity in so many parts of the world. As desirable as it would be to garner global commitment to act on pressing realities like poverty and pollution, this will not happen to the degree that the Western world mobilized in the Cold War. In two words, America's future approach to the world will be far more *decentralized* and *disaggregated* than has been true for half a century. Diversity, not unity, will mark both intellectual and political apprehension of the outside world and America's role in it.

Despite the added complexities and uncertainties produced by a flight from simplicity, this conclusion should not be regretted. A unified field theory for U.S. policy and action at home and abroad was a product more of necessity than of design. The Soviet Union was a competitor geostrategically of near-equal proportions; certainly it passed the same threshold as the United States in having the capacity to cause almost limitless destruction if not also to project power to distant parts of the globe. It was an "enemy," but one with nuclear weapons, which fact meant that it had in major respects to be tolerated, not eliminated like Nazi Germany or Imperial Japan. Its political ideology was a potent competitor in third world areas that, in particular, were rejecting the legacy of Western colonialism, and it was imposed through military power on captive societies, aided and abetted by Western analysts who proved flat wrong in discounting the resilience of resistance to tyranny. And the United States developed an instrumental role in an economy of global scope because, in the late 1940s, no other nation had the resources or the will to foster widespread economic growth. This course was important to back up Western efforts in the struggle with Soviet power and ideas, whether in Europe, Japan, or contested third world areas. And the major economic benefits conferred on the United States by this role helped generate the underpinning of popular support needed for the nation to assume a deeply engaged, committed role abroad.

Power and Position

At this moment of rupture with the past, it is critical for the American people and their leaders to be clear-sighted about the United States' situation, the challenges it faces, and the methods and tools it either has or must develop to accomplish those tasks that lie ahead. Today, it is obvious that the nation no longer needs to devote the same level of resources to military defense, that the balance between military and other instruments of national power must be readjusted, that the pattern of engagements of the past 40 years will not suffice for the future, that foreign policies must be rigorously measured against competing domestic requirements and possibilities, and that there must be new, compelling reasons to enlist the engagement of the American people in the outside world. Habit may dictate one set of policies, interests may dictate a quite different set—and it will not be possible to get from one to the other without fresh analysis, unblinkered by adherence to outdated prejudice, bureaucratic inertia, or intellectual laziness. In the post–cold war era, the United States needs a zero-based foreign policy, in which each element must justify its relevance and importance anew or be discarded in favor of another course that is more pertinent to the future, whether that course emphasizes continued involvement in different parts of the world or a greater detachment in order to master problems and needs at home.

In creating such a zero-based foreign policy, the starting point must be a strategic reassessment. There is no doubt that the United States and its partners won the Cold War, although Western leaders mute that point out of concern to avoid repeating with the Soviet Union the post–World War I experience in stigmatizing Germany. Less evident is the fact that the United States emerged from the Cold War, as from the two great hot wars of this century, not only as the world's most powerful nation according to classical calculations—this time the sole surviving superpower—but also relatively better positioned overall than any other major nation. It is a continent-sized country with a thriving economy that still produces nearly one-quarter of the world's goods and services (the historic norm of the late nineteenth and twentieth centuries); it is a vast storehouse of natural and human resources, tied to an economy that is highly productive if no longer keeping pace with some others; it is an undivided nation with a high degree of civil peace and a functioning government; and it is now recovering another quality, once lost, that is of inestimable value: the psychological sanctuary provided by two broad oceans, which was breached during the 1950s by the direct and unprecedented threat to the nation posed by Soviet strategic nuclear bombers and then intercontinental ballistic missiles.

Equally important as this statement about relative U.S. advantage is a statement about absolutes: the perception that, in the wake of the Cold War, the United States has no natural enemies. This perception has been underscored by the victory in the Persian Gulf War, which set the seal on the Cold War and its practices and preoccupations. There is, in fact, in the immediate offing no other apparent source of military threat to major U.S. interests, anywhere in the world. That will continue to be so in the absence of three possible developments: the renewed overarming of potential adversaries, which remains possible, even likely, in the Middle East with its risk of radical changes in regimes; a last-gasp aggression by a dying North Korean regime; or military actions by either the Soviet Union (Russia) or China, even though such actions would be at direct variance with these countries' compelling interests in gaining access to the global economy and Western support for economic transformation.

If this perception of U.S. security is accurate—and it is not easy to construct a case, covering at least the next several years, that would confound it—then it is also clear that today the United States has a greater range of geostrategic choice than it has had since the beginning of the Cold War and in fact since before Pearl Harbor. No doubt, the United States will want to maintain significant military forces for reasons that include guarding against unexpected but not inconceivable threats in the Middle East. No doubt, their presence at some reduced levels both on land in Europe and at sea in the Western Pacific will have considerable value, both as insurance, especially in Europe, against untoward events in the Soviet Union, and as general reassurance for many countries in the Far East. Neither the North Atlantic Treaty Organization (NATO) nor U.S. bilateral pacts with allies like Japan should become obsolete so long as the Soviet future is indeterminate. But the United States does now have latitude to decide, to a degree it has not known since it emerged full-blown upon the world stage, where to be engaged abroad and where to keep its distance.

A Geoeconomic Future

The expanding range of U.S. geostrategic choice can, of course, also be used to argue that, at least for now, the United States can lessen its engagement abroad, certainly in military terms, and that it can instead attend more to issues and challenges at home. At first look, this argument seems to be supported by two other profound developments: the progressive shift away from military instruments of foreign policy in shaping the global future, and the continuing rise in the importance of economic instruments and issues. These changes are especially relevant to a world that appears to be safe for the foreseeable future from catastrophic global war, although not from the possibility of limited regional conflicts.

Thus, as the basic East–West confrontation dissolves and the Persian Gulf War writes *finis* to an era of world affairs, there is new clarity to the importance of economic strength and practice for the shaping and conduct of global politics. The promise of the Single European Act for the European Community, the steady rise of Japan's economy and its tentative forays beyond an insular politics, and new pockets of economic prosperity and power—especially in the newly industrializing economies of East Asia—all help define an era no longer dominated either by the struggle of the past 40 years or the military instruments that were so central to its conduct.

In this world, however, the United States does not have the comparative advantage that it had before, despite its unchallenged status as strategic superpower and its overall economic potential. Already, economic bargaining across both the Atlantic and the Pacific oceans has lost a key ingredient: the special weight in the scales, favoring the U.S. position, that was for so long provided by America's once-leading export, security. Thus the two-way street in transatlantic defense trade has ceased to favor the United States, the Uruguay Round of the General Agreement on Tariffs and Trade (GATT) negotiations is not assured success on the basis of U.S. pressure to gain concessions on agriculture from the European Community, and earlier this year the United States was hard-pressed to gain contributions from allies for its efforts in the Persian Gulf.

Victory in the Persian Gulf underscored the shift from the old to the new eras by reducing Iraq's military potential and leaving the United States the preeminent outside power in the region—the region that for many years has produced most disruption in the broader security interests of the United States and other industrial countries in major part because of its precious commodity, oil. Ironically, with the elimination of the only currently extant regional threat, with the withdrawal of the Soviet Union from regional competition, and with the resulting sea change in Syria, even the military dimension of securing this most basic of economic interests has been dramatically reduced.

Indeed, U.S. success at military

containment and force of arms has produced a paradox of preeminence: its capacity to meet military challenges is unrivaled, but in the process of achieving that status it has reduced the relevance of these instruments in shaping the future of global politics. This is clearly a blessing, but it also exposes the United States as being less than well prepared to confront the world that its past policies and actions have helped make possible.

America's relatively weak position geoeconomically as opposed to geopolitically is made evident by several factors, including a widespread global dispersion of several key components of power and influence: human and technological resources, exportable capital, the efficient production of modern goods, influence over global economic decision making, and the will to mobilize economic capacity for national ends. The U.S. economy's nearly one-quarter of world output is still unmatched, but that fact confers upon the United States far less significant advantage over other countries than the one it enjoyed when the world was dominated by geostrategic issues and instruments.

Furthermore, the United States has an evident insufficiency of economic tools for influencing global economic decision making, for affecting the political behavior of other nations, or for shaping the global political–economic environment. Most obvious are the large and swelling U.S. trade deficits, which, within a decade, transformed the United States from being the world's largest creditor nation to being its largest debtor. The political leverage derived from its being a large net capital exporter has been vastly reduced. Even though it is not as vulnerable as other debtor states—its political stability and the size and weight of its massive economy provide unparalleled collateral for borrowing—the United States does lack the capacity or at least the will to mobilize large-scale resources for specific purposes. Thus, since the Berlin Wall opened the United States has committed in Eastern Europe only a tiny fraction, far less than 1 percent, of the resources it once devoted in order to contain the advance of communism in Europe and the expansion of Soviet power there. And the act of demanding financial support for the Persian Gulf War, while merited, also revealed a weakness of economic leverage and affected U.S. political stature.

If the United States wishes to have a significant impact on the world of the 1990s and beyond, it must reevaluate the tools it needs to play an effective role in foreign policy. In short, while it was building military tools that provided a backdrop to the final phase of the Cold War and permitted the stunning defeat of Iraq, the United States was also disinvesting in the domestic tools of national economic power needed to be effective in the world beyond the Cold War. U.S. actions played a major part in changing the rules of the game; but in the new game the United States finds itself not just relatively less able to compete for power and influence but potentially below the threshold of what it will require in the years ahead simply to secure its minimal interests.

The proponents of major U.S. disengagement from the outside world thus see not only a dramatically lessened need for the United States to act for strategic purposes, but also an increased need for it to turn inward in order to retool. By this reasoning, it should concentrate on building a basis for competing in the new terms that are likely to dominate relations among states for the years ahead, so that it can later choose to turn outward again.

This retooling would focus on education, infrastructure, research and development, and other components of competitiveness, not just to promote greater economic success in a global trading environment but also to produce output that will give the United States the margins for employing capital in support of foreign policy.

Yet it is not obvious that this is a real choice, that the United States can gain such a breathing space, thereby mimicking, in far less critical terms, the search for a breathing space *(peredyshka)* that is the central foreign policy preoccupation of the Soviet Union and its republics. In fact, the concept of withdrawal without consequences is an illusion. While the United States was engaged in what proved to be the endgame of the Cold War, it was also becoming progressively more involved economically in the outside world. Much of this development was obscured during the 1980s by the focus on Soviet power and the resurgence of U.S. military strength. Measured over a period of two decades, however, the change is dramatic: a quadrupling of the fraction of U.S. gross national product tied up in foreign trade, the ceding to others of primacy in determining the prices of basic factors of production and consumption (notably food and fuel), and the loss of control over setting the value of the dollar. With the revolution in communications, the outside world is no longer remote for most Americans; it is certainly no longer remote, economically, as measured in terms of jobs and standard of living.

These and other evidences of change in the U.S. global economic position have many implications, but for the future of U.S. foreign policy one stands out. At the very moment that the United States has expanded its latitude for making geostrategic choices, it has also become more constrained economically in its dealings with the outside world. To a degree never before true, it simply cannot retreat economically, yet it also cannot act as it did before. By the same token, although it is true that the geopolitical world is no longer linked together from one end to the other, that condition has developed in the geoeconomic world. There are no longer islands of economic isolation that can hope for prosperity, and that fact impinges upon the United States almost as much as any other major state; in its own self-interest it can only choose to try shaping its external environment, because it will surely be shaped by that environment.

The New Soviet Agenda

Against this backdrop, it may seem surprising that a zero-based U.S. foreign policy begins, as it did during the past four decades, with the Soviet Union. Yet the point is consistent. Despite the progressive collapse of the Soviet economy, government, ideology, and integrity, that country—along with its successor and major components—will remain a significant presence for the years ahead in each of the regions on which it abuts. Probably no development in the world today is more pregnant with possibilities, for good or ill, than the revolution sweeping the Soviet Union. Russia alone is by far the world's largest nation and the greatest repository of natural resources. The successors to the Soviet Union will still have major foreign interests and a desire to secure frontiers if not, immediately, influence abroad. Military power will not be totally dismantled, even if there are massive cutbacks and diversion of resources to civilian uses. And there is the continuing conundrum of Soviet nuclear weapons.

The prospects are bleak for a peaceful transition from a single, centralized country, with a statist economy and one-party rule, to a series of smaller entities with market-oriented economies and pluralistic politics. Strife and turmoil are more than likely; and more than likely is some spilling over onto neighboring states, if only through a peaceful invasion of civilian refugees.

The possibilities were dramatized during the brief period of the abortive coup in August 1991. In those few hours when it appeared that the clock of change was being turned back, however briefly, the West rapidly reassessed the risks and potential products of internal conflict in the Soviet Union. In Eastern Europe, anxieties rose about refugees, the loss of markets and raw materials, and the re-emergence of Communists imperfectly purged from power. Both NATO and the European Community began reevaluating their respective roles regarding Eastern Europe. In the Middle East, hostage diplomacy was suspended, prospects dimmed for Arab–Israeli peacemaking, and there was risk that the traditional Great Game of Russian–Western competition in southwest Asia would be revived. Meanwhile, hopes for a new world order, based in part on improved East–West cooperation, seemed to have died aborning.

The events of August are unlikely to be repeated. But they underscored both the uncertainties about the Soviet future and the stakes for its neighbors, not excepting the United States. At the same time, two other observations about the coup attempt and its aftermath are pertinent: despite the temporary success of hard-liners, they made no attempt to turn the Cold War back on and reiterated the importance to the Soviet Union of access to the global economy; and although developments at the center and in the republics will profoundly affect other states, whatever the outside world does there will be dwarfed by challenges that the Soviet peoples must meet on their own.

The drama of change in the Soviet Union provides a vivid illustration of the nature of the post–cold war world facing the United States, as well as the nature of useful instruments and patterns of power and influence. Most evident, in none of the events this year has there been cause for reversing the general downward trend of U.S. military spending. Even during the coup attempt, there was no apparent reason for reenergizing U.S. defense preparations. Opportunities for cooperation with the Soviet Union might have been foreclosed, but any new dangers did not foreordain a revision of attitudes about the transition beyond a world dominated by military strength and relationships.

What has become clear is the difficulty for the United States in becoming engaged in the Soviet Union, or in neighboring Central and Eastern Europe, in ways that could make a difference and promote U.S. interests. U.S. debate in late 1991 has turned mostly on whether to provide economic support for the transformation of the Soviet Union, its republics, and neighboring states. Where Moscow is concerned, this is part of what has been a basic strategic bargain. In exchange for its strategic retreat from its external empire, the Soviet Union has sought access to the global economy (ratified by President George Bush at the December 1989 Malta Summit) and direct subventions (denied at the July 1991 Group of Seven Economic Summit).

U.S. debate includes whether economic assistance, in the form either of public aid or private investment, could be beneficial and effective. Debate also turns on symbolism: whether some support should be held out as an earnest of the West's willingness and desire to see the Soviet territories progressively integrated in the global economy rather than isolated from it. Indeed, a "democracy fund" of, say, $10 billion could be held ready to provide humanitarian assistance (if needed), to promote training of workers, managers, and public officials, to help stimulate investment interest over the long term on the part of the U.S. private sector, and—in general—to symbolize U.S. and allied determination to welcome the various Soviet peoples to the outside world.

However these debates are resolved, there is also the matter of funds. Because of decisions taken several years ago, the United States does not have the latitude to appropriate moneys without deepening its budget deficit or raising taxes; there continues to be little inclination on the part of the American people to finance new ventures abroad, especially with the budget squeeze at home; and the 1990 federal budget agreement between president and Congress makes it impossible without new congressional action (subject to presidential veto) to move funds from defense to other uses. This obtains despite the evidently diminished utility of high levels of defense spending to achieve U.S. foreign policy objectives and the rising value of having funds to spend in other ways, including domestic renewal.

Of course, these decisions represent choices, not imperatives: the United States is the richest country in history, and its people are the least taxed in the Western world. Such facts do not themselves create political incentives, however, and the latter are noticeably lacking in terms of identifiable U.S. interests that the American people both understand and accept. Nevertheless, it should be clear that, although it might be good politics to persist with the budget agreement, it is surely bad foreign and domestic policy, especially when idle defense resources are needed to bolster national strength in so many other areas. Furthermore, in making judgments about national purpose, proponents of reducing U.S. engagement in the outside world in order to attend to domestic needs must confront the fact that moneys are not being spent to promote economic strength at home any more than on the new agenda abroad. The choice for major increases of funding for America's future, financed out of the defense budget, should not be either foreign policy or domestic needs but both.

U.S. reluctance to become engaged in Eastern Europe, even to be generous in opening up the U.S. market to trade, is less easy to explain. The prospects are certainly better than in the Soviet Union that moneys invested today will produce attractive economic payoffs tomorrow. Following the August coup in the Soviet Union, there should also be a clearer understanding of the value of helping the East European states meet the triple threat to their independence and stability: difficulties in the transition to democracy, the weak underpinnings for market economies, and the rise of ethnic, religious, and national strife—as witnessed most dramatically in Yugoslavia. Yet in this region, as well, U.S. economic engagement (public and private) has been minuscule in absolute terms, even though in terms of direct grants of public moneys it does not compare unfavorably with Western Europe.

It is far from self-evident to the American people, however, that the United States has a long-term interest in these countries or, if it does, why it should continue to bear European burdens at a time when its allies and other partners have the capacity to do so. The answer certainly does not lie in the arguments of the past: that this is part of the seamless web of containing Soviet power and Communist influence, two of the three cold war paradigms. Of course, if worse comes to worst in the Soviet Union and internal turmoil spills over massively into contiguous territories, that might inspire a U.S. response.

It is the remnant of the third cold war paradigm that comes into play in Eastern Europe: the importance of a growing, global economy. In the future as in the past, the direct benefits provided for the United States and the American people will be critically important, and properly so, in determining U.S. engagement. Indeed, the most compelling argument for a forthcoming U.S. response to East European needs—and to a lesser extent that of peoples in the Soviet Union—derives from the economic future: These countries represent potential markets of huge dimensions, although when those markets will be realized cannot be forecast with confidence. As America's West European allies become more engaged economically and politically in the East, it is also likely that future markets—which mean jobs and profits at home—will favor exports and investments from those countries, especially if the European Community develops special association agreements or speeds up the widening of membership. As in the cold war functioning of the global economy, therefore, creating and sustaining popular U.S. support for measures of longer-range significance require the development of a sense of future economic payoff for current efforts.

Promoting Ideology

What is happening from the old inner-German border to Vladivostok is also engaging basic Western values, especially democracy and the free-market economy. There is deep U.S. interest in these developments, in part because the evident appeal of the two Western models has helped to validate the entire cold war struggle. It will therefore be natural for the United States to continue promoting these twin concepts in many parts of the world, although so far it has shown little interest in advancing democracy in the Middle East for fear of producing potentially unfriendly regimes.

For one specific aspect of U.S. ideology—human rights—the end of the Cold War offers the United States opportunities because it relieves long-standing dilemmas. There are no longer geopolitical reasons to modulate support for human rights because of conflict with concerns about potential Soviet inroads. Thus Washington has felt free to end its support for Cambodia's Pol Pot, the world's leading butcher, now that it has no reason to counter the influence of Vietnam and hence of the Soviet Union. Vigorous debate can take place in the U.S. Congress on whether to continue extending most-favored-nation treatment to China: there is no longer need for a "China card" to play against the Soviet Union, and thus revulsion over the killings at Tiananmen Square is given preference. Of course, both in the congressional vote on China and in U.S. reluctance to press the case for democracy in the Middle East, commercial arguments intrude, reflecting the new era of geoeconomics. In the former case, China's $15 billion trade surplus with the United States was an important factor; in the latter case, the United States continues to be concerned about the security and price of oil.

It is unlikely, however, that U.S. popular commitment to democracy, human rights, the market economy, and the rule of law will on its own be sufficient to sustain an outward-looking view of the world without other, more direct evidence of either threat or opportunity. There is also risk both of disillusionment and of error. The concept "market economy" conjures up a clear picture in the West of a variety of approaches to economic organization and management, ranging across a wide spectrum of possibilities. In the former Communist countries, however, the term is still more abstract than real, a goal based upon appreciation of success rather than an agenda for action. What emerges in some countries may not look like the market-economy model as it is understood in the United States, and that development could inhibit U.S. willingness to support economic and social experimentation.

Even more problematic is the matter of democracy. Its appeal in Eastern Europe, the Soviet Union, and in many other parts of the world has been clearly demonstrated as a negative quality—the flight from oppression and tyranny. The positive quality of building a democratic society is far more difficult to achieve and far less certain of success, especially in countries that have little or no experience of Western or alternative democratic traditions. Throughout Latin America, societies are engaged in promising political-economic experiments, and more states in the hemisphere have democratic forms of government than ever before. But from Bulgaria, Romania, Albania, and Serbia eastward, transition to a politics of compromise will be long and painful, and the American people may be disappointed by the results during the next several years. These would not be the first nations to experience "one man, one vote, one time." And disillusionment in the United States, especially if several "liberated" countries fall under new tyrannies, could undermine enthusiasm for an active, ideologically sustained, foreign policy.

There is also risk of error or misjudgment in overzealous promotion of a current U.S. idea: the supremacy of the free market, with its emphasis on impersonal forces and the primacy of production over distribution. The struggle between capitalism and communism in the developed countries may be over; the struggle for social and economic justice in what we have called the Third World has hardly begun. A free-market model is now in the ascendancy and colors everything from the economic policies of the United States to the latest papal encyclical, but demands for redistribution of resources, not just sharing of economic and political philosophy, are likely to dominate North–South debate for years to come. The United States has its recent triumph over the Soviet Union in strategy, political philosophy, and economics; and a free-market economy has unchallenged practical merits in mobilizing productive resources. Nevertheless, whether in political or psychological attitudes or availability of resources, the United States is still clearly unprepared for the underlying debate with the Third World.

The United States, even more than its Western partners, also risks confusing the terms of this debate, which will often be strident, with the development of a new ideological confrontation. This could take many guises, as we have seen during several decades of North–South struggle. Today the prime candidate for ideological confrontation with the West is Islam, unvariegated in most U.S. commentary and little understood in any of its forms. Islamic political reaction against the United States and the West in the wake of the Persian Gulf War may yet become potent beyond those few countries in which it has so far appeared. Islam in different forms and places can also become a rallying point for economic and social discontents, appealing to people who have no stake in the religion as such. There is thus risk of a new ideological struggle. It can be avoided, however, if mutual efforts are made to deal with North–South economic issues on their own terms and to avoid the simplicities that so often lead peoples toward either great achievements or great wrongs. Having moved beyond an era dominated by a rigid ideological competition, the United States can hardly profit by succumbing to old prejudices born of that era or by adopting new ones that produce an avoidable confrontation.

A New World Order

The promise contained in President Bush's concept of a "new world order" can also be viewed at first blush in the negative: a world that has moved beyond cold war, beyond sterile competition, beyond the corrosive effects of communism, and indeed beyond the U.S.–Soviet nuclear age—the last-named representing one of the most stunning achievements of human history. Some observers see the promise of a new world order in a Pax Americana; others fear it for the same reason, and both are wrong because of arguments presented above: There can be no such U.S. dominance. If there is "order," and that point can be debated, it will surely not be premised on the primacy of the United States, save where, as in the Middle East, military power can still be a major arbiter of events with implications far beyond the region.

The concept of a new world order was born at a time when the United States had put together an unprecedented coalition of states to act for a common purpose. The most unlikely collection of 30 countries joined the United States in confronting and then defeating Saddam Hussein's Iraq. The coalition's purpose was not primarily military: the United States had the necessary capacity on its own, although it welcomed the efforts of key European allies. Instead the coalition served political purposes: first, to convince the American people that the United States was not acting alone to secure an asset, oil, that was more important to other countries; and second, to counter Saddam Hussein's charges that he was championing the cause of the downtrodden against the "imperialists and Zionists."

The coalition's success does not necessarily set a precedent, however. There is, in fact, no other place on earth about which so many countries care so much, because of that precious resource, oil. Thus it is most unlikely that the pattern could be repeated: U.S. identification of the threat, an initial U.S. response, U.S. development of a coalition, and U.S. management of the strategy from beginning to end. In the future, it may again be important that one nation take the lead—as was clearly so following Iraq's invasion of Kuwait; but it is unlikely that next time only costs and responsibilities will be shared and not also the power of decision. The defeat of Iraq has reduced the chances that another military coalition will be needed in the near future; but if other coalition efforts were required, it is increasingly likely that the United States would have to accept a greater degree of self-limitation in defining problems, suggesting remedies, creating strategies, and assigning roles.

Properly understood, however, this does not have to be seen as constraining U.S. power and influence; instead, it could extend and expand them. In an era dominated by issues that do not respond to military solutions—although war, obviously, is far from abolished—there is merit for the United States in using diplomatic tools that are "force multipliers," analogous to some modern combat weapons. Today, the United Nations (UN) has begun to come into its own, partly because of the changing global agenda but primarily because of the transformation of Soviet policy and attitudes. Moscow, first to understand the futility of continuing to prosecute the Cold War, was also first to understand the value in ceding to the UN sufficient sovereignty for common action that would also achieve some Soviet goals. Washington is in the process of learning a similar lesson, and the combination offers promise not evident since the UN charter was signed.

In the post–cold war era, there will also be benefit for the United States in expanded rule-making—international law—as mediated through the UN, which must not act as an agent of great power dominance but rather in areas where coalitions of states have common interests. Indeed, further codification of practice, observance of rules already accepted, and appropriate use of institutions like the UN that draw their legitimacy from international law can provide a partial paradigm, at least a reference point, for direction in a world that will otherwise have few certainties or universal practices.

The intersection of legal codes and multilateral institutions can also help provide a higher degree of predictability about world events and nations' responses to them than would otherwise be the case—a predictability that was a hallmark of the cold war era and that has been missed by some commentators as they survey the future of the global system.

This role for codes and institutions will be especially valuable as the world, including the United States, is forced to confront an emerging agenda of global issues whose time has come, partly because of the press of circumstance and partly because their importance is no longer obscured by superpower confrontation. Notably, these include proliferation, pollution, and the iron nexus between poverty and population.

Leadership in a New Age

The emotional and psychological adjustment facing the United States is not limited either to changes in agenda or in the tools most likely to be prominent in conferring power and influence. Changes in America's relative station in influencing great events will also affect its role of leadership. During the Cold War, this was an instrumental quality: if the United States did not lead, then little would follow that would promote U.S. interests. For the American people, however, it has never been clear that U.S. leadership has had value for itself, or that it should be sustained beyond the requirement for meeting U.S. needs. The answer is perhaps already evident in the relative U.S. passivity in the face of momentous events in Eastern Europe and the Soviet Union, but that conclusion may be unfair: It is not yet clear what challenges will most dominate America's apprehension of the outside world and what role will be demanded of the nation in securing its interests.

There is certainly merit in sharing leadership with other, like-minded nations, notably Japan and key allies in Europe (and the European Community). Sharing leadership, like sharing burdens, requires accommodating to the views of others, however. For the United States, it will neither be automatic nor easy to adjust to the idea of accepting the lead of another state, even a like-minded state.

Emphasis must also be placed on the term "like-minded." In the post–cold war era, the three major Western partners are likely to continue sharing a similarity of geopolitical outlook: They were held together for four decades not just by the negative influence of Soviet power and ideology but also by their shared attitudes and experiences. But it is less clear that they will now cleave together either in defining less-central issues and outcomes (as in the Middle East) or in geoeconomics. Indeed, current trends argue the opposite, whether in the failure to elevate the Uruguay Round of the GATT negotiations to the political level that its importance for the future of the global economy justifies; in the possibility that the global economic system will fall prey to the growth of regional trading blocs—with uncertain geopolitical consequences; or in the reduction of U.S.–Japanese relations in the minds of too many people to a single statistic: the bilateral balance of trade.

In all these cases, geoeconomics must be meshed with geopolitics—in short, economic issues must be integrated with broader concerns about strategic challenge and opportunity, shared democratic outlook, compatible social structures, and common global problems. In 1991, it is still too early to expect either Japan or the European Community to demonstrate the attitudes and practices of outward-looking states, with a developed and reflexive sense of responsibility for the effective functioning of the global economic and political systems. It is equally inappropriate to chastise Japan and Germany for resisting the creation of military capabilities and domestic political license in order to send forces abroad, or to criticize the European Community for inadequacy in dealing with a Yugoslav crisis that both defies easy solution and elicits little U.S. involvement.

On its agenda for the post–cold war era, the United States has a special item of unfinished business from the post–World War II era: to help nurture both Japan and Germany (the latter through the European Community) to assume political roles appropriate to their stations as major economic powers without at the same time becoming major military states. In a geoeconomic world, that would make little sense on any grounds. At the same time, in its own self-interest the United States must join other leading economic powers to fashion new rules and practices for the global economy that will preserve and extend its effectiveness without also requiring the leadership and capital surpluses of any single country.

Abroad and at Home

The end of the Cold War can also be seen as the end of an aberrant era, one uniquely marked, as argued earlier, by the dominance of a handful of paradigms. It was also an era in which preoccupation with stability in the global system distorted the balance that has been traditionally struck between that value and the continual changes in power and position among nations that are endemic to human society. The fall of the Berlin Wall symbolized the coming together of several trends in historical development: the playing out, at long last, of the endgame in Europe from World War II; the amelioration of irrational fears of one another on the part of the two superpowers, plus their mutual recognition that neither had anything to gain from continued conflict; the widespread perception of the success of Western market systems in comparison with centrally planned economies; the penetration of closed societies by modern means of communication; and the propagation and popularity of ideas fundamental to human dignity and self-realization.

Today's world is less stable and less predictable; but for all that it is a safer world, one that has moved decisively beyond the U.S.–Soviet nuclear age and also beyond the interconnection of political conditions and events that could produce a cataclysm out of a Sarajevo. In this world, the United States plays a different part, its earlier, post–World War II role having been successfully completed. It would be strange if it were otherwise.

For the United States, the premium in the future will be on clear-sighted analysis, at each step of the way, of four key factors: the changing nature of the world and its constituent parts, the individual and collective U.S. interests in that world, the tools appropriate to secure those interests, and the choices preferred by the American people—without which grounding there can be no successful foreign policies or sufficient incentive even to meet evident requirements. This analysis must be segmented, avoiding the search for simplicities or paradigms where these do not naturally exist. This is especially true where a paradigm is little more than a prejudice and produces invidious results for the interests both of the United States and of others. But the analysis must also be holistic. In the modern era, there is no merit in attempting to segregate politics or security from economics, foreign from domestic policy, or any of them from an underlying national strategy, or method, that is based on enduring democratic politics. It is no doubt true that, to be effective abroad in the years ahead, the United States must be better prepared at home, especially in strengthening those economic tools and revitalizing those social relationships that will be critical in helping the nation compete in the global economic and political marketplaces. But it is also true that, in the process, the United States and its people cannot retreat from the outside world and expect either that it will leave them alone or that they will prosper thereby.

The Crisis of Leninism and the U.S. Response

Robert A. Scalapino

NO ONE—INCLUDING the most ardent opponents of communism—accurately predicted the events that are taking place within the Leninist states today. Critics have decried the existence of extensively privileged classes in a supposedly classless society. They have deplored a political system that is fundamentally beyond the reach of law. No one was so bold, however, as to suggest that a new revolution would sweep over much of the Leninist world and that it sometimes would be led by elements occupying the very top positions in the existing power structure.

Why have many reform leaders come from the uppermost political elite? A major part of the answer is that they were in a position to realize the full extent of the system's deficiencies and, hence, to appreciate that without far-reaching changes, their nation could not be competitive with the dynamic market economies. The central motivation was first economic, then political, when it was realized that without political reform, economic reform would falter. There is, however, another factor that must not be overlooked: given the nature of the Leninist system, with power highly centralized and the society subordinated to and controlled by the party and state, a basic challenge to the old order could not easily come from any source other than the top. An old-fashioned mass revolution was a remote possibility. At a minimum, an important part of the old elite—including military elements—had to acquiesce in the course of events.

Nevertheless, once the torch was lit from the top, a diversity of elements within the society responded with an alacrity and vigor that surprised and, in certain instances, alarmed the power holders, even many reformers. It is natural that intellectuals—using the term broadly—are leading the way, because they have both the reasons and the capacity for articulating grievances. In a number of Leninist states, however, populism now is making itself felt in various ways. Workers in factories and mines are demanding improvements and rights previously denied them in a state that called itself a proletarian dictatorship. Other urban residents are voicing complaints regarding scarcities, prices, and housing. Corruption and privilege are also prominent targets. Also, in certain Leninist states, as is well known, long-suppressed ethnic divisions are erupting with great volatility.

In general, only two groups have not joined in the clamor for reform. The farmer is seldom heard from, whether because the reforms please him, as was true until recently in China, or

---

Robert A. Scalapino is director emeritus of the Institute of East Asian Studies at the University of California at Berkeley and Robson Research Professor of Government Emeritus.

because he is not interested in reform, as is rumored in the Soviet Union, or because his proclivities for being part of a political movement are limited. The more significant "outsiders," however, are the upper-middle and middle cadres and officials who have the most to lose if genuine reforms are achieved. Indeed, while the patterns of alliance regarding the reform movement differ, in almost all instances the top political elite—or that portion dedicated to reform—must find allies against the powerful, well-entrenched bureaucracy beneath them. Currently, the contest is at best a standoff, with the bureaucracy able to sabotage many reform policies. Present events reveal the serious weakness of the theory of totalitarianism. Real power is shown to be far more dispersed in most Leninist states than generally has been acknowledged.

The Crisis of Leninism

Before probing more deeply into the politics of Leninist reform, however, let me introduce the most salient cultural and economic factors that provide the basis for differentiation and commonality among Leninist states. When studying the mass response to current reform efforts in societies such as those in the Soviet Union and China, one cannot ignore cultural variations of major significance, although such a theme annoys those who insist upon monocausal explanations for political phenomena. In China, when state restraints were lifted, entrepreneurship immediately sprang up in both rural and urban areas. Although this development created certain new problems, it revealed a dynamism within a private sector that merely awaited liberation. Chinese communism clearly had not been able to create "new socialist men and women." Whether one refers to it as the Confucian ethic or applies some other label, Chinese culture made itself felt.

In Russia, however, the time span between serfdom and collectivization was relatively brief, industrialization had barely taken hold prior to the Bolshevik Revolution, and commercialism was less intensely developed than in the traditional states of Northeast Asia. It should not be surprising, therefore, that many Russians, both rural and urban, have become habituated to a surprise-free guaranteed life in which the choices and risks forced upon the individual are few. If upward mobility is limited and monotony must be endured, a minimal security is ensured. Thus, the challenge to Soviet President Mikhail Gorbachev is not only to find the appropriate economic policies, but also to change Russian culture—a task not to be accomplished quickly or easily. Even in China, to be sure, Leninism has taken its toll, as any comparative study of labor productivity in China and Taiwan or Hong Kong will make clear.

Irrespective of cultural differences, however, certain common economic problems face the Leninist states. Leaders have discovered that there is no painless route whereby the Stalinist economic strategy can be discarded. No Leninist society has yet found a way to meld a command and a market economy successfully, despite a variety of ongoing experiments. The distorted price system, the imbalance among various economic sectors, the limited incentives for productivity and innovation, and the Hobson's choice between inflation and scarcity are among the interrelated factors that produce the current economic crisis in virtually every Leninist state attempting reform.

Invariably, serious and protracted economic problems create divisions within the top political elite. Rarely, moreover, are such divisions static or neatly separable into two lines, "conservative" and "liberal." New developments produce shifts in individual positions in a highly fluid situation, and under circumstances where no one knows what to do, the differences are more subtle as well as less firmly rooted than the "two lines" thesis would suggest. Nevertheless, with some outstanding exceptions, the older generation of frontline leaders tends to be more wedded to traditional methods and more cautious in accepting novel ideas. Their inclination is toward orthodoxy. At root, they are "red," not "expert." It is within the circle of younger, better educated, more technocratically inclined leaders that one generally can find the bolder risk-takers. Generationism, however, is not an infallible guide to policy differences. In Asian societies in particular, one must pay close attention to patron–client ties and other factors making for personal identification—or estrangement.

Irrespective of the policy cleavages, one trend of striking significance can be observed in virtually all Leninist states. On the broadest front, there is a commitment to reduced military expenditures, accompanied in certain important cases by a redefinition of the appropriate military strategy to be pursued. Thus, Soviet spokesmen, acknowledging that through the mid-1980s they pursued an offensive-oriented strategy, now define their doctrine as defensive in character, with its essence captured in the phrase "reasonable sufficiency." One senior Soviet official has set forth the meaning of this concept as follows:

> For strategic nuclear forces, sufficiency is defined today as the ability to prevent nuclear attack from going unpunished in any way, even the most unfavorable, circumstances. For conventional forces, sufficiency implies a certain minimum quantity and high quality of troops and armaments, capable of providing defense. The limits of defensive sufficiency also depend on actions of NATO and the United States.[1]

Certain Soviet specialists now assert that while it was legitimate to seek parity with the United States in the past, the Soviet error was to allow itself to be dragged into a costly arms race by attempting to copy each new U.S. defense program. Soviet spokesmen recently have acknowledged that Soviet military expenditures of the past significantly surpassed U.S. estimates. Now, it is proclaimed, the Soviet Union is prepared to follow its own course, making extensive unilateral reductions in its armed forces while maintaining a deterrent sufficient to prevent any attack upon it or its allies. These words have been followed by action on both the western and eastern fronts of the Soviet Union. Significant force reductions and repositioning have taken place or are in the offing.

These actions do not threaten basic Soviet military capabilities. Past Soviet military policies led to a huge amount of waste, and a military force that was quantitatively larger but qualitatively weak in many areas, with various expensive weapon systems that quickly became outmoded. The new aim, to use the U.S. vernacular, is to create a "leaner, meaner" armed force capable of carrying out its essential defense functions by concentrating upon quality, including state-of-the-art equipment where necessary. Nonetheless, no one should doubt the thrust—to cut military expenditures sufficiently to alleviate economic strain. It is very likely, moreover, that such a policy has engendered international debate, a probability reflected in changes in top military personnel. Will the military continue to accept policies premised on austerity, with a major diversion of resources elsewhere?

Reduced military expenditures are evident in other Leninist states. In the case of China, the number of men under arms has been slashed by 1 million, although the goal of military modernization has been kept intact, with efforts to advance both nuclear and conventional capabilities. Even North Korea has acknowledged the costliness of its military expenditures to the general economy and has cut back in troop numbers while also using its military force extensively in civilian construction projects. It is in Eastern Europe, however, that the most startling developments have occurred. Indeed, the trends and pronouncements cause many observers to proclaim the Warsaw Pact dead, with certain states of the region adopting a status like that of Austria or Finland.

Whatever the future of alliances, it is clear that among and between Leninist states, the widest possible variety of strategic relations currently exists: hostility (China versus Vietnam); self-proclaimed nonalignment (China and North Korea); and variants of alliance (the East European nations and Mongolia). The separate actions of Leninist states relating to security policies pose complex new issues for the United States and its allies. To this question I shall return later.

Turning now to an assessment of the current political environment in the Leninist world, one significant feature stands out. Today, most Leninist governments are unsure of themselves and are faced with internal divisions at various levels. Moreover, groups within the citizenry at large are entering the political arena, often for the first time and uncertain about the most appropriate strategy to use in manifesting their demands. Consequently, the delicacy of the situation scarcely can be overstated. Dissidents of varying hues test regularly the frontiers of permissibility. If they overstep the boundaries (and this will be decided subjectively by those in power), they will be suppressed or punished, and the political evolution previously underway may be delayed or reversed, at least for the time being. On the other hand, if the governors mistake the political climate and assume that the old methods of coercion plus heavy doses of propaganda will suffice, they will be progressively discredited and find their hold on power increasingly precarious.

At present, two momentous changes are taking place in the world at large, each having a direct effect on the Leninist states. First, ideology is in decline virtually everywhere. The great turning point was when economics rather than politics was put in command. To concentrate on economic development is by necessity to accept a pragmatic, problem-solving approach to issues, in the course of which dogma must be abandoned. Such a transformation is dangerous for all states, but especially for the Leninist nations. If belief in eternal verities falls away, how can a people be mobilized or controlled? Thus, until recently, Soviet leaders remained reluctant to see Lenin's image tarnished or the principle of the proletarian dictatorship overturned. Chinese leaders still cling desperately to the Four Cardinal Principles and seek to respond to what they term the counterrevolutionary rebellion with an effort to restore intensive political indoctrination. Yet, the number of true believers steadily declines. Not only in China, but throughout the Leninist world (the only temporary exception is North Korea), the legitimacy of party and state no longer can be preserved through blind faith. Neither the charisma of the leader nor a recitation of the Marxist–Leninist liturgy suffices. Now legitimacy must come through successful policies. As in democracies, the average citizen asks his leaders, "What have you done for me lately?" Herein lies the true political revolution that is sweeping over Communist states.

The second and closely related change is to be found in the impact of the startling developments in communications. Historically, the capacity to insulate the average citizen from external contamination was one of the most potent sources of stability in Leninist states. It is still a powerful force in North Korea. In almost all other Leninist societies, however, access to external sources of information by a sizable body of citizens has increased geometrically. As a result, Leninist states are vastly more porous than in the past. At least the better educated citizens have some awareness of the success of the newly industrialized economies (NIEs), the experiments in greater political openness under Gorbachev, and the coming unification of Germany—to mention only the more dramatic features of recent time. Thus, contrasts and comparisons regarding one's own status and that of one's society can be made to a degree previously impossible. Naturally, this affects both political attitudes and behavior.

These conditions almost certainly doom the current effort of the Chinese government to maintain economic openness while restricting acceptable political ideas to "socialism with Chinese characteristics." To be sure, the current leaders are merely following their Mandarin predecessors. The idea of borrowing Western science and technology while holding to Chinese values is more than a century old. Yet it always has defied logic and hence has failed.

It would be a great mistake to assume, however, as some overenthusiastic observers are doing, that with the decline of Leninism the triumph of liberalism is assured. There is little on the political horizon to validate such a thesis. One recalls that some decades ago the theory of general convergence was in vogue. The argument was that the democratic, capitalist states would turn increasingly to state-sponsored welfarism and the Leninist states gradually would move toward greater political openness, with the two systems meeting in the vicinity of democratic socialism. Such a theory was overly simple and failed to pay homage to significant differences of culture, development, resources, and geopolitical position.

European vs. Asian Leninism

There is no reason to believe that all societies will gravitate toward a single political system. However, we are witnessing two fascinating trends with respect to Leninist societies. First, those Leninist states having the greatest historical contact with the central Western political tenets and lying on the peripheries of the Western orbit are taking the boldest steps away from Leninism, even experimenting with parliamentary government based in some instances on a multiparty system. Thus, a cleavage is developing between European and Asian Communist states, Mongolia excepted. The latter state, the oldest Leninist society aside from the Soviet one, always has been deeply influenced by events in Moscow. Its economic and political elite are overwhelmingly the products of Soviet training. It was expected, therefore, that sooner or later, the upheaval in the Soviet Union would be felt here.

Yet, there is another factor of great significance relating to Mongolia. One discerns the rise once again of Mongolian nationalism. The statue of Joseph Stalin, long an imposing edifice in front of the Academy of Sciences in central Ulan Bator, finally has come down. A statue honoring Genghis Khan is now being erected along with a hotel bearing his name. The famous Mongol leader is being revived—and as a hero.

Such a trend is almost certain to kindle the interest of those 3 million Mongols living in China, the overwhelming number being in Inner Mongolia, a province adjacent to the Mongolian People's Republic. Here, as in Xinjiang, China's far west where Uighurs and Kazhaks reside alongside their brethren in the central Asian republics of the Soviet Union, a commitment to ethnic separatism is manifesting itself.

The Chinese thus are compelled to declare martial law in southern Xinjiang as well as in Tibet, and watch their Mongols with wary eyes. Not the least of their grievances against Gorbachev is that he has encouraged, or at least permitted, a degree of political openness that enables ethnic sentiments to be expressed more boldly, and this is spilling over into China's border regions.

In truth, it was never absent—only suppressed. The great advantage possessed by China is that ethnic minorities represent less than 7 percent of the population, and thus can be contained by one means or another. Nevertheless, the emergence of a central Asian nationalism flying Islamic banners could be exceedingly troublesome to both Moscow and Beijing, possibly changing the political configuration of the Eurasian heartland.

On a broader screen, nationalism has had a different relationship to communism in Eastern Europe and in East Asia. In Europe, communism was a product of Soviet power, whereas in most of Asia it flew nationalist banners and was associated with "liberation," notwithstanding the massive Soviet assistance given. This is important as an additional factor accounting for the diverse trends.

China, North Korea, and Vietnam thus far have rejected the type of systemic political reform that would represent a peaceful evolution away from Leninism. On the contrary, they have proclaimed to their own people and others that the leadership of the Communist Party will be maintained and Marxist–Leninist ideology will be defended stoutly against those subversive elements represented by bourgeois liberalism seeking to overthrow socialism through "peaceful evolution."

It is true that the political current from the European Leninist front cannot be dismissed totally. Thus, the Chinese and North Korean leaders are promising to take more seriously the so-called democratic parties created and controlled by them. It is possible that in the course of time and events, these parties may play a new role, as in certain cases in Eastern Europe. For the present, however, they are little more than puppets manipulated by their Communist masters. The "dictatorship of the proletariat" (the Communist Party) continues to be championed as the necessary instrument of socialism and stability, with the latter requirement of ever greater importance to a worried elite, deeply troubled by the course of events at home and abroad. In particular, the revolt of Romania, climaxed by the execution of Nicolae Ceausescu, sent a shock wave through the Communist rulers of Asia, causing them to tighten political controls and reexamine the loyalty of their military forces.

Thus, for the present at least, an ideological–political gap has emerged between the Leninist states of Europe and those of East Asia, despite the continued hostility between China and Vietnam over Cambodia. No Asian Leninist state, however, wants to reopen the type of polemic battle that unfolded in the early 1960s. Hence, during his April 1990 visit to Moscow, Chinese Premier Li Peng was careful not to utter any words of public criticism of *glasnost* or *perestroika*. A further reduction of tension between China and the Soviet Union is in the interest of both countries, especially at this most dangerous time. Moreover, an earlier calculation by certain Chinese hardliners that Gorbachev's days were numbered, while by no means disproved, seems at least uncertain. Naturally, they, like others, will monitor carefully his chances of survival and what might follow in the event of his demise. North Korea and Vietnam also have ample reasons for not picking a public fight with Moscow, given their heavy economic and strategic dependence upon the Soviet Union. Indeed, it is Moscow that now exhibits increasing independence of action from those Asian states that have been dependencies. Its policies toward South Korea, for example, signal that North Korea no longer has an extensive veto power over Soviet actions.

Thus, while relations between the Soviets and the key East Asian Leninist states may be "normal," they are not likely to be either intimate or trusting. To be sure, a variety of circumstances, most of them domestic in nature, might occur to alter this picture. As noted, a majority of current Asian Leninist leaders would welcome Gorbachev's overthrow and the revival of orthodox Leninist politics—but even if Gorbachev were to depart, is such a scenario likely? Conversely, if—or perhaps one should say when—significant political changes occur in these East Asian states, political rapport with Moscow might be much easier, yet no amount of rapport is going to cause socialist economic interaction to replace the great need of all of these societies to tap the technology, financial assistance, and products of the advanced industrial world. Nor are certain stubborn geopolitical facts of life going to be removed, facts that breed continuing mutual suspicion among them.

While prediction is hazardous, it is logical to assume that whatever the precise outcome of the current upheaval in Eastern Europe and the Soviet Union, most Asian Leninist states sooner or later will gravitate toward what I have termed elsewhere the authoritarian-pluralist model.[2] In such a state, politics is characterized by varying restraints upon political choice and civil liberties, although the restrictions are not as severe as under the Leninist system. A single or dominant party maintains stability, whether under military or civilian rule, with the perimeters of permissible criticism or legal organized activity on the part of the citizenry relatively limited. In the social and economic spheres, however, a significant degree of pluralism is allowed. Thus, religious and educational institutions operate with some independence from the state. In the economic arena, the market dominates the scene, albeit with extensive state involvement. Among the most successful states in this category, experiments in parliamentary government are underway—South Korea and Taiwan being prime examples.

The contemporary world, it might be noted, provides ample evidence that Marx was in error in postulating that a given state of economic development would yield a given political system. Once a variety of political models became available, choices could be made on the basis of various factors. The political institutions of such South Asian states as India and Sri Lanka, for example, owe much to British tutelage and little to prevailing socioeconomic conditions or their traditional heritage. Because of two wars, Russia and Eastern Europe were thrust on the road to socialism from whence they are now seeking to retreat, with the effort to reach a modified capitalism—labeled a social and humane democracy.

In the principal Asian Leninist states, on the other hand, traditions of corporatism, a still massive peasantry, and the remnants of a first generation revolutionary elite unite to promote political conservatism. A deep fear exists—not wholly unjustified—that extensive political openness under the prevailing circumstances would lead to chaos. Yet, the external winds of change blow ever more fiercely.

Even if the authoritarian–pluralist model does represent the general course of Asian Leninist evolution, the route may be both varied and rocky, with retreats and failures occurring. Almost certainly, two broad debates will continue in much of the Leninist world, with special relevance to the Asian sector: What is the optimal mix between economic and political reform, and should the present political system be reformed or scrapped? Already, these issues are debated at home and abroad, with the Mongolian, Vietnamese, and even the North Korean political elite joining their Chinese colleagues in pondering the first issue, and Chinese intellectuals along with estranged Vietnamese and Mongolians arguing over the second issue.

The U.S. Response

The United States is more than a disinterested bystander to the crisis of Leninism. Can and should the United States develop policies providing incentives and disincentives in an effort to influence the course of Leninist societies in varying stages of evolution?

I begin with three premises. First, responses to developments in Leninist states cannot be uniform given the diversities that exist and will continue. Second, whatever the degree of separateness dictated by domestic circumstances, only policies coordinated or if possible jointly applied with Western Europe and Japan are likely to be truly effective. Third, it should not be assumed that a given course in the Leninist states is permanent or irreversible, meaning that policies that through their rigidity close doors to future opportunities should be avoided.

Worry about the fate of reforms in the Soviet Union was heightened as 1990 opened, and justifiably so. Procrastination in launching thorough economic reforms cast in doubt the public's acceptance of sacrifices and, correspondingly, weakened the will of the leadership to take bold steps.

There are several ways in which Western policies can assist the Soviet reform efforts. Rapid and far-reaching agreements on arms reduction together with decisions to forgo new weapon systems requiring a Soviet response, such as strategic defenses, would provide much-needed relief to the Soviet (and the U.S.) budget, and under certain conditions might reduce pressure on Gorbachev from the Soviet military establishment.

In making decisions on these matters, reliance upon experts is essential, but it also is critically important to ask the right questions, making certain that economic and political considerations are given equal weight with military ones in determining which policies best serve the U.S. national interest. Moreover, consultation and coordination of policies with allies in Western Europe and Northeast Asia is vital. The United States cannot and should not carry the present disproportionate share of the burden of maintaining a regional and global strategic balance. This requires that the United States and its allies move more rapidly to joint decision making, requiring nations other than the United States to be involved at the beginning, not merely the end of that process. Difficult though it is proving to be, U.S. unilateralism must come to an end.

Moreover, the United States and its allies must recast the concept of security, a process as yet begun only hesitantly. Security begins at home. The macroeconomic policies of the United States are in disarray. Current primary and secondary educational programs guarantee that a sizable portion of coming American generations will be ill-equipped for the age of high technology. The competitiveness of the U.S. private sector suffers from other deficiencies. Mobility in the vicinity of the great metropolitan areas is being slowed to a crawl, with enormous waste of energy, human and natural. The crime rate is exceeding society's ability to build new prisons. The need for reallocation of resources—national as well as state and local—should be clear.

To be sure, additional government funds are not the only answer to U.S. problems. Other measures, some of them involving changes of attitude and even culture, are required. Yet, money is an important component, compelling the United States to spend considerably less on military outlays and at the same time raise significantly greater revenues. This requires that it adopt stronger safeguards against waste and corruption in defense allocations and also expose Congressional support for defense projects within various districts that have limited utility. It also requires a review of U.S. global strategy to bring it abreast of the times, and in the process, reconsider each security commitment. We should not and will not return to isolationism. The basic instincts of the American people are sound, and they see that the most pressing issues affecting their security—indeed, our survival as a great nation—are economic and that in this area, fundamental reforms both at home and in relations with allies are past due.

I am not one of those who proceeds from this point to castigate Japan, the NIEs, and Western Europe in such a fashion as to imply that they are the basic cause of the problems of the United States. Although there is sufficient blame to be shared by all sides, the United States itself bears a sizable share of responsibility. Either there will be freer trade and financial access for all parties, or there will be managed trade and investment in the United States as elsewhere with results that are very likely to be detrimental to all parties concerned. Having moved through the scrapping of formal tariff barriers and currency adjustment with limited effect, the United States is now at the issue of tackling structural impediments in its discussions with Japan. Some have charged that this represents unwarranted interference in the internal affairs of another nation (a curious counterpart of the Chinese complaint regarding human rights issues), but structural changes are the indispensable companion to the further integration of our economies. There is no way to separate out economic and military relations with those aligned with us, because both relate fundamentally to the security of the United States.

Even as the United States wrestles with these problems, should it and other major market states lend economic assistance to those Leninist nations in the vanguard of the reform movement? The U.S. government has approved modest support for specific programs in Poland, and this support is appropriate. The exact type of economic assistance given to states requiring systemic reform, however, is of critical importance. Does the aid advance the cause of reform or deter it? Generally, massive aid in the form of grants or loans to "tide over" nations in economic difficulty and searching for new ideas provides negative incentives. Perhaps the most effective types of assistance can come from the involvement of the private sector because of the role it can play in acquisition of new technology and the upgrading of human resources. By requiring the active cooperation of the recipients, such aid will forward, not retard reform.

Where official assistance is involved, the use of multilateral agencies like the World Bank, the International Monetary Fund, and the Asian Development Bank has much merit. These agencies are not only in a position to set up the necessary economic stipulations with less political fallout, but they are vehicles whereby erstwhile Leninist economies can be brought to international economic intercourse more easily.

Whatever the form, economic assistance, like security policies, should involve closer consultation among the United States, Western Europe, and Japan. Naturally, there will be a strong element of competition where conditions for trade and investment seem favorable, and that is appropriate. Yet, to navigate this delicate period with the greatest effectiveness and to assist those socialist states that desire structural changes requires cooperation among the major market economies, including some pooling of resources. It is precisely here that the receptivity of the Leninist states is highest, even those presently resisting political change.

It must be emphasized that the primary responsibility for success or failure lies with the Leninist states and leaders immediately involved. The content, timing, and implementation of their policies, political and economic, are the crucial factors. Because virtually all of these states are committed to moving away from an autarkic economy, however, the external response is a variable of importance.

Another aspect of Western relations with the Leninist states is cultural. Here, there is every reason to encourage rapid expansion, especially in the European arena. The change in the intellectual climate of the Soviet Union and the East European states is extraordinary. To be sure, setbacks could occur if certain boundaries are transgressed. The type of total freedom known in the democracies has not arrived and may not come in certain settings. Yet, intellectual exchanges can now proceed with a degree of candor and nonpolemic dialogue not previously possible. It would be unfortunate indeed if both public and private U.S. funds were not expended to develop a larger exchange program at many levels.

What if the reforms are reversed, and in either the economic or the political arena a retreat takes place? China is a case in point. The events of June 1989 shocked the liberal world and tarnished the image of the PRC even in most Leninist states. Only Vietnam and North Korea lauded the repression of the student movement.

In reality, of course, the events of the spring of 1989 provide specificity to the general principles outlined earlier. Rising economic problems after 1985 led to divisions within the topmost elite. Thus, a divided government faced the demonstrators, making rational responses to the student demands extremely difficult. To pursue a moderate policy was to benefit individuals like Zhao Ziyang, certainly not the desire of Li Peng and his adherents. Both sides in the upheaval, to be sure, made tactical mistakes. The unwillingness of the government to engage in a serious dialogue with the movement leaders at an early date, the provocative April 26 editorial in the *People's Daily*, the declaration of martial law at a time when the movement was declining, and the brutal tactics at the end were all signs of weakness, not of strength. However, had the students decided to return to the campus and shift tactics on the eve of Gorbachev's arrival, they would have won a political as well as a moral victory.

In any case, a repressive period is now in process, albeit one replete with contradictions and uncertainties. The response of the United States, predictable as it was, reveals the underlying tension between moral concerns and strategic interests when these come into conflict. The Bush administration expressed its clear disapproval of Chinese official actions and took certain measures in accordance with this disapproval. Congress and human rights activists, among others, wanted more severe measures taken. The U.S. intellectual community, including specialists on China, have been unable to develop a unified position.

The case for the policies taken by the Bush administration is strong, in my opinion, although the first visit by national security adviser Brent Scowcroft was unwise, both in its timing and in its secrecy. Virtually everyone acknowledges that despite the victory of the hardliners, the Chinese government remains divided, with its legitimacy at low ebb, its principal leaders either aged or of questionable competence, and with very uncertain power bases. Thus, the situation has all the earmarks of a transitional era, although no one can estimate the length of the transition or the next step. Meanwhile, there are many signs that even within the government, the more committed reformers continue to exist, especially at levels below the top. The progressive Chinese intellectuals, moreover, desperately want to keep intact their contacts with the external world, and they have shown both courage and determination in this respect. There is no reason to abandon them.

It is appropriate that the low-level strategic relations previously existing be suspended. Wholesale economic sanctions, however, would not work in the absence of international consensus, and that clearly is not present. Economic decisions in this case are best left to the private sector. U.S. businessmen, like most others, are properly skeptical of new investments at this point, and it is their money along with that of the Japanese and West Europeans that will constitute the most meaningful pressure, especially because the current leaders insist that under no condition will they abandon the process of economically turning outward.

As suggested, the American people historically have demanded a moral foundation for U.S. foreign policy, thereby differentiating them from both Europeans and Asians. It can be asserted that certain U.S. policies were immoral or amoral, but the fact remains that Americans, and because of them, the U.S. Congress, repeatedly push forward the moral argument. If human rights are to be advanced in these times, however, they like economics must be internationalized. U.S. unilateralism in this field is likely to have even less effect than unilateral economic sanctions. Fortunately, the internationalization of human rights is underway, as is well known. Through such milestones as the Helsinki Agreements, this subject has been brought into the international arena, and it is now a common topic of Western dialogue with the Soviet Union among others.

In conversations with Chinese leaders, one realizes that most of them, like their North Korean and Vietnamese counterparts, are living in an earlier age. It must be remembered that however clever intellectually and skilled politically, they are the remnants of the first generation political elite, many of them peasant in origin and possessed of limited education or world experience. They have known conflict and sacrifice in the process of acquiring power, and their values and actions always will be reflective of some combination of tradition and modernity. It is thus natural that while most of them now grasp the importance of turning outward economically, they cling to archaic concepts of sovereignty, viewing the nation as a fortress not to be penetrated by foreigners. The fact that interdependence—economic, cultural, and strategic—requires the stretching of governance and the sharing of power is extremely difficult for them to accept, as is the fact that a country's domestic policies can affect both the conditions and attitudes of other peoples.

Thus, human rights are not merely a domestic matter, in China or anywhere else. At the same time, an effort by the United States to insist that its approach to this issue must command universal allegiance will fail. Only as we make further progress in internationalizing the question of human rights, establishing the criteria at that level for determining violations, will genuine progress be made. The United States can play a powerful role in this regard, but not a solo role. Meanwhile, human rights organizations should continue to deplore repression in China and elsewhere, bringing forth such facts as are available. It also is fitting that those in the category of genuine political refugees be accorded asylum in diverse open societies. In this type of situation, pluralistic approaches at the public and private levels are eminently suitable. For example, individuals and private organizations can speak or act in a manner unsuited to governments. It must not be forgotten that the Asian Leninist states, while lagging politically, have diverse constituencies warranting different approaches.

Even North Korea may not be exempt from this categorization. That society appears to be living in an earlier age, with the cult of personality dominant, an ideology compounded out of limited Marxism and excessive nationalism supreme, and mass movements directed toward economic "leaps forward," efforts to overcome technological backwardness by substituting fervor. A younger, better educated generation possessing different ideas stands in the wings, however, a small but important number of them the products of East European and Soviet education. At some point, the process of change will accelerate. Already the foundations are being laid in the growing recognition of the inadequacies of the old economic system, private debates over economic measures, preparations for tourists, and low-level trade via third parties with South Korea. In this setting, the United States is warranted in allowing expanded cultural contacts and continuing the low-level official dialogue that has opened in Beijing between embassy representatives.

Vietnam also seems mired in the political past despite recent economic reform efforts. Massive military expenditures continue, with no clear sign that the drive to dominate Indochina has been abandoned despite troop withdrawal. A sullen people view the party and government with disdain. A generational shift in leadership is underway but it has not yet affected policies fundamentally. Corruption is rampant together with the widespread cynicism that goes with such situations.

U.S. diplomatic recognition of Vietnam now would revive memories of our earlier abandonment of South Vietnam by appearing to accept Hanoi's formula for Cambodia, a formula designed to grant that country continued dominance over Indochina. Without the participation of all Khmer factions in the political process and a solution that grants minimal satisfaction to China as well as Vietnam, can there be genuine peace in that tragic country, or in the region as a whole? Pressures for policy change are growing within the United States, reminiscent of the early 1970s, although at this point the pressures are primarily from groups with special agendas. Yet, the United States currently has a certain leverage. Hanoi is desperately anxious for the United States to normalize relations with it and release current economic restrictions. Is it too much to ask that in exchange Hanoi show greater accommodation in accepting the basic principles set forth in the Australian peace proposal?

Conclusion

To distill the central propositions set forth in this analysis, three basic guidelines for U.S. policy toward the Leninist states seem appropriate at present. First, it should be accepted that today there is no Leninist community of nations. The diversities are substantial, and they still are widening. Some Leninist states, essentially those with the strongest Western heritage, are beginning an experiment with political pluralism. Others are seeking to modify Leninism in the direction of an authoritarian–pluralist system. A few recalcitrants are trying to stand firm on the old order, although the overwhelming likelihood is that the global revolution sooner or later will make such a course impossible to sustain. In any case, as noted earlier, the circumstances governing Leninism today demand pluralist policies on the part of the United States rather than a uniform line.

Second, it must be assumed that the primary responsibility for the results of the reform efforts rests with each society and its leaders. Moreover, setbacks, reversals, and failures—at least on a temporary basis—are inevitable. The task of altering Leninism, radically or even partially, is supremely difficult. It is imprudent to overestimate our capacity to assist the reformers. At the same time, to do nothing is to turn our backs on an unprecedented historic opportunity. Among other measures, consideration should be given to the creation of a diversified private U.S. group having as its major mission an ongoing study of all facets of this question as it observes the unfolding of developments in the Leninist world. This group could attempt what governments generally do not do well, namely, to look at the potential medium- to long-range implications of various policy alternatives, meeting periodically to review developments and being semi-permanent in nature, with some rotation of personnel. Such questions as these would be pondered: How much aid, and to what ends? What should be the tempo and direction of arms reductions? How can cultural relations, including educational exchanges, be advanced? How should restrictions on trade and technological transfer be handled? Many of these issues must be considered in consultation with those aligned with the United States. New policies that keep abreast of this revolutionary age are needed now.

Finally, the issue of "punishing" those states that retreat into suppression and efforts to reestablish "pure Leninism," in whole or in part, warrants equally careful treatment. Given the extraordinary fluidity and complexity of this area, the U.S. government should not take irrevocable steps, lest it be unable to adjust quickly to further changes. It can and should speak out against violations of human rights, with this issue internationalized as fully as possible. Yet actions that cut access to the very people who are struggling to sustain the reform momentum are self-defeating. Different policies are appropriate toward those Leninist nations that are deeply engaged in the battle over reform and those where reform, particularly in the political realm, scarcely has begun. Toward both categories, however, a type of pluralism can and should be developed, with governmental and private policies diverging where appropriate.

No one can predict the precise course of the revolution sweeping over the Leninist world. Yet, in terms of the great goals to which we subscribe—peace, human rights, economic development, political openness, and cooperation in facing the problems that will dominate the twenty-first century—there is ample reason for optimism. We should seize the moment.

This paper was presented originally at a CSIS Pacific Forum meeting on "An Agenda for the U.S. and Japan on Northeast Asia: Political, Economic, and Strategic Challenges for the 1990s," held in Kauai, Hawaii, November 26–29, 1989 and was updated in June 1990.

Notes

1. Soviet Minister of Defense Dimitri Kazov, as quoted during his 1989 visit to the United States.

2. Robert A. Scalapino, *The Politics of Development—Perspectives on Twentieth-Century Asia* (Cambridge, Mass.: Harvard University Press, 1989), pp. 93ff.

II. Alliances Transformed

The Emerging European Security Order

Hans Binnendijk

THE TECTONICS of the old European security order have been in metamorphosis for two years, creating political earthquakes and new fault lines on the Eurasian landmass. The security institutions straddling these fissures have had to undergo fundamental changes. They are either dying (the Warsaw Pact), evolving (the Conference on Security and Cooperation in Europe), undergoing revitalization (Western European Union), restructuring to adjust (North Atlantic Treaty Organization), or searching for new missions (European Community).

The dramatically changing political landscape makes this the sixth period of fundamental transition in European security affairs in the past two centuries. The first came with the rise of Napoleon after the French Revolution. A security alliance was eventually formed specifically to crush him. The second period began in 1815 when the Concert of Europe was born in Vienna. This flexible system of shifting alliances succeeded in maintaining the balance of power in Europe until the rise of the German empire in 1871. Bismarck's successors ushered in a third system of more rigid alliances that could not deal with regional instability and locked Europe into the tragedy of World War I. The fourth system, established at Versailles in 1919, relied at least initially on loose alliances and the rule of law implemented by a fatally flawed League of Nations. The fifth system, formed at the end of World War II, returned to rigid alliances and gave us the Cold War.

The sixth system, the new European order, is likely to have elements drawn from these previous cycles of history. As in other cases, it took a defeat—albeit not a military defeat or even one imposed from the outside—of one of the major parties to change the system. Like most preceding systems, the basic parameters of the new order will be determined within a few years of that defeat. It will have an alliance system less rigid than that of the Cold War, continuing the historical pattern of alternating fixed and more flexible systems. And, if history is any guide, the new system could last for more than a generation. The past average has been nearly four decades.

The detailed outlines of this more uncertain, more complex, and possibly less stable new order may be visible by the end of 1991. The changing nature of the risks of conflict is becoming clear. The Soviet domestic crisis creates the potential for substantial disorder. The first case of major ethnic conflict in post–cold war Eastern Europe is unfolding in Yugoslavia. Defense integration among West European nations is taking uncertain turns. And the transatlantic relationship, al-

---

Hans Binnendijk is director of the Institute for the Study of Diplomacy, Georgetown University.

though still firm, is in a holding pattern absorbing lessons from the Gulf War and waiting for Europe to define its own defense identity.

The opportunities are many and massive. With the right mix of political will and luck, the multilayered set of interlocking security institutions that is emerging may provide the flexible system that is needed to deal with the various problems that threaten the peace in Europe.[1]

This article will first review the changing threats to peace in Europe that exist after allied victories in the Cold War and the Gulf War. Next it will assess the changes that are under way in the key Western security institutions. And finally, it will offer some rules of the road to guide decision makers during the closing months of 1991.

The New Security Environment

During the Cold War, the conventionally superior Warsaw Pact forces posed the only overwhelming security threat to the North Atlantic Treaty Organization (NATO). Today that threat is gone and unlikely to return in the same form. NATO now conceives of "risks" rather than "threats," but perhaps these situations are best described as instabilities because most stem from internal disorder rather than calculated decisions to commit aggression. Risks to Europe's peace might come from a revanchist or disintegrating Soviet Union, from ethnic conflict or transition problems in central and southeastern Europe, or from escalating third world conflict involving nations armed with ballistic missiles and weapons of mass destruction. In short, Western Europe has exchanged the iron curtain for a "belt of instability" stretching from Riga in the East, through Romania to the Southeast, and ending at Rabat to the Southwest.

The Changing Soviet Dimension. President Mikhail Gorbachev has followed a zigzag course to try to preserve the Soviet Union intact and to achieve perestroika. In autumn 1990, he believed both goals were threatened by reformers seeking both independence for the republics and overly ambitious economic changes. Moving to the right, he found both the Union threatened by violent repression and no support for perestroika. At the same time Boris Yeltsin continued to gain political legitimacy while national productivity tumbled, convincing Gorbachev that the future lay with greater democracy and economic reform. Gorbachev's recent alliance with Yeltsin may be his last chance to attain his twin goals on his own terms. By devolving large measures of state authority to the republics and making secession legal but economically quite painful, he hopes to preserve the Union. By developing far-reaching economic reforms that retain an element of central control, he hopes to attract foreign aid without completely alienating the conservatives. Should his alliance with Yeltsin again falter, or should it fail to yield economic results, Gorbachev has little room left for maneuver. Polarization and possible civil war could follow.

One outcome of Soviet internal collapse could be rule by the right. It is in this case that the West might again have to worry about a risk of conflict with a revanchist Soviet Union. With Soviet forces remaining in Germany and Poland for up to three more years, there is plenty of potential for problems. But a short-warning conventional military threat exists only on NATO's flanks, where the excuses for aggression are limited. To prepare for the enforcement deadlines set up by the Conventional Forces in Europe (CFE) agreement of November 1990, Moscow has moved some 57,000 pieces of major defense equipment east of the Urals.[2] A quarter of that total will be destroyed or converted, while the Soviets have given assurances that the rest will be stored in a way that prevents rapid deployment westward. Redeployment of the remainder westward would provide months of warning time and would violate the CFE agreement. About 7,500 additional Soviet tanks and 9,000 armored combat vehicles will also be incapacitated once CFE has been ratified. The East European armed forces that were counted against Warsaw Pact totals in reaching conventional parity could now be expected to fight against Soviet troops that violate their territory. In all, the number of potentially hostile troops in Eastern Europe alone will decline by about one million.

In November 1990, the Soviet general staff calculated that the correlation of forces in Europe had turned against Moscow by a ratio of 1.6 to 1.[3] That was before they had seen the U.S. military perform in the Gulf War against predominantly Soviet equipment and Soviet-trained troops. The Western victory shocked the Soviet military, forcing Marshal Dmitri Yazov to call publicly for a review of Soviet air defense capabilities. The result may be abandonment of "defensive sufficiency," because the U.S. offensive demolished a Soviet-designed defense. Return to a more offensive doctrine would be coupled with greater reliance on high-tech weapons and a more professional army. Such a force would warrant continued NATO attention.

None of these developments affects the Soviet nuclear threat. The Strategic Arms Reduction Talks (START) will leave Moscow with both a significant hard-target kill capability and a relatively invulnerable intercontinental ballistic missile (ICBM) force. That may not be true of the U.S. ICBM force after START. In addition, the pending short-range nuclear force talks (SNF) are on hold, with Washington increasingly unwilling to negotiate reductions bilaterally that it plans to make unilaterally anyway. Moscow may take a tougher line on future nuclear reductions because the Soviets may need their own flexible response doctrine to offset conventional force asymmetries. Now may be the time for Washington to develop a more aggressive program for nuclear arms reductions that will more clearly define the nature of minimum deterrence, both in European and strategic nuclear systems.[4]

Conventional or nuclear threats to the West appear much less realistic than risks associated with Soviet domestic upheaval. Economic turmoil coupled with relatively free emigration conjures up visions of a horde of Soviet refugees marching westward. In addition, if the Soviet Union should collapse, new ethnic and border clashes might break out throughout the area. The potential for civil war raises the added concern that Soviet nuclear weapons might become bargaining chips in the conflict. Most nuclear weapons have been removed from trouble spots, but with tens of thousands of warheads, not all could be guaranteed in safe hands. A senior Soviet general recently knocked on wood three times after explaining Soviet nuclear command and control procedures to his stunned Western audience.

These dramatic scenarios of Soviet civil war, chaos, and a return to hardline rule need to be considered by Western security analysts. The most likely outcome, however, is that Soviet leaders will try to put off conflict and simply muddle through.

Eastern Europe in Strategic Limbo. The demise of the Warsaw Pact was widely applauded throughout central and southeastern Europe, but there is little to take its place. The Conference on Security and Cooperation in Europe (CSCE) was initially regarded as a possible substitute, but its limitations have now been recognized. The nations of central Europe had also hoped for NATO membership but they are beginning to understand that this would push the Soviet Union too far and that membership is closed to them at least for now. NATO's June 6, 1991, Copenhagen declaration that "coercion and intimidation" aimed at the countries of central and southeastern Europe would be treated as a matter of "direct and material concern" is probably as much of a commitment as these countries will receive from the West.[5] Associate status in the European Community (EC) might provide some vague security commitments, but full membership probably remains years away. Regional security has failed before in Eastern Europe, although some regional security cooperation in areas like air defense will prove useful. None wants Swedish-style neutrality.

These countries are, thus, in a strategic limbo with no obvious defense arrangements, and they may have to rely on a series of "negative-security" pacts until NATO or EC membership eventually opens to some or until the CSCE matures. These pacts would bind each country not to take certain steps that might threaten the security of the other country. Romania has already signed such an agreement with the Soviet Union, in which Romania pledges not to join another alliance.

The countries of central Europe will resist making similar pledges, but they may agree that no foreign troops should be stationed on their soil. The Soviets would reciprocate by agreeing not to station forces in these central European countries in the future.[6] If the West is asked to guarantee such a no-troops pledge, however, it may in fact be providing some degree of military commitment to Hungary, Czechoslovakia, and Poland. Meanwhile, these countries will pursue economic, political, and cultural ties with the West and hope that this reinforces the deterrent effect of the "shadow of NATO."

Unfortunately, the region in strategic limbo is also the most unstable part of Europe.[7] Its problems range from civil war between Serbs and Croats in Yugoslavia to the possibility of conflict between Hungary and Romania. Most states remain politically and economically fragile during their transition from communism. Democracy and peaceful transfer of power are not yet the norm. If violence erupts, the West could feel compelled to become involved either to stop slaughter or to prevent neighboring states from intervening in favor of ethnic minorities. Close U.S.–Soviet consultations are required to avoid the dangerous misunderstandings that are inherent in the current situation of vague commitments. The West's ability to aid central and southeastern Europe and to manage conflict there could be the single most important security task it faces this decade.

The New Risk from the South. The Gulf War has dramatized for most Europeans that risks to their security will increasingly come from the South. The sight of ballistic missiles landing in Tel Aviv, the threat of chemical warfare, the risks of nuclear proliferation, and the sophistication of advanced weapons available to developing countries seriously concern European decision makers. So do terrorism and the constant flow of immigrants from the Maghreb.

The Gulf War demonstrated that Europe alone, as it is now organized, is incapable of dealing with many of the new threats. Although it was able to help enforce the economic embargo on Iraq through naval activities coordinated by the Western European Union (WEU), it was unable to reach internal agreement on what to do next. The French broke ranks with a last-minute unilateral peace initiative. The Belgians were unwilling to sell artillery ammunition to the British. The Germans hesitated before honoring the NATO commitment and sending Alpha jets to a threatened Turkey. And European reliance on U.S. airlift, sealift, command and control, intelligence, and manpower was painfully clear for the world to see. Europe's military and political gaps will not be filled easily. So although Europe emerged from the war impressed by U.S. resolve and military capability and perhaps even more reliant on them, it also emerged with a strong desire to find a more united and equal voice in foreign and security policy.

The Gulf War has also had the effect of creating two separate categories of what in the NATO context used to be called "out-of-area issues." The first is problems on NATO's periphery. Inspired by the Iraqi threat to Turkey, this category includes potential conflicts involving neighboring countries that could directly threaten NATO countries. In these cases, NATO might take a more direct role. The second category includes the more traditional out-of-area problems where vital interests of NATO members are at stake. NATO officials hope to deal with these cases primarily through joint intelligence and policy coordination but not necessarily through direct NATO military action.[8]

NATO Tries to Adjust

In the days of the Cold War, NATO's mission was often described by using Lord Ismay's famous dictum that its purpose was to keep the Soviets out, the Americans in, and the Germans down. Perhaps the new purpose of European security is to pull the East up, bring Europe together, and continue to keep the Americans in. A more detailed list of goals would include the following:

- deter any residual Soviet threat;
- provide some collaborative structure for Western security ties with the Soviet Union;
- encourage democratization in the Soviet Union and Eastern Europe;
- extend a degree of stability to Eastern Europe through assistance, conflict resolution, and if necessary peacekeeping;
- keep Germany as an integral part of the Alliance and the European Community;
- avoid renationalization of European armies;
- maintain strong U.S. ties with and influence on European defense efforts; and
- organize Western responses to crises, aggression, and arms proliferation outside the NATO area.

The institutional instruments needed to accomplish these tasks are more complex than the NATO of the Cold War. No single organization can do the job, and a multilayered set of interlocking institutions is needed. Europe's security priority must be to adjust existing institutions to accomplish these goals and to create new institutions if necessary.

NATO's role in this effort will be, first, to hedge against a renewed Soviet threat; second, to keep German and other armies as part of an integrated European command; and, third, to maintain a U.S. commitment to Europe. But staying in nearly the same place during a period of rapid transition has required significant movement. NATO can accomplish the same goals with less military capability but perhaps at the cost of spending more political capital to hold the Alliance together. The broad outlines for NATO's transformation were developed in the London Declaration of July 6, 1990, which declared that:

- the Warsaw Pact would no longer be considered an adversary;
- conventional forces would be smaller, highly mobile, more versatile, increasingly multinational, and more reliant on reserves and force reconstitution; and
- nuclear forces would be truly weapons of last resort.[9]

Since then, a three-tier review has been under way to implement the London Declaration. The reviews are to be completed prior to the November 1991 NATO summit, which is expected to put the new NATO policies in final form. At the most senior level, the NATO Council has struggled with fundamental political issues such as redefining NATO's basic functions. It has made little progress on key issues such as extending NATO commitments eastward, using NATO troops for peacekeeping in Eastern Europe, and extending NATO operations out of its area to deal with North–South and proliferation issues. The French have resisted any expansion of NATO's functions, so Europe will probably have to rely on other institutions for this purpose.

The Strategic Review Group, chaired by Britain's Michael Legge, is considering alternatives to existing NATO doctrine. Forward Defense will be discarded in favor of a doctrine that allows for mobility and some forward positioning. Flexible response will be recast to make it consistent with reduced tactical nuclear force deployments and the new "last resort" policy. But NATO continues to shy away from discussions of nuclear issues. In general, Legge's review will recommend a broader approach to security issues in which military force is not dominant and crisis management is a more important tool. Preliminary work on the review has been completed and negotiations are under way with the French.[10]

The most progress has been made by the Military Committee and the Supreme Headquarters Allied Powers in Europe (SHAPE), although logically broad strategic parameters should be set before military details are decided. On May 28, 1991, NATO announced a revamped concept that included the following.

- A mobile immediate reaction force numbering 5,000 capable of responding to crisis in 72 hours;
- A Rapid Reaction Corps 50,000 to 70,000 strong designed to respond in less than one week. The corps would be commanded by the British and include two British divisions, two multinational divisions, and U.S. ground, air, and air transport units.
- A base force of seven multinational corps designed to defend Western Europe. Included would be three German corps (one in the eastern part of Germany), one Dutch corps, one Belgian corps, one mixed Ger-

man and Danish corps, and one U.S. corps. A U.S. division would serve in a German corps and vice versa.
- An augmentation force, made up primarily of U.S. units, designed to reinforce NATO's base force.[11]

Under this concept, NATO troops might be reduced by 350,000, of which nearly half could be Americans. By the mid-1990s (after Soviet troops leave Germany), the United States would have in Europe a corps headquarters, two army divisions, and corps support elements. This would yield a new U.S. force level of about half of the current 320,000 troops or less. The position of Supreme Allied Commander, Europe (SACEUR) would continue to be held by an American, at least for now.[12]

The NATO reforms will change the institution enough to enable it to survive in the new environment. All nations of Western Europe—even the French—want NATO to remain. The adjustments should also help Europe in future transatlantic burden-sharing debates. Significant progress was made at the May 1991 meeting of NATO defense ministers in consolidating NATO's position, but the debate over the European defense identity continues.

The European Defense Identity

The founding fathers of the European Community had a vision of a United States of Europe with its own independent defense identity. Several events during the past two years have raised the prospect that their vision might be achieved before the end of this decade. Inertia following the ratification of the Single European Act and the talks on monetary union led to the formation in December 1990 of a second Inter-Governmental Conference (IGC), which is assigned the task of drafting a Political Union Treaty by the end of 1991. The Germans want political union as the price for monetary union. Others want monetary union in order to benefit from the strength of the deutsche mark, and coincidentally they want to anchor a united Germany firmly in West European institutions. The changed threat perception with regard to the USSR allows Europe to contemplate a more united role, and the prospect of U.S. troop withdrawals may compel them to consider it. Above all, Europe's weak response to the Gulf crisis has forced it to find ways to strengthen its institutional ability to respond to future crises.

The bidding was opened by the Italian foreign minister, Gianni de Michelis, who suggested an early EC–WEU merger. The president of the EC Commission, Jacques Delors, provided a more comprehensive approach in an address in London on March 7, 1991, when he called for the insertion of the mutual defense clause of the WEU's Article 5 into the Political Union Treaty. With an EC mutual defense commitment, the WEU would eventually emerge as the key institution for European security. Delors also suggested that the WEU should be a "melting-pot for a European defense embedded in the community."[13] The Delors proposal is generally considered overly ambitious.

Franco–German collaboration has been a driving factor in setting the agenda for the establishment of a Common Foreign and Security Policy (CFSP) within the EC. In joint statements, the two countries have called for cooperation among the 12 EC members to present common positions on security issues in the NATO coordination process. Issues to be discussed by the EC would range from multilateral arms control to armaments cooperation. They have also called for the European Council (summits of the Twelve) to provide guidelines to the EC. Ultimately, after 1996, they envision absorption of the WEU by the EC.[14] Until that time, the WEU would serve as what WEU Secretary General Wim van Eekelen has called a "temporary bridge" between NATO and the EC.[15]

The current draft of the IGC Political Union Treaty foresees a two-stage process. In the short run, it envisions an organic relationship between the WEU and the EC, the nature of which is unclear. In the longer run, it would set as a goal a common EC defense policy, with a review in 1996 to reconsider merger of the WEU and the EC. The British and Dutch have objected to much of this plan. Final decisions on these matters will be taken in the IGC in the context of trade-offs with issues on monetary union.

A key set of issues to be decided in 1991 relates to the role and orientation of the WEU. The phoenix-like WEU is a nine-member European defense organization originally designed to hedge against postwar German rearmament. Its efforts to coordinate European naval operations in the two recent Gulf crises have made it a focal point for the European defense identity. It has no military forces or command structure of its own, but proposals are being discussed to allow some European troops dedicated to NATO's new Rapid Reaction Force to be at the same time the core of a WEU-based force of the same name. Van Eekelen has suggested a series of arrangements by which ambassadors would represent their countries in both the WEU and NATO, and he has also promoted coordinated WEU–European Council meetings so that the WEU can be a bridge between NATO and the EC as well. But transition measures do not solve the underlying problem that the United States and Britain want the WEU to become the second pillar of NATO, whereas France and to a lesser extent Germany want it under the direct control of the European Council. The bridge is under pressure from both directions. France moved aggressively to push its view when it set a precedent by calling a WEU meeting in the middle of the April 1991 EC summit and later reportedly proposed an EC rather than a NATO Rapid Reaction Force.

The United States has viewed many of these developments with alarm. Despite years of support for a European pillar within NATO, the United States is concerned that movement toward a European defense identity will bring about U.S. political and military isolation within NATO and that eventually a new European defense organization will compete with NATO. If developments go the wrong way, they could force U.S. troops out of NATO and perhaps even destroy the Alliance. William Taft, U.S. ambassador to NATO, speaking in London on February 9, 1991, warned that Americans would be suspicious of those who "mess" too much with familiar security structures.[16] A harsh U.S. diplomatic note to European capitals followed on February 22, warning against a European caucus in NATO that might move decision making on defense issues from NATO to the EC. The United States does not mind if the WEU presents a coordinated position in NATO councils, but it fears that the EC has a history of reaching agreed positions that leave little negotiating flexibility, a development the United States would find intolerable in the defense area. Washington does not want to repeat within NATO the experience of the General Agreement on Tariffs and Trade (GATT) debate over the Common Agricultural Policy. Secretary of State James A. Baker III summarized the U.S. position by saying "one of our key goals must be to insure that NATO remains the principal venue for our consultations and the forum for agreement on all policies bearing on the security and defense commitments of its members."[17] Similarly, SACEUR General John Galvin is concerned that a parallel European command structure established either in the WEU or the EC would be expensive and confusing and would undermine the U.S. role in NATO.[18] The message is clear. The United States has changed its signals on a European defense identity from green to blinking amber.

With this display of U.S. concern, Europe is recalculating its position. The British, under Prime Minister John Major, are pursuing their newly articulated desire to be "at the heart" of the European process. But Britain remains concerned that EC procedures would paralyze decision making on defense and drive a wedge in the transatlantic relationship. They believe that strengthening the WEU provides a viable alternative. Given Major's success in providing EC leadership on the Kurdish problem, Britain is now strongly placed to influence the evolution of a European position.

The French position is more complex and somewhat contradictory. First, the French give great importance to NATO and the U.S. commitment to Europe. Since the Gulf War, President François Mitterrand has developed close personal ties with President George Bush and now consistently praises NATO and the United States in his foreign policy speeches. Despite NATO reforms, however, France resists moving closer to NATO's integrated command structure. France also supports efforts such as the European Confederation (CSCE minus North America), a stand that is likely to alienate the United States. Second, France emerged from the Gulf War impressed with Europe's weak response and convinced of the need to maintain its independence of action. Yet France champions deep political unity within the EC that would deny it a good deal of freedom of action. Third, France supports a European defense policy and a European army. Yet the one institution currently established for that purpose, the WEU, is dismissed by the Elysée as too close to NATO. The French want to retain the U.S. insurance policy without making premium payments.

Germany has emerged from unification and the Gulf crisis looking primarily inward and secondarily toward Eastern Europe. It must deal with over 30 percent unemployment in the five new *Länder* and instability along its eastern borders. To reassure Western Europe during unification, Chancellor Helmut Kohl linked Germany to French concepts of European integration. His personal vision includes a European army and a European currency. Foreign Minister Hans-Dietrich Genscher, however, wants to maintain an option to expand the European Community eastward that is incompatible with an early EC defense commitment. Kohl and Genscher also differ on whether Germany should allow its troops to perform out-of-area operations sanctioned by the WEU or NATO, and a constitutional amendment to allow such deployments is unlikely to receive the required two-thirds vote. Because of these divisions and uncertainties in German policy, the British have made special efforts to divert the Germans from the current

43

pattern of Franco–German cooperation. They appear to have been partially successful, because Kohl stressed in Washington during his visit of May 1991 that Germany did not want NATO diminished or replaced by a new European security system and that the WEU should be NATO's European pillar.[19]

Other Europeans are also uneasy with current plans for defense integration within the EC. In addition to wanting to avoid transatlantic tensions, the Dutch are concerned that the larger countries will dominate the European Council. The neutral Irish do not want to undertake an EC defense commitment. The Danes and Greeks are in the EC but not the WEU. The Turks feel isolated now and would object to being excluded from a new, stronger European defense community. The Portuguese value good transatlantic relations above all. Even the Italians are having second thoughts and are backing away from an early EC–WEU merger. NATO Secretary General Manfred Wörner has contributed to the debate by announcing seven principles to guide development of Europe's defense identity.[20] So Europe proceeds into the IGC Political Union talks with determined caution.

As Europe's caution waxes, it is possible that U.S. concerns will wane. Guidance to the WEU by the European Council might not differ significantly from what happens now because the WEU would be taking orders from nearly the same group of leaders. A single European voice in NATO would not be a disaster, as long as rigid positions were avoided. And a WEU structure that could command elements of the NATO Rapid Reaction Force might prove useful in cases where U.S. involvement would be detrimental. Convergence of transatlantic views on the nature of the European defense identity and its relationship to NATO is entirely possible.[21]

Additional Security Arrangements

In addition to NATO and the WEU, several other security institutions will contribute to the new European order.

Of these, the CSCE's function is perhaps most complex. Its unanimity rule and the Soviet veto make it useless as a true collective security organization to replace NATO. But it could be very useful to provide a collaborative structure for Soviet–Western relations; promote conflict prevention and perhaps peacekeeping in Eastern Europe; and encourage democratization in the East. During the November 1990 CSCE summit in Paris, the organization received a secretariat (in Prague), a conflict prevention center (in Vienna), and a center for democracy (in Warsaw). Progress will be slow, as shown by the organization's inability to act early in the Yugoslav crisis. But because its 35 member states include countries from both Eastern and Western Europe as well as North America, the CSCE usefully complements the more traditional European security structure.

The United Nations (UN), too, might prove useful in Europe, as it already has in the case of Cyprus. The Security Council demonstrated new effectiveness in the Gulf War, and UN peacekeeping forces have much experience. They might be used for conflict management in Eastern Europe, but the UN has traditionally been cautious about involvement in civil war or in any conflict when contending parties do not agree on the UN's role. The Chinese and Soviet vetoes also remain a factor. So although the UN might be useful when the occasion calls for it, it cannot be relied upon to provide continuing security for Europe.

Regional security proposals are springing up all over Europe to deal with local problems and to fill gaps left by the larger institutions. Nordic states, which already have the Nordic Council, muse about recreating the medieval Hanseatic League to provide a security framework for the Baltic republics (should they get independence). The three central European states already cooperate on security matters with meetings such as the one held recently in Visegrad. Romanians suggest that a Balkan League might bring peace to the area. Bulgarians see a future in a regional association with Greece. The Italians promote the Pentagonal group, which includes countries of the former Austro–Hungarian empire, and which Poland may soon join. The as-yet-unformed Conference on Security and Cooperation in the Mediterranean (CSCM) would give the countries of southern Europe a forum for discussions with the Maghreb countries. Franco–German military cooperation continues despite low initial marks for the Franco–German Brigade. Each of these proposals responds to local needs and fills gaps in the existing structure.

The Road Ahead

Europe in the 1990s might be seen as a set of concentric circles.[22] At the center are the nine nations that share membership in the EC and the WEU. As both institutions are strengthened, additional functions, such as implementing the Schengen agreement on borderless immigration, will be added. A second, wider circle would include the neutral EC members, a group likely to expand as European Free Trade Area (EFTA) countries join the EC. A third concentric circle includes the "hopeful three" of central Europe (Poland, Hungary, and Czechoslovakia), who are eager to join all of Western Europe's institutions. This group may be enlarged if the Baltic republics, Slovenia, Croatia, and others shed existing bonds and turn westward. A fourth group of states is likely to be on the outside, looking in. These would include the Soviet Union, the Balkan states, and probably Turkey. The United States and Canada are tied to this European model through NATO and an enhanced relationship with the EC.

Movement in the Europe of the 1990s will be generally toward the center circle. The inner core seeks to deepen its internal bonds. Many neutrals in the second group are reconsidering the value of neutrality in the new European order. Members of the third circle wait for their reforms to mature and for the Soviet Union to digest its current problems before they plunge to the center. The fourth group may be isolated from the rest of Europe, a situation that could cause long-term problems.

As these developments mature during this decade, some rules of the road might prove useful so that transatlantic ties remain strong and nations are not isolated as Europe deepens its integration process.

First, the United States should seek to make NATO a more attractive home for the European security identity. The London Declaration and recent NATO reorganization were steps in this direction. Eventually NATO will take on more characteristics of a bilateral European–North American alliance. The future model is a barbell with equal weights on both sides, rather than the current model of a wheel with the United States at the hub. The WEU should be actively encouraged to represent the European side, and NATO procedures may have to change to enhance the WEU's voice. The WEU's movement to Brussels and double-hatting WEU and NATO permanent representatives would be useful steps in this direction.

Eventually the United States might consider strengthening Europe's role by alternating the SACEUR position with Europe, although the consensus for now is that SACEUR should remain an American. If alternating roles were agreed to, a U.S. deputy could retain nuclear authority for the United States when SACEUR is a European.

Making NATO a more attractive home for a European defense identity also means making it more attractive for the French. At present, France appears unwilling to deepen its involvement in NATO and has generally created problems during the recent review. But after the changes that have taken place in Europe, there should be some convergence of French and NATO doctrine. In the nuclear area, for example, the dramatic decline in the number of theater warheads and the absence of viable targets in Eastern Europe mean that NATO's former doctrine of flexible response should move dramatically in the French direction. If agreement can be reached that use of nuclear weapons as a "last resort" means as a measure of desperation and not necessarily late in a war, then there might be opportunities for agreement on a key issue that has kept France and the rest of NATO apart. If Europe gains more control over NATO and doctrinal differences are reduced, France might eventually be lured further into NATO.

Second, Europe needs to be sensitive to U.S. fears of political and military isolation. The key is European patience. The defense integration process should be furthered step by step, so that the United States can be convinced at each stage that the next step will not harm NATO. Thus, while Europe can state its long-term visions, deadlines should be avoided. The current plan to reconsider an EC–WEU merger in 1996, for example, should be kept vague so that it is not seen by the United States as a deadline. As each step unfolds, it is to be hoped that the United States will learn that the European voice in NATO is not confrontational but in fact provides the United States with a stronger, more united partner. At the outset, however, the IGC talks on political union should limit the EC's role to security issues that do not clash with NATO's principal defense mission. Assigning defense functions to the EC at this stage could signal that Europe is taking a separate path. Similarly, military planners should continue to integrate U.S. forces into multinational European forces at every opportunity to avoid isolation of the substantially reduced U.S. contingent.

Third, the U.S. campaign to warn Europe of the limits of European defense integration has thus far had a positive effect, but accelerating the campaign could be counterproductive because it would be seen as interfering in Europe's internal affairs. Having delivered its message, the last remaining superpower should now have the confidence to stand back and let Europe decide how it wants to make its internal decisions.

Fourth, development of a European force of 50,000 under the WEU's command could enhance Europe's defense identity and provide a capability for intervention without a superpower. Such a capability might prove useful in Eastern Europe or the Middle East. It would be relatively inexpensive if NATO's new Rapid Reaction Force were reconfigured in time of crisis to drop the U.S. component. German and French participation would have to be worked out in advance. U.S. airlift, logistics, and intelligence capabilities would be needed at the outset to mobilize the force. Some degree of NATO consent would be required because troops would be pulled out of the NATO integrated command and the force's actions might eventually involve NATO in the conflict.

Fifth, the grey area of Western commitment to central Europe will suffice if no Soviet threat to the area reemerges. But should it reemerge, then vague commitments are more dangerous than no commitments at all. One need only remember the confusion about commitments to Poland in 1939, South Korea in 1950, and Kuwait in 1990 to conclude that Western intentions—one way or the other—should be made absolutely clear in the event of a real threat.

Sixth, the West needs to consider the tremendous costs of policy reversals or disintegration in the Soviet Union. A new world order backed up by UN enforcement is impossible without the Soviet Union. The Soviet nuclear threat remains. The Soviets are potentially powerful in Eastern Europe and parts of the Third World. Disintegration of the Union might give the West additional geostrategic advantages, but those advantages would be outweighed by the spillover risks of civil war and large-scale ethnic strife in a nuclear power. Although the West certainly cannot bring stability to the Soviet Union, it can help. The Grand Bargain may be overly ambitious, but a phased Western financial plan tied to specific economic milestones must be developed both to encourage further reforms and to ease the Soviet Union's transition to a free market. The imposition of political conditions will be needed to make the plan feasible in the United States.

Steps also need to be taken to assure the increasingly nervous Soviet military that the West will not threaten Soviet forces and that Soviet military institutions will benefit from improved relations. NATO should conduct relations with the Soviet Union in a manner that will promote Soviet integration in Europe, not its continuing segregation from it. And the CSCE military doctrine dialogue might be intensified to further expose Soviet officers to Western security policy.

Finally, NATO should reconsider its prohibition of out-of-area operations. It would be dangerous to set up a mechanism that *requires* NATO to make decisions on third world disputes because agreement would be difficult in most cases. But if agreement can be reached, there is no legal obstacle to NATO's use of force beyond its treaty region. As the traditional threat from the Soviet Union fades, it is precisely the instabilities to the South that will increase in importance. By automatically taking itself out of the picture, NATO diminishes its overall usefulness. A place to start might be with instabilities on NATO's immediate periphery.

Conclusions

In the coming years, the perilous certainty of the Cold War will give way to the uncertain instability of a new European order. European security institutions are adjusting fairly well to the new environment and will form a flexible set of capabilities to meet the new challenges. The experience of 1914, when such instabilities were mismanaged by rigid alliance systems, is unlikely to be repeated.

New problems now exist for the transatlantic partnership: how to manage the Soviet decline; how to provide security for Eastern Europe; how to respond to future out-of-area problems; and how to handle the emerging European defense identity. So far, answers to the first three appear to lie to a large degree beyond the purview of NATO. The new and revived institutions like the WEU and the CSCE may have to take up the challenge, or NATO will have to expand its mandate. Yet NATO, even with its existing mandate, remains crucial to Europe's peace. Efforts spurred by the Gulf War to develop a new European defense identity must proceed carefully, using cautious rules of the road. If the United States supports Europe's long-term vision of its future, and Europe in turn respects the U.S. fear of isolation, adjustments can be made to retain a healthy transatlantic relationship.

Notes

1. For further discussion, see Hans Binnendijk, "What Kind of a New Order for Europe?" *The World Today* 47 (February 1991), pp. 19–21.
2. Michael Z. Wise, "Soviets Accept Limits on Arms in Europe," *Washington Post*, June 15, 1991, p. A–16.
3. Briefing in Moscow with members of the Soviet General Staff, November 1990.
4. Such a minimal deterrence program might include cuts to about 4,000 relatively invulnerable strategic nuclear warheads per side (i.e., real reductions by more than 50 percent after START I) and about 500 air-delivered weapons each in Europe for the United States and the USSR.
5. Thomas L. Friedman, "NATO Tries to Ease Military Concerns in Eastern Europe," *New York Times*, June 7, 1991, p. A–1.
6. François Heisbourg, "The Future Political and Security Architecture of Europe" (Paper presented to the Rome Conference on the Future of European Security, Rome, May 3, 1991).
7. See John Orme, "Security in East Central Europe: Seven Futures," and Jan Zielonka, "East Central Europe: Democracy in Retreat?" *The Washington Quarterly* 14 (Summer 1991), pp. 91–105 and 107–120, respectively.
8. Klaus Wittmann, "Work on NATO's Future Military Strategy" (unclassified briefing for the International Institute for Strategic Studies, London, April 16, 1991).
9. For the text of the London Declaration, see *Survival* 32 (September/October 1990), pp. 469–472.
10. Author's interviews at NATO Headquarters, Brussels, April 1991.
11. Paul L. Montgomery, "NATO Is Planning to Cut U.S. Forces in Europe by 50%," *New York Times*, May 29, 1991, p. A–1.
12. Alan Riding, "NATO: Still the Armorer for Europe," *New York Times*, May 30, 1991, p. A–3.
13. Jacques Delors, "European Integration and Security," Alastair Buchan Memorial Lecture (International Institute for Strategic Studies, London, March 7, 1991).
14. Franco–German Non-Paper (working paper), January 1991.
15. Also see "WEU's Role and Place in the New European Security Architecture" (Presidency's conclusions to the extraordinary meeting of the WEU Council of Ministers, Paris, February 22, 1991).
16. William Taft, "The US Role in the New Europe" (Address to the International Institute for Strategic Studies, London, February 9, 1991).
17. Friedman, "NATO Tries to Ease Military Concerns," p. A–8.
18. Author's interviews at SHAPE, Mons, Belgium, April 1991.
19. Helmut Kohl, "The Agenda of German Politics for the Nineties" (Speech at a luncheon sponsored by the Center for Strategic and International Studies, the American Institute for Contemporary German Studies, the Atlantic Council, and the Georgetown University School of Foreign Service, Washington, D.C., May 20, 1991).

20. Based primarily on author's interviews at NATO Headquarters, Brussels, April 1991. Wörner's principles, set out in a speech to the Atlantic Council in Washington, D.C., on June 25, 1991, were: (1) NATO is the essential forum for consultation and decision making on defense matters; (2) The new system must maintain the strategic unity of all its members; (3) It must strengthen the transatlantic link; (4) It must maintain transparency in the decision-making process; (5) Complementarity must be preserved; (6) NATO nations must not be marginalized; (7) The integrated military structure must be retained.

21. This convergence was in evidence during the NATO defense ministers' meeting on May 28, 1991. The ministers stated that "the efforts to develop a European Security identity and defense role should lead to a strengthened European pillar within the alliance." Riding, "NATO," p. A–3.

22. A related model has been proposed by Edward Mortimer of the *Financial Times*.

Germany, Japan, and the False Glare of War

*Daniel Hamilton and
James Clad*

IMAGINE BEING IN a room lit by lamps of familiar intensity and power. Suddenly, piercing illumination shines in from an unexpected direction, casting the surrounding forms in disturbing shapes and throwing distorted shadows on the walls. The flash from the Gulf War has had that effect on the perception in the United States of its position in the world. The war seemed to sharpen U.S. perceptions of friend and foe alike, clarifying underlying realities of power while exposing divergent assumptions about those supposed pillars of a "new world order"—the United States, Germany, and Japan.

Those assumptions, which concern the respective roles and responsibilities of the world's most influential countries, matter far more in the longer term than an expeditionary war in the Middle East, no matter how successful. And the United States stands a good chance of getting these key relationships right if it moves as decisively now as it did in the Gulf to burn away the disorienting fog that has accompanied notions of a new world order ever since the collapse of the Cold War.

For several years now, the United States has been groping its way through this haze, trying to discern the dimensions of the new house it inhabits. Judging from U.S. public reaction to Germany and Japan both during and in the aftermath of the Gulf hostilities, the war's brief and unnatural illumination has not helped Americans to see their way around much better. Indeed, it has blinded them to the architecture of the new world.

The war has brought home at least one clear lesson. Although the United States is no longer the undisputed world leader, it is still the only country that retains all the attributes of power: military, political, economic, technological, and demographic. It also enjoys a more varied and intimate range of ties with all the major powers than any other nation.

This range and diversity enables the United States to employ leveraging influence with all major powers, whether it acts in concert or alone. Like no other country, the United States has the power of international initiative and of global agenda-setting. It has the potential to emerge from the Gulf War as the world balancer; not the sole superpower or the world's policeman but the best-equipped broker.

The authors are senior associates at the Carnegie Endowment for International Peace. James Clad, an Asian specialist, is a former diplomat and correspondent for the *Far Eastern Economic Review*. Daniel Hamilton, a European specialist, was deputy director of the Aspen Institute Berlin from 1982 to 1990, where he directed an international project on "The Role of Germany and Japan in the 1990s."

The war's partial exorcism of the ghost of Vietnam is, of course, reinvigorating the U.S. belief in itself. Yet this reinvigoration must be based on assimilation of some provisional lessons from the Gulf War.

The Diffusion of Power

The most important lesson is that although the war's outcome was the result of the application of concentrated military power, the conflict's origins were the result of a diffusion of power in the broader sense.

As the discipline imposed by the Cold War dissipates, international tensions are driven more and more by the encroachments of regional powers. Bolstered in part by arms brokering that stemmed from the old rivalries, nations hitherto of less importance, such as Iraq, have grown in stature and confidence to the point at which they can pose challenges to the longer-established players.

Apart from that, the very nature of power itself has changed. To be effective, power measured by access to resources must be translated into power over outcomes. This translation occurs through a process of political negotiation in which attributes such as will, commitment, skill, and domestic cohesion outweigh crude calculations of military or economic power balances. Although the Gulf War has reminded the world of the occasional utility of military force, use of that force by the United States proved strikingly successful for two reasons. One was the legitimization of the use of force through intense, methodical diplomatic efforts to build and sustain a multilateral coalition through collective security mechanisms. Although the war demolished the fashionable notion that military power had gone the way of the dodo in a world that had seen the "end of history," the use of that force came sanctioned only as a last resort. The other reason was the financial engagement of sources unwilling or unable to send combatants.

Beyond the specific characteristics of the recent war lies a larger realization. Even in the first weeks after the fighting it was possible to detect how transient the military issues were by comparison to the mundane agenda of trade, investment, and other issues that count immeasurably more for the success, or shortcomings, of the United States as a nation. Already it is clear yet again that tight security relationships do not, on their own, reduce economic and political friction among allies.

In short, the once clear hierarchy of issues in world politics, in which the "high" politics of military security dominated the "low" politics of economic and social affairs, continues to fade, despite the forceful resolution of the invasion of Kuwait. By returning so quickly to an international agenda dominated by economics, and by renewed recognition of how deficits determine defense spending, the United States is acknowledging the self-correcting hand of a world in which security no longer equates to weaponry.

Erstwhile Partners in Leadership

A second lesson from the war is that Japan and Germany, erstwhile partners in the new world order, still shy away from exercising the roles of partnership-in-leadership that the United States had envisaged for them. Neither seemed ready to grasp the wider significance of the Gulf conflict. Neither has thought through its stake in a victorious result.

On the face of it, Japan's response to the Gulf crisis demonstrated that, despite its formidable economic and financial weight, Tokyo still hesitates to present a confrontational face to any adversary. Nor does it find it easy to abandon its occasionally neurotic habit of financial appeasement. Japan seemed to be offering too little, too late.

Meanwhile, Germany's relatively inept reaction to the Gulf War has also demonstrated that many Germans, like the Japanese, remain transfixed by years of postwar conditioning to view their country as an economic giant but a political dwarf. Like the Japanese, Germans remain susceptible to bouts of self-pity and urgent moralizing. And, fortunately, they still seem to be greatly inhibited by the Hitlerian legacy—just as Japan's trauma of defeat powerfully inhibits the seduction of the call to arms.

The reaction of both countries to the war shows that both will avoid leadership roles until they are able to define such roles as in their own national interests. This can only occur through their own domestic processes and on terms hammered out with partners and neighbors.

In the meantime, their foreign commitments are unlikely to reach beyond what their publics will support, what their institutions and neighbors will tolerate, or what their military and economic capabilities can sustain. After all, neither Germany nor Japan is a superpower. Both, instead, have become weighty intermediate powers, selectively strong in selected dimensions. And both prefer to argue that they remain too small or too vulnerable to play a larger role in global affairs, even if they realize they have grown too rich and too big to pretend that their abstinence carries no consequences.

At the same time, none of these caveats should obscure the strides made by each nation as it attempted to come to grips with questions of national direction posed by the Gulf War. When tallied, these moves point to a sea change in outward orientation, even if U.S. opinion has been almost totally oblivious to actions they took that were not only directly helpful to the allied cause but also unprecedented in the history of both countries since 1945.

Consider Germany's response. After initially treating the whole affair as an inconvenient distraction from unification, Germany agreed to donate $10.7 billion in multilateral aid for the U.S.-led coalition. It also served as the hub of war logistics and supply from Europe. Further, it agreed to the first significant deployment of its military forces outside German territory since World War II when it contributed jets and troops to a North Atlantic Treaty Organization (NATO) multinational rapid deployment force near the Turkish–Iraqi border. It is likely to change its constitutional restraints on the use of German armed forces abroad and, with Teutonic thoroughness, it now wants to clean away any stench caused by German "merchants of death" in the Gulf (especially sellers of chemical weapon precursors) by imposing a rigid new export control regime that could be extended throughout the European Community.

Japan reacted to the Iraqi invasion by pledging aid to countries affected by the seizure of Kuwait. Later, this support was extended to helping those affected by the international trade embargo. However fumbled in its later implementation, Prime Minister Toshiki Kaifu's promise to send noncombatant, Self-Defense Agency forces to Saudi Arabia marked a new departure. And the follow-up pledge from Tokyo of $10 billion toward the war effort, coming on top of its initial $3 billion donation, ultimately won parliamentary endorsement on March 7, 1991, albeit some weeks after the fighting had stopped.

But inside Japan, public debate was galvanized by Tokyo's offer of C–141 transport planes to move refugees out of Jordan (an offer never implemented; inconveniently, the refugees never appeared in sufficient numbers). This recalled Japan's last controversy over forward deployment when, in 1987, Tokyo declined to participate in naval patrolling during the Iran–Iraq War.

On a per capita basis, German contributions to the Gulf effort outweighed those from Japan, despite the fact that Germany had concurrently to find $30 billion to facilitate the withdrawal of Soviet forces from central Europe and additional billions to secure democratic, market-oriented reforms in Eastern Europe. Bonn must also shoulder the massive costs involved in the reconstruction of former East Germany, which are likely to amount to $600 billion over the course of this decade.

On the other hand, Japan's contribution of financial help toward the war amounted to 26 times that of South Korea, even though Seoul had good reason to respect wars to resist aggression sanctioned by the United Nations. In East Asia, only Singapore and Taiwan helped in cash or kind, although some under-the-table contributions also came from smaller Southeast Asian countries. And no other Asian nation has taken such a highly visible role in postwar patrolling as Japan.

From a captious perspective, Japan's visible, initial, and prewar contribution looked lame. Even New Zealand's three million people sent transport aircraft, service crews, and military medical teams totaling over 100 personnel to work alongside U.S. and British forces in the Gulf.

Yet seen in broader terms, Japan must receive due credit for financing an enormous part of the war's cost—a direct saving to the U.S. Treasury—and, in the postwar phase, for contributing naval capability. On the diplomatic side, it also deserves points for seeking an active role in promoting other initiatives aimed at increasing stability in the Middle East. Thus, its contribution was neither derisory nor (given the distance the Japanese public had to move) even very dilatory. Both Germany and Japan, therefore, not only broke important new ground during the crisis but also made extremely important contributions toward the U.S.-led, collective effort. And both paid in their contributions faster than any other country pledging financial support.

In rushing to advance a new order, the United States should be cautious about pushing Japan and Germany into military roles. If in the future it wishes to see Japan and Germany projecting armed power around the world, it must first think through the intermediate steps, working closely with each nation. After all, just a few months ago fears arose that a united Germany would seek to become a military superpower. Anxiety about a dominant Germany continues to hover just below the surface throughout Europe. And worries abound that Japan may feel obliged to deploy a blue water navy well down into Southeast Asian waters. After all, the size of the Japanese economy means that even its relatively restrained defense spending on a percentage of GDP basis has resulted in the world's largest military budget in cash terms.

Should Japan and Germany in fact convert their military potential into actual capability, then the balance of power would change dramatically, instantly destabilizing the regions in which each country lies and transforming German and Japanese domestic politics. The leaders of neither country want this. Nor do their neighbors. Neither should the United States.

Rather than viewing the Gulf War as a litmus test of loyalty, with both allies bringing home a poor report card, the war should be seen instead as a time of rapid learning. The crisis amounted to a forced march into the complexities of a world that, despite its shift toward economic competition, cannot kick the habit of conflict. The war's effect, therefore, was that of a salutary shock stimulating overdue internal debate in both Germany and Japan over future global roles and responsibilities. And the lively discussions in each of these democratic, prosperous countries has ignited much new thinking about the move from relatively passive participation in the cold war world to willing participation as principal buttresses of the post–cold war era.

Soon after the Gulf War each nation took cautious yet significant steps toward a broader international role. Germany sent Bundeswehr troops to build camps for Kurdish refugees in the Iran–Iraq border area. Japan's decision to send four mine-sweepers and two support vessels to the Persian Gulf also amounts to a sea change in attitude, one that only the catalytic effect of the earlier period of executive indecision (and embarrassment over that indecision) could have permitted in either country.

It must be remembered that formerly dependent countries do not find it easy to accept a more central political and economic position. The key remains the creation of a framework through which German and Japanese energies can prosper side by side with broad U.S. interests. And the vision, as before, remains one of a pluralist world—associative, collaborative, and managed. This requires many adjustments. It posits the basic trade-off of more equitable burden-sharing arrangements among allies matched by U.S. willingness to accept a commensurate increase in decision making by its partners. It also requires abandoning nearly two centuries of U.S. tradition (for the United States has always been unilateralist at heart, acting first and asking acquiescence later).

The United States must learn to persuade where it has been accustomed to command. This will be a particularly difficult lesson to learn in the wake of a victory such as it has so recently experienced. Yet it is precisely at this time, when nations around the globe recoil at the thought that any single country might seek to control the new world order, that the United States should counter perceptions that it is prepared to announce what might be called the Ring Lardner doctrine ("'Shut up,' he explained"). Nor will it be enough, as William Safire has done, to label Japan and Germany as mere checkbook powers: the days are fast passing when either country can offer a blank check to an alliance of undefined scope.

It is important to remember how rapidly the Gulf War came upon Germany and Japan as both were struggling to adjust to accelerating changes in the latter 1980s. For Germany, the conflict followed so closely on the heels of national unification and the disintegration of the old central European order that the demand for a further reorientation fast enough to suit either the United States or the swift-moving exigencies of the crisis simply overloaded the German capacity to cope.

For Japan, the crisis caused only the most recent of its many hesitant responses to its own rising importance in the Asia–Pacific region. For example, only within the last three years has Japan felt confident enough to play Asia's spokesman at the Group of Seven (G–7) economic summits. Insistent urging from the Reagan administration for Japanese rearmament has already collided with deeply entrenched political habits and prejudices, both within Japan and throughout Asia.

Just as Germany's political system has been breathlessly playing catch-up with global and regional realities, so has Japan's. As the primary potential beneficiaries of the transition to a new world order, both nations are expected by a range of neighbors to shoulder considerable burdens of adjustment.

The Soviets expect support for German unification to be repaid with greater economic assistance and a German–Russian "partnership of destiny"; East European reformers expect German aid, blueprints for economic and social modernization, and support for their efforts to join the European Community; West European partners expect Germany to spearhead the drive toward deeper European integration; Americans press Germans to shoulder greater global responsibilities as a "partner in leadership."

Japan has been deluged with similar requests—to rescue indebted countries, to use the aid weapon to express disapproval of repression in Yangon or Beijing, or to bankroll recovery programs for ailing U.S. client states, as in the Philippines. The Soviets, looking East, see trade-off chances in a restoration to Japan of the Kuriles in return for increased aid. Now, in the aftermath of the war, the United States wants Japan to apply pressure on Beijing to slow Chinese exports of certain conventional or even nuclear or chemical-capable weapons, for instance, the recent sales of missiles to Pakistan. Japanese public opinion is prepared to have Tokyo take a more assertive line in policing the Missile Technology Control Regime.

In important ways, therefore, German and Japanese leaders have already sought to meet expectations. Yet anxieties building in Bonn and Tokyo center less on aggressive new global roles than on what might be called anti-imperial overstretch.

The Nature of Alliances

A third lesson from the Gulf War concerns underlying assumptions about alliances. Desert Storm has vented a great deal of emotional clutter that had been building in U.S. relations with its two weighty allies.

Alliances, it is often said, rest on common cold-blooded national interests, not on emotional bonds between peoples. Nations have permanent interests, not permanent friends. Or so one hears—most recently from Henry Kissinger.[1] Yet it will be difficult if not impossible to comprehend the future direction of U.S relations with Germany and Japan if the United States does not understand the emotional underpinnings of its postwar friendships with these two countries and the manner in which this foundation might now deteriorate.

During the postwar era Germany and Japan drew strength and direction for their policies from their respective bonds with the United States. Each invested heavily and successfully in the partnership. Americans, too, were repeatedly refreshed by the success of their engagement in both countries. The Japanese and German economic, political, and moral recovery appealed to the pragmatic, can-do spirit of the United States. In American eyes, each country's success implicitly justified the U.S. role in the world. As Germany powered the European Community and as Japan's trade and investment network meshed with Asia and the Pacific, the United States viewed the unfolding events with the benign countenance of a senior partner. The United States promoted Japan's reentry into Asian affairs during the 1950s and 1960s via the creation of the Asian Development Bank and other regional initiatives. It also played a decisive role in building German democracy, promoting Germany's postwar rehabilitation and integration into the Atlantic Alliance, and facilitating German unity.

The belief that the United States can serve as a model for others remains central to its own self-image. Just as many Germans and Japanese idealized U.S. society in the early postwar period, the United States has idealized its role in Germany and Japan. It is a habit the pupils have outgrown far faster than their mentor.

The truth is, U.S. success has bred political superficiality. Despite the passage of time and obvious divergences in geographic, political, social, spiritual, and economic experience, the United States continues to idealize its place in the life of Germany and Japan. This has led to equating these junior partners in quite unjustifiable ways. Time and reality have now caught up with the idealized images, sparking an emotional shake-up that could damage the shared interests that bind the United States closely to both Japan and Germany.

New signs of restiveness are evident in each country. On the one hand, Germans and Japanese show disquiet with the U.S. inability to get its own economic house in order. They are correspondingly uneasy with their own, continued dependence. Both Germans and Japanese, although they now argue pro forma that their first priority remains an open international economic and monetary system, insist that they must also narrow their exposure, sheltering themselves from global economic and financial instabilities.

The German conclusion is to negotiate tougher terms of economic engagement within Europe and between the European Community and the outside world. Although committed to multilateralism, German leaders believe that various multilateral structures in their present form are no longer suited to the new realities. They are less hesitant about using Germany's new clout to retool old institutions, shape new ones, and achieve terms of engagement with major partners more beneficial to their perception of German interests. The tough stance taken by the German Bundesbank and the German government on European monetary union does not reflect a new hesitation toward such a union; it heralds a new assertiveness in defining European unity on German terms.

The Japanese conclusion is to redouble efforts, long evident now in corporate planning decisions, to locate manufacturing plants outside Japan and, generally, to get a foot over the moat before the trading bloc fortresses pull up the drawbridge. Coupled to this has been an approach that uses financial aid as a substitute for clearly stated policy, notably in Asia. And yet the Japanese grumble about U.S. assumptions that Tokyo's checkbook power will bolster U.S. priorities, as in China and the Philippines.

Americans, on the other hand, are frustrated by German and Japanese unwillingness to accept their "responsibilities" and carry their fair share of regional and global burdens. Pointed U.S. criticism of German and Japanese actions and dark populist suspicions about their presumed intentions simply amplify a bitter frustration erupting across the U.S. political spectrum that U.S. generosity over four decades has not been repaid with support for U.S. leadership. These views feed on a sense that the United States for too long has carried more than its fair share of the common defense. It flows also from a sense of "being had"—that the United States has maintained the international economic order only to be bested, by the Japanese in particular, by so-called allies that do not play by the rules.

Particularly galling, from this perspective, is a German and Japanese habit of characterizing U.S. policy either as naive or as overly bellicose. German and Japanese politicians sometimes find it necessary to defend their working arrangements with Washington as a struggle to restrain the impulsive and profligate Americans. The notion of Americans as loose cannons has a strong, residual resonance in both nations. The U.S. experience in Indochina during the 1960s and 1970s as well as the U.S. invasions of Grenada and Panama reinforce a distrust of U.S. readiness to resort to arms. Given that both the Germans and Japanese have been at the receiving end of those arms, and that they still perceive them to have been indiscriminately applied, it is not surprising that this depiction finds ready acceptance in both countries.

But this only gives the wider U.S. audience another reason for grievance. And so it continues. The rapidity of communications allows domestic politicking in Japan or Germany to play straight back into the U.S. arena. Their attitudes toward Americans—somewhat akin to humoring a slightly crazy, aggressive old aunt—only lead to more recriminations.

This dialectic of disparagement encourages a climate in both Germany and Japan that seeks further distance from the United States. To be sure, much of the mutual criticism has a patently unfair feel to it. Yet in the life of nations objective facts count for less if trust begins to erode. In the eyes of an ever-increasing number of Americans, Germany and Japan have become deeply suspect. They have acquired a reputation, fairly or unfairly, of being unwilling to take risks. They seem oblivious to their responsibilities for the common defense. As often as not they seem free-riders on the international economic and trading system. When a crisis erupts, Americans see Bonn and Tokyo as ducking behind a bogus constitutional commitment to peace.

On the German and Japanese side, myths and myopia have also multiplied. A deeply rooted cultural arrogance, dormant in much of the postwar period, periodically reemerges in both countries, leading to disdainful attitudes toward the U.S. cultural, economic, and political experience. These attitudes will erupt in future disagreements over substance, with each controversy tearing at the fabric of old associations.

In addition, the Gulf War revealed clearly that German and Japanese leaders have their own expectations regarding their new roles and responsibilities that may differ in crucial respects from the expectations of their U.S. partner. As Americans become less indulgent, Germans and Japanese become less deferential. Their leaders feel less inhibited about using their new clout to achieve new terms of engagement with the United States.

Germany and Japan Are Not Identical

Perhaps the most long-lasting of the many, galvanic effects of the Gulf War will be a settled understanding of how Germany and Japan *differ*. Outside the administration, much of the foreign policy debate in the United States has lumped the two countries together in a highly indiscriminate way. Criticism in the Congress often blurs the most elementary distinctions between these countries and assumes that their interests in the Gulf must converge with those of the United States.

A closer look at the differences is imperative. German hesitancy about wholehearted participation in the coalition, while disturbing, was based in part on the country's divided moral response to its past. Japanese hesitancy contained no such elements. Yet Germany is only 11 percent dependent on Middle Eastern oil, compared to 12 percent for the United States and 65 percent for Japan.

Japan did not contribute to help resist international aggression; it contributed mostly to avoid another U.S. (and European) round of Japan-bashing. And while initial German contributions may have been motivated by similar concern, German public opinion, at first uncertain, quickly hardened into support for the Gulf effort. In Japan, opinion remained ambivalent until the last stages of hostilities, when a strong wish to be on the winning side supplanted ethical agonizing over the war's human cost.

Arms sales to Iraq were another complicating factor. Germany's were significant, whereas Japan's sales were negligible. Indeed, despite the popular image of Japan in the United States as a single-minded exporter, Tokyo has erected the world's most restrictive export regulations for weapons-capable materials, such as chemical weapons precursors. German restrictions look tough on paper but, in practice, have been weakly enforced.

Divergent reactions to the Gulf reflect the different frameworks within which each country operates. German unification in 1990 was achieved with the acquiescence of all of Germany's neighbors—a tribute to German postwar policies of reconciliation carried out with neighbors in both East and West. The Japanese did not conceptualize their diplomacy in the same way as Germany but the same, postwar rehabilitation remained (and still remains) a guiding objective. Germany has no enemies while Japan has no friends of the size and importance of the United States.

German energies have become embedded in a dense network of multilateral institutions to which it has surrendered significant aspects of sovereignty and freedom of economic maneuver; Japan remains more autonomous within a more fluid and less structured East Asian environment, tied moreover via its primary relationship to a non-Asian power. Germany is emerging as Europe's central power, but its ambitions and its weight are balanced by other powers of consequence. In Asia and the Pacific, there is no equivalent structure to channel Japanese energies and no balancing powers, save the United States.

Other points of divergence may become significant. United Germany is now a sated territorial power whereas Japan still has outstanding territorial issues with the Soviet Union. Excessive preoccupation with trade disputes with Japan could leave the United

States unprepared for the economic consequences of the European Community's 1992 program, which will create a $5 trillion market of 340 million persons anchored to a formidable deutsche mark. Furthermore, Germany is much less dependent on the U.S. market than is Japan.

The Alliance After the Gulf War

Flushed with victory in the Gulf, the United States should pause. A more balanced scorecard reading of the war's results is available, one that will illuminate the lessons better than the sharp light of conflict. The war's aftermath has the potential to lead the United States to a better understanding of the proper balance between military power, economic prowess, and political will. It can also throw a broader light on the views of crucial U.S. allies. The present allocation of responsibilities and distribution of resources and power remain fixed in the past. The present expectations about roles fail to bring the Germans, Japanese, or Americans to reflect directly about the global foundations of their security, their economic prosperity, their political objectives, or their position in the world. By treating the alliance as a caricature of good and bad allies, the United States is still following the script of the late, unlamented old world order. To redress the damage, several shifts in mood must take place.

- First, the United States should acknowledge that both Germany and Japan made considerable efforts both to assist the immediate Gulf War effort and to lead their respective publics to see the wider aims involved.
- Second, while acknowledging both countries' very considerable internal difficulties, which obstructed a ready identification with U.S. aims, the United States should be explicit *now* about its future expectations of each.
- Third, the United States must make every effort to distinguish the unique characteristics of Germany and Japan. Reticence may wear a similar face in both countries but the similarities go no further. The State Department knows this. The White House knows this. Unfortunately, harsh words from Congress show that the public and its representatives do not.
- Fourth, the United States must keep a unique episode in perspective. It cannot sustain—let alone build—a new world order on the basis of a narrow quid pro quo defined by a you-owe-me, I-owe-you relationship with its primary partners. The U.S.-supported initiative to develop the G–7 preparatory committee into a more institutionalized mechanism to deal with future crises points in the right direction for including both countries in world order management. The idea will take time to come to fruition; Germany especially must proceed cautiously given French misgivings about altering too rapidly the shape of the globe's top-level management structure as reflected in the composition of the UN Security Council. Yet even with formalized, G–7 political collaboration, "looping in" the Japanese and Germans will still fail if the U.S. attitude to this results less from a broad vision of shared burdens and responsibilities than from a chief scout's attitude to seeing that all dues are paid.

The generative and degenerative possibilities in a world emerging from the Cold War and the Gulf War are such that German and Japanese power will be pivotal. Historic insecurities generated by domination by both in the past have been supplanted by contemporary uncertainties about where Germans and Japanese will now direct their power, and whether they will use it to promote collective efforts or to sustain more assertive and independent roles. Despite a growing awareness of their new clout and despite undertones of criticism about U.S. leadership, Germany and Japan continue to look to the United States for cues regarding their own regional and global roles and responsibilities. Although each country has become central to any redefinition of the global economic and political order, the United States will remain the natural and indispensable partner when it comes to nudging Germany and Japan toward roles and responsibilities commensurate with their enhanced weight.

If, as this paper argues, a readjustment of global management is not a matter of if but of when, inevitable concessions confront U.S. policymakers. Yet at the same time tremendous possibilities of leverage also await the United States: despite talk of U.S. decline, the nation remains the principal partner for both Europe and Japan. It retains better ties with each than they do with each other. Americans find themselves courted by Europeans to join an "Alliance of the Occident" against the economically menacing Orient. At the same time, the Japanese and Northeast Asians talk about *Nichibei* or a type of condominium. They envisage an association with the United States that will dominate the world economy.

Either way, the broker is being wooed. The trilateral relationship is replacing East–West confrontation as the defining axis of wealth and power in the post–cold war era. U.S. engagement in Asia and Europe during the Cold War prepositioned the United States to become a fulcrum. It would be sadly ironic if, in its haste and concern about competitiveness (and in pique over slow-moving allies), the United States were to slow its engagement in Europe and Japan just when the potential for enhancing its position in the post–cold war world has never been higher.

The authors are responsible for the views expressed in this article. These views do not reflect, nor should they be taken as expressing, any institutional viewpoint of the Carnegie Endowment.

Note

1. Henry Kissinger, "False Dreams of a New World Order," *Washington Post*, February 26, 1991, p. A–21.

The Japan–U.S. Bilateral Relationship: Its Role in the Global Economy

Raymond Vernon

THE CONVENTIONAL WISDOM of 1990 portrays Japan and the United States on a collision course. According to a view shared widely in both countries, the United States is on the way down, and Japan is on the way up. The United States is giving up to Japan its mantle of technological superiority, dominance over international finance, and leadership as the home of the world's leading enterprises.

My views differ from conventional wisdom in two critical respects. First, the future of U.S.–Japanese relations is far from being so fully determined; and although it is filled with risks and dangers, the future still offers opportunities for collaboration and cooperation. Second, the strong disposition of U.S. and Japanese representatives to use bilateral discussions in an effort to settle their differences is dangerous and misguided, a practice more likely to precipitate the risks than to realize the opportunities in their relationship.

Raymond Vernon is Clarence Dillon Professor Emeritus of International Affairs and Herbert F. Johnson Professor Emeritus of International Business Management, Harvard University. His most recent book is *Beyond Globalism: Remaking American Foreign Economic Policy* (New York: The Free Press, 1988).

Japan Ascendant

The perception of Japan as the ascendant partner in the bilateral relationship has been prevalent for a decade or longer, and was foretold fully in a remarkable book by Herman Kahn that was published 20 years ago.[1] Kahn foresaw that the Japanese economy would grow to be one of the largest in the world, when measured by its gross national product, with per capita incomes that rivaled those of Europe and the United States. He anticipated that Japan and the United States would continue to share some interests, as they have, including a joint concern for global economic growth, protection of the global environment, and the maintenance of defense capabilities sufficient to hold China and the Soviet Union in check. Kahn also envisaged the possibility that the two countries would develop a partnership to preside over the non-Communist Pacific area, with Japan playing the role of economic overlord, and the United States the role of political and military leader. This is an idea that occasionally emerges in today's political discussions. Finally, although Kahn regarded nothing as absolutely certain, he did foresee stressful bilateral relations between Japan and the

United States, especially in areas in which the two countries would continue to compete.

It would be a mistake not to give Herman Kahn his full due as a seer, but there is little risk that his prescient views will be forgotten. Other effective publicists on both sides of the Pacific, including Ezra Vogel, Clyde Prestowitz, and James Fallows, since have affirmed the rightness of Kahn's remarkable projections. When trying to fathom likely developments in the U.S.–Japanese bilateral relationship, however, one must do more than extrapolate the past. Two sets of changes must be taken into account in appraising the ways in which that bilateral relationship will develop in the 1990s. The first set emanates from within each of the two countries, the second set from changes in the global environment.

Japan's Changing Interests. Kahn's expectation that Japan would prove a dominant actor in the non-Communist Pacific area obviously is consistent with the reality of the 1990s. Japan is a dominant power in the Asian Development Bank, and a dominant investor and trader in Southeast Asia. In addition, Japan's growing influence on the Pacific coasts of North and South America adds to its strength in the Pacific region.

Missing, however, is a lesson that every economic power eventually is obliged to learn. A nation that exports a substantial part of its savings and develops a considerable market abroad acquires stature and power in the process. Still, as that nation's stake in foreign countries grows, its autonomy declines. Unlike the exploitative hegemon of history, the modern hegemon intertwines its own well-being with that of the foreign countries with which it deals. On reflection, that proposition may seem self-evident, but it is overlooked too easily.

In Japan's case, a surge of exports to North America in the first half of the 1980s sharply altered the geographical composition of its export trade. In a brief period, the North American share of Japan's exports was lifted from about 25 to about 36 percent, where it since has remained. In the latter half of the decade of the 1980s, Japan was pouring its capital into the United States at the rate of about $60 billion annually, so that its aggregate stake in the U.S. economy reached about $300 billion by the end of the decade.

In power terms, the effect of these trends was evident. Because the United States had become dependent on Japan's savings, Japan was in a position to inflict great pain on the U.S. economy. Japan only could use that power, however, if it were prepared to risk giant losses, including a massive impairment of capital and a loss of critical markets.

Meanwhile, Japan's increasing stake in other areas has reduced its autonomy further. Between 1983 and 1987, Japan's long-term capital commitments in the European Community (EC) grew by over $140 billion, increasing at about the same rate as in the United States. At the same time, Europe provides Japan's largest market outside of the Pacific Rim, accounting for about 16 percent of Japan's exports.

Herman Kahn's picture of Japan's future, therefore, needs to be refined in major ways. Japan is indubitably a Pacific power, but its new status in the world is inescapably a source of weakness, as well as strength. As with Britain and the United States in earlier eras, the change in Japan's status has required an increase in its global commitments. Like the United States and Europe, Japan's future is intertwined deeply with that of the rest of the world.

Japan's Changing Policies. Japan's policies have evolved in ways that reflect its changing interests. Until the early 1970s, the country's foreign policy was essentially passive or reactive. Japanese foreign policy consisted mainly of fending off measures that restricted Japanese exports, resisting pressures to open the Japanese market, conducting foreign economic relations through bilateral deals when possible, and spending on military objectives and on foreign aid only to the extent necessary to avoid the acute displeasure of the United States. Where global institutions and global programs were concerned, Japan left initiatives and responsibilities to others.

Japan's growing economic interests in the 1970s and 1980s, however, have given the country a major stake in the maintenance of effective international regimes for the conduct of trade, payments, and investment. Today, it would be hard to find a country with a stake greater than Japan's in furthering the central objective of the International Monetary Fund (IMF), the General Agreement on Tariffs and Trade (GATT), and the Organization for Economic Cooperation and Development (OECD). That objective is to maintain in the world a system of open and stable markets.

After 1971, with the abandonment of fixed exchange rates, the stability of the U.S. dollar and European currencies became matters of deep concern to Japan. In the two decades since, Japan has found itself a key player in every major global arrangement relating to exchange rates: in the IMF, where the country has developed a decisive role in the financing of heavily indebted developing countries; in the OECD, where Japan's concurrence in agreements on export financing has proved critical; in the Bank for International Settlements, where its concurrence on issues of solvency and supervision of international banks has been indispensable; and in the U.S.–Japanese–German triangular consultations on measures to stabilize the U.S. dollar, where the yen–dollar relation has been paramount.

Japan's greatly augmented role in world affairs has been accompanied by new initiatives and greater assertiveness in international bodies. Occasional references in the Japanese media to the so-called mad dog Americans have matched in their ugliness occasional U.S. references to Japan as a so-called enemy to be contained. In a turnabout long overdue, Japan has taken the United States to task in the GATT, alleging that U.S. threats to deny Japan access to U.S. markets are a violation of GATT provisions. Japan's special commitment of $10 billion to supplement World Bank and IMF funds for heavily indebted developing countries has been another illustration of an initiative that would have been unlikely in the 1970s.

To be sure, some surveys see the new accents in Japanese policy as a ringing affirmation of Kahn's view of Japan as an emerging superstate. Kahn, however, saw Japan as using its power to dominate the Pacific, and not to become a participating member in global institutions. Indeed, I have been unable to find a single reference in the Kahn opus to either the IMF or the GATT. A Japan that finds itself anxious to improve the world's economic institutions is bound to take a different direction in its foreign policies than a Japan bent mainly on the domination of the Pacific.

This is not to say that Japan will

turn its back on opportunities to build up its influence in the Pacific or elsewhere. Like the United States in Latin America, Japan almost surely will try to carve out a special place for itself in Southeast Asia; and, like the United States, it almost certainly will discover the limitations of such a strategy. Like the United States, too, Japan also will revert to bilateral negotiations whenever it feels such an approach would serve its interests. In the U.S. case, such bilateral approaches mainly have served to clamp down the flow of goods from exporting countries. In contrast, in the Japanese case, they principally will aim to secure preferential access for Japanese products in foreign markets. In spite of such regional and bilateral efforts, however, Japan seems pushed inexorably by its growing global interest of supporting multilateral organizations, such as the GATT, OECD, and IMF, as channels through which Japan may shape its economic relations. Japanese influence in such organizations is bound to increase, but its interest in influencing their future will not be vastly different from those of the United States and Europe.

Japan's Internal Developments. Four decades ago, John Foster Dulles was referring to Japan as "a basket case," and scarcely a dissenting voice was to be found. Today, the only observers who are prepared to pay any attention to the possibility that Japan may stumble are the Japanese themselves. The rest of the world seems persuaded that Japan has mastered the secret of perpetual growth without pain.

Herman Kahn was one of the earliest of those who were convinced that Japan could overcome practically any difficulty. Although in most respects history is on his side, Kahn has yet to be proved correct on one issue. His 1970 guesses were much too sanguine about the ability of the Japanese to use their high incomes to create a livable environment.

As Kahn had predicted, the Japanese have been making many determined environmental efforts, including the introduction of vigorous antipollution measures, the upgrading of sanitary and health facilities, and the improvement of retirement plans. Despite efforts to curb urban air pollution, however, Tokyo's atmosphere has remained one of the world's most polluted. Despite elevated income levels, most Japanese live in cramped houses and apartments, suffer long commutes to work, have limited access to parks, beaches, and other outdoor commons, and face prohibitive housing costs.

These shortfalls appear to be a source of discontent among young Japanese, especially those who have traveled abroad and formed firsthand impressions of living conditions in Europe and North America. They have learned quickly that Japan's high per capita income, as a measure of its living amenities, is altogether misleading. The high internal prices of consumer goods reduce Japanese incomes by about one-third, when compared with the United States, while the paucity of leisure time and shortage of living space widen the amenities gap even further.

To the outside observer, two added factors seem relevant in gauging the reactions of the Japanese people. One is growing restiveness among Japanese women with the restraints on the economic and social roles they usually are required to accept; the other is increasing concern among Japanese wage earners over an inescapable increase in the national tax burden. The Japanese workforce has realized that the tax burden cannot fail to mount, as the society undergoes dramatic aging in the coming decades. The fact that the percentage of Japanese citizens over 65 years of age will have risen from 10 percent of the population in 1984 to 21 percent in 2015, for instance, carries striking implications. Accordingly, the years ahead point to some significant changes in Japan's economic performance that would affect measurably the country's bilateral relationship with the United States.

One possible scenario is that the savings rate of Japanese households, which has been declining slowly in the past decade, will continue to fall. That development could come about as the aging Japanese population demands more amenities. If that occurs, the Japanese economy would lose some of the critical cushion that previously has allowed it to maintain a high rate of investment, without risking a high rate of inflation.

Another possibility is that the Japanese public may resist further increases in military expenditures and foreign aid, believing that the economy cannot afford such expenditures. A reaction of that kind would be even more likely if the Soviet Union and the People's Republic of China continue to maintain a relatively unthreatening posture toward Japan, and if the tensions between the United States and Japan regarding trade and technology issues continue to grow.

At the same time, however, the Japanese government likely will be highly sensitive to the need to nurture and protect the vested interests that Japanese banks, insurance companies, and manufacturing enterprises rapidly are establishing all over the world. Like the United States, the United Kingdom, and Germany, Japan will come to recognize that the well-being of its citizens increasingly will depend on how other economies are faring. Accordingly, the Japanese tendency to pull away from the United States in response to domestic pressures could be diluted or offset by Japan's need to collaborate with the United States on projects in order to protect their joint interests in world markets.

U.S. Frustrations

The central problem of the United States is to reconcile an unchanging desire to remain the world's leading military and political power with a growing national realization that U.S. economic and technological resources are limited.

The East European revolution inspired by Mikhail Gorbachev could provide the United States with a graceful way out of this dilemma, allowing it to shrink dramatically the U.S. defense establishment and to redeploy a so-called peace dividend to meet some neglected needs at home and abroad. The United States likely will make such shifts slowly and cautiously. Worries over Gorbachev's durability will serve to curb such efforts as will vested U.S. economic interests, including the cities, states, single enterprises, and whole industries that have a stake in maintaining a large defense establishment.

The frustrations that the limited resources of the United States generate for its leadership are bound to continue. While East Europeans face the severest trial and greatest opportunity of their modern history, the United States only can scrape together a few hundred million dollars to affect the outcome. While Japan marshalls $10 billion to help developing countries reduce their overhanging debt and enthusiastically supports a major expansion in IMF quotas, the U.S. government is obliged to plead poverty. U.S. housing and education needs are underfunded chronically, and the growth of U.S. domestic industry depends increasingly on European and Japanese business investments.

Yet, retreating to an economic or military "Fortress America" is not a realistic U.S. option. The United States cannot yet bring itself to modify its leadership image on the political and military front. Besides, U.S. firms based in foreign countries and foreign firms based in the United States have become so critical to the U.S. economy as to prevent such a withdrawal. With most large U.S.-based multinational enterprises typically relying on foreign subsidiaries to generate 30 to 40 percent of the parent company income, one can anticipate that such enterprises will support a continued U.S. presence abroad.

The so-called Fortress America possibility is obsolete, rendered inoperative by the modern technology of transportation and communication. There is no longer any serious hope of relying alone on U.S. technology in order to build the world's most advanced fighting force. Nor is there any serious hope of controlling the movement of capital and technology across U.S. borders. The formidable problems encountered in attempting to control the movement of people and goods across U.S. borders attests to these difficulties.

Apart from international links in the fields of investment and technology, the United States also is anchored to the rest of the world by the U.S. dollar. The dollar serves double-duty, being the world's key currency at the same time that it serves the U.S. economy. In the latter 1980s, for example, foreign governments' holdings of U.S. dollars exceeded $300 billion, and were showing no signs of shrinking. At that time, the dollar claims of banks outside of the United States came to something like $2,000 billion. Nor can the U.S. government easily alter the situation, because U.S. banks and other financial intermediaries would struggle to avoid having the U.S. dollar withdrawn from its leading role. The United States, therefore, is both master and slave in its role as the provider of the world's leading currency.

The idea of a Pacific partnership with Japan does not seem to offer much prospect of resolving these U.S. dilemmas. Such partnership, although attractive, cannot provide easy answers to the country's complex frustrations regarding the mismatch between limited resources and global interests. Europe, Canada, and Latin America continue to occupy a dominant position in the external economic interests of the United States. Moreover, until *perestroika* is on a much firmer footing within the Soviet Union, Europe will continue to occupy a central position in U.S. military interests.

The United States, therefore, seems committed inescapably to the pursuit of a policy that attempts to be global in its reach rather than autarkic or regional. The inevitable inconsistencies and contradictions of U.S. economic policy likely will prove even more pronounced, as the country attempts to maintain a global position without adequate resources to sustain it. Still, it is difficult to picture a set of circumstances that will persuade the policymakers to accept more limited horizons for the exercise of their influence.

Mismatched Policy-making

During the decades ahead, for the United States, Japan, and all other industrialized countries, an increase in the exposure of national economies seems inescapable. With the globalization of markets, the multinationalization of enterprises, and the increase in environmental concerns, Japan and the United States are bound to engage in more frequent and concerted dialogue. Most bilateral interchanges likely will prove relatively routine and trouble-free. Governmental agencies with specialized functions, such as tax collection, bank supervision, or air traffic control, will continue to develop and explore their cross-border contacts, operating at various levels of their respective bureaucracies.

Some bilateral issues, however, will be lifted out of such humdrum channels and dealt with at higher levels. As a rule, these will be domestic policy issues, such as the protection of Japanese rice farmers from competition or the promotion of the U.S. aircraft industry. In these and other instances, it will be a challenge for both countries to avoid rancor and bitterness.

The high level of tension that heretofore has characterized practically all such bilateral U.S.–Japanese negotiations perhaps could be explained by the intrinsic importance of the subject matter under discussion. Similar heated debates between the United States and Germany or France, however, have generated far less tension. Understandably, many Japanese believe that the underlying problem carries racial overtones. I am convinced, however, that the explanation is to be found in the fundamental incompatibility of Japanese and American styles of conducting their bilateral discussions.

Historians and sociologists repeatedly have explored factors that have produced the obvious mismatch, and some of their observations are worth recalling. On the U.S. side, the highly fragmented distribution of power in the federal government provides the backdrop. When President Bush speaks with Prime Minister Toshiki Kaifu about trade matters, he speaks only for the executive branch, not the U.S. government. As foreign governments have been slow to learn, that fragmentation pervades the three main branches of government, including the executive branch. Although that fragmentation of governmental power reflects American values, it gives an ephemeral and uncertain quality to U.S. economic diplomacy. What one agency might present as a position of the United States may, in the end, prove to be only an opening gambit unsupported by the rest of the U.S. government. For example, a 1987 proposal made by the U.S. trade representative for all governments to abolish agricultural import restrictions over a ten-year period could not possibly have had the firm commitment of the U.S. Department of Agriculture, much less that of the Congress.

Another U.S. value that creates confusion is the idea that a professional bureaucracy should operate under the firm control of its political masters. This is a laudable principle, fully consistent with the notion that the legitimacy of any government derives from the mandate it receives from the electorate.

The application of that exemplary principle, however, generates some difficult international problems. The new crop of cabinet ministers and bureau chiefs ushered in by new administrations are transient recruits from law firms, universities, newspapers, and state governments, assigned to temporary duty in Washington. As a rule, such political leaders do not remain in their jobs for longer than two or three years. Accordingly, one political scientist aptly has described the U.S. government as a "government of strangers." Such politicians have a limited capacity for consensus-building, and few of them spend much time attempting to build the internal agreements necessary for the development of international positions.

Still, the results of a revolving-door bureaucracy are not all bad. With little time to spare, little effort to build consensus, and, sometimes, little appreciation of all the difficulties in their own proposals, U.S. officials are much quicker than those in most other governments to launch new initiatives in response to international problems. Often, the ability of officials to launch a new policy or redirect an old one depends on extraneous factors, such as the official's force of personality or access to the president, rather than on the merits and durability of the policy. As a consequence, the capacity of the system to pursue an unwavering course over time has been limited.[2]

Contrast these patterns of operation with those of the Japanese government. The permanent Japanese bureaucracy has a much more powerful hand in the shaping of governmental policies. True, that power does not go unchallenged altogether in Japan. Even before a succession of scandals in the late 1980s began undermining the power of the Liberal Democratic Party (LDP), the Japanese *Diet* and political parties appeared to be gaining rapidly in strength, relative to the bureaucracy. Moreover, U.S. scholars energetically debate whether the dominant financial, industrial, and commercial enterprises of Japan may be exerting more power in the framing of national policies than the Ministry of International Trade and Industry (MITI) or the Ministry of Finance.[3]

However that debate resolves itself, it is indisputable that the Japanese bureaucracy plays a dramatically different role in Japanese policy-making than that of its U.S. counterpart.

Nevertheless, the Japanese bureaucracy secures its power at a high price and retains it through the deeply ingrained practice of touching all bases before any international position is taken. Occasionally, Japanese negotiators will take an action that seems to breach that rule; but that is the exception and usually is taken under great pressure from the opposing government.

Operating under an imperative for consensus, the style of Japanese negotiators differs markedly from that of their U.S. counterparts. In most international gatherings and to the vast annoyance of the Americans, the Japanese participants usually do no more than observe and report. Occasionally, they will make formal gestures of open-mindedness and goodwill, but subsequent meetings often reveal that they were without real substance. Meanwhile, within the Japanese establishment, a national position slowly is being hammered out among the competing interests. As a rule, the final product of those internal battles is devoid of principle, reflecting only a small shift in the center of gravity of the interests that contributed to it. When the Japanese negotiators eventually produce the mouse that is the product of their protracted discussions, the U.S. instinct is to cry foul.[4]

One hardly could find two less compatible styles of policy-making. On the Japanese side, one finds a long trail of commitments in principle, embodied in treaties and agreements, followed by a snail-like movement in the general direction defined by the principles. On the U.S. side, traditional adherence to such principles is obscured by the mercurial shifts that repeatedly shock the Japanese. An examination of the past 40 years illustrates the bewilderment and frustration that the process has produced. From 1952 to 1957, U.S. policymakers repeatedly urged the Japanese to reduce their trade barriers, in accordance with GATT provisions. In 1957, however, the pressure was turned on Japan to curb its increasing exports of textiles to the U.S. market, in gross violation of the spirit of the GATT. Throughout the 1960s, the United States supported a regime of fixed exchange rates and convertible currencies. Then, in 1971, the United States abandoned fixed rates, and violated its commitments to Japan by slapping a discriminatory 10 percent duty on Japanese imports. In 1986, after decades of inveighing against the evils of the so-called managed trade proposals put forward by France and others, the United States demanded an agreement from Japan to guarantee U.S. semiconductor producers a share of the Japanese market. In 1989, after a century of supporting the principle of national treatment for foreign-owned businesses, the United States abruptly began to discriminate against Japanese-owned enterprises that were seeking to do business in the United States. Meanwhile, after interminable representations from the U.S. side, the Japanese began the slow and laborious process of modifying their practices in the general direction the United States had sought for so long.

Because these disconcerting patterns appear to be the consequence of well-entrenched institutions and values in Japan and in the United States, it would be unrealistic to assume that either country will alter significantly its behavior in the immediate future. The challenge, therefore, is to find a way to deal with their shared problems, and by means that would not require the bilateral confrontations of the past.

Beyond the Bilateral

Over the years, the bilateral discussions between the United States and Japan have fallen into a familiar pattern. Rarely have they involved an exploration of common problems and opportunities. Typically, they have had their origins in a complaint by the United States that Japan was behaving unfairly toward U.S. interests and a demand that Japan should change its practices. That opening gambit has been followed by a long, drawn out succession of meetings on the U.S. complaint, followed by a series of apparent Japanese concessions.

Some of the issues on the agenda of bilateral U.S.–Japanese discussions have been of primary concern to the two countries, and have not affected the interests of other countries. The most contentious issues, however, have involved substantial interests of other countries as well.

Many of the complaints have been based on the contention that Japan was violating a particular provision of the GATT. Subsequent U.S. proposals for remedy affected the interests of third countries. For instance, in proposing to Japan that it should set aside some proportion of the Japanese semiconductor market for U.S. exports and should stop dumping its computer chips in third-country markets, the United States obviously was stepping on the toes of other countries.

Even issues not governed by any agreement have had direct effects on the interests of third countries. In the so-called structural discussions between the United States and Japan launched in 1989, each country raised issues regarding the other's economy that were global rather than bilateral in their impact. The United States questioned Japan's restrictive distribution system, its strong propensity to exclude foreign service companies, and its tortuous antiforeign local ordinances. In turn, Japan pointed to the dangerously low U.S. savings rate, U.S. underinvestment in education, and the heavy U.S. emphasis on short-run financial returns.

With bilateral discussions between Japan and the United States so heavily handicapped by incompatibilities of structure and style, an obvious alternative would be to search for multilateral opportunities. For example, both the semiconductor issue and the structural discussions would have been far more appropriate in a multilateral forum. To be sure, the provisions in the Omnibus Trade and Competitiveness Act paint the United States into a corner by forcing the president to deal with Japan on a bilateral basis. But, the early 1990s will produce a number of major occasions for the reconsideration of U.S.–Japanese relations in a multilateral setting. These are opportunities that both countries would do well to seize.

One such occasion is the round of negotiations accompanying the European Community's remarkable program for completing the integration of its internal market by 1992 (EC–92). On many issues arising in connection with that process the interests of Japan and the United States are on the same side. Both countries, for instance, want to persuade the Europeans to maintain as open a border around the new Europe as it will be possible to negotiate. A temptation for the United States will be to accept any EC arrangement that will seem to serve U.S. interests in the short run, even if the arrangement is opportunistic, and even if it slights Japanese interests.

The problem is illustrated by the EC's principles in granting foreign banks the right to do business inside the European market. Those principles have been drafted in such a way as to raise the possibility that U.S. banks eventually will gain greater access to European markets than their Japanese competitors.[5] Presented with an opportunity to better its competitive position over the Japanese, the U.S. side may prove unable to resist the temptation to "take the money and run." Yet, the occasion could be used much more fruitfully by attempting to develop a global *modus vivendi* on such issues, including an international mechanism to adjudicate disputes over banking issues.

The multilateral approach to issues such as these already has generated some impressive successes, as illustrated by the various governmental agreements that have been reached since 1975 to increase the safety of international banks. These agreements, sponsored by the Bank for International Settlements, have brought the EC, United States, and Japan together in a series of unprecedented accords on measures to tighten up the supervision and increase the capital of such banks.[6]

Another opportunity for shifting the bilateral issues between the United States and Japan into a more promising environment is provided by the ongoing negotiations sponsored by GATT under the title of the Uruguay Round. Although the United States traditionally has been the principal proponent for strengthening GATT powers, it has tried almost invariably to avoid recourse to the GATT in handling bilateral U.S.–Japanese disputes. Presumably, the idea has been that the coercive powers of the United States in the bilateral relationship would be stronger than those that the United States could exercise in GATT. That never has been a self-evident proposition, and it may be even less so in the future.

It would be too much to expect that either Japan or the United States would give up bilateral channels wherever they thought something could be gained by the maneuver. Still, the case for shifting U.S.–Japanese discussions to multilateral channels is already strong, and will increase in strength if the dispute-settling mechanisms of international agencies can be reinforced. In recent years, there has been a visible movement in this direction, as quarreling parties have been turning increasingly to such mechanisms. A notable step was taken in that direction when Japan uncharacteristically invoked the GATT mechanism to complain about U.S. threats to apply the super-301 provisions of its trade law, under which the United States reserves the right to determine unilaterally what is fair in trade practices.

Conclusion

Bilateral relations between Japan and the United States promise to remain critical for both countries in the foreseeable future. On economic issues, however, the bilateral approach inescapably will continue to generate interactions of a destructive kind. What may prevent such developments from turning into more active hostility is that neither country can inflict great harm upon the other without imposing great costs upon itself in the process.

Likewise, there are few bilateral issues that do not intimately affect third countries as well. As a result, most of the disputes that arise between Japan and the United States involve issues in which third countries have a legitimate interest, suggesting the desirability of shifting to multilateral settings wherever the choice exists.

In the case of Japan and the United States, however, the reasons for avoiding bilateral efforts to resolve large problems or disputes are strengthened greatly by the basic incompatibilities in the decision-making processes of the two governments. As a result, when the United States and Japan engage in two-way conversations, it appears that they cannot hear each other.

Inadequate as existing multilateral institutions may be for the development of policy and the settlement of disputes, therefore, they are measurably superior to the bilateral channels of Japanese–U.S. relations. Japan already shows small signs of recognizing this critical point, and it is time for the United States to recognize it, as well.

An earlier version of this paper was delivered to a conference of the CSIS Pacific Forum on "An Agenda for the United States and Japan on Northeast Asia," November 26–29, 1989.

Notes

1. Herman Kahn, *The Emerging Japanese Superstate* (Englewood Cliffs, N.J.: Prentice Hall, 1970).

2. Raymond Vernon and Debora L. Spar, *Beyond Globalism* (New York: Free Press, 1989), p. 15 et seq.

3. Richard J. Samuels, *The Business of the Japanese State: Energy Markets in Comparative & Historical Perspective* (Ithaca, N.Y.: Cornell University Press, 1987), pp. 231–237.

4. Clyde V. Prestowitz, Jr., *Trading Places: How We Allow Japan to Take the Lead* (New York: Basic Books, 1988), pp. 46–70.

5. For a description of the relevant provisions, see Sidney Key, "Financial Integration in the European Community," International Finance Discussion Paper No. 349, Federal Reserve Board, Washington, D.C., 1989.

6. Ethan B. Kapstein, "Resolving the Regulator's Dilemma: International Coordination of Banking Regulations," *International Organization* 43:2 (Spring 1989), pp. 323–347.

III. Regional Policies

East Central Europe: Democracy in Retreat?

Jan Zielonka

EASTERN EUROPE IS no longer good news. After a short period of euphoria evoked by the spectacular collapse of communism, concern is growing that even Poland, Czechoslovakia, and Hungary are drifting away from the intended safe harbor called democracy. As two U.S. observers put it at the end of 1990:

> The winterscape of Eastern Europe is forbiddingly dark. The fervor for freedom that spilled into the streets last year and fueled the 20th century's most remarkable round of democratic change has run low. In its place, there is a dark awareness of freedom's costs, destitution and demagoguery.[1]

The initial warning came from Hungary in the spring of 1990. There the first free national elections after 40 years produced nasty infighting between major political contenders, the Alliance of Free Democrats (AFD) and the Hungarian Democratic Forum (HDF). The latter party won the elections and formed a new coalition government, but the infighting continued with opposition parties issuing scathing reports on the government's alleged mismanagement of the country's affairs, and the governing parties questioning the "Hungarianness" of some leading members of the opposition. In the meantime, the frustration among ordinary Hungarians grew, as demonstrated by the taxi and truck drivers' strike in October 1990, which caused nationwide chaos and greatly undermined the credibility of the new Hungarian political elites.

In Poland, a major split within the Solidarity movement provoked even greater polarization than in Hungary, with the subsequent presidential elections producing packages of empty slogans, waves of ethnic hatred, and the dangerous phenomenon of Stanislaw Tyminski, the electoral dark horse who skillfully employed a combination of aggressive populism, economic demagoguery, and a charlatan-like appeal. In the end, Lech Walesa won the elections, but only at the cost of ending cohesion within the former alliance of democratic forces.

For some months, Czechoslovakia—or more properly now the Czech and Slovak Federal Republic—looked like an oasis of peace and common sense in the region. But in the fall of 1990 there was a major conflict within the new governing party, the Civic Forum, followed by a heated controversy between the Czechs and Slovaks that prompted President Václav Havel to ask for emergency authority to rule by decree. The Civic Forum subsequently split into two factions.

In the meantime, the economic, environmental, health, and housing statistics in all three countries have been

---

Jan Zielonka is associate professor of international relations at Leiden University.

giving increasingly alarming signals. In the Soviet Union a dangerous shift toward authoritarian rule has gradually been taking place, making all east central Europeans particularly uneasy. And the war in the Gulf deprived Eastern Europe of Western attention as well as resources, dashing hopes for increased Western help for the transition effort.

Adam Michnik, editor of the Polish newspaper *Gazeta Wyborcza* and a longtime Solidarity adviser, described the current trend in extremely pessimistic terms:

> This is the ideal time for demagogy. Demagogy that aggressively attacks the government may be successful, which must lead to destabilization. Destabilization elicits chaos. Chaos generates a new poverty and a new dictatorship. All postcommunist countries will face this. Everywhere phantoms from the past awaken: movements that combine populism, xenophobia, personality cult and a vision of the world ruled by a conspiracy of Freemasons and Jews.[2]

Does Michnik's pessimism represent a prophecy or an emotional overstatement? Will east central Europe share the fate of many Latin American nations that shed their dictators but failed to establish durable democracy? After a period of rising freedom, is the pendulum swinging back toward authoritarian resurgence?

I will argue in this article that the transition of east central Europe toward democracy can be neither smooth nor painless. Despite all alarming developments, however, there are few reasons to believe that the region is so to speak condemned to despotism, and that the pendulum of history is now swinging away from democracy. Arguments predicting an authoritarian future are often simplistic, and they minimize the democratic achievements so far and their durable consequences. Moreover, the West can do much more than it has so far to strengthen the course of democracy in the region.

Authoritarian Temptations Reconsidered

Despite all their problems, solid foundations have already been laid for a new democratic system in all three countries under consideration. They peacefully completed free presidential, parliamentary, and local government elections, providing victories for the political forces that pushed through the democratic transformation of 1989.[3] They prepared the ground for both a multiparty system and a system of checks and balances between the executive, the judiciary, and the legislature. They abolished state censorship and allowed various types of nongovernmental associations to flourish. Likewise they implemented important reforms in the areas of human rights, education, and culture. They reformed the army and police and reoriented their foreign policies by developing close cooperation with leading democracies. Last but not least, in all three countries economic reforms have been initiated aimed at transforming the command into a market-oriented economy and, in particular, reinstating rights to private property.

All these achievements can hardly be undone by sheer political manipulation or by a quiet coup by any self-appointed dictator. Of course, there are still numerous threats on the road toward democracy. After all, as Ralf Dahrendorf observed: "The only common feature to all transitions is the tension arising from being threatened every single day."[4] But the existence of threats does not presuppose an ultimate failure of democratic aspirations. In particular, one should warn against all simplistic theories about the dictatorial temptation. Democracy in east central Europe is threatened by various, often conflicting factors, and it is very difficult to say which type of scenario is truly dangerous.

On the one hand, democracy could be strangled by populist mobilization of the masses fueled by the marketization of the imbalanced economy and fostered by ethnic or egalitarian hatred. On the other hand, democracy may also be threatened by the indifference and apathy of citizens who abstain from political participation and from all sorts of economic expansion.

Another possibility is that excessive governmental powers, combined with restrictions imposed on political parties, could jeopardize democratic developments. Democracy can also be killed, however, by the unrestrained partisanship of many small and largely ideological parties that, unable to form a stable coalition, would paralyze any normal functioning of the state.

There could also be a threat from old-regime supporters who maintained positions in various segments of the economy, media, security apparatus, and local administration. This old *nomenklatura* could undermine democratic efforts through instigating waves of strikes, fabricating disinformation, and utilizing authoritarian tendencies in the Soviet Union. On the other hand, democracy would also be threatened by anti-Communist purges, political witch-hunts, and all sorts of retaliation that would undermine the principles of the rule of law.

Fueling ethnic infighting is dangerous, but so is ignoring ethnic concerns and aspirations. Democrats should prevent a resurgence of chaos and anarchy, but corporate behind-doors agreements by the elites might also prove disastrous.

In short, the process of building democracy is a balancing act in which one-sided scenarios and emotional overstatements have no place. Authoritarian temptation has not one but many faces, and all existing stereotypes should, therefore, be judged with extreme caution.

Exaggerated Skepticism

Those who believe that democracy is in trouble in east central Europe refer to three major factors to justify their skepticism: (1) the alarming economic situation of the region; (2) the frightening populist rhetoric of the successive political campaigns; and (3) the lack of democratic tradition in the region, or worse, an awakening of the "phantoms of the past," as Adam Michnik put it. All three factors can indeed bring democratic dreams to an end, but not necessarily. In fact, a careful examination of the arguments of the skeptics indicates that there are far fewer reasons to be worried than might appear at first glance.

Skeptics are right in claiming that economic health is indispensable for the success of democracy: economic problems have repeatedly been exploited by various types of dictators in the Third World. Skeptics tend to forget, however, that in east central Europe dictatorial solutions for economic problems have already been tried for many years and with very discouraging effects. Not surprisingly, therefore, most Poles, Hungarians, Czechs, or Slovaks seem to identify economic welfare with the existence of stable democracies in Western Europe, the United States, and Australia rather than with the authoritarian rule in South Korea, Singapore, and Taiwan.

More important in this context is a

possible misreading of some economic data. Statistics are cited to prove the depth of the misery among the population that is expected to lead to an explosion: falling real wages, unemployment, a catastrophic drop in production, and a general collapse of living standards. To a considerable extent, however, economic decline in east central European countries reflects the impact of determined efforts to speed up the pace of economic transformation and is helping to cleanse them of the distortions and inefficiencies of centrally planned economies. For instance, a fall in production in deficit factories, however painful it may be in the short term, may yet lead to longer-term benefits.

Moreover, some statistical figures are highly misleading. For instance, skeptics are fond of repeating the rapidly rising figures of unemployment in the region, but they usually fail to mention that most comparisons refer to the Communist era, when unemployment officially did not exist. When governments in east central Europe first began to register the jobless and offer unemployment money, thousands of people who had never held jobs signed up, including housewives.

Focusing on the rhetoric and language of political campaigns in east central Europe can also be misleading. Aggressive populist slogans were indeed disturbing during the successive electoral campaigns last year, especially in Poland and Hungary. However, careful postelection surveys conducted by the Hungarian Social Science Information Centre revealed that the HDF's tremendous effort to mobilize its supporters through populist appeals during the first round of local elections did not succeed. The HDF's supporters were motivated less by ideological commitment than by economic grievances. Among the opposition parties, the great winner in the local elections was not the ideologically driven AFD, but the Alliance of Young Democrats (AYD), which tried to present itself as a party of expertise and pragmatism. Populi rhetoric is always frightening, but it seems to carry little appeal for the Hungarian electorate, which looks for pragmatic rather than ideological solutions to the country's problems.

Presidential elections in Poland have also been run according to the liberal versus populist dichotomy. But the opinion polls conducted by Krzysztof Jasiewicz from the Polish Academy of Sciences revealed that only tiny minorities within Polish society may be described as "populist," with most of the people expressing moderate, centrist views.

Referring to the lack of democratic tradition in east central Europe can also be misleading. One may ask, in particular, which period of time is under consideration? We can trace the existence of the Polish and Hungarian diets back into the seventeenth century and earlier. The Czech parliament created by the constitution of 1920 reflected in part the new state's Austrian and Hungarian heritage.

If one refers to the interwar period of this century, then there were indeed examples of dictatorial rule in Hungary and Poland, but not in Czechoslovakia. Moreover, the international setting of authoritarianism in Poland and Hungary at that time differed very much from what it is today, making all simple analogies rather dubious. As Timothy Garton Ash put it:

> If more or less authoritarian regimes flourished in East Central Europe between the wars this was partly because there were examples of authoritarianism else-

where in Europe, which could also somehow be associated with the dream of modernity. Today, there are no such examples, and modernity is unambiguously associated with democracy.[5]

Referring to the lack of democratic tradition in east central Europe since World War II does not make the argument any stronger. People in that region may be unfamiliar with the procedures of democracy, but they are all too familiar with the mechanisms of authoritarianism. Will they follow a populist demagogue offering them a well-known repertoire of repression that has already brought their countries economic misery, ecological destruction, and a decline of moral standards? One should also keep in mind that postwar dictatorship in east central Europe flourished within an entirely different ideological environment. Today we experience a remarkable intellectual domination of liberalism with its praise for democracy and criticism of all dictatorial aspirations.

Pillars of Democracy

If so many prognoses about east central European fortunes can be misleading, what are the true pillars of democracy in the region? In my view, there are four of them: (1) a developed civil society; (2) a stable party system; (3) a system of checks and balances between the executive, the judiciary, and the legislature; and (4) further progress of market-oriented economic reforms.

Civil Society. Although the concept of civil society is rather vague, all students of democratic transitions recognize the importance of intermediate groups and voluntary associations that broaden collective participation beyond the political realm of the state. The existence of business and producer units, trade unions and peasant cooperatives, independent media, and professional associations as well as associations of students, youth, and women, self-help groups, and religious and ethnic institutions has repeatedly been seen as the common denominator of effective democracy in various parts of the world.[6]

In east central Europe civil society has for decades been absorbed by the all-embracing party-state, making it difficult for groups and individuals to define autonomous identities and interests. After all, Marxist–Stalinist striving for a "perfect unity of mankind" required nothing less than the "suppression and elimination of the civil society."[7]

The opposition to Communist rule in the 1980s tried hard to reestablish social links and to overcome atomization of citizens by creating a network of independent grass-roots initiatives.[8] These efforts reached a peak in the critical year 1989, which was accordingly characterized as "the springtime of societies aspiring to be civil."[9] Yet it proved easier to abolish communism and to rewrite constitutions than to create a Western-style civil society.

Independent associations are now allowed to flourish. In Hungary, for instance, no less than 4,000 of them have recently been registered. But this growing organizational infrastructure remains passive and does not provide an important bridge between the new elites and various segments of society.[10] Apathy and passivity on the part of the populace is striking, regardless of successive campaigns organized by the elites. New associations do not mushroom spontaneously; they are often manufactured by political parties and state institutions attempting to establish direct links with the electorate.

Emerging groups are not, as is frequently the case in the West, tied to specific material interests; instead they emerge on the basis of rather vague ideological commitments related to questions of religion or national history. The media have gained a new freedom: no party can now control them directly. Nonetheless, radio, press, and television are still used by the elites as a weapon in the ongoing political struggle rather than as a vehicle to provide unbiased information to and communication with various segments of society. Local, small groups and institutions are suffering most from financial shortages, and they are proving unable to assert themselves against the mainstream of national politics and the central administration.

For the time being, this relative weakness of civil society is not necessarily alarming. A mature civil society cannot be created by an overnight decree; it takes years, if not generations, before a dense network of associations can emerge and assert itself. Portugal and Spain, for instance, had long had similar problems before successfully accomplishing their transition. Nevertheless, in east central Europe a weak civil society will continue to undermine democratic efforts in at least three important ways.

First, critical gaps between "high politics" and day-to-day realities, between national and local perspectives, between the macro and the micro levels of change, between "us," the ordinary people, and "them," the elites, can only be bridged by further development of civil society. The continuous existence of the gaps mentioned will perpetuate social apathy as well as reluctance to be actively engaged in the democratization effort. It will also erode public trust in successive governments, regardless of their effectiveness, profile, and intentions.

Second, economic transition from central planning to incentives and market competition needs a vigorous civil society. Economic reforms that are essential for democracy cannot be only a matter for governments and their experts. The success of market reforms requires crystallization of material interests across various organized segments of society actively participating in the process of change.

Third, a weak civil society will make it difficult to move from a very competitive to a more compromising style of politics, which, after all, represents an important feature of a stable democracy. As Peter Mair observed:

> In Eastern Europe, the absence of strong organizational networks, the weakness of stable collective identities, and the extraordinary openness of electoral markets suggest that highly competitive and potentially destabilizing politics may well be encouraged.[11]

In Western Europe, Mair and others argue, it was the density of organizational networks of civil society that encouraged an accommodationist political style in more plural societies (such as the Netherlands or Switzerland) and a consensual style within the more homogeneous political cultures (such as the Scandinavian countries).

Party Politics. Rudolf Tökes described today's party politics in Hungary as "an endless series of intellectually underwhelming confrontations among smaller than life-sized politicians with oversized egos."[12] This description can also be applied to other countries in the region.

An amazing number of groups have registered as parties. For instance, more than 100 of them have formed in Czechoslovakia, including some with fancy names such as the Union of Beer Drinkers. They are all engaged in bitter competition, however, with little support from the population at large. Even the largest parties have few members. In Hungary, for example, the six parliamentary parties have approximately only 250,000 dues-paying members. Electoral support for them is also low, as illustrated by a low electoral turnout and by the success of independent candidates in the elections.

Most parties appear unable to act as effective political organizations, formulating coherent platforms or enforcing their political will. They have weak internal structures and amorphous political programs. They are often led by well-known personalities but suffer from internal divisions and a lack of discipline. (Here also, there are parallels with the first years of democratic politics in Portugal and Spain in the 1970s and 1980s.)

Parties have been unable to establish close links with any specific groups within the electorate and therefore have failed to create any durable electoral loyalties. Only agrarian parties traditionally have a relatively strong social base in the countryside, but there are indications that this base is shrinking. All the larger parties find voters throughout various segments of society, but there is little evidence that any social group identifies itself with a specific party.

Most parties emerged from broad civic movements united in their struggle against communism under banners carrying patriotic and moral slogans. The end to communism, however, implied the end of solidarity within these movements, and the infighting began. Infighting as such can be healthy, but the issues that have created conflicts are worrying because successive disputes have been only vaguely related to economic reforms and other essentials of democratic transformation. Infighting often results from personal animosities (those who now have power versus those who want it; those who have a Marxist past versus those with supposedly clerical or nationalist credentials; those who are charismatic versus those who rely on their expertise). Many conflicts emerge from differences in political style and symbolism (populism versus corporatism; acceleration versus wisdom; moral stance versus effective stance). New parties also engage in strife due to ideological differences on such issues as religion and ethics, the national tradition and the ethnic question, Pan-Slavism and Eurocentrism.

This situation is obviously an unhealthy state of affairs for a democratic body politic. Communication between citizens and party elites will remain difficult, thus affecting both the accuracy and the legitimacy of political decisions. Immoderate and ideological party politics will be conducive either to sheer paralysis or to a disorderly sequence of ill-calculated reforms that end in failure. Parties will be unable to articulate and aggregate major policy options and will have problems accommodating potential protest voters. Elections instead of giving voice to the principal political cleavages and conflicts of interest in society will tend to be a sort of referendum on the performance of the incumbent government. As a consequence, the countries in the region may experience a constant flux of new parties in government. Moreover, because of this electoral instability, different parties will control different institutions causing additional conflicts and subsequent confusion. Hungary is already split in this way.

The national government is run by the HDF and its coalition partners; the larger cities are ruled by the AFD and the AYD; while former Communists, running as independents, managed to retain local control of the provinces.

In short, democracy building in east central Europe would require crystallization of a stable party system. Parties should improve their organizational structures and specify their programs by addressing the most crucial problems of the transition rather than engaging in factionalism and clientelism. They should establish better links with the electorate and define their profile more according to material values than to ideological sentiments (more easily said than done, of course).

Balance of Power. East central Europe will soon have to make a choice between a presidential system of government and a parliamentary one. A presidential system was established during the Communist rule in Czechoslovakia and Poland, but the system is now under review, and opposing political forces are raising conflicting arguments. In Hungary, a group of reformed Communists have tried to strengthen presidential powers and to introduce direct presidential elections. Their effort failed, however, and the parliamentary system seems now to be widely accepted, although its functioning causes many problems.

Debate about the best possible model of government for the emerging democracies is crucial, but it is far from being conclusive. Advocates of a parliamentary government argue that it is more conducive to stable democracy than a presidential model because it creates a better bridge between ruling coalitions and the public. This in turn helps to form the necessary public consensus behind painful economic policies that will be unavoidable in the years to come. Presidential government, on the other hand, brings with it the dangers of demagogic election campaigns, makes political parties weaker, and introduces an undesirable element of winner-take-all politics into societies that need mechanisms of conciliation instead.

Supporters of the presidential system argue that parliamentary governments tend to be unstable during transition periods due to frequent conflicts between immature parliamentary parties and to a lack of effective leadership. The success of democracy depends on governmental action rather than parliamentary debates. In the transition period, when party identification is weak and public opinion highly volatile, the institution of a directly elected president with extensive powers can provide leadership to conflicting parties and push through necessary reforms regardless of any parliamentary deadlocks. Naturally, there is a danger of abuse of power by a president. But as Vernon Bogdanor put it:

> To deprive someone of the power to do evil is also to deprive them of the power to do good. Anyone who looks at the past history of Central and Eastern Europe and, in particular, at the failure of democratic institutions in the inter-war years, must, surely, come to the conclusion that the greatest danger which these countries face is weak government.[13]

This debate on presidents versus parliaments shows that there are no blueprints for a governmental system trying to build democracy.[14] It is important, however, that the major weaknesses of any model chosen be reduced, if not eliminated. Thus if a choice were made for a parliamentary system with proportional representation, measures should be taken in particular to reduce factionalism and clientelism among small parties and to improve the effectiveness of the government. Here the German model provides a good example with its "constructive vote of no-confidence" and a provision that parties must win more than 5 percent of the popular vote to gain any seats in parliament.

If a choice were made for a presidential system, then the French model provides a good example by combining a directly elected president with a cabinet system in which the prime minister and his government are responsible to parliament.[15] The French system allows both for strong government, because the president has the power to break the deadlocks that can so easily arise in a multiparty political system, and for parliamentary checks on government if that is what the electorate wants.

Both a presidential and a parliamentary system should be balanced by a strong judiciary that not only prevents abuse of power by the executive but also protects minorities and individuals from the tyranny of the majority. The judicial system in east central Europe is undergoing profound changes aimed at increasing judicial independence, removing the discredited *nomenklatura* officials from important posts, and reorganizing the system of courts as well as the Ministries of Justice. The legal system is also being reviewed in order to strengthen civic and human rights and to remove from the legislation all glaring vestiges of Communist ideology. The degree of success in implementing these changes will be of crucial importance for democratic prospects in the region.

All these systemic changes will not compensate for the lack of proper individual performance by parliamentarians, members of the executive, and judges. If today the public in east central Europe has low confidence in their parliaments (on average less than 50 points on a 100-point scale), the unprofessional conduct of many individual members of parliament is partly to blame. In the future, parliamentarians must be better able to discern what the public wants and express it to government. They must also be able to recognize the limits of what is governmentally feasible and explain that to each other and to the public.

A special responsibility will rest on the shoulders of those heading a cabinet or holding a presidential office. Even well-constructed government systems can be misused because of personal ambition, abuse of power, or simple ineffectiveness. One must hope that those elevated to the highest offices in Poland, Czechoslovakia, and Hungary will meet the historic challenge of democracy.

Economic reforms. Economic crisis was one of the factors that enhanced democratic aspirations and subsequently caused the fall of communism in the region. Communist regimes, especially in Hungary and Poland, tried hard to improve economic efficiency, but in the late 1980s it became increasingly apparent that economic reforms were doomed to failure unless accompanied by profound political changes. This, of course, strengthened the course of democratic opposition, which was then able to negotiate serious concessions from the regime that led to free elections and the victory of democratic forces.

It would be no exaggeration, however, to say that the democratic groups came to power basically unprepared to restructure the economy of a country. Their programs were clear about why the old system ought to be replaced but much less specific on how to achieve economic transformation. By now, they all agree that there is no alternative to the market in the long run and believe that denationalization, deregulation, and taxation should replace the old policy of central planning and income distribution. But they are still far from reaching consensus on the pace, scope, and social costs of reforms, and they are confronted with difficult dilemmas as to how to organize privatization, proceed with price reforms, or introduce a stock market. Moreover, reformers have to cope with the enduring "heritage" of communism: lack of competitive self-supporting spirit, low work ethic, and egalitarian sentiments. For instance, the late 1990 opinion poll of the Association for Independent Analysis in Prague revealed that almost 40 percent of the Czechoslovak population expect that the state is going to take complete responsibility for their standard of living.

Democracy is not a synonym for prosperity, yet 75 percent of Hungarians think just that, as indicated by research conducted in November 1990 by two sociologists, Simon János and László Bruszt. Democracy merely opens the doors to successful economic reforms by reintroducing economic freedoms, legitimizing economic policies of elected governments, and allowing criticism of all misguided steps or ideas. Nevertheless, introducing a market system always takes time and imposes severe costs on a society. There is also a risk that reforms might fail due to various, often unpredictable circumstances.

The time factor might prove to be crucial: new parliamentary institutions can be put in place within months, but economic reforms take years. The Spanish and the immediate postwar German cases of transition indicate that the time gap between democratic transformations and economic improvements can eventually be bridged within four years. These four years, and in the case of east central Europe possibly even more, represent a very tough test for the emerging democracies. Ralf Dahrendorf called it

a test of the valley of tears: People are asked to accept that democracy begins with government policies which make their daily lives harder. Now that they are able to voice their grievances, they are asked to hold back and wait until the new institutions deliver goods.[16]

Again, there are no blueprints for passing the "valley of tears test." Nevertheless, democracy might indeed fall victim to economic troubles unless at least three conditions are met.

First, privatization, demonopolization, and marketization of the economies in the region must proceed without any further delay. Governments should stop merely talking about reforms, they should begin to implement them. Poland represents a good example of a determined effort to restructure its economy through stabilizing and achieving the full convertibility of Polish currency, reducing the monthly inflation rate to single figures, balancing the budget, and eliminating shortages on the domestic market. Even this ambitious program, however, has been slow in privatizing state-owned enterprises. During the first year of reforms, only 5 of the more than 7,000 enterprises were sold for shares. Czechoslovakia and Hungary, the latter especially, are still much more cautious in taking decisive steps in the direction of a market economy. But postponing genuine reforms will not allow any escape from the "valley of tears test"; it will only force democrats to go through the test under even worse circumstances.

Second, market reforms should envisage a social net that will protect the weakest segments of society from poverty, mass unemployment, and wild competition. Democracy cannot flourish under the inhuman conditions known during the nascent stages of capitalism in the nineteenth century. Democrats would be well advised, however, to abandon any possible illusions they may have about a happy middle ground of a "social market" that releases them from tough economic choices and unpopular steps. Egalitarian rhetoric promising everybody a job with a steadily growing income might reap some extra electoral votes but in due time it will prove a disaster. Reducing state distributive functions, encouraging economic competition, and diversifying consumption patterns is needed for reforms to succeed, even if it leaves many people disadvantaged.

Third, democracy building and economic restructuring may have different time schedules, but this does not imply that democracy might better be suspended for a while in order to allow economic reforms to proceed. Democracy should allow for an effective government that is able to foster economic changes. A certain degree of public constraint, self-denial, and discipline is also needed for reforms to succeed. Those who blame democracy for slowing down economic changes should be reminded that inefficiency has many parents—and more often than not of authoritarian origin. Moreover, discipline and public self-denial are usually stronger when based on a democratic compromise rather than on an iron fist policy that suspends democratic aspirations.

The Need for Western Help

Foreign aid has always been crucial in fostering democratic transitions in Europe. The Marshall Plan made the German transition possible, and Greece, Portugal, and Spain have benefited from early entry into the European Community. Today, there is a general consensus among Western policymakers that democratic restructuring in east central Europe deserves to be helped as well, and by the end of October 1990 the Group of 24 industrialized nations (G-24) had committed itself to a $21 billion package of aid and credits over the next two years to the *entire* area of Eastern Europe. The problem is that even this amount of help meets only a small portion of East European needs (estimated at $270 to $370 billion over the next five years), and there are no prospects of admitting Czechoslovakia, Poland, and Hungary to the European Community.

The amount of aid offered so far contrasts sharply with the relative scale of the Marshall Plan. In the four years after the war, the United States invested $5 billion a year in the European Recovery Program—2 percent of its gross national product (GNP). Today the 2 percent figure applied to the GNPs of 7—not even 24—of the strongest industrialized nations (G-7) would amount to no less than $200 billion in aid a year.[17] Of course, there is no need to spend that much on east central Europe, especially if one considers the enormous problems of poor countries in the Third World. Besides, fostering democracy is not necessarily a function of financial aid.[18] Nevertheless, the comparison with the Marshall Plan indicates the modest level of

Western readiness to bear sacrifices aimed at transforming the region that, after all, has been a source of its cold war obsession for several long decades.[19]

Several factors explain the limited scale of Western commitment to the building of democracy in east central Europe. First, time and again the West has been confronted with other major problems erupting in various parts of Europe and the world. East central Europe is important, but Gorbachev's perestroika is considered even more important, and the latter seems to have run into real trouble. Germany, which would be in a position to help the most, is overburdened by the costs of its own reunification. The Gulf War has attracted both overwhelming Western attention and its resources. When the United States was funding the Marshall Plan, there was little doubt that Western Europe represented America's greatest concern. Today the same cannot be said about east central Europe.

Second, the collapse of communism in East Germany, Czechoslovakia, Hungary, and Poland produced enormous confusion among Western policymakers. They are divided in assessing the impact of the change that has taken place and are unable to reach consensus about the future security and economic and political architecture of the old continent. In addition, some important institutional decision-making frameworks are being eroded (the North Atlantic Treaty Organization most notably), other frameworks are undergoing a profound change (the European Community and the Conference on Security and Cooperation in Europe in particular). In this situation, short-term considerations and national factionalism prevail, undermining the efforts toward a long-term collective strategy that would be needed for the creation of any major aid program.

Third, the policy of helping democracy in east central Europe is not a vote winner in Western states. Communities of ethnic Poles, Hungarians, Slovaks, and Czechs in Western Europe or the United States are small and unable to exert any significant pressure. Major lobby and interest groups are not directly concerned about the fate of east central Europe. In fact, the recent controversy about the ways of investing the expected peace dividend showed that the interests of some of these groups are in conflict with the policy of democratic aid. The idea of including east central Europe in the European Community, in particular, does not make Western trade unions and various groups of producers happy. In the past, anticommunism (on the Right) and disarmament rhetoric (on the Left) could appeal to voters. But today the idea of aiding democracy building cannot count on the same constituency.

Failure to come up with a substantial aid package for democracy building in east central Europe may have serious negative implications for Western countries as well. Most important are the security implications of any instability resulting from an eventual collapse of democracy. The cold war division of Europe was unjust, but it was fairly stable to the extent that the successive explosions in east central Europe could easily be contained within the region. But today the European security system is in a state of flux and full of uncertainty about who threatens whom, who will oppose whom, and who will gain or lose from the actions of states involved in potential local conflicts. As a consequence, the possible eruption of chaos and violence in Poland, Czechoslovakia, or Hungary can have unpredictable consequences for the entire European continent.[20] Collapse of democracy in east central Europe will also dash hopes for possible Western economic expansion in this region. This expansion has only just started, but, as the recent London report by the Centre for Economic Policy Research showed, for example, Eastern Europe could provide profitable use for between $1,350 and $2,910 billion in capital imports over the next decade.[21]

Finally, a collapse of democracy in east central Europe will further weaken the democratic course within the Soviet Union, and the West has an obvious interest in preserving the policy of perestroika. Reformers in various parts of the Soviet federation would be unable to legitimize their campaign if democratic efforts in Poland, Czechoslovakia, and Hungary were to produce anarchy, poverty, and ethnic violence.

In summary, the demise of communism in east central Europe does not guarantee the instant advent of democracy. We cannot rule out a revival of autocratic patterns in the face of rising nationalism, populist demagoguery, or economic mismanagement. East central Europe has always displayed a mixture of hope and despair, of democratic progress and autocratic temptation.[22] Yet the trend toward freedom and democracy seems now to be crystallized, and it can hardly be reversed without a major political battle affecting the entire European continent. As Pierre Hassner put it: "Democratic legitimacy is both indispensable and implacable. [This constitutes] the message of hope that communism has left to us from beyond the grave."[23]

Notes

1. Blaine Harden and Mary Battiata, "In Eastern Europe, the Horizon Is Getting Darker," *International Herald Tribune*, December 26, 1990. See also James Walsh, "Populism on the March," *Time*, December 24, 1990, or Morton Kondracke, "Freedom Bummer," *New Republic*, November 26, 1990.

2. Adam Michnik, "The Walesa I Know Is Unpredictable and Incompetent," *International Herald Tribune*, November 23, 1990.

3. Parliamentary elections in Poland are still pending, while in Hungary and Czechoslovakia the president is elected by the National Assembly.

4. Ralf Dahrendorf, "Transitions: Politics, Economics, and Liberty," *The Washington Quarterly* 13 (Summer 1990), p. 142.

5. Timothy Garton Ash, "Eastern Europe: Après le Déluge, Nous," *New York Review of Books*, August 16, 1990, p. 56.

6. See, e.g., Guillermo O'Donnell and Philippe C. Schmitter, *Transitions from Authoritarian Rule: Tentative Conclusions About Uncertain Democracies* (Baltimore, Md.: The Johns Hopkins University Press, 1986), p. 49, or Larry Diamond, "Beyond Authoritarianism and Totalitarianism: Strategies for Democratization," *The Washington Quarterly* 12 (Winter 1989), p. 148.

7. Leszek Kolakowski, "Marxist Roots of Stalinism," in *Stalinism*, Robert C. Tucker, ed. (New York: W. W. Norton, 1977), p. 294.

8. Some opposition groups went as far as to promote a comprehensive vision of a "Self-Governing Commonwealth." See, e.g., the first National Program of Polish Solidarity adopted in the fall of 1981.

9. Timothy Garton Ash, "Eastern Europe: The Year of Truth," *New York Review of Books*, February 15, 1990, p. 20.

10. Religious organizations represent here a notable exception. See Krzysztof Pomian, "Religion and Politics in a Time of Glasnost," in *Restructuring Eastern Europe*, Ronald J. Hill and Jan Zielonka, eds. (Aldershot, England: Edward Elgar, 1990), pp. 112–127.

11. Peter Mair, "(Electoral) Markets and (Stable) States," in *Markets Against the State*, Michael Moran and Maurice Wright, eds. (London: Macmillan, forthcoming 1991).

12. Rudolf L. Tökes, "Politics of the 'Second Transition' in Hungary: Elite Perspectives and Policy Arenas" (Paper presented at the seminar "Overcoming Obstacles to Democratization and Institution Building in Europe," organized by the Institute for East–West Security Studies and the Netherlands Institute of International Relations, "Clingendael," The Hague, The Netherlands, November 9–11, 1990), p. 35.

13. Vernon Bogdanor, "The Emerging Democracies: Should They Adopt a Presidential or a Parliamentary System?" (Paper presented at the seminar "Parliaments and the Transition Towards Democracy," organized by the East–West Parliamentary Practice Project, The Hague, The Netherlands, September 13–17, 1990), p. 10.

14. See, e.g., Donald L. Horowitz, Seymour Martin Lipset, and Juan J. Linz, "Debate: Presidents vs. Parliaments," *Journal of Democracy* 1 (Fall 1990), pp. 71–91.

15. The French presidential system seems to be better suited to East European circumstances than the U.S. presidential system which, among other unique characteristics, is based on a diffused party system that is not known in Eastern Europe.

16. Ralf Dahrendorf, "Roads to Freedom: Democratization and Its Problems in East Central Europe," in *Uncertain Futures: Eastern Europe and Democracy*, Peter Volten, ed., Institute for East–West Security Studies, Occasional Paper Series no. 16 (New York, 1990), p. 13.

17. See Robert A. Levine and David A. Ochmanek, *Toward a Stable Transition in Europe: A Conservative/Activist Strategy for the United States*, RAND Note N-3106-AF (Santa Monica, Calif.: The RAND Corporation, 1990), p. 40. It should be noted that in 1990 the U.S. Congress has approved a mere $370,000,000 in economic aid to Eastern Europe. See Ronald Linden, "The New Eastern Europe and East–West Relations," Radio Free Europe Research, Report on Eastern Europe, Munich, November 16, 1990, p. 31.

18. For instance, Hungary's membership in the Council of Europe enhanced legislative changes in that country, especially in the area of human rights.

19. As Robert E. Hunter observed: "The United States alone invested more than $2 trillion in containing Soviet power and condominium in Europe, but so far has been prepared to commit in its aftermath sums that can only be styled paltry." "The Future of European Security," *The Washington Quarterly* 13 (Autumn 1990), p. 62.

20. For a detailed analysis of this problem see Jan Zielonka, "Europe's Security: A Great Confusion," *International Affairs* 67 (January 1991), pp. 127–137.

21. See Richard Portes, "For Eastern Europe, the Short Term Will Decide," *International Herald Tribune*, November 15, 1990. Also Eoin Belton, "Eastern Europe Gateways Beckon to Small Savers," *Daily Telegraph*, January 18, 1991.

22. As a Hungarian sociologist, Elemér Hankiss, observed: "This odd mixture of freedom and servitude, hope and agony, may have been one of the basic characteristics of East European societies and political cultures in the last few years." *East European Alternatives* (Oxford: Clarendon Press, 1990), p. 273.

23. Pierre Hassner, "Communism: A Coroner's Inquest," *Journal of Democracy* 1 (Fall 1990), p. 6.

Who Killed the Third World?

Richard E. Bissell

ONE OF THE most dramatic theories of 1990 has been that the East–West thaw is eliminating U.S. and Western interest in the Third World. Leaders of developing countries have a nightmare: that the industrialized countries are sealing up their collective hearts, picking up their aid purses, and heading off for Eastern Europe. In this nightmare, the poor and hungry of the Third World are left alone, beside the road, without resources and without a cause to attract attention from the rest of the world. The scenario is a dramatic one, heightened by a series of diplomatic events this year, and made more poignant by a sense of revolutionary good news about emerging democracies yielding such bad news for the majority of mankind.

The problem is that this nightmare is only half true. The Third World, as a political movement, has disintegrated; it was on its deathbed, however, well before the liberalization of Eastern Europe. It is important to understand why and how, so the industrialized world can respond positively to the opportunities in both Eastern Europe and the developing countries of Latin America, Asia, and Africa.

Richard E. Bissell is assistant administrator at the U.S. Agency for International Development, and the author or editor of several books on problems of the developing countries. From 1984 to 1986, he served as executive editor of *The Washington Quarterly*.

The Rise of Third-Worldism

The Third World movement has its origins in a specific phase of independence for most post-colonial less-developed countries (LDCs).[1] In the early phases of independence, most countries experienced a heady nationalism, born out of a misplaced confidence that a new state automatically could succeed to the authority and resources of the colonial power as easily as it raised a new flag. For Africa and Asia, the effort to create a Third World coalition reflected an awareness that arrived a few years after each state's independence—that in fact each country did not possess the economic and political resources to move international events greatly. Even India, the subcontinent giant with enormous resources, embraced the bargain of the disaffected newly independent at the inaugural meeting of the nonaligned states at Bandung in 1957 in order to gain a place on the world stage.

This movement toward third-worldism, then, has as its source a sense of relative powerlessness, a negative phenomenon that some leaders understood could be turned into a positive outcome. Even Latin American leaders, most of whom did not experience twentieth-century political discontinuities, recognized the potential in a coalition of the majority (demographically speaking), and although they never showed unbridled enthusiasm for the Third World effort, generally they joined. In most international organizations Latins maintained a separate caucus, but found a way to strike a bargain with the rest of the LDCs. For the Latins, the fact that they had been independent far longer did not mitigate the fact that they did not fare equally in the postwar power sharing dominated by the northern hemisphere.

Who joined the Third World? By coining the name, adherents clearly expected it to include countries not in the First (capitalist) or Second (socialist/Communist) Worlds. Did that mean China could be admitted? China was certainly a member until it obtained its permanent Security Council seat in 1971; then it became unclear. Other countries on the periphery caused dilemmas—South Korea, Turkey, and Israel, among others—but none were important enough to unsettle the vision that came to be known as the Group of 77 (G-77), for the number of initial members. The number, which actually grew in subsequent years despite the fixed appellation, mattered because it was greater than the combined votes of the East and West blocs at the United Nations (UN). Thus was born the idea of the automatic majority in the UN General Assembly, and the illusion of power that held sway in much of the 1970s.

As the Third World movement was political in origin, it required an ideology to maintain it. Given the great diversity of states in the movement, it was unlikely to have a spontaneous ideological worldview based on historical experience. Therefore, the movement looked for an ideology that would explain what its members did share in common: powerlessness, poverty, and a need to get their issues on the international agenda. The members needed to explain to their own people and to the world why their political independence had not delivered them from difficulty. Independence, it turned out, had been a chimera, and it was not clear why.

The answer was found in the social structural analysis of the "dependency school" of both East and West.[2] This analysis placed the Third World in a structurally inferior position on the periphery of global affairs, and thus established a myth-structure in which the LDCs were only pawns and a worldview commanding structural transformation. Economically, the world was seen as driven by the historical advantages of and the drive to dominate by the industrialized countries and their multinational corporate minions. Politically, criticism focused on the hegemony allegedly established by the powers of the First and Second Worlds in the wake of World War II. The central theme of thirdworldism was the inability and futility of individual LDCs taking control of their future until a radical change had been wrought in the international power balance. In the West, this sometimes was called "third world socialism," owing to the major redistributive element in the ideology. The emphasis on the redistribution to the poorer nations of economic goods in terms of capital and income was matched in a less tangible way by calls for a political reordering to give at least equality, if not dominance, to the Third World agenda.

This ideology had adherents in the First and Second Worlds as well. For the Communist bloc, the Third World represented useful allies, albeit somewhat unruly at times. It became messy for the Soviet Union when various friends in the Third World embraced Marxism, with endorsement from Moscow, only to turn out to be opportunistic dictators in Marxist clothing. For the Kremlin, the reflection of its own ideology in some Third World thinking was gratifying, as it was useful in isolating the West in the UN and the specialized agencies.

In the First World, many adopted the ideology of third-worldism. Their sense of the righteousness of the Third World's struggle was reinforced by the U.S. pursuit of an unsuccessful policy in Vietnam, and considerable skepticism that the West as a whole offered a useful development model to the Third World. The abandonment of the Rostow "stages of growth" model for development left a vacuum in U.S. thinking.[3] In the 1960s, the United States scaled back its aid presence in areas outside Vietnam and abandoned broad-scale approaches, seeking instead to tend modestly to the hunger and hurts of the poorest. U.S. universities, given their protests over involvement in Vietnam, were delighted to provide intellectual horsepower for the ideology of third-worldism. The work of many U.S. academics reflected a convenient combination of highly abstract views of their world and selective readings of grass-roots reality in the LDCs.

After the independence decade of the 1960s, the 1970s was a decade of test for the Third World. The LDC reality was not a pleasant one. Governments were not prepared for the periodic emergence of adverse terms of trade in commodities produced by developing countries. Popular disappointment with the fruits of independence led to the widespread rejection of governments modeled on the West. The assertion of "authentic roots" of government led in some cases to narrowly based regimes that could be justified only by Leninist principles, although most were ineffective, even as instruments of coercion. The reach of the state tended to decline. In other cases, as in parts of Asia, authentic sources of governance led to rather more efficient governments able to mobilize economic performance although generally at the cost of civil liberties. In a sense, General Park Chung Hee's Korea was as politically authentic as Field Marshal Jean-Bédel Bokassa's Central African Empire. The results were just very different, despite their professed solidarity with a shared international ideology.

If the economic rewards of third-worldism were paltry, the political rewards were numerous for a decade. The 1970s were driven by a desire in the First World to accommodate the Third World agenda. "North–South" meetings became a staple of international life. UN power structures were amended to accommodate the interests of the majority. Meetings of the UN Conference on Trade and Development (UNCTAD), where demands for changes in global economic structures were explored, were unceasing. Western equity holdings in the Third World were reduced. Nationalizations in key sectors attempted to ensure that Third World governments never again would be threatened by multinational companies operating in their countries.

At the end of the decade, however, a visceral stocktaking occurred. For the men, women, and children of the developing countries, there had been few improvements in the standard of living. Certainly, the gap in the quality of life between the developed and the developing countries was growing, although government officials seemed to be doing well with frequent trips to New York and Geneva. The problems of governance in the LDCs and their internal economies were worsening. Basic government and social services were disintegrating. There were more palms to grease with bribes. The stocktaking in the West was more dramatic, based on decisive events. The double ratcheting of oil prices in 1973 and 1980 raised enormous alarm that the West's economic influence was dissipated. The emergence of premodern political systems, as represented by the caricature regimes of Idi Amin in Uganda and the ayatollah in Iran, suggested to the West that it was time for another approach. The decisive years for all sides were 1979 and 1980, when forces emerged to push aside the Third World agenda.

The Erosion of Third-Worldism

Hindsight shows clearly what was not understood at the beginning of the 1980s—or since then, by many. No vote was taken in an international body to disband the Third World. Rather, the Third World lost its adherents. Defections from the cause increased during the 1980s. Events disapproved the value of its ideology. Politically, the international community chose contexts other than third-worldism to address a series of issues where sensible compromises were reached without the North–South confrontations of the 1970s. In effect, the developing countries discovered what can be achieved through cooperation rather than confrontation with the rest of the world. To be sure, several successes were needed to show how it was done.

The first significant sign of the erosion of third-worldism was a decision by an increasing number of states to internationalize their economies. The export-driven growth in East Asia, demonstrating that poor countries did not inevitably lose in the existing international structure, challenged the rest of the developing countries. In looking closely at the growing Asian economies, others realized that internal measures were as important as international networks. When leaders asked how to get advice on internal reforms, they found that they had well-trained individuals in senior positions and access to advice from the World Bank and the International Monetary Fund. The gradual adherence of those leaders to internal reforms was essential, and although the rewards of such reforms were not always instantaneous, leaders learned that they were essential for the eventual satisfaction of the people's desire for an improved quality of life.

Reform took on many different hues. In some cases, the focus was on relations with the external world—moving from an overvalued exchange rate to an undervalued one, simplifying regulations, eliminating tariffs and controls that were disincentives for exports, and allowing indigenous companies to keep foreign exchange earnings for the import of new technology. In all cases, internal reform was essential to establish confidence in the long-term future of the economy and the social system. East Asia, for example, found ways to create incentives for entrepreneurs to keep their money at home, while in Latin America governments struggled with a malfunctioning system of ineffective controls that put a premium on getting money out of the legal economy and into bank accounts abroad.

As each country in the Third World coalition began to measure its own ability to build domestic confidence and open linkages abroad, the elements of unity among the LDCs began to diminish. First, some countries were successful in their economic reforms, and thus began to move away from poverty. With the injection of assistance from the World Bank, regional development banks, and bilateral donors in support of these reforms, economic growth began to pick up, most visibly after the global recession of

1981–1982. The United States and others aggressively maintained a policy line in favor of open markets, ensuring export opportunities for developing countries even as the U.S. trade deficit continued to grow. In certain sectors, such as sugar and textiles, the United States could not be of great assistance owing to domestic pressure groups. The drive for open markets was far-reaching, however, as enshrined in the progress made by the General Agreement on Tariffs and Trade (GATT) on reduction of tariffs.

Many LDCs discovered excitedly that economic policy reform brought with it increased control over their own futures. With the guidance of their own well-trained experts, governments were able to negotiate for the future. In some cases, they decided to create and pursue their own reform programs, as in Nigeria. In many others, they turned to the World Bank for collaboration and financing, getting at one and the same time a review of their macroeconomic frameworks and a place to borrow much of the money required to finance changes. In turn, the World Bank helped to spark the creation of consultative groups, country-specific gatherings of aid donors that reviewed reform plans and pledged financing. Although there often were sharp differences of perspective between Bank economists and developing country officials, these were not any more than one would expect from a dialogue between lender and borrower.

The payoff of economic reform was not merely a set of policies pleasing to the eye of the World Bank. For governments in the developing world reform was a gamble, and if it did not fairly quickly result in perceptions of improved living standards for the man in the street, the government would be overthrown. On the other hand, many governments perceived the potential positive payoff as very attractive: the chance to demonstrate their leadership abilities and to cement the loyalty of a citizenry that had become quite jaded about governance in general. Therefore, the World Bank and donors became increasingly sensitive to the extent to which policy adjustments could impoverish people on the way to prosperity. For example, the move to market prices of basic grains might result in higher income for farmers, but it also would raise the price of bread for people in the cities. Riots in capital cities were not healthy for governments. Likewise, reduction of government employment in an attempt to balance the budget easily could result in fewer education and health services. It should be noted, parenthetically, that in some countries such reductions made no difference; reductions in force in Guinea following Sékou Touré's overthrow in 1984 revealed that the vast majority of paid government employees never showed up for work anyway. It was clear, however, that reform would be dead politically if it were perceived as increasing the general hardship. Governments and donors gradually appreciated that particularly vulnerable parts of the population, such as the landless or women and children, required the alleviation of the symptoms of poverty that accompanied some policy adjustments.

A second type of payoff from reform was the increasing control enjoyed by people and enterprises over their own fate. Not only were governments freer to control their national destiny, but people gained control through deregulation of the economy and society. By simply reducing the number of "gates" in a government through which an action must pass increased the efficiency, honesty, and individual accountability. The now-legendary studies in Peru undertaken by Hernando de Soto raised the issue of the time occupied in legally incorporating a business: 287 days, working eight hours a day, in contrast to Miami, where it could be done in four hours.[4] Fortunately, the Peruvians have begun to loosen up their problem, and such examples have become commonplace throughout developing countries. By freeing individuals and businesses to pursue their own fortunes, instead of waiting on government, many processes of economic growth were unleashed. Most important for many in Latin America, reform did not mean a return to the traditional, government-sanctioned crony capitalism where a few families were given control of economic activity; instead, reform constituted a generalized unleashing of entrepreneurial energy and broad-based aggregate growth.

The 1980s also eroded third-worldism's tolerance and even support of nondemocratic regimes. The opening up of economies required the opening up of societies generally. Much of the Third World rhetoric had dwelt on the inefficiency of multiparty systems, unguided pluralism, and the dangers of empowering people at the grass roots. In the 1960s and 1970s, politics had been an elite sport; in the 1980s, the requirements of mobilizing popular support for economic reforms compelled a more broad-based politics. Thus, President Ronald Reagan's speech at Westminster in 1982 on democracy-building found a remarkable resonance. The subtle change in the focus of the United States from the rights of the prominent few to the participatory freedom of the people at large, helped catalyze a profound political transformation of the international policy community. Free elections were held first in Latin America. The rapid weakening of the Leninist models in China and the Soviet Union accelerated the change, reaching avalanche proportions by 1989, when the countries of the Third World already had realized that their societies had to choose between democratization and collapse, both political and economic.

The latest payoff of reform was the steady integration of the economies of the developing world into international trading regimes. Internal reform required external reform at a later stage, although as recently as 1986, one informed observer could comment that "Third World states will still find great difficulty adopting a capitalist international trading system or confining themselves to a trading strategy in world politics."[5] In retrospect, it is clear that the difficulty encountered by most developing countries was merely perceptual—failing to recognize the major trade opportunities of the 1990s. This too has changed. For example, former trade hard-liners, such as India and Brazil, have shown interest in new approaches to intellectual property rights. This is hardly surprising now that India is a major exporter of computer software, based on the third-largest pool of software programmers in the world. Likewise, Mauritius has developed textile and computer industries that are competitive worldwide; with those sectors as leaders, economic growth is rising by nearly 10 percent annually. There are still major problems with agricultural monocultures devoted to tropical crops. Countries are learning, however, that they should not rely solely on cocoa, sugar, or coffee, and where they must, that they must add value to products in order to pick up the processing markup. Ecuador, for instance, ships tons of shrimp each year, but only recently began to break into the precooked shrimp market in Europe. Other countries will follow in food processing and agribusiness.

The diplomatic arena as well has felt the impact of changing perspectives in the G–77. The Special Session of the UN General Assembly on International Economic Cooperation in April 1990 was a remarkably low-key affair. The bias was clearly a G–77 one, but in a way that did not rebut the basic premise that each developing country ultimately is responsible for its own affairs rather than being at the mercy of a hostile international system. Redistributionist calls, so common in the 1970s, were virtually absent. A more limited approach to South–South issues emerged in the efforts of the G–15, a group created during 1988–1990 by Peru, Algeria, Yugoslavia, and India. The conclusions of the first summit in June 1990 were fairly anodyne, with the usual calls for global review of economic distress among the developing countries, but the focus generally was on South–South cooperation. The same atmosphere pervades preparations for the upcoming September 1990 international conference on the least-developed countries, organized by UNCTAD. Discussions are serious rather than confrontational. Agenda items are meant to be result-oriented, rather than merely rhetorical. Even where an agenda item is raised that clearly is beyond the mandate of the conference, such as international debt issues, the tone is more mournful than militant.

In 1990 we live in a world different from that of 1960, 1970, or 1980. International solidarity no longer is organized along North–South lines. The old division between "haves" and "have-nots" is muddied, not least by the many "somewhat-haves" and countries with a mixture of both.

What Succeeds Third-Worldism?

Some would argue that the failure of third-worldism was that rhetoric does not fill stomachs. In a way, that is true, although even in the 1970s, there was a significant flow of funds to the LDCs. The enormous flow of public sector borrowing from commercial banks produced statistics that indicated all was well. Unfortunately, such flows funded a kind of economic development that was neither broad-based nor sustainable. It was narrowly based in being siphoned off by the first hands to touch the money (namely, those in government). It was unsustainable because the private sectors in the LDCs effectively were being strangled. Well-motivated governments could feed people for a year, but few in the 1970s created the markets and institutions to feed a generation.

The real failure of the Third World movement was psychological. By blaming the rest of the world for the ills of the LDCs, people were left feeling powerless. This was convenient for the autocratic leaders of most LDCs, but it was logically wrong, and an increasing number of people came to recognize that it was morally wrong as well. To deprive people of their ability and rights to control their lives was a clear transgression of striking social and political consequence. Those who made short-term gains out of such an ideology were overthrown in the 1980s.

Not all promoters of the Third World have disappeared. Even within LDC governments, there remain institutional pockets devoted to maintaining the vocabulary and agenda of the 1970s. Foreign ministries, devoted to the old conference circuit, often are the last to be converted. The countries of East Asia certainly have moved beyond the old confines. India has become divided in its approach: with rising international economic engagement (exports rose by 35.5 percent and imports by 27.9 percent in 1989–1990)[6] and a middle class of 150 million people alongside the largest concentration of below subsistence people in the world, where does it play its chips? On the other hand, Arab countries are mesmerized by their regional revolutionary forces and the problematic future of oil. The way to integration into a global society is not through the confrontation of the past; instead, most LDCs today are shifting to broad-based competition in the marketplaces of the 1990s, where all can win. The United States, both as a government and in partnership with the American people, will have three major opportunities to build a new relationship with the developing countries in the 1990s. The first opportunity will be to work together on new societies, open to participation by all and characterized by honest government, as a leader in the global movement for democratic governance. The second opportunity will be partnership on a strategy of broad-based economic growth with the objective of improving the welfare of the people, something requiring resources and talent from both the public and private sectors of both the developed and the developing countries. The third opportunity is shared stewardship of the environment: the heightened sensitivity over the environment has taught us, above all, that we do share one planet and one future. The stewardship agenda is fully compatible with economic and democratic progress.

It is no coincidence that the demise of the Third World movement occurred during a decade of strengthening democracy. The determination of the Reagan administration to support democracy-building around the world, first in Central America and Eastern Europe, but also in Namibia and elsewhere, implied the downfall of third-worldism. With the wave of democratization sweeping the world, the U.S. role must change from that of high profile leadership for democratization to a more subtle, supporting role. In the 1990s, democracy is no longer the revolutionary force of the turn of the decade but it does have to be institutionalized country by country and the United States cannot afford to be inactive. Nongovernmental organizations are likely to play a key role in assisting democracy abroad, ranging from the U.S. National Endowment for Democracy to the International Foundation for Electoral Support. In all, the U.S. government spends about $50 million in direct support of democracy-building abroad each year. That figure easily can be justified at a level twice as high, in order to accommodate Eastern Europe and the global challenge of governance. Elections are only the first step; building participatory institutions (legislatures, honest civil services, and administration of justice) is a much more arduous and expensive process. It is also a long-term process. If people take increasing responsibility for their political futures, they also will take the initiative on economic matters.

This brings us full circle to the mistaken thesis raised at the beginning of this article. The move toward democracy and open markets in Eastern Europe is not a threat to the countries of the erstwhile Third World. The most important mobilization occurring in both regions is internal, not external. The power to mobilize resources is far greater within any country than outside it. Foreign aid can be only a catalyst, and not a solution in itself. It can stabilize an economy, but the long-term investment in a society must be generated overwhelmingly from within. The movement toward democracy in all regions is a crucial step in raising confidence in government and a stable economy. It is only one step, with many to follow, but it is the most important and necessary one. Democracy is contagious, as well demonstrated in Eastern Europe and in Latin America, and remaining nondemocratic forces are right to feel threatened by global popular democratic aspirations.

The race for free markets also is essential for long-term development. It will be tempting for some people to demand immediate payoffs from economic change. Bread riots will occur. The most important change has come, however, when people have focused on the long term and on economic change for their children's generation. That is an investment mentality that bespeaks a confidence in the future of a society. The rest of the world can provide a catalyst for that confidence, with small amounts of money, but it can never create the confidence. Each government and its private sector institutions must earn that confidence from its own people, which is a protracted process. In this, there is no competition between Eastern Europe and the developing countries. All countries are involved in a process of generating and maintaining the confidence of their peoples. Today, they reinforce one another, across national boundaries, with a spirit of self-determination and direction, in sharp contrast to the "solidarity" of blame and recrimination so pervasive in the Third World era.

Is this new breeze from the developing countries good for the United States? The G–77 structure was bad for the United States because it cast the government, economy, and society of America as villains in a morality play. Its demise creates new opportunities for a far less stilted dialogue and diplomacy. Greater diversity in the developing world, and a broader commitment to democracy, free-market economics, and pragmatism create new sympathies with an American public that today sees the values animating its political and economic life at stake—and thriving—elsewhere in the world. As U.S. international trade grows, and as the American public becomes more sophisticated about the world, people recognize the artificiality of North–South divisions. An increased U.S. presence abroad, whether in Eastern Europe or the developing countries, will be beneficial for global cooperation only if the U.S. private sector plans to remain for the long haul. Quick, short-term profits do not exist in most countries, but the preference of the U.S. financial sector for Western Europe means that it misses bigger markets in developing countries. If the U.S. private sector genuinely wishes to compete abroad, it will have to be in countries that currently are perceived as weak. Others, particularly the Japanese, are searching for those long-term niches where the returns will be great. The U.S. private sector should do no less.

In their pragmatism, Americans want to develop mutual interests with those people in developing countries who are dealing with the real world, not a world as seen through a G–77 prism. The movement toward democracy and honest government will do wonders for establishing common values with Americans. Although economic confidence is important, the need to rebuild credibility between the poorer countries and the United States involves more than the debt crisis and the elimination of communism. People in both North and South want the confidence that they can work together on real problems, rather than shoot at shadows on the wall. The needs of the Third World movement created an increasingly distorted prism, and drove Americans away. In the disintegration of that prism, Americans will find their fates once again interwoven with the future of the developing countries.

The views in this article are the author's own and do not necessarily reflect the position of the U.S. government.

Notes

1. See Richard E. Bissell and Michael Radu, eds., *The Post-Decolonization Era in Africa* (New Brunswick, N.J.: Transaction Press, 1979).

2. See, for example, Immanuel Wallerstein, *The Capitalist World Economy* (New York: Cambridge University Press, 1979) and Roger A. Coate, *Global Issue Regimes* (New York: Praeger Publishers, 1982). For a critique, see W. Scott Thompson, ed., *The Third World: Premises of U.S. Policy* (San Francisco, Calif.: Institute of Contemporary Studies, 1983 revised).

3. Walt Rostow dominated U.S. government thinking on development in the 1960s with *The Stages of Economic Growth* (Cambridge: Cambridge University Press, 1960) and *The Economics of Take-Off Into Sustained Growth* (New York: St. Martin's Press, 1963).

4. Hernando de Soto, *The Other Path* (New York: Harper and Row, 1989) and "The Informals Pose an Answer to Marx," *The Washington Quarterly* 12:1 (Winter 1989), pp. 165–172.

5. Richard Rosecrance, *The Rise of the Trading State* (New York: Basic Books, 1986), p. 205.

6. *Financial Times*, June 6, 1990, p. 6.

Regional Order in the 1990s: The Challenge of the Middle East

Richard N. Haass

FOR GOOD REASON, much of what is being said and written about the 1990s concerns Europe. It is Europe more than any other area that has held the key to the global balance of power in this century, and it is this continent more than any other that is experiencing fundamental change. What is at issue is not some rearrangement of the furniture, but the architecture of the house itself.

Although the questions concerning where Europe is now or is heading are of great interest, and although my topic is closely associated with them, it addresses neither developments in Europe nor the future of East–West relations. Rather, it deals with the likely impact of what might be called the mellowing of the Cold War—intentionally avoiding the theological question of whether the Cold War is actually over—on other parts of the world. More specifically, it addresses the prospects for regional order, and above all order in the Middle East, in the 1990s.

Richard N. Haass is special assistant to the president and senior director for Near East and South Asian Affairs of the National Security Council.

What Kind of Mellowing?

The phrase "mellowing of the Cold War" is borrowed from George Kennan, who in his famous telegram and subsequent article on containment predicted that the successful frustration of the Soviet Union's push for influence beyond its borders would inevitably lead to fundamental political and social change within its borders.

Now, 40 years on, we are seeing many of Kennan's predictions come to pass. The Soviet Union is a much changed place in many respects. Internal political change, planned and otherwise, has been and continues to be nothing short of fantastic. These developments have important consequences for what was once called the Third World and in particular for the Middle East—used here as a shorthand to define the area stretching from "Marrakesh to Bangladesh."

What is likely to be the result, for the Middle East as elsewhere, of the decline of the Soviet Union and the mellowing of East–West relations? Above all, and despite the exceptions that will certainly arise, it is feasible to anticipate a period of diminished tension and reduced competition between the United States and the Soviet Union. It is not difficult to suggest just why this is likely. Most of the explanation derives from changes in the Soviet Union. It now has available to it fewer resources and more important priorities closer to home. The fact that the West was able and willing to compete effectively, whether in the deployment of missiles to Europe or in the several manifestations of the Reagan Doctrine, signaled that competition would be expensive and more often than not a losing effort. At the same time, the reduced role for ideology in Soviet foreign policy diminished the importance of the so-called Third World as either a social and political laboratory or as a locus of contest with the West.

The level of superpower competition has not been reduced simply because the Soviet Union no longer deserves the description of superpower. To a lesser but still significant extent it is also a function of changing U.S. policies and perceptions. The United States faces a future of more constrained resources coupled with competing demands at home and abroad. Ironically, the success in winnowing states in Eastern Europe and Central America from communism or some other tyranny has created new demands for the security assistance program, hitherto less than universally popular. The increased strength of U.S. allies in Europe and the Asia–Pacific regions will bolster arguments that burdens ought to be more evenly distributed. And reduced Soviet activism and the sense that cold war competition for its own sake, that is, in the absence of important intrinsic local interests, is an anachronism, will also work to reduce U.S. involvement. The net result of these changes within and between the United States and the Soviet Union will be to reduce the significance of regional outcomes to the central balance.

There will, of course, be exceptions. One already exists in Afghanistan, where both the United States and the Soviet Union continue to support their respective protagonists with military and economic aid despite the departure of Soviet forces more than a year ago. The Soviet Union also continues to back governments in countries ranging from Cambodia and North Korea to Ethiopia and Cuba. These examples, however, are more residues of the past than harbingers of patterns to come. Indeed, if the thesis articulated here is correct, such commitments of resources where strategic stakes are modest or absent are likely to be more exception than rule in the future.

This may be a good thing on the whole for the superpowers themselves. Less competition should translate into less cost (empire and wars are not inexpensive) and less risk of escalation that could embroil the great power patrons in direct combat—something that in the nuclear age could well prove a calamity for all involved and even for those that are not.

Not all the results of less involvement are bound, however, to be good for the United States and the Soviet Union. There could well be a loss of political influence, military access, and markets, especially for the Soviet Union, which often has little more than arms to offer countries that understandably see little reason to emulate unsuccessful economic practices or unappealing politics. The United States should fare much better if political and economic concerns come to the fore. Recent events and the ascendance of democratic, market-oriented states would suggest this is already the case.

The more relevant question, though, is not the impact on the great powers of a greater distancing from regional conflict but rather its impact on those who cannot distance themselves from such conflicts, namely, the regional states themselves. Here reality is quite complex.

At first glance, a mellowing of the Cold War would appear to constitute an unmixed blessing for the Middle East and other regions. This assessment would stem from the belief that much of the turmoil in the Middle East and other regions can be traced in part or in whole to great power machinations and in particular to their provision of military or other support to one or another protagonist. According to this school of thought, regional states would do very well (or would at least be far better off) if left to themselves.

There is a degree of truth in this. The Soviet Union bears a good deal of responsibility for arming and encouraging governments and movements that resorted to violence to realize political aims. Another notion, however, bears consideration. The relative distancing of the United States and the Soviet Union from regional disputes may not always be a good thing for those in the Middle East and other regions or for those with a stake in settling or more modestly managing these disputes. To the contrary, and unless regional states and regional organizations themselves act with unprecedented vision, the future could be one of more rather than less conflict at the regional level.

This conclusion may not be self-evident; an explanation follows. Historically, the United States and the Soviet Union have engaged in conflict management. Although the stated intention was to prevent crises from erupting in the first instance, the real focus became one of limiting and bringing to an end those crises that did occur. The motives for doing so were clear and have already been alluded to—namely, to protect the investment in one's ally, to avoid having disagreement over some regional issue spill over and poison other more central aspects of the relationship (a fear of linkage), and, most important, to avoid having a regional dispute escalate and become the cause of global confrontation.

These motives, however, came into conflict with other motives, namely, the promotion of national interests. Such interests ranged from gaining access to military facilities and markets to promoting the welfare of like-minded governments or would-be governments. Behind this was a pervasive sense of ideological competition and rivalry. Considerations of world order and such intangible but far from unimportant factors as national prestige and reliability often transcended any more immediate or intrinsic strategic interest or economic claim.

Not surprisingly, there were numerous attempts by Moscow and Washington to resolve this tension between conflicting objectives. The best known, if least successful, was the 1972 Basic Principles Agreement signed at the first Nixon–Brezhnev summit meeting. The principles themselves—supporting peaceful coexistence, eschewing unilateral advantage, and exercising restraint—were ambiguous and general enough to have little effect other than to add to the disillusionment with détente that set in following the 1973 Middle East war. At that time, the Soviet Union appeared more interested in gaining advantage than in exercising restraint, at least until direct U.S.–Soviet confrontation became a possibility. In short, the Soviet Union did not participate in crisis avoidance but did support crisis management when events threatened to get out of hand.

A number of specific agreements have also been designed to delimit U.S.–Soviet competition in one or another region. The 1962 Agreement on Neutrality for Laos was one such instance. The 1988 Geneva Accords that provided a basis for Soviet withdrawal from Afghanistan also come to mind. So too does the arrangement for bringing stability to southern Africa and to Angola and Namibia.

More often than not, however, relations between the superpowers in the realm of regional competition and disputes were more informal than formal, more implicit than explicit, and more oriented toward management than avoidance. Certain patterns emerged: they avoided confronting directly each other's military forces; they accepted limits on the ability of their friends and allies to create a new status quo that would be intolerable to the other power; they demonstrated a degree of respect for areas of interest vital to the other; they accepted limits on direct intervention except when coming to the aid of a seriously threatened or soundly defeated friend. It is almost possible to speak of an understanding in which the two dominant powers of the day jointly managed international relations in a manner in which the core interests of either remained unthreatened.

Such patterns emerged on many occasions. The Cuban missile crisis is a case study in Soviet acceptance of limits in an area close to the United States. During the Vietnam conflict, the United States was reluctant to attack North Vietnam, in part out of respect for Soviet and Chinese interests. In South Asia, India was able to play midwife to the state of Bangladesh but not to dismember what is today Pakistan. In the Middle East, Israel was allowed to restore the status quo ante in 1973 but not to decimate the Egyptian army. And throughout its presence in Afghanistan, the Soviet Union was careful not to challenge Pakistan too directly lest it force the United States to escalate its own involvement in the struggle.

The principal point is that the United States and the Soviet Union are less likely to do such work in the future. In part this is for reasons already mentioned, namely, less will and declining resources, especially in the case of the Soviet Union. The trend of diminishing great power control, however, has less to do with the great powers than it does with changes taking place within the various regions themselves. Even in the Middle East, the Persian Gulf, and South Asia— regions where the United States retains important intrinsic interests including support for Israel, promoting the stability of moderate friends, and ensuring access to oil—the ability of outsiders to influence events is generally declining.

International Deregulation

There are several reasons for this change. Wealth, technology, and arms now come from too many sources for either the United States or the Soviet Union to be in a position to dictate local decisions. Also, many once developing states are now relatively developed in areas of direct military significance. Denial of military or political support is thus a less credible sanction than it was. So too is the threat to intervene. Beyond any falling off in the willingness of either the U.S. or Soviet publics to support lengthy and expensive interventions, it is a fact that the costs of such interventions are sharply up in those regions where local military capabilities have vastly improved. Moreover, if the costs of such armed interventions are up, the prospects are down that a simple show of force or the dispatch of a gunboat can turn the tide. As the British learned in their war with Argentina, establishing local military superiority can prove to be no easy task. Overall military superiority and nuclear weapons count for little when faced with significant local opposition halfway across the world.

To some extent these impressive local capacities are the result of U.S. and Soviet largess. Years of providing arms and know-how have had an impact. To an increasing degree, however, the strengthening of local capabilities reflects additional factors. Sources of advanced arms can be found not only in other so-called major powers (France, the United Kingdom, China) but also in countries such as India, South Africa, Brazil, and Israel. And many countries have themselves developed impressive indigenous sources of militarily significant technology. The consequence is clear: more and more countries are increasingly independent of the United States and the Soviet Union when it comes to their own security. The leverage once derived from being the sole or principal supplier is much less than it was. The result is that the ability of the United States and the Soviet Union to regulate, much less dictate, regional order is bound to decline.

Where is all this likely to lead? We are moving toward a world in which power is increasingly diffused and in which the ability of great powers to regulate regional order as they once did is reduced. The cause and consequence of what might be termed international deregulation are clear. We are seeing the emergence of competing and increasingly powerful regional states around the world. The result is a world in which, in addition to the five declared nuclear powers, several countries possess an unacknowledged nuclear weapons capability and many more are working to develop one. The Central Intelligence Agency (CIA) estimates that more than 20 countries may be developing chemical weapons and at least 10 are working to produce biological weapons. The CIA also projects that by the end of this decade at least 15 developing countries will be producing their own ballistic missiles. And lest anyone forget, all this proliferation of unconventional weaponry is taking place in a context of improving conventional arsenals.

One more point should be added here. It is true that these developments are global, but it is more accurate to say that they are most visibly, and dangerously, taking place in the area that embraces the Middle East, the Persian Gulf, and South Asia. It is here that we find Libya, Egypt, Israel, Syria, Iraq, Iran, Pakistan, and India—each and every one of them states that possess impressive conventional military inventories as well as one or more unconventional military capabilities and the means to deliver them.

This evolution, or more accurately revolution, is dangerous. Weapons of mass destruction, if used, will result in widespread civilian deaths. Fortunately, with few exceptions, most previous conflicts in the Middle East were largely confined to battlefields. One awful exception—the Iran–Iraq War, which resulted in mass civilian as well as military fatalities—provides a picture of a possible future.

Nevertheless, weapons of mass destruction can be counterproductive even if they are not used. Their very existence can become a casus belli; so, too, can attempts to develop them. Preventive attacks on emerging but still immature capabilities can lead to war. In a crisis, the conviction that such weapons must be destroyed before they are used could prompt preemptive attacks that by definition would detract substantially from crisis stability.

Not everyone will subscribe to these possibilities. It has and will continue to be argued in some places that these weapons will automatically provide for deterrence—much as they have for the United States and the Soviet Union over the past half century. This assessment is, nevertheless, too sanguine to be taken at face value. It misreads the history of deterrence between the United States and the Soviet Union. This textbook deterrence has been threatened on more than one occasion. One lesson it offers is that the transitional period from a balance of conventional weapons to one of unconventional weapons brings with it special dangers. In addition, the United States and the Soviet Union were stable political systems, possessed military capabilities with important similarities, and enjoyed diplomatic relations, a history with virtually no direct conflict, and established, if limited, patterns of cooperation. Neither desired territory held by the other. By way of contrast, in much of the Middle East, the Persian Gulf, and South Asia, states are often headed by regimes of uncertain staying power, governments do not recognize one another, and countries make claims to one another's territory, possess fundamentally different military capabilities, and have a history of recurring war. No one should assume that deterrence can be re-created.

Policy and Security

What, then, can and should be done? Let me suggest an agenda for both local states directly involved and others with a stake in the stability of this critical part of the world.

The proliferation problem could be attacked directly. This means continued efforts designed to stem or slow the emergence of capabilities. It is neither accurate nor useful to say it is too late to try to do so. Proliferation is not some seamless web, but rather a set of developments that varies from country to country and according to particular technologies. Arrangements such as the nuclear nonproliferation treaty, the biological and toxin weapons convention, the Committee on Disarmament, the Missile Technology Control Regime, the Australia Group, bilateral and multilateral diplomatic efforts—all have an important and continuing role to play in discouraging the spread of nuclear, chemical, biological, and missile capabilities.

One related issue gaining salience is the complementary approach of regional weapons-free zones. Egypt, for example, has proposed a zone free of unconventional weapons in the Middle East, while Israel has proposed separate zones free of chemical weapons and nuclear weapons, respectively, for the area. Thus far, such ideas have gained little currency—a result of important differences over what weapons and countries to include and how to negotiate and verify any agreement. Nevertheless, such arrangements merit additional consideration, even if their ambitious scope argues against near-term prospects for success.

Also available are more indirect means of affecting the calculations of governments that are considering acquiring or developing one or another unconventional capability and the means to deliver it. The provision of security assistance, arms transfers, and, in special circumstances, firm security commitments provide alternative paths for countries to meet their legitimate security requirements without having to resort to producing, acquiring, or using unconventional weapons of their own. Depending upon circumstances, these same tools could be denied (or their denial threatened) as a disincentive for states considering acquisition, development, testing, and/or use of various unconventional capabilities.

Policies designed to prevent acquisition or development of unconventional capabilities will not, as we are seeing, necessarily succeed. When they do fail, the challenge to policymakers is not over. Rather, it is simply different. Managing proliferation is no less important or urgent a task than preventing it in the first place.

Management can embrace several dimensions. None is more basic than conflict resolution itself. In the Middle East, this argues for moving ahead on the sort of step-by-step, gradualist process championed by the United States. The policy promoted by the United States is designed to bring about a comprehensive political settlement based upon certain principles—Resolutions 242 and 338 of the United Nations Security Council (UNSC) and the guiding concept of territory for peace; security and recognition for Israel and all states in the region; and satisfaction of legitimate Palestinian political rights. As a first step, the United States continues to believe the best approach is both to bring together Israelis and Palestinians to negotiate the terms for elections and to initiate a negotiating process leading to interim and ultimately final status arrangements. At the same time, Israel and the Arab states are being encouraged to take political and economic steps that would increase mutual confidence and break down some of the barriers now separating them.

One beneficial result of the mellowing of the Cold War might be enhanced U.S.–Soviet willingness to work together to resolve regional conflicts. It is not an objective of the United States to exclude the Soviet Union from participation in diplomatic efforts designed to alleviate regional tensions. To the contrary, the United States recognizes that the Soviet Union retains a capacity to affect diplomatic prospects in the Middle East, the Persian Gulf, and South Asia. It recognizes, too, that these conflicts retain the potential to endanger U.S.–Soviet relations. The United States is prepared to accept Soviet involvement so long as it is constructive and the local states involved accept a Soviet role. The bigger problem may be, however, as the overall theme of this essay suggests, that even working together the United States and the Soviet Union will be unable in many instances to persuade regional states to overcome their differences.

A Future of Conflict?

In short, a good many conflicts will persist. Not every situation is ripe for solution; often one or another protagonist lacks either the will or the ability to agree to formulas or procedures that are available and reasonable. When this is the case, no amount of diplomacy is likely to prove successful in eliminating the root causes of the dispute. It may be possible, however, to settle parts of a dispute or, failing that, at least to agree to disagree in a manner that does not include conflict while at the same time possibly setting the stage for more ambitious diplomacy. Even limited political breakthroughs can have considerable utility if they are a prerequisite for regional arms-control arrangements.

Many key regional pairs—India and

Pakistan, Israel and its Arab neighbors, Iran and Iraq—would do well to adapt and adopt many of the arms-control and confidence-building measures developed by the United States and the Soviet Union. These can focus on conventional forces and might include such procedures as prior notifications of military exercises, arrangements for mutual observation of exercises, dedicated communications links between civilian and military authorities, and rules of the road to avoid incidents at sea, on the ground, or in the air. These measures can also involve unconventional forces and include understandings about basing locales, field- and flight-testing, and alerts. Where politics precluded formal undertakings, many of these arrangements could be informal and tacit.

A strong case also exists for creating a context in which political relationships can be stabilized. Regional organizations can work to resolve political differences. These same organizations can contribute to regional stability by promoting economic relations or cooperation on such international problems as narcotics, terrorism, and the environment. And there is a role for modest but still important undertakings in the realm of tourism and cultural and educational exchange. Peoples can sometimes show their governments the way.

The United States has an important role in all of this. Its arms-control efforts and accomplishments set a powerful example. It has already eliminated biological weapons, is committed to the elimination of chemical capabilities (and is taking practical steps in that direction), and is reducing its nuclear arsenal. The United States can also work to promote conflict resolution, be it with the Soviet Union when the two countries agree or with local states directly. It can continue to work with others to discourage proliferation through incentives, denial, and sanctions. And the possibility remains of selective sharing of defensive technologies to counter the effects of unconventional weapons if all else fails. None of this promises to solve the proliferation problem in the Middle East or elsewhere, but it does offer a realistic path to coping with its consequences. In a world of increasingly diffused power, this may be the most to which anyone can realistically aspire.

An earlier version of this paper was delivered to the Washington Institute for Near East Policy on April 30, 1990.

Old Quarrels and New Realities: Security in Southern Asia After the Cold War

Rodney W. Jones

THE SWEEPING CHANGES that have disrupted familiar cold war patterns and ended the East–West military confrontation over Europe have forced India and Pakistan, the two larger powers of southern Asia, to begin a reassessment of their interests and alignments. Since 1989, the Soviet military withdrawal from Afghanistan, the upsurge of nationalist-democratic revolutions in Eastern Europe, the collapse of the Warsaw Pact, and the ratification of German reunification by the great powers have fundamentally changed the security structure and political map of Europe. The shift from U.S.–Soviet strategic confrontation to increasing cooperation has shaken long-held assumptions about the structure of world politics. Most recently, the failed coup of August 1991 in Moscow caused the collapse of communism in the Soviet Union and forced a change in the very nature and extent of the Union.[1] These far-reaching developments acutely affect the prospects of India and Pakistan.

The Iraqi invasion of Kuwait in August 1990 and the coalition war against Iraq that abruptly freed Kuwait in early 1991 portend similarly significant developments. The effects on the economic situations of both India and Pakistan have been particularly traumatic. Unprecedented Soviet endorsement and Chinese acquiescence in the action against Iraq, authorized by the United Nations (UN) but led by the United States, contradicted all previous expectations of how the major powers would react given their often divergent interests in the oil-rich Persian Gulf region. The international coalition against Iraq, which involved Syrian, Egyptian, and Saudi Arabian as well as British and French expeditionary forces, with Iranian and implicit Israeli support, scrambled Middle Eastern alignments and opened new possibilities for diplomacy.

India and Pakistan were unable to respond coherently to this regional upheaval. Indian workers trapped in Kuwait were rescued with difficulty, and Delhi's economic relationships with Kuwait and Iraq were disrupted. Polarization inside Pakistan between supporters of Iraq and supporters of Saudi Arabia injured Islamabad's credibility with both Arab camps.

After the cease-fire, the UN-sponsored hunt for newly declared and concealed Iraqi production facilities and

---

Rodney W. Jones is a foreign affairs officer in the Bureau of Strategic and Nuclear Affairs, U.S. Arms Control and Disarmament Agency, Washington, D.C., and an adviser to the U.S. delegation in the Strategic Arms Reduction Talks (START).

109

stockpiles of weapons of mass destruction—apparently including the whole range of nuclear, chemical, germ-warfare, and missile capabilities—stimulated "new world order" hopes for other areas of proliferation such as North Korea and the Indian subcontinent. The stated willingness of hold-out nations such as France, South Africa, and, most recently, the People's Republic of China to join the Nuclear Non-Proliferation Treaty (NPT), and the new resolve of Brazil and Argentina to bring their nuclear programs under exclusively civilian control, indicated that the post–cold war constituency for nonproliferation was growing.

Dramatic as the external changes are, they have done nothing to reduce the rivalry between India and Pakistan. Those countries are no less adversaries today than before. If anything, the events of the last decade deepened their hostility. Each alleges it has been the victim of "low-intensity war" and "subversion" by the other. Both continue to be plagued by an array of political crises and internal security problems, some of explosive proportions, as in the case of the conflicts in Kashmir and Indian Punjab. Both are facing economic crises, aggravated in both India and Pakistan by the effects of the Iran–Iraq and Gulf wars, and in Pakistan also by the loss of foreign aid. Each is afflicted by government or regime instability, internal political violence, and secessionist movements.

Even so, there are signs of fresh thinking and of rational economic policy initiative in the governments of both South Asian countries. It is too early to judge whether these tentative signs mean southern Asia itself might cross a watershed comparable in regional terms to the recent geopolitical changes in European and East–West relations. But some evidence exists that a fundamental rethinking of economic policies has gotten under way and this could happen to security policies too.

This essay explores how the national leaders of India and Pakistan are responding to the rapid changes in East–West relations and to the consequences for their regional situations. What are the Indian and Pakistani assessments of the altered roles of the superpowers? Will India and Pakistan regard the decline of U.S.–Soviet confrontation as a net gain for their own security, or will they expect it to unleash even more violent trends in central and southern Asia? Can Delhi and Islamabad extract a financial or trade windfall from the emergence of market economies in Eastern Europe, or will they fall further behind in international trading competition? Will newly fashionable economic assistance to Eastern Europe or the USSR divert assistance away from poorer countries such as India and Pakistan? Will the post–cold war situation encourage India and Pakistan to resolve their bilateral conflicts or will it lock them in a spiral of increasingly desperate measures?

Superpowers in Transition

In Delhi and Islamabad, the most basic factor in reassessing foreign relations now is the change in world standing and relative influence of the two superpowers. The U.S. image of strength has increased, while the Soviet image of power has given way to one of weakness. Although Soviet strategic nuclear capability could obliterate any adversary, the Soviet Union's internal crises of authority, economic stagnation, and power sharing in center-republic relations have seriously weakened it. Moscow's bid for Western economic and technical assistance and for integration in international financial institutions will probably further limit Soviet power externally.

The formidable U.S. role in building a multilateral war coalition against Iraq established the perception that the United States alone now has the will and both the military and economic means to operate globally as a superpower. Realistically, U.S. strength on the global scene will not depend just on unilateral U.S. initiatives but also on both continued U.S. ability to mobilize domestic and broader Western support and on Soviet restraint. The perception of a major power's international influence is often much simpler abroad, however.

Thus, this major shift in the balance of international power between the United States and the Soviet Union must eventually have a deep impact on the diplomatic priorities of India and Pakistan. Even though Indian governing officials have been conscious of Soviet weaknesses in the past and thus never were prone to exaggerate Soviet power, the present decline of Soviet fortunes and degree of internal paralysis exceeds anything that even informed Indians would have expected.

From a Western standpoint, the shift in relative power between Washington and Moscow draws heavily on the triumph of democratic aspirations and self-determination in Eastern Europe, but also farther afield from the return home of Cuban forces and Soviet disengagement from former clients in eastern and southern Africa and in East Asia. It derives in part from the economic success of the advanced industrial countries of the West, including Japan, and the newly industrializing countries (NICs) of Southeast Asia. It reflects widening acceptance of the ideas that political and economic freedom go hand in hand and that command economies are prone to serious distortions and ultimate failure. Awareness of the comparative advantage of economies based on market principles and of integration in the international trading system is simultaneously breaking through the dogmas both of the Communist countries and the once-colonized Third World.

In South Asia, the effects of declining Soviet power and rising U.S. prestige have been painfully disorienting to the traditional foreign policy elites. In both India and Pakistan, foreign policy makers and bureaucrats had successfully inculcated a high degree of doctrinal commitment and continuity among their intellectual supporters in the universities and communications media. Thus, as a general rule in South Asia, the deepest disagreements among political parties and institutionalized centers of power have been over domestic issues that daily affect the struggle for power, not over foreign policy matters.

The current decline in superpower competition, however, drastically reduces a key source of developing country leverage—the option of playing one superpower off against the other. Because India and Pakistan have both exploited the cold war tension between the superpowers to achieve their own ends—usually in opposite directions—the new situation will probably induce each to adjust its posture significantly. Although Pakistan's loss of leverage on Washington is more obvious and by far more wrenching than India's loss of leverage on the Soviet Union, the new situation may be serious for India as well. What will future leverage on a decentralized "Union of Sovereign States" mean? Thus, contrary to what one might expect, many seasoned South Asian leaders will initially mourn rather than welcome the attenuation of bipolar East–West rivalry. A whole regional vocabulary of great power relations will no longer be meaningful and will have to be discarded.

More important for India and Pakistan's future than their loss of leverage on superpower patrons, however, will be the substantive content of their future relationships with all of the important external powers and their access to international financial institutions such as the World Bank, the International Monetary Fund (IMF), and the Asian Development Bank. After the Cold War and as regards the West, at least, the substance of such relationships will have more to do with how open India and Pakistan are to foreign trade and investment and how willing they are to privatize their inefficient public-sector industries and commerce.

India's Current Political Dilemmas

In July 1991, India formed a new Congress party government under P. V. Narasimha Rao, a seasoned but aging national leader, the first prime minister from the South. Rao was chosen as a compromise candidate to replace the former prime minister and Congress leader Rajiv Gandhi, who was assassinated in May 1991 during the first phase of the national elections. Despite the relative weakness of the new Rao government (with 226 Lok Sabha seats, less than half of the 507 total, its tenure rests on alliance with minor parties and on the exhaustion of all parties from the huge cost of competing in nationwide elections), it moved boldly but desperately in the economic sphere to propose restructuring India's trade, industrial licensing, and tax regulations, and to cut certain central budget items severely.

This Indian move responds to awareness that market economics will dominate the post–cold war environment. But its timing and character must be understood also in its domestic political context. Rao assumed charge at a time of cascading political and economic crisis in India. The death of Rajiv Gandhi appeared to have ended the three-generation dynastic line of Indian prime ministers from the Nehru family. No political leader of comparable stature and India-wide recognition remained. The Rao government itself was the beneficiary of the sympathy vote after the assassination, and Congress actually improved its share of the vote in the second phase of the election, still winning less than a bare majority of seats in Parliament.

During the previous three years, India had solved only one pressing problem—the 1990 extrication of its military from Sri Lanka, where Indian armed forces had been deployed in 1987, ostensibly as a "peace-keeping force" (IPKF). But the IPKF had failed to end the civil war and had suffered serious casualties at the hands of Tamil guerrillas.[2] India experienced the pain of overseas involvement in a guerrilla war, and public pressure rose for withdrawal. The situation was resolved, but the net result was negative.

Another abiding set of problems stems from extremist demands for autonomy or independence, which have often precipitated internal warfare. Two of these "internal security" situations in India could trigger wars with Pakistan. Sikh extremism in India's state of Punjab, dating from about 1980, actually increased in virulence in the few weeks leading up to the May 1991 national polls—causing more than 200 deaths, the assassination of eight local candidates, and the cancellation, unwisely, of elections in that state.[3]

In Kashmir, Muslim militant organizations rose against the politicians and civil authorities in January 1990 and drove them from Srinagar and other towns. Indian redeployments of regular and special security forces to restore law and order were ineffective, and by late that year, privately organized arms and volunteers reportedly had begun to flow from Pakistan to support the insurgents. Less pressing but potentially serious insurgencies continued in parts of Assam and the tribal states of eastern India.

Another set of problems was the spread of Hindu–Muslim communal conflict and its impact on the relative electoral strength of India's main political parties. The specific issue was rival religious claims to a sacred site in Ayodhya, in Uttar Pradesh. Today Ayodhya contains the Babri Masjid (mosque) attributed to Babur, who invaded from central Asia and founded the Mughal dynasty in the early sixteenth century. Ayodhya is also believed to be the location of the legendary capital of the kingdom of Ram, a god in the Hindu pantheon. The activist Hindu temple movement (Ram Janmabhoomi Mandir) claims that the site on which the mosque was built was Ram's birthplace and that the mosque sits on the foundations of an ancient temple attributed to Ram, creating an emotionally charged political issue.

The dispute, still unresolved, has been the source of recurrent rioting and bloodshed, reportedly causing some 2,000 deaths over the course of a year.[4] It was one factor in the downfall of Indian Prime Minister V. P. Singh's Janata Dal coalition government. His electoral cooperation with the Hindu revivalist Bharatiya Janata party (BJP) narrowly defeated the Congress party led by Rajiv Gandhi in the 1989 elections. But Singh's unwillingness to endorse the Hindu claim at Ayodhya and his surprise announcement in August of support for a new "backward castes" job reservation policy led the pivotal 85-member BJP group in Parliament to distance itself, allowing Congress-inspired factional maneuvering to topple the Janata Dal government on November 7, 1990.

The national spread of this emotional dispute was a key rallying point for the BJP in the 1991 elections and partly accounted for its substantial gains: the BJP share of parliamentary seats rose from 85 in 1989 to 119 in 1991 and its voting strength doubled nationwide, virtually introducing a two-party national system.[5] In addition, the BJP not only won control of a major state legislature for the first time but also took over the pivotal state government of Uttar Pradesh— the keystone of the Hindi-speaking heartland of Indian politics as well as the former base of the Nehru family.

The rise of the BJP to new nationwide prominence has major foreign and security policy implications for India. Although its ideology has been moderated somewhat to broaden its appeal, the BJP articulates a sectarian vision of Hindu majority rule and seems implicitly to clash with the secularism of the Indian Constitution. Traditionally a high-caste, urban middle class party of professionals and civil servants, the BJP leans toward private business enterprise and is staunchly anti-Communist. At the same time, it is allegedly anti-Muslim and the most hawkish of India's major parties against Pakistan. India's recent difficulties in Kashmir have probably increased support for the BJP. Its most prominent leaders spoke out openly during the campaign in favor also of an Indian program to develop nuclear weapons.

India's New Economic Policy

On July 24, 1991, Dr. Manmohan Singh, the new finance minister in Narasimha Rao's cabinet and a respected planner-economist, announced a series of economic and budget policy measures that were quite radical by Indian standards. The overall thrust of these new measures seemed to be intended to liberalize India's trade and tariff regulations, stimulate exports, move to a deficit- and debt-reduction path, and restore India's creditworthiness.[6]

The new measures were preceded in early July by a 20 percent devaluation of the rupee against the U.S. dollar and the pound sterling. They featured some relaxation of capital and import licensing controls (the "license Raj") that have impeded foreign investment and domestic industrial expansion in India and that, allegedly, have allowed enormous graft to spread among some administrators in positions to hold up or facilitate the approval of licenses. Foreign firms can, under the new regulations, own up to 51 percent of the equity in a joint venture in India. The new policy measures lift the antimonopoly ceilings on new investment that inhibit large domestic firms from engaging in new projects, introduce new incentives for non-resident Indians (NRIs) to repatriate hard currency earnings to India, and offer other penalty-forgiving schemes intended to attract "black money" (unreported income) into the regular economy. To reduce the central government's widening expenditure-revenue deficit, certain corporate taxes were increased and fertilizer subsidies were reduced.[7] Shortly after, the defense budget figures reportedly showed real defense expenditures would be curtailed.[8]

It would be gratifying to say these policies sprang only from enlightened Indian decision making. In fact, however, India is now virtually compelled to change course by its internal economic crisis, rising external and internal indebtedness, mounting inflation, and exhaustion of foreign currency reserves. These conditions got suddenly worse in the winter of 1990–1991 due to the war over Kuwait, which raised India's cost of imported petroleum and related products considerably while cutting foreign remittances. India's hard economic decisions apparently come at this point primarily because of the confluence of new Indian elections and IMF conditions for multibillion dollar loans. The loans were necessary to rebuild Indian hard currency reserves and protect the government's commercial creditworthiness.[9]

The post–cold war milieu makes it easier both for the IMF and the World Bank to adopt tough "conditionality" policies and for India to accept them. International lending policies that require recipients to accept new financial discipline and economic policy adjustments do not single out southern Asia; they are based on a worldwide approach. The credibility of this approach has been bolstered by the acceptance in the USSR as well as Eastern Europe of the necessity of restructuring command economies.

The need for a changed course in India, if hundreds of millions of its citizens are to have a chance for more than bare subsistence, has long been recognized abroad. The disparity between India and the more successful developing countries in real gross national product (GNP) per capita has widened dramatically. India's world ranking on economic measures has dropped from that of a giant to more ordinary proportions, as illustrated by a recent report in the *Economist:*

> In 1950 India accounted for 2% of world exports and 6% of third-world exports; by 1980 the respective figures were 0.4% and 1.4%. In 1955, just before India began its industry-based growth strategy, it was the world's tenth biggest industrial power; less than 20 years later it ranked 20th. The world's other poor behemoth, China, could claim average annual growth in real GNP per person of 5.2% during the years 1965–87. India's score over the same period was 1.8%.[10]

Factors that contributed to this decline were India's long adherence to Fabian socialist doctrines, disproportionate public-sector investments, and, not least, the protectionist leanings and oligopolistic practices of India's oldest and largest private business houses. The panoply of controls and vested interests that resulted perpetuated a structure that could not easily be changed, except under threat of its collapse. Today, the internal and external credit underpinnings of these arrangements have indeed come close to collapse.[11]

The economic liberalization theme had emerged earlier in the 1980s. It began with less conviction under Indira Gandhi in 1980–1982, Rajiv Gandhi gave it new panache in 1985, and it was advanced in a low-key fashion by V. P. Singh in 1988–1989. These moves coincided with dawning Indian awareness that China's surrender of the myth of autarky, its opening to international trade, and its internal economic liberalization, however uneven, paid dividends in rapid economic growth after 1979. Indeed, China's break with old economic thinking may have been, for Delhi, the first clue that the Cold War would wane. China's similarity to India in huge population and level of industrialization seemed more relevant than the extraordinary economic takeoff of the NICs of Southeast and East Asia. But now the lessons of export-led growth in South Korea, Singapore, Hong Kong, and Thailand are also sinking in.

It remains to be seen whether the Rao government will have the staying power to implement these measures and to extend liberalization into other areas that need it, such as the ratio of public- to private-sector investment, the internal financial system, labor policy, and public subsidies.[12] Rajiv Gandhi's efforts in the mid-1980s were stymied by reactions within the Congress Party and the existing administrative system. But knowledge that a dynamic economy is crucial not only for improved standards of living but also for influence and status in the post–cold war environment could prove a basic incentive for Indian governments to stay on the new course. In addition, the affinity of the BJP for a free enterprise economy will, if that party continues to thrive, press in the same direction.

Pakistan's Predicaments

For Pakistan, the transition to the 1990s will be arduous. Although the Soviet military withdrawal from Afghanistan in February 1989 was a landmark achievement—a tribute in large part both to Pakistan's resolve and to its skillful diplomatic efforts—the remaining problems are formidable. The effect of the Afghan trauma on Pakistan will not be relieved until normalcy is restored in Afghanistan and the accumulated four million Afghan refugees in Pakistan have the option to return to their homeland.[13] This prospect currently seems remote.

The highly fragmented *mujahidin* (Afghan resistance) movement has been unable to unite either militarily to overthrow the Najibullah regime in Kabul or politically to agree on what a legitimate government should be. Thus, Pakistan's future domestic tranquillity remains hostage in special ways to the continuation of the warfare in Afghanistan. As spillover within Pakistan, drug running, arms smuggling, and the predatory attacks of armed gangs in the big cities and, in Sind, along the north-south road axis of communications, are persisting manifestations of the intra-Afghanistan conflict.

Pakistan has had to come to terms, abruptly, with a measure of new isolation in its international relations. In part, this is an obvious consequence of the success in expelling the Soviet military from Afghanistan. What mattered most to the rest of the world was that expulsion of Soviet forces. Thereafter, political and military interest in Pakistan as the frontline state dropped sharply. The installation of Benazir Bhutto, a Western-educated and progressive young woman with personal flair, as prime minister briefly attracted Western attention, but this interest too was dissipated with removal of her government on August 6, 1990.

Benazir Bhutto's removal came just days after Saddam Hussein invaded Kuwait. The interim government of Pakistan immediately made a commitment to the international coalition—or more precisely, to Saudi Arabia—of about 5,000 soldiers to assist in internal security and to help guard the holy places of pilgrimage. But domestic controversy inside Pakistan over the issue—Saddam's resistance to the rest of the world had a powerful emotional appeal in Pakistani cities—inhibited deeper involvement.[14] The mobilization of an international response to Iraq's aggression raised international concerns about nuclear and chemical weapons dangers to a new pinnacle.

Then the United States abruptly cut off almost all aid to Pakistan. The occasion was the annual presidential certification to Congress under the Pressler amendment, due in October 1990. President George Bush was unable in this case to certify that Pakistan did not "possess" a nuclear explosive device. An automatic aid suspension shut off all U.S. assistance not already in the pipeline. The cutoff preceded the election and installation of the new Pakistani government of Prime Minister Nawaz Sharif and thus deprived Sharif of the opportunity to try to head off the rupture.

As a result, predictably bitter "anti-Americanism" is percolating through Pakistan. It joins the ordinary Pakistani's sense of outrage over supposed Western antagonism to Islam with anger at alleged previous U.S. betrayals of security commitments to Pakistan. These feelings were given a freer reign by the regime of Zulfikar Ali Bhutto after Pakistan's dismemberment by India in 1971. They increased in the 1977–1979 period in reaction to repeated U.S. denials of arms assistance to Pakistan on nuclear nonproliferation grounds and peaked following the rupture of U.S. relations with Iran after its Islamic revolution in early 1979. The catalysts today are the perceived Western humiliation of Muslim Iraq, plummeting U.S. concern for an acceptable settlement in Afghanistan, and the U.S. cutoff of aid, including replacements and spare parts that Pakistan needs to sustain training and defense preparedness against the threat it perceives from India.

Meanwhile, the Kashmir problem rose to the top of the local security agenda again in 1989–1990 and has remained there since. The Kashmir dispute is so acute that it evokes the specter of nuclear war in the subcontinent—a risk that seemed to become technically realistic in the late 1980s. Recent reports suggest that Pakistan has already adopted a policy of limited nuclear deterrence against Indian attack, a posture first hinted at by President Zia ul-Haq, but associated explicitly with outgoing Chief of Army Staff Mirza Aslam Beg.[15] In an about-face from her previous denials that Pakistan had a nuclear weapons capability, former Prime Minister Benazir Bhutto recently told reporters that Pakistan knows how to build nuclear weapons: "Pakistan has sufficient nuclear information that in the event of a [nuclear] threat it could rapidly produce a deterrent. . . . The Americans always knew what stage we were at, the Indians knew roughly where we stood." Although the political party motivation for this statement is transparent, the admission is the first from a high-level Pakistan government leader, serving or former, and thus cannot be brushed aside completely as no change in the equation. If she returns to power, she will find it hard to retreat from this assertion.[16]

Indian defense analysts have long worried that once Pakistan acquired nuclear weapons, it would endeavor to detach Kashmir by using its nuclear threat to deter India's superior conventional military power.[17]

The government of Prime Minister Nawaz Sharif, installed in November 1990, must now deal with these issues. Nawaz Sharif, a youthful businessman from Lahore, presides over a National Assembly coalition of moderate Muslim League and conservative Islamic elements known as the Islami Jamhoori Ittehad (Islamic Democratic Alliance). The components of this IJI coalition are strongest in Punjab and the northwestern provinces. The IJI draws heavily on urban middle class business, commercial, and professional groups—constituencies that have rapidly expanded in size for over two decades and that the Zia regime specifically encouraged. The IJI components are much weaker in rural Sind, the home base of the Bhuttos and other Sindhi landlord families, where chronic political violence has seriously disturbed industrial productivity, commerce, communications, and agriculture since 1983.[18]

Soon after he took office in November 1990, Nawaz Sharif launched a national economic liberalization policy. Features of this policy were even more dramatic than India's the following year. For example, domestic controls over the convertibility of the rupee to the dollar were lifted, along with a relaxation of import controls. Pakistanis were free for the first time in memory to purchase dollars for rupees and take them outside the country without restriction. This devalued the rupee on the open market but thereby removed the largest incentive for black market currency exchange transactions. The devaluation of the rupee should boost Pakistani export competitiveness, although at the cost of higher domestic inflation. In addition, if restrictions on investment return are removed, and provided the violence in Karachi and Sind can be stopped, these measures could attract overseas Pakistani capital back into the country.

Sharif's new economic policy promised to privatize public-sector firms, beginning with nationalized banks. Much of the nationalized sector in Pakistan is the result of the quasi-socialist policies of the first Bhutto regime in the early 1970s. In contrast to India, there is little ideological support in Pakistan for nationalized enterprises as such. Zulfikar Ali Bhutto, however, instituted the practice of using the nationalized sector as a huge job patronage system for retiring military and civil service officers, elements of unionized labor, and People's party loyalists. This pattern was maintained by the conservative Zia regime, but with a different set of party loyalists. Thus, intense resistance to dismantling and privatizing the production units can be expected. Private investors, including former owners, may not easily be persuaded to infuse new capital into these organizations.[19]

Implementation aside, the message these policies send is that Pakistan expects to nurture and reward private investment, at least as long as the present government prevails. If Pakistan had to devise a strategy to compensate for the loss of external assistance from the United States and other donors, it is hard to imagine an approach that could produce new investment from abroad more rapidly than by securing the overseas availability of returns on that investment through currency convertibility. Retrospectively, we may find that Iranian, Japanese, and South Korean private investments in Pakistan's energy and manufacturing sectors took off in the 1990s.[20]

Earlier we noted that Pakistan probably now faces, as a result of the Soviet exodus from Afghanistan and the U.S. foreign aid cutoff related to nuclear proliferation, a greater degree of near-term isolation in international affairs. But another, post–cold war factor, the loosening of Soviet control over central Asia, holds potentially significant, longer-term, and still undefined possibilities for Pakistan.

Even before the Soviet coup attempt of August 19, the central Asian, basically Muslim republics of Kazakhstan, Uzbekistan, Kirghizia, Tadzhikistan, and Turkmenistan had signed an agreement, based on the decentralization in the draft Union treaty, to create among themselves a unified regional economic community or Common Market. Such an entity today would hold some 50 million people—about half Pakistan's current population, but in a much larger territory. The failure of the Soviet coup and subsequent moves toward an even looser confederation of republics probably makes such an association even more likely.

This development could present distinctive new opportunities for Pakistan. First, the successor state to the Soviet Union, the emerging Union of Sovereign States, will be weakened and probably will not be as threatening as it previously was, either as a Communist or as an expansionist military power. Thus, it could become a more natural partner for Pakistan, politically as well as geographically.

Second, the departure of the Baltics and possible departure of other western republics would increase the relative importance of the central Asian republics and could shift the center of interest of the new Union toward Asia. In this context, the Muslim affinities of the central Asian republics would increase incentives for political and economic relations with the other Islamic countries, including Pakistan. With its capacity to export educated professionals, technicians, and business entrepreneurs, Pakistan may be able to position itself to play a role in the development of the central Asian republics. It could even, in this manner, potentially contribute to the stability of the successor to the Soviet Union.

Such an evolution in Pakistan's external relationships could also increase the perceived importance of Pakistan in the Middle East and could be beneficial to China, reinforcing Pakistan's existing western and eastern regional relationships. Such relationships could compensate Pakistan, eventually, for a lessening of its ties with the West.

The future of central Asia, however, contains great uncertainty and may produce new dangers for Pakistan—and for India—that would require unprecedented changes in their foreign policies. The descent of Yugoslavia into civil war—primarily between Serbs and Croats, but with several other ethnolinguistic conflicts that could erupt—and the violent conflict between Armenia and Azerbaijan over the Armenian enclave of Nagorno-Karabakh, could be a portent of internal conflicts in and between former Soviet republics closer to southern Asia. Such conflicts between distinctive central Asian nationalities—notwithstanding common religious background—could be very awkward for Pakistan in seeking closer relations in that region, even as Pakistan has found it difficult, historically, to deal with Afghanistan.

Defense Concerns and the Arms Buildup

Despite the added threat posed by the Soviet military presence in Afghanistan through most of the last decade, military crises recurred between India and Pakistan. The most serious was probably the emergency triggered by India's huge forward deployments in the Brass Tacks military exercise in the winter of 1986–1987 and the high-altitude skirmishing along the undemarcated "line of control" on the Siachen Glacier in Kashmir. Since these crises have continued into the 1990s, there is no evidence yet that the post–cold war environment itself will be a source of relief.

The festering sore of Sikh terrorist violence in Punjab, India's defense planners believe, opens gaps in India's security for Pakistani subversion or open military invasion. Pakistan's defense authorities worry about the reverse—Indian interference in politically volatile Sind. Armored columns crossing the desert from Rajasthan could, with surprise, quickly sever Sind from the country to the north. Sind, Punjab, and Kashmir form a politically explosive chain of past battlefields along the border between the two countries.

India and Pakistan used the 1980s for a major military modernization and buildup of new forces, certain features of which are highlighted in graphs 1, 2, and 3. Although this buildup in the subcontinent was much less massive than that in the Middle East, especially in proportion to the size of the countries involved, it nonetheless created the prospect of a much larger and more lethal Indo-Pakistani air and ground war. The South Asian buildup included the acquisition of more capable, longer-range arms by both sides, increased mechanization of the infantry, and the expansion of indigenous arms production and maintenance capabilities. Far more dependent than India on outside resupply for war material and spare parts, Pakistan put new emphasis during the 1980s on making itself self-sufficient in certain fields of defense production. Through its relationship with China, for instance, it obtained fighter aircraft maintenance and tank-engine rebuild facilities.

At the same time, Indian military forces became capable of rapid air and sea deployment of ground units across neighboring waters for the first time, giving India a limited military power projection capability beyond the territorial confines of the subcontinent.

Moreover, as the graphs on air, naval, and armored combat equipment indicate, although the decade's growth in aggregate numbers of major battle systems was impressive enough (graph 2 shows roughly a doubling of heavy armor and artillery, and graph 1 indicates a one-third increase in combat aircraft), the real story is the increased proportion by 1990 of high-performance or advanced technology systems in each profile, especially India's. It is important that both countries first deployed "nuclear-capable," high-performance, fighter-bomber aircraft in substantial numbers during these years. In India's case, such aircraft now make up roughly half of the total combat air inventory.[21]

Not depicted in graphs but symbolically even more important in demonstrating nuclear delivery capability were India and Pakistan's ballistic missile military research and development activities. India flight-tested the Prithvi short-range missile in March 1988 and demonstrated the Agni intermediate-range, nuclear-capable ballistic missile prototype in May 1989. Pakistan claimed to have tested short-range Hatf ballistic missiles in 1989 and reportedly obtained mobile ballistic missile launchers, presumably from China.[22]

Firepower and ground force mobility stand out as features of the military modernization on both sides during the decade. By 1990, both air forces (see graph 1) had acquired tactical aircraft with long ranges (even without extra fuel tanks or aerial refueling) and substantial ground attack capability (e.g., India's 80 Jaguars and 80 MiG–27s); both had deployed state-of-the-art fighter/interceptor aircraft (the U.S. F–16 in Pakistan, and the French Mirage–2000 and Soviet MiG–29 in India); and both sides have acquired a repertoire of modern air-to-air missiles and supporting avionics.

In the balance between regular combat air forces, India increased its margin of superiority over Pakistan notably, from a ratio of 2:1 in 1979 (then all "vintage aircraft" on both sides), to better than 3:1 in 1991, specifically in the categories of "high-performance" and "nuclear-capable" aircraft (i.e., modern fighter-bombers and interceptors).[23]

Not shown in the graphs but relevant to military projection and support of ground forces is the buildup of air transport fleets, an area of major achievement for India. Indian military fixed-wing air transport capacity (nearly 200 transport aircraft) exceeds Pakistan's by a multiple of more than 10. It provides the capability to resupply and reinforce Indian units in the valley of Kashmir, outposts or staging areas along the Himalayas, and in Assam.

Both countries investigated airborne warning and control systems (AWACS) in the 1980s. At the height of Soviet intrusions during the Afghanistan conflict in 1986–1987, Pakistan urged the United States to sell or lease to it aircraft with long-range radars that could detect incoming Soviet bombers in time to alert its interceptors. No deal was concluded. India looked at British and Soviet airborne early warning (AEW) systems, but finally reverted to its own research and development (R&D) program for integrating radar and data-processing technologies in transport aircraft. India has long had a high-altitude photo-reconnaissance capability in the MiG–25 that allows it to monitor military infrastructure and force concentrations in Pakistan.

In ground forces (graph 2), mobility and increased firepower were incorporated by 1990 in increased numbers of deployed heavy tanks (e.g., 700 Soviet T–72s with 120 mm guns in India), self-propelled heavy artillery, mechanized infantry fighting vehicles,

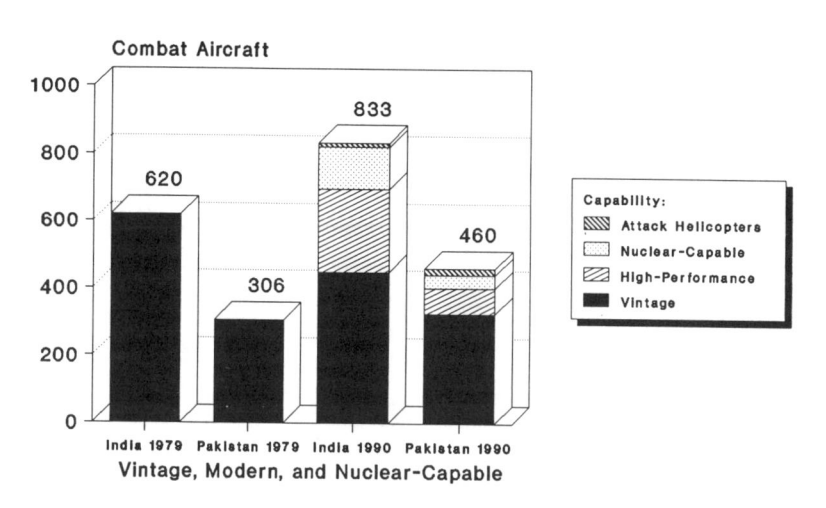

Graph 1
Combat Aircraft Capabilities: India and Pakistan, 1979–1990

Combat Aircraft

- India 1979: 620
- Pakistan 1979: 306
- India 1990: 833
- Pakistan 1990: 460

Capability:
- Attack Helicopters
- Nuclear-Capable
- High-Performance
- Vintage

Vintage, Modern, and Nuclear-Capable

Source: IISS, *The Military Balance 1979–1980* and *1990–1991* (London: Brassey's for IISS, 1979 and 1990).

armored personnel carriers, antitank guided weapons, and transport helicopters. India has an embryonic helicopter gunship assault force based on the Soviet Mi–25, a significant asset for support of maneuvering armored formations on the ground and for counterattack against enemy armored penetration on the flanks. Pakistan recently acquired a fleet of Cobra AH–1 antitank helicopter gunships.[24]

Since 1987, military exercises on both sides have emphasized the coordination of multidivision armored and infantry maneuvers, new field radio communications, and improved interservice communications to integrate tactical air support by the regular air forces.

In the naval sphere (graph 3), the most important trends in the last decade were in the acquisition of submarines; terminally guided, antiship missiles (e.g., Exocet, Sea Eagle, and Harpoon); and, in India's case, two aircraft carriers, now equipped with Harrier attack aircraft for fleet defense and coastal attack and with helicopters equipped for antisubmarine warfare. India also acquired five long-range marine reconnaissance (Tu–142M Bear F) aircraft from the Soviet Union some years ago; these provide distant early warning for its larger naval vessels and can alert and vector its recently formed maritime squadron of Jaguars to naval or coastal targets. Pakistan's relative weakness in naval forces was more apparent at the end of the decade.

India is attempting to create independently operating naval fleets for control of the approaches to its western and eastern coasts and to demonstrate effective sovereignty over remote island groups, the Laccadive Islands 250 miles to the west and the Andaman and Nicobar islands over 600 miles to the east. As an adjunct to the

Graph 2
Armor and Artillery: India and Pakistan, 1979–1990

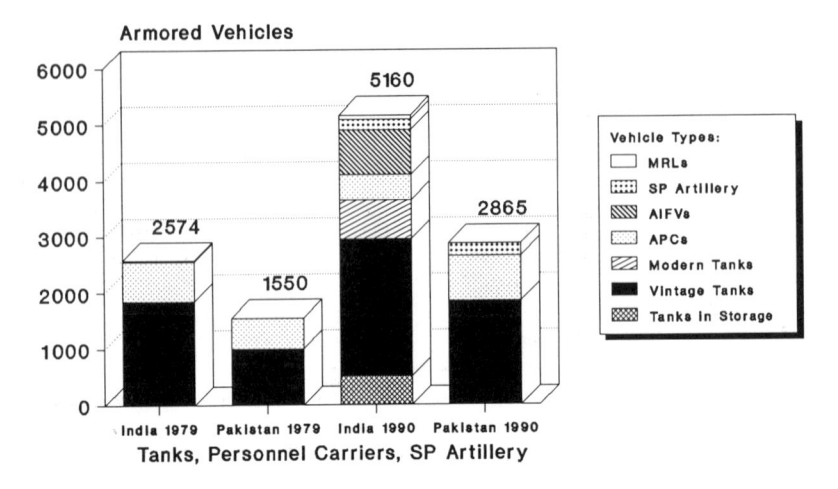

Armored Vehicles

Vehicle Types:
- MRLs
- SP Artillery
- AIFVs
- APCs
- Modern Tanks
- Vintage Tanks
- Tanks In Storage

India 1979: 2574; Pakistan 1979: 1550; India 1990: 5160; Pakistan 1990: 2865

Tanks, Personnel Carriers, SP Artillery

Source: IISS, *Military Balance*.
MRL—multiple rocket launcher
SP—self-propelled

navy, India has also recently formed two 1,000-man units of marines, suggesting that coastal assault missions beyond India's borders are envisaged. Finally, India's expensive lease arrangement with the Soviet Union to train Indian sailors in operating one or two nuclear-powered, guided-missile submarines symbolizes strategic ambitions.[25]

Past Indo-Pakistani wars have been brief, with occasionally intense battles in specific battlefield salients. Except for India's sweep into East Pakistan in 1971, war operations scarred relatively small populated areas. The more sophisticated weaponry absorbed in the 1980s implies that future conventional warfare between India and Pakistan is likely to be more intense. Technically, each now has greater incentive than before to attempt preemptive operations in the early stages of hostilities.[26]

A conflict between them now is more likely to entail high rates of consumption of ammunition and other expendables, rapid depletion of major equipment, and possibly far greater military and civilian casualties than heretofore, even without escalation to nuclear war. And conflict between them could now apparently escalate to the nuclear level.[27]

A New Look in Indian Defense Policy?

At the turn of the decade, there have been mixed signals on defense in key areas. On the one hand, India's announcement in August of a "real" (dollar-denominated) drop in the defense budget might imply that the buildup of the 1980s will not be sustained and could level off or decline.[28] Also on a hopeful note, Pakistan Prime Minister

Security in Southern Asia

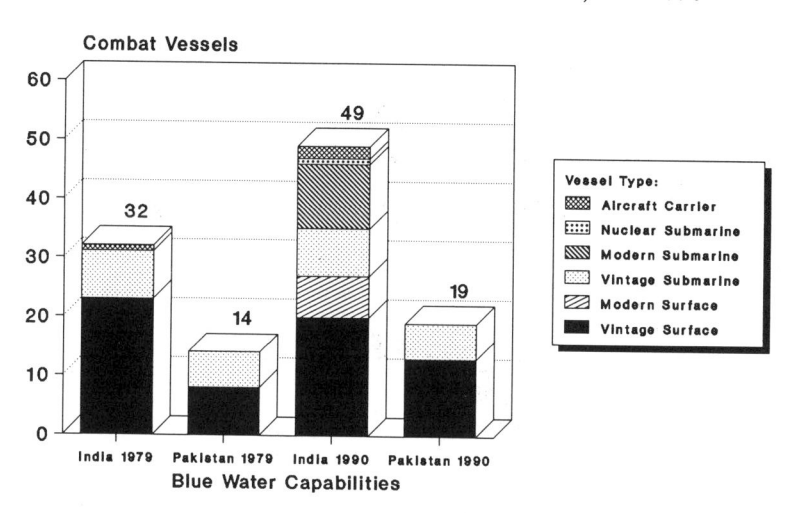

Graph 3
Naval Combat Vessels: India and Pakistan, 1979–1990

Combat Vessels

Vessel Type:
- Aircraft Carrier
- Nuclear Submarine
- Modern Submarine
- Vintage Submarine
- Modern Surface
- Vintage Surface

India 1979: 32   Pakistan 1979: 14   India 1990: 49   Pakistan 1990: 19

Blue Water Capabilities

Source: IISS, *Military Balance.*

Nawaz Sharif proposed on June 6 a new nonproliferation initiative in which the major powers could assist India and Pakistan to reach an agreement precluding nuclear weapons. On the other hand, India closed the last decade with its first ballistic missile demonstrations and lease of a Soviet nuclear-powered, guided-missile attack submarine. Moreover, during the last two years a concrete and more operationally specific discussion of an Indian nuclear weapons program has emerged.

At first glance, continued Indian programs for the development of nuclear-powered submarines and ballistic missiles, not to speak of a production and deployment program for nuclear weapons, are hard to square with a drop in real defense expenditures. Presumably, the announced defense cutback adds credibility to India's negotiations with the IMF. It may also be meant to signal to the West that India's reading of the post–cold war environment, and specifically of the U.S. suspension of military assistance to Pakistan, permits Delhi politically to scale back rearmament. It may indicate, secondarily, that India's needs for major conventional equipment (e.g., aircraft and tanks) are satisfied, at least for the near term. But is the defense cutback more apparent than real?

The answer may lie in information about the Indo–Soviet (rupee–ruble) relationship and the location of defense line items in the non-defense budget, neither of which are published. The reported defense cutback preserves a high level of rupee expenditures, essentially constant with what has been published for the year before. Moreover, the 28 percent reported drop is in the dollar-denominated value, which corresponds to rupee devaluations over the preceding year. Because the buying power of the rupee for servicemen's salaries and non-imported goods and services has not dropped in the same manner, the actual cutback is probably more equivalent to the level of inflation, currently about 10 percent.

Published defense figures tell only a part of the story. Some years ago India excluded pension figures, defense road development, certain air transport, and other significant defense-related items from the defense portion of the central budget. Defense-related aspects of space, electronics, and nuclear programs—the ballistic missile R&D projects, for example—have long been excluded by bureaucratic definition from published defense categories. All that aside, the cancellation and reprogramming of funds from a high-cost but unsuccessful indigenous defense production program, for example, the program to produce a main battle tank, could offset the drop.

The Nuclear Dimension

A nuclear missile procurement and deployment program would exceed the incremental R&D costs and thus could not so easily be hidden. Among the new reasons for concern, however, is that former Indian Chief of Army Staff Lieutenant General K. Sundarji, the most colorful and dynamic military figure to have occupied that position, now openly advocates from his retirement that India deploy nuclear weapons.[29] His scheme might be satisfied by a relatively small number of mobile launchers and long-range ballistic missiles equipped with nuclear-fission (not H-bomb) warheads capable of reaching Chinese urban areas.[30] He claims that a finite deterrent, second-strike posture will result in a stable relationship with China and presumably Pakistan. Sundarji apparently is the first senior Indian military figure to discuss Indo–Pakistani nuclear warfare scenarios openly and frequently.

General Mirza Aslam Beg, who recently retired as Pakistani chief of army staff, also drew attention to Pakistan's missiles and implicitly to its nuclear capability while he was still in office. Nonetheless, Pakistan's official line has been strikingly different. Beginning before the Soviet invasion of Afghanistan and throughout his tenure, Zia ul-Haq launched a series of proposals on nuclear nonproliferation, essentially agreeing in principle and in advance to any kind of nuclear weapon ban, or nonproliferation constraints, that India was prepared to accept, whether bilateral, regional, or international.[31] Nawaz Sharif's proposal on June 6, 1991, reiterated Pakistan's continued backing for all of the previous proposals and added a new one to the effect that the United States, the Soviet Union, and China should consult together with India and Pakistan to arrive at a solution that would keep the region free of nuclear weapons.[32]

Regrettably, this proposal was immediately rejected by the lame duck government of India's Chandra Shekhar, preventing further bilateral discussion at that time. A delegation of senior Pakistanis visiting the United States, partly to explain the Nawaz Sharif initiative, may have stimulated an interesting shift in U.S. congressional sentiment. For various reasons, the nonproliferation sanctions in U.S. foreign assistance legislation tend to single Pakistan out and bypass India. A vote with a twist on the Pressler amendment in the U.S. House of Representatives, however, resolved that aid should be provided to India only if the president can certify that India is not developing "additional" nuclear explosive devices.

Because Pakistan has been a major U.S. aid recipient but India receives very little bilateral U.S. aid, this House action was more symbolic than a substantial assertion of evenhandedness. Nevertheless, it signaled that the U.S. congressional mood had stiffened on antiproliferation measures after the Gulf War toward India as well as Pakistan. Moreover, it implied that there is some U.S. understanding that a solution of Pakistani nuclear proliferation is unlikely to be attainable in separation from a solution of Indian nuclear proliferation. A key question now therefore is whether the Rao government will take a fresh look at Nawaz Sharif's June 6 "five-nation" construct and respond in a positive and concrete way.

Looking Ahead

The passing of the Cold War prompts a natural curiosity about southern Asia's future, given the past impact of East–West competition on relations with and within the region. The Cold War's demise is the most dramatic—although it is only one—of a number of international factors driving Delhi and Islamabad toward a reorientation of their foreign, domestic, and security policies. The more immediately compelling post–cold war factors for South Asia are the crumbling of Soviet political and military power, the muting of the East–West ideological clash and bipolar orientation in international affairs, and the reinvigoration of international action against the proliferation of weapons of mass destruction triggered by the Gulf War. Less compelling in the short term, but no less relevant to the future security of southern Asia, are the strong international movement toward market economics, the increasingly potent demands for political participation and self-determination, the emergence of international cooperation as a prerequisite for economic rejuvenation in most economies—developed, developing, and post-Communist alike—and the success of arms-control and confidence-building negotiations in Europe that have strengthened the possibilities for new forms of collective security.

How are these developments affecting southern Asia, how are India and Pakistan responding, and what can the rest of the international community now do to help solve the problems of that region? Can the new realities assist with remedies for their old quarrels, or will they accentuate them?

For India, the weakening of the Soviet Union and calming of the U.S.–Soviet rivalry pose considerable new uncertainty. There are, first, domestic implications for India that include the object lesson of subnational entities successfully asserting independence and causing the disintegration of a federal union. This is not a new problem for India and one that it handled successfully in the past. But the fate of the Soviet Union may remove the taboo from regional or ethnic claims to independence in other heterogeneous states.

Second, India cannot count bilaterally on the Soviet successor state to offer the former level of support in security affairs. Moscow is cutting its foreign burdens drastically. Although the Indo–Soviet Friendship Treaty of 1971 was just renewed in August 1991, the restoration last year of friendly Soviet relations with China after over two decades of serious Sino–Soviet tension must devalue, for India, the prospect of Soviet aid to India against a renewed Chinese threat. India can no longer assume that playing the Moscow card will evoke special attention in the West. That the end of the Cold War made the political doctrine of East–West nonalignment obsolete is well understood in New Delhi.

India's repositioning has already begun. The West looms much larger in India's reckoning than before. India's restructured economic policy, opening to direct foreign investment, and defense budget cuts make a virtue of necessity but are also being packaged for maximum political appeal to the West. India's economic ties with Moscow, including low-interest, long-term Soviet credit for Indian arms purchases and the rupee-ruble commodity trade, are too entrenched and too mutually valuable to revise quickly. But Moscow and Delhi both are likely to want to place their future exports to each other on a hard currency basis. This means that the value and volume of their bilateral trade probably will diminish relative to their respective trade with other partners. Indo–Soviet trade might not shrink in absolute terms because India probably will retain certain comparative advantages in the Soviet Union's successor states and could gain from playing a part in their future development. India's motivation for this could also be spurred by competition with Pakistan.

A big question mark in India's assessment of its future relations concerns the effects of the global changes on China and the character of the Chinese relationship with Pakistan. To outward appearances, the Chinese threat to India has declined over the last two decades, even as China's broader international relations have been normalized. But India's fear of China—of the Chinese nuclear potential and of China's material support for Pakistani security—remains a key factor in Indian defense and nuclear programs. India took steps under Rajiv Gandhi to improve the long-chilled relationship with Beijing, and Gandhi played down and thereby reduced the salience of the threat from Chinese nuclear weapons to India. But the outbreak of a major conflict in Kashmir could sweep away these limited steps. The emergence of China as a major arms supplier to the Middle East, with sales to Iran, Iraq, Saudi Arabia, and Syria, is also a concern to India, which has been reticent about selling arms.

A long-standing concern in the theoretical literature has been that the reduction of U.S.–Soviet strategic rivalry and weakening of bipolar alliance structures could actually accelerate nuclear proliferation. Although usually it is Germany and Japan that are referred to in this context, such a danger in southern Asia is not theoretical but real. The weakening of the Soviet Union as a source of Indian security reassurance against China will tend to increase India's incentives for nuclear weapons. A flagrant Chinese provocation that revives Indian concern about the Chinese potential for nuclear blackmail would probably convince Delhi to nuclearize. This stimulus seems unlikely today, however, because China is less interested than ever in being perceived as a menace by any major country, including India. But China's interest in Pakistan and therefore in the Kashmir problem remains a related source of Indian uncertainty.

Pakistan's new sense of isolation and embitterment could incite further disruptions in its relations with the United States and Western Europe. The changes in the Soviet Union could lead to future economic opportunities for Pakistan in central Asia. But instabilities in the domestic and interstate politics of that region could make it hard for Pakistan to devise a coherent approach toward those states. It would be a long time in any case before the fruits of such new opportunities could compensate for current Western support. For near-term compensation, Pakistan is more likely to concentrate its energies on enlarging its political and commercial ties with neighboring China and Iran and further cultivating those with Saudi Arabia and the smaller Gulf states.

Perceived isolation from the West and adversarial relations with the United States will almost certainly increase Pakistan's proclivity for nuclear weapons. This could mean that the remaining barriers are solely technical and political—the supposed advantages, for example, of adhering as long as possible to a policy of ambiguity. In the past, Pakistan's main motivation for nuclear capability has been deterrence of India. If the end of the Cold War means that Pakistan must guarantee its security largely by itself, and if Pakistan is convinced the perceived threat from India cannot be removed by a political settlement, the incentive for producing nuclear weapons may become irrepressible.

If there is a flashpoint, it is likely to be Kashmir. To prevent war over Kashmir, India's two primary concerns continue to dictate its hard line. One is to avoid a breakaway in Kashmir that could excite other separatist movements in India. The other is India's strategic interest in being able, in Ladakh, to man and defend its frontiers with China. The predominantly Muslim-populated capital of Srinagar and the surrounding valley of Kashmir provide the only practical overland access to Ladakh. In Delhi's view, India's *raison d'état* outweighs any international norm that could legitimize Kashmiri self-determination. Thus India will defend Kashmir by military means, at very high cost if necessary, even in the face of a nuclear threat from Pakistan. It would invade Pakistan, or at least occupy the plains in Pakistan that command the southwestern approaches to Kashmir, at the moment its position in the valley is seriously jeopardized.

This moment could arise at any time because Indian police forces and administrative authorities have lost political control in Kashmir, probably irretrievably, and law and order there is badly disrupted—although regular Indian military bases and lines of communication still remain secure.

Pakistan is unlikely to contest India's physical control of the valley by sending in its army because India would immediately expand the war to Pakistan. Political sympathies in Pakistan for the liberation of Kashmiri Muslims run so strong, however, that private volunteers, money, and guns are migrating to Kashmiri resistance organizations. No elected government of Pakistan will try to interdict this traffic because it would fall if it did.

Like the Kurdish problem, Kashmir has no obvious or easy solution. The main roles for members of the international community are to keep an eye on the situation and make their opposition clearly known both to any decision to initiate war and to other extreme measures, especially when the situation heats up to crisis levels. In time, political evolution within Kashmir and new ingenuity in Delhi may create new possibilities for legitimacy and pacification. To achieve a political solution, India may find that granting a significant measure of self-governing autonomy and subsidy is unavoidable. This could be dovetailed with provision for separate military reservations in sparsely populated areas that allow India to maintain its defensive positions. Lifting the barrier to domestic private investment in Kashmir may also help over the long term.[33]

The instability in Punjab essentially requires a political solution that allows the Sikh community a measure of autonomy within local and state politics and reassurance against punitive discrimination in recruitment to the national services. Ironically, this may mean that a secular central government finally grants a sectarian political concession to Sikh communalism in Punjab while refusing a reciprocal concession to Hindu communalists in both Punjab and Haryana—a constitutionally untidy but possibly necessary paradox of religious pluralism. It is a sustainable compromise because at the national level the Sikh community is a tiny minority, while Hindus at the national level constitute an overwhelming majority and accordingly need no special protection.

Economic policy reform and integration in the international trading system could go a long way toward enabling India and Pakistan to ameliorate their internal security problems and the external threats they perceive to be linked to them. Economic growth, job creation, and the expansion of internal resources will not necessarily extinguish social conflict but are prerequisites of the institutional and political confidence as well as the material wherewithal needed to manage social conflict successfully and reduce it to tolerable proportions.

This is partly a question of opening wide the domestic manufacturing and transport sectors to the international trading and investment systems and letting a multiplicity of home-grown and foreign firms do their natural work. Many foreign enterprises that would be relevant to the subcontinent but that are unfamiliar with South Asian conditions may therefore step in slowly, but the process will gather momentum if the conditions warrant it. Success may also depend on letting the fate of public-sector firms depend entirely on their competitive performance by cutting off anything beyond start-up subsidies. The initial adjustments will inevitably be painful but far less painful today than if they are postponed.

Natural market forces will not suffice to deal with the domestic effects on Pakistan of the war in Afghanistan or with the opening up and development of Afghanistan itself. The violence in Karachi and Sind, which now extends to kidnapping foreign businessmen for ransom, has about the same effect on foreign investment in Pakistan as the terrorist hijacking of airplanes has had on tourism to certain countries. Thus, some new source of inspiration or initiative may be required to get to the roots of the problem. Assuming the violence can be brought under control, it would be a useful project for Pakistan's wealthier neighbors to sponsor a study and financial consortium for the stimulus of economic investment, transport, and market links among Afghanistan, Iran, Pakistan, and the smaller Gulf states.

For the nuclear issue, Nawaz Sharif's June 6 "five-nation" proposal contains the kernel of a promising two-step or tiered approach. The decline of the Cold War should make such a multilateral approach more feasible. It would require the United States and the two adjoining nuclear great powers—the Soviet Union and China—to join as guarantors in a nuclear weapon-free arrangement covering the territories of India and Pakistan and, perhaps, certain neighboring states and contiguous regions.

Such an arrangement would be unthinkable if the Soviet Union still occupied Afghanistan or if the Sino-Soviet conflict were still in full swing.

But Gorbachev removed both. The prospective appeal of the "five-nation" approach today is suggested by the increasing readiness of China as well as the Soviet Union to accept new measures to strengthen the nonproliferation regime. The Soviet Union has long been, along with the United States, committed to the NPT regime. China is now moving in that direction. Both the Soviet Union and China have begun to give serious consideration to controlling missile proliferation, if not the exact approach developed in the Western-sponsored Missile Technology Control Regime (MTCR).

The tiered approach is a response to India's long-standing concern about the potential nuclear threat to itself from China and to India's insistence that any regional nuclear weapon–free zone scheme not be limited to South Asia, nor to the subcontinent, but rather encompass all of Asia, including China. Thus, Chinese participation seemed to be necessary to achieve a solution that would cover both India and Pakistan. The senior Pakistani visitors to Washington mentioned earlier suggested that both the Soviet Union and China, as well as the United States, expressed sufficient interest in the concept to encourage Prime Minister Nawaz Sharif to announce the initiative.

The Pakistani formulation is deliberately open-ended and thus does not prejudice any of a number of specific alternative arrangements. One way to get the talks going is to organize diplomatic discussions serially, in bilateral channels, between each of the participants. More important than the mechanism, however, is to get them going. This should be tested early with the Rao government. If Indian resistance to talks does not soften, the serious underlying issue is whether economic benefits should be linked to military security issues to get talks moving. It may no longer be permissible to divorce these issue areas from each other. It certainly was not possible for the United Nations to do so in Iraq after the war.

Controlling nuclear proliferation and reducing the risk of major conventional and nuclear war is a matter of great concern outside the subcontinent as well as within it. It is worth recalling that India and Pakistan, although they have been at war three times and are deeply emotional rivals, have signed peace agreements, generally maintained diplomatic relations, and carried on numerous official dialogues. Their situation is quite different in this respect from the technical "state of war" between the Arab confrontation states and Israel, or between the two Koreas. The problem during peacetime has never been diplomatic recognition or how to break the diplomatic ice. It has been to convince the authorities on both sides to identify and agree on compromises that are politically difficult for one or both to accept. In the nuclear area, India and Pakistan must do this together. But, in the nuclear area, the international community can ill afford to wait for this to happen spontaneously. Catalysts are needed.

New realities combine uneasily with old quarrels in the region, bringing the risk of war and nuclear confrontation closer even while stimulating some new thinking about an attenuation of conflict and a piecemeal process of overcoming the sources of domestic and regional instability. The post–cold war agenda for the international community in southern Asia is formidable. The chief objectives must be to prevent a war over Kashmir, reduce the emerging risk of nuclear war, support the strengthening and implementation of the new economic and trade policy realism in Delhi and Islamabad, and help facilitate, to the extent possible from outside, political solutions of the causes of internal communal, ethnic, and terrorist violence. In the near term, preventing the outbreak of war over Kashmir will take precedence, but every opportunity to check the nuclear proliferation threats should be pursued. The economic development priorities need sustained emphasis and may be crucial in the long run to solving the deepest internal conflicts. The ability of Delhi and Islamabad and of interested members of the international community to address this agenda creatively and effectively will determine whether South Asia slides deeper into despair and nuclear conflagration or joins the more hopeful movement of history evident in so many other parts of the world.

The views contained in this article are solely the author's and do not necessarily represent those of ACDA or any other U.S. government agency. An earlier version of this article was presented at the U.S. Institute of Peace conference on "Peace and Deterrence," Washington, D.C., July 9–10, 1990.

Notes

1. Although alternatives to the formal name of the Soviet Union have been discussed, and the new Union may settle on the "Union of Sovereign States," the familiar name Soviet Union is retained in this article, except where the context explains an alternative.

2. Rajiv Gandhi's assassination itself apparently resulted from Sri Lankan Tamil guerrilla retaliation against his use of India's military forces against the Tamil secessionists in the northern part of Sri Lanka.

3. Note that Sikh extremist behavior and terrorist actions spring from a minute fraction of the larger Sikh community and have not undermined the loyalty of the Sikh community as a whole to the nation of India.

4. "Death Among the Blossoms," *Economist*, May 25–31, 1991, pp. 39–41.

5. For an election report, see *India Today*, July 15, 1991, pp. 20–28.

6. See "The Economy: Bold Gamble," *India Today*, July 31, 1991, pp. 10–21.

7. See Sudeep Chakravarti and R. Jagannathan, "Ending the Licence Raj: New Economic Policy," *India Today*, August 15, 1991, pp. 10–17.

8. See Brahma Chellaney, "Military Growth in India Over," *Washington Times*, August 7, 1991.

9. See *Economist*, June 8–14, 1991, p. 78, and July 27–August 2, 1991, p. 36.

10. See issue of June 23, 1990, pp. 27–31, for a feature story on then–Prime Minister V. P. Singh's reckoning with these issues and the statistical information quoted.

11. India's external debt in hard currencies—which apparently does not include ruble obligations to the Soviet Union—has reached over $70 billion, equivalent in value to nearly one-quarter of India's total gross domestic product (GDP). See *Economist*, July 27–August 2, 1991, p. 36. This external debt has risen more than threefold, from $21 billion, since 1981. The proportion owed to foreign commercial banks has remained low, at about one-fifth. The fact that a larger proportion had been derived from international aid reassured commercial lenders until recently. *Economist*, June 8–14, 1991, p. 78.

12. For a report on the problems of implementation of economic reform in both India and Pakistan, see Steve Coll, "S. Asian Reformers Face Tough Hurdles," *Washington Post*, September 8, 1991, p. A–21.

13. For an insightful summary of the internal effects of the Afghan conflict on Pakistan, see Mahnaz Ispahani, "Pakistan: Dimensions of Insecurity," *Adelphi Papers* 246 (London: Brassey's for IISS, 1990), pp. 43–45.

14. This occurred despite the fact that Pakistan's relationships historically with Iran and Saudi Arabia are much closer than those with Iraq; indeed, the past dilemmas for Pakistan in balancing its relations with powers in the Gulf have arisen mainly from the hostility between Tehran and Riyadh.

15. See the report by Steve Coll, "Pakistani

Army: A New Cadence," *Washington Post,* August 15, 1991, p. A-34.

16. Benazir Bhutto attributed her new knowledge to discussions with nuclear scientists "who owed loyalty to [her] father," former Prime Minister Zulfikar Ali Bhutto. She reportedly claimed that while she was in office, she had been kept in the dark by Ghulam Ishaque Khan, who became president of Pakistan upon the demise of General Zia ul-Haq. She also surmised that Khan today keeps the new prime minister, Nawaz Sharif, in the dark. See Steve Levine's report, *Guardian,* September 2, 1991, p. 8.

17. For an early exposition of this possibility, see "Military Implications of a Pakistani Bomb," chap. 6 of Major General D. K. Palit and P.K.S. Namboodiri, *Pakistan's Islamic Bomb* (New Delhi: Vikas Publishing House, 1979), especially pp. 115-116.

18. That year Sindhi frustrations with the increasing competition of Urdu-speakers and Punjabis for land and jobs in the province gave momentum briefly to the Sindu Desh (Sind independence) movement.

19. See Coll, "S. Asian Reformers Face Tough Hurdles."

20. The current scandal in Washington and London over the discovery of massive fraud in the Pakistani-founded but Abu Dhabi-financed private Bank of Commerce and Credit International (BCCI) also provides an interesting case study of the international migration of entrepreneurial initiative and assets. Agha Hasan Abedi, the Pakistani head of BCCI, lost his private United Bank in Pakistan to Bhutto's nationalization in 1972 and started BCCI in 1974. During its ascendancy, BCCI reputedly was one of the five largest banks in the world.

21. Apparently the aircraft concerned—the Anglo-French Jaguar, U.S. F-16, French Mirage-2000, and Soviet MiG-27 lines—were not specifically configured for nuclear delivery during manufacture by their foreign suppliers. Neither country is known to have equipped such aircraft for nuclear weapon carriage. Retrofitting such aircraft for nuclear delivery would, however, pose no insurmountable problems for Pakistani and Indian technicians. Rough-and-ready delivery by military cargo aircraft would not require sophisticated retrofits at all.

22. The burgeoning literature on missile developments in the Third World remains less than clear on the operational capabilities of missile programs in India and Pakistan. See, however, Martin Navias, "Ballistic Missile Proliferation in the Third World," *Adelphi Papers* 252 (London: Brassey's for IISS, 1990); Aspen Strategy Group, *New Threats: Responding to the Proliferation of Nuclear, Chemical, and Delivery Capabilities in the Third World* (Boston: University Press of America, 1990), chap. 3, especially p. 101; Leonard Spector, *The Undeclared Bomb: The Spread of Nuclear Weapons* (Cambridge, Mass.: Ballinger, 1988), chap. 2; Rodney W. Jones and Harald Müller, "Preventing a Nuclear Sarajevo: Proliferation in the Middle East and South Asia," *Arms Control Today* 19, no. 1 (January/February 1989), especially pp. 18-19; Aaron Karp, "Ballistic Missile Proliferation in the Third World," chap. 7 in Stockholm International Peace Research Institute, *SIPRI Yearbook 1989: World Armaments and Disarmament* (Oxford: Oxford University Press, 1989).

23. Indian planning must, of course, take Chinese as well as Pakistani military forces into account. The main Chinese threat, however, consists of ground rather than modern air forces and is relevant only in the hypothetical case of a combined Chinese and Pakistani war against India. Consequently, the ratio with Pakistan is the principal concern. Because India also has a significant naval air strike force (land-based Jaguars and sea-based Harrier "jump-jets") that can attack Karachi, and Pakistan's naval air capability is negligible, the effective ratio of modern combat aircraft is actually closer to 4:1 in India's favor.

24. According to a recent report, the Cobras are virtually grounded by uncertainty over the U.S. resupply of spare parts since the aid cutoff of October 1990. See Steve Coll, "Pakistani Army," *Washington Post,* August 15, 1991, p. A-34.

25. The proliferation concerns are analyzed in Ben Sanders and John Simpson, "Nuclear Submarines and Non-Proliferation: Cause for Concern," *PPNN Occasional Paper no. 2* (Southampton: Centre for International Policy Studies, University of Southampton, July 1988).

26. A remarkable conjecture for its time that

reflects these trends is Ravi Rikhye's *The Fourth Round: Indo-Pak War 1984* (New Delhi: ABC Publishing House, 1982).

27. For a discussion of past conventional warfare patterns in South Asia and conjecture on how India would plan for nuclear operations, see the author's "India's Nuclear Strategy: A Threat to World Peace?" *NBC Defense and Technology International* (May 1986), pp. 66–72.

28. See Chellaney, "Military Growth in India Over."

29. See, for example, "The Nuclear Threat" in his column called "Brasstacks" in *India Today*, November 30, 1990, p. 94.

30. The August 1991 scare of potential loss of central control over Soviet strategic nuclear weapons resulting from the independence moves of constituent republics might give pause to any Indian consideration of where and how India might deploy strategic missiles on its territory.

31. The only Zia proposal that took root was the bilateral accord, each side pledging it would not attack the other's nuclear facilities. At Zia's urging, the agreement was first announced orally by Rajiv Gandhi in Zia's presence to the Delhi press in 1985. It was committed to writing as a formal agreement under Benazir Bhutto and V. P. Singh's respective governments and entered into force after it was formally ratified by the Pakistan Senate in January 1991.

32. Address to the National Defence College by Nawaz Sharif, prime minister of Pakistan, Rawalpindi, June 6, 1991.

33. The investment market might be part of the long-term political solution for poverty-ridden Kashmir. Investment by non-natives in Kashmir, which has a special constitutional status in India, is virtually prohibited. What would happen if the barrier were removed? Non-Indian foreigners would probably have little or no incentive to invest. But Indians at home and non-resident Indians abroad might be attracted to do so because of the prestige and beauty of that part of the subcontinent. An influx of resources and growing employment would probably change the outlook of at least some of the Kashmiri youth, from whom the latest agitation sprang.

In Search of a Latin America Policy: The Elusive Quest

William Perry

DURING THE MONTHS preceding the 1988 U.S. presidential elections there sprang up a veritable cottage industry of studies and reports aimed at influencing the Latin America policy of the incoming administration. Because of the increased salience of hemispheric affairs over the past decade, this now traditional form of activity assumed unprecedented proportions. Among the prominent participants were the Americas Society, the Association of American Chambers of Commerce in Latin America (AACCLA), the Center for Strategic and International Studies, the Council for Inter-American Security's Committee of Santa Fe, the Heritage Foundation, the Inter-American Dialogue, and the Sanford Commission.[1]

Although the ideological orientation of these groups spanned the relevant bands of the U.S. political spectrum and much, of course, was to depend on which party eventually won the elections, their diverse efforts shared a surprising amount in common. The general elements of this consensus were spelled out in an article coauthored by Dr. Abraham Lowenthal, generally regarded as the intellectual guru of the administration of Jimmy Carter, and Ambassador José Sorzano, the penultimate chief for Latin American affairs at the National Security Council under President Ronald Reagan.[2] The views of these two disparate experts may be summarized as follows:

- Latin America will be of greatly increased importance to the United States in coming years not only on account of security questions, but also because of debt, trade, narcotics, immigration, and the environment.
- If Latin America's deep and prolonged depression is not ended soon, the consequences could be disastrous: violence and repression, radical politics and insurgencies, the crumbling of democracies, expansion of drug trafficking, and a swelling of emigration to the United States.
- The new administration and the Congress should move quickly to confront this emerging crisis.

The clear implication was that the United States urgently required a bold and comprehensive new approach to the hemisphere. While not discounting the enduring importance of Central American security problems, such an initiative also would embrace the

---

William Perry is senior associate on South American Affairs with the CSIS Americas Program. Prior to coming to CSIS, he spent two decades as a specialist in hemispheric affairs with academic institutions and in government service, including with the Senate Foreign Relations Committee and the National Security Council.

emergent debt, trade, drugs, terrorism, immigration, and support for democracy issues, raising them to the front rank of a new U.S. foreign policy agenda for the 1990s. A departure of this scope and nature would have to overcome both a pervasive pattern of inattention to Latin American affairs evident over the past 50 years and the bitter partisan differences of the past decade.

It is hardly surprising that regional specialists of every stripe tout the importance and critical condition of their particular area of concern, or that they lament the inattention of others to the object of their affection. Specialists on Latin America, however, made a particularly compelling case: the nations of Latin America and the Caribbean stand at a historical crossroads, and this situation does create unprecedented demands on U.S. policy.

Politically, the region comprises a great arena in the struggle for democracy in the developing world. If the nations of the hemisphere succeed in institutionalizing modern, workable democratic systems, truly historic progress will have been made in their integration into the broad Western community of nations. If they fail, however, the United States will be confronted by a seething mass of frustration and discontent along its southern borders that for decades to come will affect adversely U.S. society and complicate its foreign policy.

Economically, the stakes are equally high. Successful development in Latin America would mean the definitive emergence of a host of promising partners whose proximate and largely symbiotic patterns of production and consumption could contribute significantly to the enhanced prosperity and competitiveness of the United States. The alternative is continued regional stagnation and decline—producing ever-higher human costs, undermining prospects for democratic government, injuring the economic interests of the United States, and precipitating increasingly serious social problems in this country.

In view of the course of regional events over the past decade, the security importance of the region requires little elaboration. A stable, democratic, and prosperous hemisphere would alleviate many valid U.S. security concerns, reduce the amount of resources that both the United States and its neighbors devote to the common defense, and also facilitate regional cooperation in coping with continuing threats.

Likewise, an improved diplomatic climate that would result from a politically and economically healthier hemisphere could be expected to enhance prospects for collaboration among the United States and its regional neighbors on general foreign policy matters. This would strengthen Washington's hand in dealing with adversaries, friendly competitors, and Third World nations around the globe. An additional benefit would be the reduction of the considerable controversy that is occasioned by regional issues on the domestic U.S. political scene.

With so much at stake for the United States in Latin America, the challenge for U.S. policy is great. In testimony before the Western Hemisphere Subcommittee of the Foreign Affairs Committee of the U.S. House of Representatives last March, the author posed the basic questions:

> Can we (now) overcome our people's and policy-makers' ingrained habit of taking this hemisphere for granted? Do we clearly see both the opportunities and dangers of present circumstances?

Will we recognize that now, and for the foreseeable future, what happens in Latin America and the Caribbean probably will affect the average American more directly than do events in any other region of the globe? Will we elevate hemispheric affairs to that same priority we routinely accord those of Europe and Asia? Can we summon the will to act toward realization of bright opportunities before the all too obvious tide of negatives send events spinning out of control? Will the new Congress and the new administration take the initiative? Can we forge a realistic, effective bipartisan policy which is supported by the American people—especially with respect to devisive issues like Central America (but also toward broader regional concerns that have emerged in recent years)?[3]

The Bush Administration's First Year

Almost one year later, it is clear that neither the administration nor the Congress has risen to the challenge outlined in these questions. Instead of an enthusiastic and definitive "yes," it has settled for the long familiar "no" or, at least, "not yet." The reasons for this disappointing response are many. There is the long-standing problem of the preoccupation of the present generation of U.S. foreign policy specialists with other regions and issues, a situation aggravated by the truly portentous and promising course of events in areas in which they are truly experienced and interested. The East–West focus of the policy community is reinforced by enduring partisan differences and by the unenviable reputation that the Western hemisphere has generated in recent years.

A significant new departure in U.S. policy toward the hemisphere would have required presidential leadership, a comprehensive strategy, and many specific tactical initiatives toward the myriad, interrelated set of problems and opportunities confronting the United States in the region. The arduous forging of real bipartisan agreement on the need for and specific elements of such an initiative would have been necessary. From the first day of the new administration, a powerful theme offering inspiration to the United States and hope to the hemisphere also would have had to be articulated.

Instead, the new administration has offered a truce aimed at the avoidance of controversy over hemispheric issues. The bipartisan agreement reached with the Congress in March 1989 basically glosses over problems, defers necessary steps, and, in any event, deals only with one country, Nicaragua. Clearly, the kind of bold, comprehensive, new U.S. initiative toward the hemisphere urged unanimously by Latin America specialists of both parties has not emerged.

Given recent experience and the wider course of international events, it is not particularly surprising that the Bush administration seems purposefully to have attempted to deemphasize Latin America on the U.S. foreign policy agenda. The central axis of policy-making under the current administration stretches from the cupola of Secretary of State James Baker's department to the president's own door. The new team divides the universe of foreign policy issues into two distinct categories. There are those issues that can be addressed with a significant prospect of near-term success, rebounding to the political credit of the administration. There are other problems that are controversial, difficult or impossible to resolve, and full of political pitfalls. The Bush administration evidently decided early on that most hemispheric issues tend to fall into the later, or loser category, making a comprehensive new initiative toward Latin America neither feasible nor desirable, and impelling merely *ad hoc* attention to hemispheric problems, as absolutely required.

Evidently, the secretary of state's first priority with respect to regional issues was to attempt to liquidate the friction generated in Congress over Central America policy during the Reagan administration. Toward this end, Secretary Baker appointed as his assistant secretary of state for inter-American affairs a Democrat whose principal qualification was his experience in dealing with the Congress on Central American controversies. Baker then moved quickly to forge a bipartisan agreement that aimed to put off further congressional controversy as long as possible, and, at least, until after the Nicaraguan elections of February 1990.

The administration's aversion to becoming embroiled in controversy over Latin America became even clearer in its handling of the twin crises in Panama—those produced by the annulment of the May 1989 elections and the attempted coup d'état against General Manuel Noriega in October. In both instances, the prime objective seemed to be to avoid direct U.S. action and the adverse political consequences of involvement in another Central American quagmire. As in the case of Nicaragua, reliance on local and multilateral fora was preferred over any form of unilateral U.S. action, despite minimal prospects of thereby achieving nominal administration objectives.

Similarly, there has been little inclination to anticipate emerging troubles, such as narcoterrorism so long in the making in Colombia and Peru. Despite administration rhetoric on the defense of democracies and the war on drugs—and the provision of limited aid in acute circumstances—no comprehensive initiative has been forthcoming. In addition, the administration seems unresponsive to the creative ideas of others, such as the surprise proposal for a multinational drug force offered by Jamaican Prime Minister Michael Manley.

The drug war and, when possible, Panama tend to be delegated to the Department of Defense, whose traditional reluctance to undertake bold new initiatives on such matters seems to fit well with overall administration preferences. Secretary of Defense Richard Cheney, however, now seems to be rethinking these increasingly pressing issues with a view toward adopting a more protagonistic approach. On the lingering debt question, the Department of the Treasury takes full responsibility (except for the case of Mexico, as explained below). The questions are handled by the Department of Commerce, whose Secretary Robert Mosbacher has demonstrated surprising interest in the hemisphere, and by the United States trade representative (USTR).

A few regional issues have not been adjudged losers and, thus, merit treatment by the administration at the highest levels. Mexico and regional summitry are the most obvious examples. The reforms being undertaken in Mexico by the government of Carlos Salinas are received with great relief in the United States. It is both possible and politically profitable to build upon this development to make real improvements in the historically difficult U.S.–Mexican relationship.

The Texas cast of the new administration strongly reinforces this inclination. Likewise, in bilateral consultation with democratic leaders of the region and at summits celebrating democracy or considering problems of universal domestic and international concern, such as drugs, President Bush and Secretary Baker take the forefront and deserve high marks for their efforts.

Given the apparently early decision to pursue a largely reactive strategy with a premium on damage limitation, this pattern of conduct by the new administration is not surprising. It also explains, in large part, the slow pace of appointments, the lack of legislative initiatives, and the absence of both a positive overall theme for and comprehensive coordination of the administration's approach to the hemisphere during its first year.

Democrats in Congress have reacted with relieved acquiescence to the Latin America policy of the incoming Bush administration, much as the administration must have hoped. Some members of Congress have criticized the timidity of the drug policy and the hesitation evident during the coup d'état attempt in Panama. Nevertheless, it is difficult to envision a majority of Democrats favoring more drastic action on drugs, especially if it were to involve loss of life, or more direct intervention in Panama, especially if it were not painless and immediately successful. Senate confirmation of administration appointees also has been slow, and there have been more than the usual number of complaints about the quantity and quality of the political appointments to regional embassies. In general, however, the Democrats in Congress seem content that the Bush administration has not pushed the controversial aspects of its predecessor's Central America policy.

Whatever concern may exist in Congress about the failure of administration leadership on Latin America policy is quite muted—on the Republican side of the aisle, by the fact that a Republican administration is calling the shots, and on the Democratic side, by the fact that it is not their responsibility.

Whether the administration's strategy proves to be wise and successful remains to be seen. Whatever its piecemeal accomplishments, such an approach is seen as substantially inadequate by those who believe that a major new initiative was required in order to get out in front of serious problems in the region and realize longer-term opportunities now in evidence. Obviously, the issues facing the United States in the international arena do not divide themselves neatly into those that can be treated easily with domestic political gain and those that cannot. Of course, calculations of what is practical and at what political cost are important and must inform any administration in the formulation of its priorities for international action. However, an administration's calculations must take the long-term as well as the short-term view and it must be willing to undertake the difficult and unpleasant as well as the easy and gratifying.

There are, after all, matters that do not admit much prospect of short-term gain but should be worked assiduously in order to set the stage for significant advantage over the longer run. This is related to the so-called vision thing that dogged the Bush presidential campaign. Basically, with reference to this hemisphere, the question is: Does there exist an eventually attainable situation in the region that would be significantly more favorable to U.S. values and interests, and toward which U.S. policy should now be working?

Furthermore, there are issues entailing domestic political liabilities and of dubious tractability that demand treatment nevertheless, because of their potential to get immeasurably worse. Most Latin America specialists would argue that the Western Hemisphere is teeming with issues in both of these categories, which the United States will sooner or later discover to its pleasant surprise, or bitter chagrin.

Building Effective Strategy

What lessons have been learned over the last year and, indeed, from all past experience? What are the obstacles to a more effective policy? What would be required to articulate and implement the kind of policy that would receive the support it needed at home and perform as required in the field? Finally, what would such a policy look like?

Some of the obstacles are familiar and long standing. At present, neither the people of the United States nor its foreign policy elite are prepared for the crucial role to be played by Latin America and the Caribbean in the external relations and domestic affairs of the United States. Two generations of analysts and policymakers have been trained with an overwhelming orientation toward the affairs of the Northern Hemisphere, many of whom see the Western Hemisphere only as a potential diversion from the staple concerns of U.S. foreign policy in the postwar era. Retooling the foreign affairs vision of the country and its infrastructure to incorporate Latin America and the Caribbean will take time.

The existing pool of Latin American specialists in the United States has not proven to be as helpful as one might have hoped. The study of Latin America long has existed outside the mainstream of U.S. foreign policy thinking and heavily partakes of utopianism, clientitis, parochialism, and radical chic social thought. Moreover, the existing Latin American studies establishment evidences enormous difficulty in showing the realism and practicality necessary to contribute to policy that would be aimed fundamentally at promoting U.S. interests, as most people in the United States perceive them. A whole new school of thought on Latin America, with a balanced, realistic, and forward-looking vision of the region's affairs and of its relationship with the United States, must be forged.

In terms of Latin America, distinct differences between the Democratic and Republican Parties must be acknowledged. Although nearly everyone recognizes the need for a more bipartisan approach to the region, few have been willing to address the differences squarely, which is the essential first step in harmonizing partisan views.

The beliefs and perspectives that tend to bind liberal Democrats include the following. They favor a greater show of concern and understanding for the characteristics and problems unique to Latin American democracies, and for their inevitable differences with the United States on matters of both domestic policy and international politics. Toward that end, they are inclined to frequent meetings and consultations with Latin America's democratic governments and politicians. Essentially, they would seek to cultivate better and more tolerant relations between the United States and a neutralist, Third World Latin America.

Generally, liberal Democrats evidence a strong aversion to U.S. interventionism, especially the use of military instruments to resist radical changes or to protect U.S. interests. They are prone to believe that when such changes are in train, they are necessary and comprise little, if any, threat to real U.S. interests. When serious conflicts do arise, liberal Democrats are inclined to emphasize appeals to regional opinion, multilateral fora, and negotiations as the vehicles for their resolution. On the other hand, archetypical liberals are capable of punitive attitudes toward rightist authoritarian regimes and are prone to sanctions in retribution for human rights infringements.

In the economic sphere, Democratic preferences tend toward increased economic aid, enhanced multilateral lending, and, under current circumstances, the granting of maximum feasible levels of general debt relief. On matters of trade, however, they hardly can be so forthcoming, given the protectionist sentiments of key Democratic constituencies. Whereas Democrats are restrictive on commerce, they tend to be more permissive on immigration issues and more tolerant of biculturalism in the United States. Generally, their attitudes toward the drug problem reflect a certain ambivalence—manifesting genuine outrage at the trade and its consequences, but also reluctance to countenance the sometimes unpleasant results of harsh countermeasures, especially if the United States has a hand in them.

The archetypical conservative Republican position tends to anticipate and work toward the gradual integration of the hemisphere into the Western community of nations—if, and when, those nations are ready. Often less sensitive to the distinctive features of local societies, Republicans easily are capable of ignoring the region, if U.S. interests are not at play. On the other hand, it could be argued that Republicans of this stripe only are setting a standard of realistic self-interest that Latin Americans will have to learn to live with, if they wish to enter the mainstream of international affairs. Republicans tend to believe that Latin America should pursue reform and modernization on an evolutionary basis, if it is to win the place it desires in the highly competitive international environment. Social change might be necessary in Latin America, but Republicans are wary of its banners being taken over by anti-American and antidemocratic elements, especially those with extraregional links.

According to this worldview, power politics are to be played as they would be anywhere else in the world: as U.S. interests would require. Consultations and multinational fora are to be preferred up to the point at which hostile adversaries and vital U.S. interests are involved, when the use of all the instruments of a great power's foreign policy would be justified, including force or the threat of force.

In economic affairs, conservative Republicans would favor reliance on freer trade and investment over additional loans and aid, and only limited debt relief based on economic reform and improved performance of local economies. Republicans are less tolerant than Democrats of widespread emigration to the United States and are skeptical of biculturalism. They also are prone to adopt an unambiguously harder line on drug trafficking and terrorism, even if it means that strong methods must be employed by the United States.

The differences between these two worldviews undoubtedly are important. They are not, however, unbridgeable. A bipartisan foreign policy does not require, after all, a unanimity of views—that would be utopian.

Rather, it requires an ample majority with a basic consensus about essential goals and priorities.

If there is a sliver of the Republican Party that is tolerant of military dictatorships or that believes that Latin American countries can be bullied or their governments changed because they are not constituted in the image of the United States, it is not likely to fit into any realistic bipartisan consensus. Likewise, if there is a wing of the Democratic Party that believes that the region is some kind of fairyland outside the normal international system, where real threats to regional democracy and U.S. interests do not exist, that eschews U.S. involvement, and that denies the necessity of choices—often between the lesser of two evils—then it cannot play either.

The author believes, however, that an ample majority of U.S. citizens and their elected representatives in the Congress and administration fall well between the Neanderthal and utopian extremes outlined above. Thus, a good measure of harmonization of partisan differences in support of a broad, new initiative toward the region should be possible. Clearly, however, a new level of commitment and reasonableness—to say nothing of civility and respect for the differing views of others—would be required in order to generate this bipartisanship. The advent of a new administration undoubtedly presents the best opportunity for such an effort.

The most daunting obstacles to achieving such a consensus remain Nicaragua and, perhaps once again, El Salvador. Something such as the bipartisan agreement reached in March 1989, committing the United States to support local negotiations and the election process in Nicaragua without the prospect of military assistance to the contras, was indispensable. Still, it also might have included an undertaking by the Democratic leadership to reconsider the Party's historical position on such aid, based upon the Sandinista government's performance during those elections and its attitude toward the peace process, including its support of the Salvadoran rebels. A position of this nature would have committed the Democrats to nothing specific, but would have strengthened greatly the prospects of Sandinista compliance with nearly universal U.S. expectations.

Similarly, with respect to a new crisis that seems to be emerging in El Salvador, would it not be possible for the Republicans to agree publicly to a specified cut in aid to the government of Alfredo Cristiani if the murders of the Jesuit priests are not brought to justice by a specified deadline? Such an agreement might be strengthened by a tougher Democratic stand toward the ongoing assassination campaign led by the armed Salvadoran leftists and the support that the Sandinista regime obviously supplies to the rebels.

In times of crisis, the administration must take responsibility for effective and appropriate action. With regard to Panama, however, would it not be possible to circulate an open letter in Congress calling on the president to take whatever measures are necessary in order to secure Noriega's removal? A growing number of signatures would put the Congress on record and would give the president a bipartisan consensus from which to act with confidence. The mere existence of such a letter might prove helpful in terms of convincing the Panama Defense Force that the United States is serious about Noriega's removal.

Although controversies in Central America are certain to endure, it must be recognized that the capacity of the

United States to confront them effectively would increase if the administration acted from a wider hemispheric policy upon which there was general accord. Given widespread agreement on the need to defend democracy and to combat the scourge of drug trafficking throughout the hemisphere, the outlines of a bipartisan initiative in this crucial area are not impossible to imagine. Significant additional assistance to the democratic governments of the Andean region and certain Caribbean countries could be found, if pressure were generated to consult real U.S. interests. Democratic concerns about direct U.S. involvement in the strong measures that would be required might be assuaged by channeling military assistance and responsibility for direct action through some multinational agency, as suggested by Prime Minister Manley. Such an approach also might bolster and update the role of the Organization of American States and the flagging U.S. cooperation with Latin American nations under the Rio Treaty.

On economic matters, too, it is not terribly difficult to conceive of a basis for accord. Basically, the Republicans in Congress and the administration would have to agree to become more active on the question of debt relief. In exchange, the Democrats would have to recognize that the finite amounts of relief available would have to be directed on a priority basis, to countries that have made the reforms necessary to draw real, ongoing benefit from any such U.S. financial commitment. The trade question would be a bit more difficult, but the administration might become somewhat tougher with recalcitrants and a bit easier with those who are opening their economies, thereby assuaging Democratic concerns over unfair competition, while simultaneously promoting Republican policies in favor of freer trade and markets.

Looking to the Future

This brief article is not the place for a detailed description of the many elements of U.S. policy toward the hemisphere demanded by present and future circumstances. An effort to forge such an approach would require, first and foremost, the recognition of its necessity in the higher reaches of the administration and Congress. It would presume vision, leadership, and an energizing theme, for the United States and the hemisphere as a whole. Imagination, hard work, and the restraint of partisan passions on behalf of the common good also would be necessary. Perhaps it is unrealistic to expect such an initiative now or in the immediate future; eventually, however, circumstances in the hemisphere will compel such an effort and the United States had best make itself ready.

Sound, positive, and practical ideas, mustered to the service of enlightened self-interest, are the stuff of which good policy is made. Sadly, given the historical orientation of this nation's foreign policy infrastructure, this is an area in which the United States is sorely lacking as regards the Western Hemisphere. The transition period is the time when a new administration must grapple with this deficiency. That opportunity was largely lost.

Once an administration is already underway, the policy planning staff at the State Department is probably the only entity in the government that has time for real thought. Happily, the role of this staff in the current administration seems to be considerable. Constant contact with the academic community, research and public policy institutions, business, labor, and other private entities with ongoing regional involvement and the administration's political constituencies are required, however, if this policy planning staff is to play its unique role in an effective manner.

The best source of ideas, of course, is the people who are recruited for posts in the administration. Giving proper priority to Latin America means attracting individuals for service, in the embassies and key positions in the executive branch, whose Washington and field experience demonstrate the seriousness of the United States about the region and also guarantees good performance in the policy arena. In addition, these are precisely the people most likely to have, and to be capable of evaluating, ideas that might contribute to the success of this nation's policy.

Once a qualified, compatible team is in place, the question of coordinating the many arms of U.S. policy becomes paramount. In this regard, an active, disciplined interagency process, wide consultation, when practical—especially with the Congress—and experience on the part of key policymakers is indispensable. Finally, leadership from the president and the cabinet secretaries and cooperation among them and between them and the Congress is necessary in order to raise the priority of any set of issues and to see them effectively addressed. It is to be hoped that all these important considerations will be kept in mind in the continuing quest for a policy toward the Western Hemisphere that is adequate to the enormous task already at hand.

The views expressed herein are the author's own and do not necessarily reflect those of any institutions with which he presently is associated.

Notes

1. Most salient here were Georges Fauriol, *The Third Century: U.S. Latin American Policy Choices for the 1990s*, Significant Issues Series, X:13 (Washington, D.C.: Center for Strategic and International Studies, 1988); F. Lynn Bouchey et. al., *Santa Fe II: A Strategy for Latin America in the Nineties* (Washington, D.C.: Center for Inter-American Security, 1989); Charles L. Heatherly and Burton Yale Pines, eds., *Mandate for Leadership III: Policy Strategies for the 1990s* (Washington, D.C.: The Heritage Foundation, 1988); Abraham F. Lowenthal, ed., *The Americas in 1989: Consensus for Action* (Landover, Md.: The Aspen Institute/University Press of America Inc., 1989); and the *Report of the International Commission for Central American Recovery and Development* (popularly known as the Sanford Commission report), (Durham, N.C.: Duke University Center for International Development Research, 1989).

2. Abraham F. Lowenthal and José Sorzano, "For U.S., a Rare Opportunity in Latin America," *Christian Science Monitor*, January 17, 1989, p. 19.

3. William Perry, "U.S. Policy Toward the Americas in the 1990s and Beyond: Challenge and Opportunity," testimony delivered before the Subcommittee on Western Hemisphere Affairs, Foreign Affairs Committee, U.S. House of Representatives, March 1, 1989.

After the Cold War: U.S. Interest in Sub-Saharan Africa

David D. Newsom

SINCE THE MOVE toward independence in sub-Saharan Africa during the late 1950s, a principal theme justifying official U.S. actions in that continent has been the perceived threat posed to U.S. interests by the activities of the Soviet Union and its Communist allies. Will the current improvement in relations between the United States and the Soviet Union, by reducing the effectiveness of that theme, lead to decreased public and congressional support for U.S. activities in Africa? Those activities include diplomatic representation in almost all countries, official economic and military assistance programs, U.S. statements on African issues, reciprocal visits by government officials, participation in Africa-related international organization activities, and private sector trade and investment.

This essay probes the U.S.–African relationship of recent decades in order to speculate about its future. It tests the hypothesis that the Communist threat has been, in fact, the paramount rationale for U.S. engagement in Africa and searches for alternative justifications for U.S. official programs.

David D. Newsom previously served as U.S. ambassador to Libya, Indonesia, and the Philippines, and as under secretary of state for political affairs. He is now the Cumings Professor of Diplomacy at the University of Virginia.

U.S. Objectives in Africa

Although stated in different terms to suit varied political climates, the officially pronounced objectives of U.S. policy in Africa have remained much the same over the last 40 years. The objectives have included countering the Soviet threat, preserving the U.S. military's access to facilities, promoting democracy, freedom, and self-determination, respecting African nationalism, opposing apartheid in South Africa, and supporting the security and economic needs of developing nations. The United States also has emphasized the importance of African resources for the U.S. economy and the significance of the large African bloc in the United Nations (UN) in the pursuit of U.S. global policies.

In a speech before the Boston World Affairs Council on February 15, 1984, then Secretary of State George P. Shultz outlined traditional U.S. policy objectives in Africa.

> We have a significant geopolitical stake in the security of the continent and the seas around it. Off its shores lie important trade routes, including those carrying most of the energy resources needed by our European allies. We are affected when Soviets, Cubans, and Libyans seek to expand their influence on the continent by force, to the detriment of both African independence and Western interests.

Shultz also highlighted Africa as a key source of raw materials, underscored the African role in the UN, and recalled the African links with the U.S. civil rights movement.[1]

To determine the priority given by an administration to any one of the objectives, including that of countering the Soviet threat, is not a simple matter. The order of attention given in a speech or statement may be a reflection of the policies of the executive. It also may be a reflection of what is considered most likely to be effective with the public and the Congress. Whatever an administration's principal goals, they must be presented in a manner that will assist in gaining both the authorization and the appropriation of the necessary funds from the legislative branch. Congressional approval depends also on factors beyond those directly related to policy, such as the personalities, individual interests, and constituencies of committee and subcommittee chairpersons, policy differences between the Senate and the House, and occasional differences between the authorizing and appropriating committees.

Furthermore, open committee sessions tend to be dominated by controversial issues or rhetorical efforts to "make a record." The process tends to be complicated by occasional, deep policy divisions within an administration as well as within the Congress. Although administrations generally endeavor to present a coherent policy, statements by administration witnesses tend to stress the special responsibilities of the relative executive departments. For example, State Department spokespersons emphasize the need for responses to African political and economic realities while Defense Department representatives argue the need for military aid to support friends and to counter Soviet assistance. Although the White House does not testify, it sometimes informally makes clear that it has different views on particular issues.

Conflicting Perceptions of U.S. Interests in Africa

The stated official objectives of the United States in sub-Saharan Africa have been sustained since the 1950s by shifting combinations of three diverse and sometimes conflicting perceptions of U.S. interests in that region. First is the perception that sub-Saharan Africa is an important theater of U.S.–Soviet competition. Suggestions that the continent is otherwise strategically important have been countered by global strategists inclined to believe otherwise. G. Mennen Williams, assistant secretary of state for African affairs in the Kennedy administration, frustrated by his inability to win broad support in the Congress for Africa programs, commissioned an academic study on the strategic importance of Africa, hoping thereby to gain arguments to support his wider Africa policy. He was deeply disappointed when the professor who undertook the study concluded that "the United States has no strategic interest in Africa."[2]

That view today is still shared by many. William H. Lewis, writing on U.S. military assistance to Africa, has reported,

> In contrast to the emphasis on the linkage of the Horn of Africa to security concerns in Southwest Asia, most of the rest of sub-Saharan Africa is downgraded as a region of significant strategic U.S. interest in formal presentations before the legislative branch.[3]

Similarly, in a recent analysis of U.S. global priorities by William Hyland, Africa does not loom large. The only Africa references are to the war in Angola and to South Africa, not in terms of strategic priorities, but "as a policy matter . . . reduced to narrow debates about whether sanctions work."[4]

Despite such assessments, others argue that the continent is and remains important in the East–West confrontation, with a corollary that the United States is placed to exercise pressure and influence in several ways. There are four different points of view:

- Global strategists rally support for countries such as Somalia and Kenya that provide the United States access to military facilities or related cooperation, arguing that such cooperation is stabilizing in Africa and allows for the deployment of U.S. forces in the Indian Ocean.
- Those who see Soviet and Cuban inroads in Africa as part of the overall Communist threat to the West advocate strong measures to roll back those adversarial penetrations. For example, they have pressed administrations to link any movement toward the independence of Namibia to the withdrawal of Cuban troops from Angola.
- Those unsympathetic with liberation movements that seek to replace friendly non-Marxist governments point to Soviet assistance to such movements as proof of their essentially Communist character. These analysts view the African National Congress (ANC), for example, as a Moscow-directed force undermining the pro-Western regime in South Africa. In this case, the internal character of a nation is less important than its perceived geopolitical orientation.
- Those who have regarded declared Marxist governments such as those in Mozambique (before recent changes in direction) and Angola as part of the Soviet threat encourage the United States to back groups seeking their overthrow. During the past 30 years, a pattern has developed that involves not only the advocacy of official covert aid to such groups, but also public relations efforts to win public and Congressional support by enhancing the non-Communist images of the groups' leaders. Such campaigns have been conducted on behalf of Moise Tshombe in Zaïre in the 1960s, of C.O. Ojukwu in Nigeria in the 1960s, and of Jonas Savimbi in Angola in the 1980s.
- A fifth group regards the East–West confrontation as arising from unresolved African conflicts that provide opportunities for external exploitation. Whether concerned primarily with the Soviet aspect or with the broader question of stability in the continent, those in this group are active advocates of a strong U.S. role in conflict resolution whether, as in the past, between Somalia and Ethiopia or, more recently, as between South Africa and Mozambique.

Public and congressional support for U.S. activities related to the Soviet presence in Africa has been strongest in cases such as the Cuban troops in Angola, where activities could be linked directly to Moscow or a Soviet satellite. Efforts by conservative legislators to portray as equally inimical to U.S. interests the African guerrilla and liberation movements that receive support from the Soviet Union have created more controversy because such legislators have less broad support. Their efforts do illustrate, however, the capacity of a small, but determined and well-organized, group to affect policy—even if not always in the manner intended—when others are less preoccupied with a region.

For many years, the African bloc in the UN was an important adjunct to U.S. anti-Communist policy in that body. This was especially true during the period prior to the U.S. rapprochement with the People's Republic of China in 1972, when the African nations supported, longer than any other group, the Republic of China on Taiwan as the official representative of China. In the UN, many African nations still support the United States on East–West issues such as Afghanistan. However, the United States' enthusiasm for the African bloc in the UN has waned in recent years as many Africans supported UN General Assembly resolutions defining Zionism as a form of racism and tended to vote against the U.S. position on key issues.[5]

The 10 issues chosen by the State Department to judge the degree of concurrence with U.S. views at the UN were Israeli credentials, the International Court of Justice jurisdiction on Nicaragua, condemnation of foreign intervention in Cambodia, criticism of human rights abuses in Iran, change in name of the Palestine Liberation Organization, a Soviet resolution on international peace and security, external debt and development, foreign intervention in Afghanistan, genuine and periodic elections, and the program budget outline. No division votes were taken on the last three. On the first 7, 8 African countries voted with the United States 3 times; 17 voted with the United States twice; 15 concurred with the United States once; and 7 opposed the United States or abstained on every issue.

As indicated in the statement by Secretary of State Shultz, a corollary to East–West concerns is the declared U.S. interest in stability in Africa. From the time of the support for the unity of the former Belgian Congo in 1960, "stability" has been the term used in support of aid to friendly nations threatened by internal unrest fomented from the outside. In recent years, Libya has been seen as the primary threat to stability. Its activities have been regarded as expansionist and destabilizing, whether one regards Mu'ammar Qadhafi as a surrogate of Moscow, as a terrorist maverick, or otherwise. The United States has sent strong messages to Libya, including a military strike, and has provided assistance to the government of Hissein Habre in order to thwart Libyan efforts in Chad in 1987. The successful repulse of Libyan forces was seen both as a victory for the West and as a block to Libya's territorial ambitions. In the future, it is likely that U.S. assistance to nations threatened by Libya will win strong public and congressional support.

A second current in the making of U.S. policy in sub-Saharan Africa relates to the leading U.S. role in efforts to end apartheid in South Africa. Those who believe the U.S. role to be instrumental focus almost exclusively on the apartheid issue. Many congressional leaders have come to support full disengagement from South Africa and restrictive policies toward nations friendly with the Pretoria government in order to dismantle apartheid and to bring majority rule to that country.

Chairman Howard Wolpe of the House Foreign Affairs Committee's sub-committee on Africa has written:

> Post-Reagan American policy should be based squarely on a clear definition of U.S. national interests. These interests lie first and foremost in moving South Africa away from apartheid and regional destabilization in order to

prevent an expansion of violence and superpower conflict and to contribute to a stable and accountable political order that will permit the realization of the entire subcontinent's vast economic, political, and human potential.[6]

A third rationale for U.S. engagement in Africa derives from a recognition of Africa's serious economic and social needs. This current calls for strong support for economic assistance on the basis of need rather than on political considerations, rapid involvement to avert or respond to disasters, and an emphasis on human rights. In this view, the continent's internal conflicts stem more from poverty, drought, famine, and refugee flows than from East–West conflict. The application of human rights standards in relation to U.S. assistance programs to African countries, except for South Africa, arises out of the worldwide U.S. interest in how governments treat their peoples. In Africa as elsewhere, the relationship of aid to human rights violations has been imperfect. Congress has canceled aid to countries such as the Central African Republic under President Jean-Bedel Bokassa (where hundreds were reportedly slain by Bokassa himself) and to Burundi because of ethnic massacres, but continues to authorize aid to countries such as Somalia and Zaïre. In these latter cases, cooperation with the United States in providing access to military facilities justifies assistance despite reports of human rights abuses. As one examines the aid allocations in Africa, it is difficult, on the other hand, to identify countries that have been particularly rewarded for good human rights records. Experience has demonstrated, especially in connection with U.S. aid programs, that it is more difficult to reward and encourage political reform than to punish violators. One of the stated objectives of the African Development Fund is to establish a flexibility in assistance that will permit rewards to countries that have put into effect economic reforms; no similar flexibility appears to be sought to reward countries that have made improvements in human rights.

An examination of over 30 years of executive presentations to Congress in support of policies toward Africa and of the transcripts of congressional hearings on African programs, suggests that no one perspective concerning U.S. interests in Africa has prevailed. When Washington has displayed greater levels of interest in the region, usually it has been through the coalescence of the three different currents of opinion. Military assistance and economic support funds (ESF) have been allocated to countries that either have provided the United States with access to military facilities (Kenya, Somalia, Morocco, and Liberia), have been threatened by Libya (Chad, Senegal), or are supporting U.S. efforts against a Soviet surrogate (Zaïre). An exception to the general practice of U.S. assistance is Botswana, which receives aid because of its democratic character and the threat from South Africa.[7] Economic assistance, on the other hand, appears to be apportioned on the basis of need and performance, rather than strategic cooperation, although anti-Communist Zaïre still receives the largest share.[8]

Although each current of interest has been important in stimulating an increased U.S. presence in Africa, the most constant theme over many years has been the need to oppose Soviet ambitions in the continent. If an administration did not stress this in its initial statements to the Congress, individual members raised the question. The East–West confrontation theme appeared to assure the greatest justification for broad-based and long-term support for an Africa policy. When the relevance could be demonstrated clearly, it rallied not only those who were convinced of the Soviet threat in Africa, but also those of lesser ardor who did not wish to be on the other side of that issue. Support for some of the principal U.S. initiatives in Africa, from the introduction of UN troops during the Congo crisis (1960–1964) to the more recent negotiations linking the withdrawal of Cuban troops from Angola and the independence of Namibia, depended heavily on justifications drawn from the Cold War context.

Those directly involved in the administration of economic assistance to Africa tend to deny the centrality of the East–West context. Reports on development assistance also tend to concentrate on development policies rather than on their political rationale. The recollection of policymakers who have defended programs in the Congress, however, is often at variance with the less political, bureaucratic reports on such programs. The Congressional Research Service has reported:

Prior to 1975, the provision of aid to sub-Saharan Africa was not justified by the goal that had shaped aid programs to other parts of the world, that of forestalling Communism. Some references in hearings and official documents had been made to attempts by the Soviet Union or Chinese Communists to gain influence, but this had never been a primary concern. In fact, some administration witnesses before Congress had complimented the Africans for resisting Communist overtures.[9]

Yet, in the same report, Congressional sources suggest that Ethiopia's provision of troops in support of the UN action in Korea was an important rationale for the first allocation of U.S. aid to the Addis Ababa government in 1951.[10]

Assistant Secretary Williams, writing on the Congo crisis, holds that U.S. involvement was a policy victory.

Ending the secession did more to restore African confidence in the United Nations and the West—particularly the United States—than any other event in the preceding six years. That the UN was able to end the secession when it did was very fortunate, for African confidence in the UN and the West was under severe trial. Had the UN not succeeded, Africans would have been ready to turn to the Communists for help.[11]

Writing of later U.S. initiatives in Africa, Martin Lowenkopf has commented that

East–West considerations largely account for the fact that Africa is on the very short lists of claimed foreign policy successes of the last two presidents (majority rule in Zimbabwe for Carter, the Angola–Namibia accords for Reagan) and is credited with having played a role in one major failure (when SALT II was 'buried in the sands of the Ogaden' if Zbigniew Brzezinski's rhetorical response to Soviet intervention in the Ethiopian–Somali conflict of 1977–1978 is to be accepted).[12]

Africans and Africa experts in the United States frequently have chafed over the emphasis given to East–West issues in the expressions of U.S. policy. They have stressed the intrinsic importance of the continent, urging greater attention to African development, to the elimination of apartheid, and to a recognition of the dignity and independence of African nations. Africa expert I. William Zartman has written on the need to pursue a more active Africa policy.

> It was once thought that independence would allow African societies to continue the progress begun under colonization, and that takeoff into development and democracy was merely a matter of time. It is clear now that, at best, the time involved is severely extended and that, at worst, the possibilities of economic growth, political participation, and social promotion are most uncertain. These developments change the terms of U.S. interest in Africa but they do not change its nature. The increasing challenges of the coming years mean that the United States will need to pay more attention to Africa for the United States' own good.[13]

The argument that the United States must pay attention to Africa "for its own good" has not received the wide support required to mobilize a national constituency in favor of a substantial U.S. role in Africa. To be effective, policies must have a sufficient measure of public and congressional support. A historical review of U.S.–African relations suggests that, leaving humanitarian concerns aside, such support has been manifested through the linkage of African issues to wider strategic concerns.

Justifications for U.S. Policy

The period of greatest U.S. attention to Africa occurred during the Kennedy administration. President John F. Kennedy displayed great enthusiasm and support for the independence movement in Africa. His administration encouraged visits by new African leaders, launched the Peace Corps in Africa, and supported multi-year economic assistance commitments to African countries. President Kennedy's rhetoric changed from that of the Cold War outlook of the Eisenhower years to focus on "those people in the huts and villages of half the globe struggling to break the bonds of mass misery."[14] Conscious of African and black American attitudes toward apartheid, he kept his administration at arm's length from Pretoria. President Kennedy believed his policies responded to a continent historically linked to the United States, but also served to preclude Soviet advantages in newly independent states, the latter a problem that was much on the public's mind. Kennedy's assistant secretary of state for African affairs recalls,

> During my nearly five-and-a-half years in the State Department, wherever I spoke, I could be sure of the question: 'How are you doing in Africa as compared with the Communists?'[15]

During that period, many of the new African states, aware of the U.S. preoccupation with the Communist threat, played on it in order to gain increased aid. Although the strategic, political, and humanitarian objectives merged during the Kennedy years as they seldom have since, Communist ambitions were stressed when the administration sought support for UN actions in the Congo crisis or funds for the rebuilding of a road from Tanzania to Zambia.

In the decades following the Kennedy administration, notwithstanding other considerations, containment of the Soviet Union has been a constant basis for the justification of policies in Africa. The paramountcy of the East–

West issue was diminished somewhat in the early 1970s when the United States and France responded to the drought in the Sahel and when the United States joined other UN members in imposing sanctions against the Ian Smith regime in Rhodesia (now Zimbabwe). The shift resulted, in part, from the Nixon administration's preoccupation with other issues, such as Vietnam and Watergate, the growing strength of the Congressional Black Caucus in the House of Representatives, and the influence of Senator Hubert Humphrey, the then chairman of the Senate Foreign Relations Committee's subcommittee on Africa, who used his influence as chairman to stress the importance of issues such as agriculture, food, and population.

The revolution in Portugal in 1974 brought the East–West issue once more to the fore in Africa. Liberation movements supported by the Soviet Union had been active in both Mozambique and Angola, the two principal Portuguese colonies. When independence came, these movements made successful bids for power, outmaneuvering movements supported by the West. Cuban troops, with Soviet help, were moved to Angola, establishing, for the first time, a Soviet-backed military force on the continent. In that year's congressional hearings, officials of the State Department's Bureau of African Affairs, faced with the continuing issue of Rhodesia and the new developments in the former Portuguese colonies, emphasized the need for the United States to find peaceful solutions to African conflicts, to strengthen the front-line states against South Africa, and to provide assistance to Mozambique. The Congress, however, had other priorities, and two ensuing actions demonstrated the divisions that can occur over policy toward Africa—each related to the Soviet factor in African policy.

The first was the Byrd amendment on Rhodesian chrome. The UN sanctions against the regime of Ian Smith, which were supported by the United States, banned the purchase of minerals from Rhodesia. The chrome lobby in the United States was able to circumvent the ban by an amendment, offered by Senator Harry Byrd, that permitted the importation of Rhodesian chrome so long as the only alternative source was the Soviet Union. The amendment was opposed by the Bureau of African Affairs, but quietly encouraged by the White House.

In the second example, Congress moved in the opposite direction. An amendment, introduced by Senator Dick Clark, banned covert action to oppose the Marxist government in Angola. The Clark amendment passed in 1976 over strong opposition by the White House. It was repealed during the Reagan administration.

Both actions illustrate congressional preoccupation with the relationship of the Soviet Union to Africa. In the case of the Byrd amendment, that preoccupation was used to advance a special economic interest.

In the Carter administration, opinion was divided on the emphasis to be given to the Soviet presence in Africa. Early in the administration, differences arose over whether to extend military assistance to Somalia in its war with Ethiopia. Somalia had moved out of the Soviet camp and a Marxist government recently had come to power in Addis Ababa. The State Department favored a more neutral approach, in contrast to the view of the National Security Council staff that opposition to the Soviet and Cuban presence should guide U.S. policy. At that time, U.S. action was confined largely to rhetoric.

The Reagan administration placed strong emphasis on the Soviet factor. As indicated by the Congressional Research Service report,

> Rationales for aid changed somewhat after 1975 with the establishment of Marxist regimes in Mozambique and Angola, and later in Ethiopia. When the Reagan administration entered office, there was initially a very strong emphasis on security as a rationale for aid, with some attempt made to bring African countries into an East–West conflict framework. The emphasis softened considerably with time.[16]

Despite the last sentence, however, the report later states,

> Even if the economic strategy of U.S. assistance is increasingly influenced by accelerated development thinking, however, U.S. political interests have dictated that a U.S.-centered or security-oriented approach to African aid remains important. This can be seen in the concentration of aid on countries of special importance to the United States and in the growth of military assistance to several strategically located countries.[17]

The major accomplishment in Africa of the second Reagan administration was the conclusion of an accord between Angola, South Africa, and Cuba for the independence of Namibia and the withdrawal of Cuban troops from Angola. This accord, established in the Brazzaville Protocol of December 1988, was justified as much by the removal of the Cuban troops as by the independence of Namibia. The Reagan administration probably judged correctly, when it established the policy in 1981, that the only way to gain congressional support for the independence of Namibia was to link that issue to the withdrawal of Cuban troops from Angola. Accordingly, the administration stepped up aid to the anti-Communist Jonas Savimbi of the National Union for the Total Independence of Angola (UNITA).

During the Reagan presidency, African leaders who were received on official visits were generally those known as anti-Communists. The bulk of military and economic assistance went to those few states that either provided the United States access to military facilities, such as Somalia, Kenya, and Morocco, or assisted in U.S. covert actions, such as Zaïre. So dominant was the Soviet theme in U.S. policy-making in Africa that it was mentioned in connection with the famine in Ethiopia. Assistant Secretary of State for African Affairs Chester Crocker declared in March 1985 to Congress:

> I believe that the U.S. response says volumes to the Ethiopian people and to all of Africa. It speaks to our humanitarianism, to our direct relevance to Africa's most pressing problems, and to the failures of collectivist strategies and reliance on Soviet military aid when it is the economy and the poor who need help .... It is a strong and powerful message. We think it is the best of America and the strongest and most telling response we could make to the years of Soviet arms, Soviet ideology, and Soviet indifference to poverty that have dominated Ethiopia.[18]

The Post-Cold War Era

For 30 years, concern over Soviet activities in Africa has been a major factor in the presentation and support for U.S. programs in the region. The primary Soviet involvement was through military assistance to African nations. At the peak, in the four years from 1979 to 1983, Soviet deliveries to sub-Saharan African nations were estimated at nearly $5 billion. The bulk of this went to three countries: Libya, Ethiopia, and Algeria. This figure apparently does not include equipment sent to liberation movements. Economic aid was less. In 1984 (the last figure available), the sub-Saharan total was $536 million of which $268 million was earmarked for Ethiopia.[19] With the coming to power of Mikhail Gorbachev, Soviet policy changed. Although military and economic assistance has not ended, it is declining. As demonstrated by Soviet cooperation in the Angolan–Namibian settlement, Moscow now is more prepared to assist constructively in conflict resolution.

If improved U.S.–Soviet relations remove the East–West dilemma from Africa and, therefore, the rationale for significant U.S. programs in the African continent, will other U.S. interests emerge to justify the American presence in Africa?

The strong sentiment against apartheid in South Africa may provide a powerful base for support for active U.S. policies in Africa. The force of this issue was illustrated in the passage, over a presidential veto, of the Comprehensive Anti-Apartheid Act by the Congress in 1986. The anti-apartheid movement was able to muster valuable public support from wide and dramatic television coverage of riots in the South African townships and to cultivate the backing of a number of Republican congressmen from the South who had come to believe that their party would gain from embracing the anti-apartheid legislation.

The anti-apartheid cause has generated support for economic and military assistance programs to the frontline states that border and face military threats from South Africa. That cause does not have an appeal as broad as the anti-Soviet one, however, because a number of members of Congress, concerned about the Soviet threat, have ambivalent attitudes toward South Africa and are reluctant to espouse actions that appear to be directed against Pretoria. Such legislators see in South Africa a nation friendly to the United States, strategically placed, and confronted by a Communist threat from the ANC. In view of U.S. dialogue with the ANC and the Soviet Union's apparent interest in peaceful change within South Africa, displayed in discussions with the Pretoria government, the force of this argument in policy-making may diminish.

Nevertheless, some analysts have warned of the fragile nature of support for anti-apartheid measures. John Marcum has analyzed the composition of the majorities that voted for the Comprehensive Anti-Apartheid Act of 1986:

> Interviews with both advocates and opponents of such measures revealed more concern for being on the 'right side' of the issue than for strategic and realistic thinking about how best to facilitate fundamental reform at tolerable cost.[20]

The anti-apartheid movement is a coalition of active and interested groups growing out of the interests of the black community, churches, labor unions, and human rights organizations. These groups have led the lobbying for sanctions against South Africa, disinvestment, and a general reduction in official relations. Efforts of the anti-apartheid groups on behalf of assistance to other parts of sub-

Saharan Africa outside of the front-line states are less noticeable.

Although exceptions exist, the black community as a whole has never organized, as have some other ethnic groups, a strong national lobby on behalf of an active U.S. interest in black Africa. In part this is due to the concentration of many of America's black leaders on domestic issues within the United States and, in part, due to the absence of the strong economic base enjoyed by other ethnic groups.

If opposition to apartheid will not provide an alternative to the Soviet threat as a rationale for U.S. assistance programs in Africa, will not a broad appeal to humanitarian considerations?

The U.S. response to emergencies in Africa—which in this decade have included drought, famine, locust plagues, and massive refugee flows—often has been prompt and dramatic. U.S. efforts have matched, if not exceeded, those of other countries and, as in the case of the Ethiopian famine, have been directed toward countries regardless of their political orientation. Relief efforts are administered to a large extent through private voluntary agencies such as Catholic Relief Services, Church World Service, Africare, and CARE. Relief supplies are provided by the United States government through Public Law 480 Title II commodities. In the presentation to the Congress for fiscal year 1990, the Agency for International Development estimated the need for such commodities at $72 million in 20 countries. Of this amount, the largest quantity is scheduled for Mozambique, the second largest to Burkina Faso.

Such efforts have broad appeal, but they are short-term and often have few long-term development benefits. Emergency assistance often is inspired less by a perceived policy need than by the demand for a reaction to television coverage of human privation. A few individuals, such as the late Congressman Mickey Leland, as well as church organizations and academics have created pressure for a U.S. commitment to long-term recovery in Africa, but broad public support for humanitarian considerations is inclined to disappear once the scenes fade from the news.

Development assistance to Africa has faced the same obstacles as foreign assistance to other areas of the world: the general unpopularity in the Congress of foreign aid; the allocation of the majority of available resources to select countries (such as Israel and Egypt) for special political reasons; and the belief that many nations are unable to make effective use of the aid provided. Moreover, African development assistance has been the subject of debate among those who favor a "top–down" approach, advocates of a "bottom–up" approach, proponents of security-oriented economic aid, and those who emphasize internal reforms as a prerequisite to effective aid.[21] Nevertheless, ceilings on the number of eligible African countries have been removed and most African countries receive U.S. development assistance, either on a bilateral or regional basis. Development assistance is today the largest share of total U.S. aid to Africa.[22] Of the total of $554.5 million in development assistance requested for fiscal year 1990, $181.9 million is allotted to three regional accounts. A total of $50 million has been set aside to contribute to the Southern African Development Coordination Conference (SADCC), founded by the front-line states to reduce their economic dependence on South Africa. Another $55 million will go to the African Development Fund in order to encourage economic reform in sub-Saharan Africa.

Although the climate for U.S. private trade and investment in many African countries has improved over the early independence years, remaining high risks and the lack of confidence preclude anything more than low interest in the region on the part of U.S. business. As Carol Lancaster has observed,

> With the long period of economic mismanagement and political instability much of the continent has experienced, neither domestic nor foreign investors show much inclination to risk their money in Africa. Even with sustained economic reform and greater political stability, it will take time to create an atmosphere of confidence sufficient to attract investors.[23]

Current U.S. investment is largely in the extractive industries. The overall number of companies involved is being reduced as firms disinvest from South Africa. In 1986, imports from all of Africa, primarily petroleum products and minerals, comprised only 2.6 percent of total U.S. imports; exports to Africa made up only 2.7 percent of all U.S. exports. Private sector activity is not likely to sustain a significant U.S. presence in Africa. In 1973, a proposal was introduced in the Congress to create an Export Development Credit Fund "to finance exports by American firms to the poorest of the developing countries." The proposal, however, was stricken from the foreign aid legislation on the floor of the House by a vote of 240–137.[24]

Alternative bases for U.S. support for programs in Africa do exist, but only short-term humanitarian concerns have the same broad base of public support as that provided by the East–West rivalry. Support for development assistance, humanitarian aid, and anti-apartheid measures in Africa is likely to continue while limited U.S. military assistance will be allocated to those countries that provide U.S. forces with access to military facilities. Concerns over human rights and democratic institutions are likely to be reflected more in negative rather than positive actions. However, in the absence of a potent Soviet threat, it is difficult to see a basis for major U.S. initiatives in Africa involving substantial commitments of resources and requiring broad domestic support.

A U.S. Constituency on African Affairs?

In order to make future predictions, it is necessary to look at both negative and positive factors relating to support for Africa in the United States. Many African economies are in serious trouble and, for their own political reasons, African governments often resist the kinds of economic reforms that Western experts believe are necessary to bring about economic recovery. The unresolved massive debt problem continues to depress growth and hinder the effective use of external aid. African countries now have the world's highest population growth rates, a further impediment to economic growth. Corruption plagues many African countries, further discouraging investment, especially by the U.S. private sector.

Furthermore, serious human rights problems continue to generate concern in the United States, especially in two countries of strategic importance, Somalia and Zaïre. In addition, African rhetoric can offend Americans. On July 4, 1986, former President Jimmy Carter walked out of a reception at the U.S. embassy in Harare, Zimbabwe, when David Kariamazira, Zimbabwe's minister of youth, sport, and culture, attacked the United States for rejecting economic sanctions against South Africa and for bombing Libya. As a result of the incident, the Reagan administration suspended the disbursement of aid to Zimbabwe for an extended period.

These concerns are likely to remain. Regardless of the current preeminence of the East–West rivalry, the concerns could become significant issues in some countries. For example, the record of internal oppression and the human rights practices of Somalia and Zaïre now are subordinated to strategic considerations but might not be in a future, nonstrategic climate. The democratization of African governments will continue to be of interest to Washington and will generate support for U.S. programs.

On the other hand, there are positive indications of a continued interest in Africa and support for U.S. activities, even if they have less broad appeal than in a Cold War context.

Although domestic concerns will continue to compete with foreign affairs for attention in the American black community, significant organizations in the community as well as other anti-apartheid groups will continue to be important points of pressure on policymakers, especially concerning South Africa. If meaningful reforms commence there, divisions may well occur in the United States over their impact and scope and the degree of open support to be given by Washington. Nevertheless, the interest and demand for peaceful change in South Africa will remain. Washington likely will continue to bolster the security of the front-line states, so long as they are threatened by South Africa.

In the United States and in Africa, the perception will remain that the United States can play a useful role in conflict resolution, for the cases of Angola, Namibia, the Western Sahara, Ethiopia–Eritrea, and others. U.S. mediation will depend on the degree to which African nations wish the United States to be involved. Just how active the United States is likely to be in resolving disputes that do not involve the East–West rivalry remains to be seen.

U.S. economic interests in Africa, although not as extensive as in other regions, remain important. The degree of U.S. initiative in trade will depend to some extent on whether American firms sense a genuine improvement in the African economic situation. Beyond that, increased U.S. economic engagement in Africa will depend on the degree to which African countries are able to restructure their economies, leading them to genuine recovery and the ability to compete in the global context.

The East–West confrontation in Africa has diminished, with the varied policy implications cited above. The Cold War may be over, but many significant vestiges remain in Africa.

It is too soon to proclaim victory for the West, capitalism, or democracy in Africa. The Brazzaville accords calling for the independence of Namibia and the withdrawal of Cuban troops from Angola are being implemented, but the last Cuban soldier has yet to leave Luanda. The internal Angolan conflict between government forces, supported by the Soviets, and those of U.S.-backed UNITA has yet to be resolved. Soviet influence remains strong in Marxist Ethiopia, although the Ethiopian government displayed unprecedented cooperation with the United States during the Mickey Leland rescue effort.

On a broader scale, the deployment of Soviet armed forces provides continuing justification for the U.S. pursuit of port access rights such as those in Berbera, Somalia and Mombasa, Kenya. The future of U.S. access to these facilities will depend more on the perception in Washington of the continued need to support U.S. naval forces in the Indian Ocean not only to counter Soviet strength, but also to meet contingency plans of the Central Command in the Middle East. So long as the United States enjoys access to these facilities, U.S. geostrategic interests will provide a justification for official assistance to Somalia and Kenya.

The normalization of relations with Marxist governments such as Ethiopia and Angola will take time; some in the Congress may insist on the removal by democratic means of the current leaders before that can take place. Senator Orrin Hatch, an important conservative, has served notice on this point:

> On June 27, 1987, Congress unanimously approved H.R. 1827, signed into law by President Reagan on July 11, which condemns the Soviet–Cuban build-up in Angola and calls upon the United States to adopt those policies which will facilitate a negotiated settlement leading to free and fair elections. Last October, 51 members of the U.S. Senate, including 21 Democrats, sent a letter to President Reagan urging him to continue support to UNITA (the Angolan opposition movement led by Jonas Savimbi) until all Cuban forces have withdrawn from Angola, the Soviet Union has stopped supplying the Marxist MPLA regime, the MPLA has agreed to genuine national reconciliation and a date has been set for free and fair elections.[25]

In the case of Ethiopia, the current limits on relations are compounded by the continuation of unresolved problems from the close ties of the United States with the previous government of Emperor Haile Selassie. These include questions of compensation for the nationalization of U.S. companies and Ethiopian claims arising from the U.S. decision to stop the delivery of military equipment when the emperor was overthrown.

Conclusion

Periodic talks on African issues have taken place between representatives of the United States and the Soviet Union, with the most recent in June 1989. Apart from cooperation on Namibia and Angola, the talks have led to no agreements on the resolution of other African issues. From what is known of the talks, they consisted mainly of a review of the assessment of each of the issues in Africa. Soviet diplomacy remains active in the continent; a breakthrough in dialogue even has been achieved with the staunchly anti-Communist government of South Africa.

Nevertheless, a total coincidence of approaches to African issues between the United States and the Soviet Union seems unlikely. The Soviets will continue to have points of view distinct from the United States toward liberation issues, different obligations to traditional friends, and responsibilities as a permanent member of the United Nations Security Council. In the future, Moscow may not be as active or confrontational, but neither will it be completely out of the picture.

Continuing Soviet activities in the continent still will provide a basis for administration requests for assistance to Africa and serve as a criterion to assess the orientation of African leaders. This will be especially true in the event that the Cubans and the Angolan government do not implement fully their part of the Brazzaville accords. Furthermore, those who see liberation movements such as the ANC or Namibia's South West Africa People's Organization (SWAPO) as Communist, because of past support by the Soviet Union, will continue to oppose U.S. cooperation with them, and will point to their actions as evidence of continuing Soviet presence and aggressive policy in Africa.

In the last analysis, the justification of African programs on the basis of a Soviet or Communist threat will depend on the U.S. public's perception of the relationship with Moscow. If that relationship proceeds to the point at which the Congress, reflecting changed perceptions, no longer seeks or accepts the Soviet threat as a justification for programs, policymakers in the executive branch will need to find other premises to justify an active U.S. presence in the continent. That time, however, has not yet come.

Notes

1. U.S. Department of State, *Realism, Strength, Negotiation: Key Foreign Policy Statements of the Reagan Administration* (Washington, DC: Government Printing Office, May 1984), p. 19.

2. From the personal recollection of the author. To his knowledge, the study was not published.

3. William H. Lewis, "U.S. Military Assistance to Africa," *CSIS Africa Notes* 75 (August 6, 1987).

4. William G. Hyland, "Setting Global Priorities," *Foreign Policy* 73 (Winter 1988–1989), pp. 22–40.

5. In the 43rd United Nations General Assembly (1988), African nations, on the average, voted with the United States in only 9.5 percent of the plenary votes. See: *Report to Congress on Voting Practices in the United Nations*, submitted by the Department of State pursuant to Public Law 100–461 and Public Law 98–164, April 20, 1989, pages II-3 and II-4.

6. Howard Wolpe, "Seizing Southern African Opportunities," *Foreign Policy* 73 (Winter 1988–1989), p. 63.

7. In the request for military assistance to sub-Saharan Africa for fiscal year 1990, the four largest recipients are Kenya and Somalia (which provides U.S. access to military facilities), Chad (threatened by Libya), and Zaïre (which assists in funneling clandestine aid to the anti-Communist forces of Jonas Savimbi in Angola).

8. A level of $33 million in development assistance is proposed for Zaïre in the fiscal year 1990 budget; the next largest recipients are Kenya ($30 million), the Republic of South Africa ($21.6 million to be allocated to South African blacks), Senegal ($22 million), and Cameroon, Malawi, and Mozambique ($20 million each).

9. Congressional Research Service, *U.S. Aid to Africa: The Record, the Rationales, and the Challenge*, prepared for the House Committee on Foreign Affairs, Subcommittee on Africa (January 7, 1986), p. vii.

10. Ibid., p. 21.

11. G. Mennen Williams, *Africa for Africans* (Grand Rapids, Mich.: William B. Eerdmans, 1969), p. 97.

12. Martin Lowenkopf, "If the Cold War is Over in Africa, Will the United States Still Care?" *CSIS Africa Notes* 98 (May 30, 1989).

13. I. William Zartman, "Why Africa Matters," *CSIS Africa Notes* 86 (June 30, 1988).

14. John F. Kennedy, *Inaugural Address*, January 20, 1961. See U.S. Department of State, *Bulletin*, February 6, 1961, pp. 654–656.

15. Williams, *Africa for the Africans*, p. 71.

16. Congressional Research Service, *U.S. Aid to Africa*, p. vii.

17. Ibid., p. 83.

18. Statement by Assistant Secretary of State Chester Crocker before the Senate Foreign Relations Committee on January 17, 1985, as cited in the U.S. Department of State, *Bulletin* 85:2096 (March 1985), p. 24.

19. Abraham S. Becker, *The Soviet Union and the Third World: The Economic Dimension*, RAND Occasional Paper OPS-005.

20. John A. Marcum, "Africa: A Continent

Adrift," *Foreign Affairs* 68:1 (Winter 1989), p. 172.

21. For a full development of this debate, see Congressional Research Service report, *U.S. Aid to Africa*, p. 80ff.

22. The estimated obligations for fiscal year 1990 were Development Assistance, $554.5 million; Economic Support Funds, $152.1 million; PL 480 (food aid) Title I, $106 million and Title II, $67.6 million; IMET (military training), $9.1 million; and Military Assistance (MAP), $25.7 million.

23. Carol Lancaster, *U.S. Aid to Sub-Saharan Africa: Challenges, Constraints, and Choices*, CSIS Significant Issues Series 10:16 (1988), p. 12. See also her essay appearing in this Winter 1990 issue (13:1) of *The Washington Quarterly*.

24. Congressional Research Service, *U.S. Aid to Africa*, p. 48.

25. Orrin Hatch, "The Lessons and Challenges of Angola," *Washington Times*, June 13, 1989, p. F4.

IV. Updating Policy Instruments

Can Arms Control Survive Peace?

James E. Goodby

THE EAST EUROPEAN revolutions of 1989 and clear signs of instability in the Soviet Union have prompted some respected and highly qualified observers to ask why we bother to negotiate arms-control agreements with the Soviets. At a time when East European governments are demanding that Soviet troops be sent home, why bother with the arcana of treaties? In the *Washington Post* of February 9, 1990, Charles Krauthammer asked "What on earth are we doing still at the conventional arms talks in Vienna? . . . who needs all these negotiated categories and compromises?" On May 20, 1990, writing in the *New York Times*, Thomas L. Friedman said that "many Soviet and American citizens have been asking themselves lately: In the postcold-war world, why should I care about arms control any more?" He added that "the most immediate threat to the United States–Soviet relationship is not the possibility of one side's suddenly raining nuclear missiles on the other . . . the talks over conventional arms levels in Europe have been almost totally overtaken by events."

James E. Goodby is distinguished service professor at Carnegie Mellon University. He was the head of the U.S. delegation to the Stockholm Conference on Disarmament in Europe, vice chairman of the U.S. delegation to the strategic arms reduction talks (START), and ambassador to Finland during a 35-year career as a Foreign Service officer.

This latest wave of doubts about the merits of force reductions achieved through negotiated agreements has lent credibility to a view that arms control is no longer relevant to international security relations. Impatient with long-drawn-out negotiations and discouraged by the bickering attendant upon the ratification and implementation of arms-control treaties, many advocates of arms control prefer nonnegotiated, reciprocal, or parallel force reductions—"arms control without agreements."[1] This was true even before the dawn of the new era in U.S.–Soviet relations pronounced by Presidents George Bush and Mikhail Gorbachev at their Malta summit. The idea has gained even more supporters since then. Of course, some skeptics always have doubted whether the results of arms control are worth the effort, and some military people and defense analysts always have asserted that force structure decisions should be kept in the hands of U.S. decision makers, not shared with others through the process of arms control.

Arms-control processes surely must change with changing times, and their relevance must be reexamined. Before discarding arms control and the negotiated treaty method of accomplishing its purposes, however, it is prudent to look more closely at what arms control could do in the new era and at arms control without agreements. Defenders of the negotiating process also

161

need to consider whether the management of treaty implementation could be improved. The latter question is especially important now that two major new ground-breaking arms-control treaties are expected to be completed this year.

The Treaty Approach and Alternatives to It

Arms control is popularly considered to consist of limitations on and reductions of weapon systems and armed forces. There is, however, another form of arms control that is aimed at monitoring, regulating, and assessing the *operations* of military forces. Operational arms control is important for what it can do to deter surreptitious preparations for an attack, to clarify ambiguities, to reduce the level of incidents when the military forces of two or more nations are operating in close proximity to one another, and generally to create a security regime in which cooperation replaces at least some aspects of confrontation. Many agreements exist in this area that have not taken the form of treaties—the 1986 Stockholm document on confidence- and security-building measures in Europe, for example—but all of them have been meticulously negotiated and reduced to the precise language of commitments. The ratification procedure, however, has not been invoked.

When it comes to actual force cuts and limitations, the presumption in U.S. law is that the Senate will be asked to give its consent to ratification. The requirement in the Constitution that such consent to ratification must be based on mustering the votes of two-thirds of the Senate—in effect, to support an agreement negotiated with a sometimes bitter adversary—has presented recent U.S. administrations with a daunting challenge. The evidence of the past several months is that it is far easier to reduce U.S. forces unilaterally through budget cuts than through negotiated treaties, even though the latter would result in reducing the forces of other countries as well.

The alternative to some form of negotiated arms control is, in fact, uncoordinated force cuts and unilaterally determined modernization programs—the two sides of the restructuring coin. Obviously, such restructuring will not yield automatic improvements in stability. Worse still, the results of haphazard cuts could be a military relationship between the major powers that is even less stable than the one that exists today. Throughout the nuclear age, stability never has been achieved to the satisfaction of military planners; new weapon systems never have been able to overcome the dilemma of how to improve the security of one country without impairing the security of others. There will be reductions in the levels of U.S. defense spending and hence in levels of armaments, but whether the result will be a more stable and controllable international situation is anybody's guess.

In theory, reciprocal, nonnegotiated reductions should be able to achieve a stable military balance. Exercising restraint in the procurement of new weapon systems could be an even more important achievement of a coordinated, but nonnegotiated arms-control regime. This prospect certainly deserves more attention by governments. In practice, however, it is very difficult to coordinate force structure planning. In the United States, the sharing of power by the executive and legislative branches complicates the process of force planning. Despite *glasnost*, Soviet force planning still is shrouded in secrecy. Neither government has shown much appetite for inviting the other into what could amount to a joint force planning exercise. The sharing of some general information on trends might well occur in the predecision phase of force planning—a situation far from coordinated restructuring.

What is true for the United States and the Soviet Union is likely to be true also for other pairs of countries or alliances. Even in NATO, force planning decisions are mainly the product of national decisions rooted in domestic considerations, despite incentives and pressures for coordination among close allies. Furthermore, in circumstances such as those prevailing in Europe, informal understandings about force levels are not likely to become a substitute for long-term treaty obligations, which almost certainly will be a necessary part of a political settlement. This is evident from the discussions in and around the two-plus-four talks. For example, on May 17, 1990, an obviously well-informed senior administration official spoke of conventional and nuclear negotiations as "part of creating a context of progress in East–West relations in which we might hope to persuade Mr. Gorbachev that Germany's relationship in NATO is a sensible notion." It is the main answer to those who question why we bother with the negotiations on Conventional Forces in Europe (CFE) at this time. Another answer, mentioned by the secretary-general of NATO, is that only by securing treaty rights can we limit and verify the levels of Soviet forces in the Soviet Union.

Both negotiated measures and arms-control-without-agreements are liable to the same vulnerabilities. The fact that arms-control-without-agreements may be imposed by the harsh realities of declining budgets does not insulate it from the same pressures that can operate against any form of arms control. Threats to any arms-control regime, whether negotiated or not, will arise if the existing mood of accommodation gives way to sharp confrontation. When Soviet Premier Nikita Khrushchev decided to raise the level of tension during his 1961 campaign to weaken the Western position in Berlin, he broke a three-year nonnegotiated moratorium on nuclear weapons tests with a series of nuclear explosions in the atmosphere, including the largest ever detonated. A massive shift in strategic assumptions would have the same effect. An informal, even undeclared arms-control regime of sorts existed from 1963, when the United States removed its Jupiter missiles from Turkey, until 1983, when U.S. intermediate-range missiles again were deployed in Europe. A shift in West European assumptions about the deterrent effect of NATO's nuclear and conventional forces led to a decision to abandon that regime. Over time, perhaps because of a more or less benign strategic environment, some of the involved parties could begin to think of any arms-control regime as irrelevant to their needs. Moral pressures on governments to refrain from the use of chemical weapons was probably more effective in perpetuating an arms-control regime in this area than the Geneva Protocol which codified that obligation. Those pressures, and the language of the Protocol, were insufficient to prevent the use of chemical weapons when some governments concluded that the preservation of a non-use regime was an irrelevancy, at best. Arms-control-without-agreements is even more vulnerable to changing circumstances than arms control registered in a formal treaty because there are no formal laws or treaty obligations to restrain governments. Of course, this very flexibility is seen by some as a main advantage of reciprocal, informal reductions.

The particular faults of the treaty approach are many—ponderous negotiations, premises overtaken by time, and sluggish adaptation to change. The informal reciprocal approach avoids these pitfalls. This method, however, has yet to prove that it is capable of doing all the things that arms control is supposed to do. Stability and predictability at lower force levels, with some limits on systems that seem to cause special security problems (for example, multiple independently targetable reentry vehicles or MIRVs), are some of the features that come to mind in considering the purposes of arms control. Only a bargain struck and a contract recorded are likely to deal with these specific needs. It is difficult to escape the conclusion that parallel, reciprocal, or unilateral force reductions will not—except by chance—achieve these purposes of arms control. In these areas, we are stuck with negotiations and formal agreements—whether "treaties" or not is a separate matter—and we should think about how to make the process work better than it has in the past.

Overcoming the Drawbacks of the Treaty Approach

The problems with negotiated formal agreements on arms control can be overcome partially. Some "problems," of course, should not be liquidated because they are part of what makes a formal agreement different from and superior to informal understandings. An obligation to do things in a certain way for a certain amount of time may be awkward, but is one way of dealing with instability and unpredictability. What could be avoided, as we have witnessed recently, are the protracted, nonserious negotiations of the past that have given arms control a reputation for frivolity.

There may be innovative approaches to negotiations that also could expedite matters. Senator Sam Nunn (D-Ga.) has mentioned "two-tier" negotiations, for example, in which one level of talks would be exploratory and general in nature, the other formal and detailed. Perhaps the new era in U.S.–Soviet relations will make that easier to do than in the past. Clearly, the new state of East–West relations requires a fresh look at how arms-control negotiations are conducted.

The other major problem that needs review and remedial action could be described as the management of arms-control agreements. Governments have not given this aspect of their responsibilities the high-level attention it deserves except when something goes wrong and political pressures mount to "do something." The result is that the leadership qualities of foresight, judgment, and a sense of proportion have been lacking in the implementation of treaties; second or third order issues have become magnified because they were not attended to in time. This shortcoming of negotiated formal agreements also can be overcome and must be if the Strategic Arms Reduction Talks (START) and CFE treaties are to do what is expected of them. The problems of treaty management should be reviewed and improved methods of management proposed before START and CFE are completed. These two treaties may be the most significant arms-control treaties of them all. If we cannot manage them properly, the future of arms control in any form will be in doubt.

The literature of arms control does not shed much light on the management of arms-control treaties. Most of what has been written on the subject deals with compliance problems—not the sum total of treaty management by any means.[2] Treaty management also should include such tasks as effective oversight of treaty-related activities, anticipating problems and planning to deal with them, and exploiting the beneficial, and perhaps transitory, effects of an arms-control treaty, both within and outside the field of arms control.

Arms-control treaties nearly always have been in some kind of trouble. Nothing suggests that the START and CFE treaties will be any easier to manage successfully than previous arms-control agreements. To the contrary, these agreements will be more difficult to administer than any of the others by orders of magnitude. The special characteristics of these two agreements are unique; new and different problems of implementation will certainly confront their adherents from the very beginning. Challenges to the smooth operation of the treaties will arise from special factors such as the following:

- The treaties may be transitional instruments in a rapidly evolving security environment;
- The treaties' provisions may be applied to deeper reductions and more stringent constraints on military operations than those for which they were designed;
- In the case of CFE, multilateral participation with equal rights for all participants will pose complex coordination problems;
- Intrusive and vigorously exercised verification systems for both treaties will conflict with perceptions of national sovereignty;
- Regulations affecting a wide spectrum of military operations will raise legal and other issues for defense establishments; and
- Formal and frequently used consultative machinery will require constant attention by political leaders.

In addition to these special management problems, experience in implementing other arms-control agreements shows that other, more "normal" difficulties will arise.

- Disputes over treaty implementation. Whether these be over verification provisions or over definitions of weapon systems, such disputes will occur and will become politically contentious.
- Modernization of weapon systems. As various nations replace weapon systems limited by the treaties, disputes will arise over capabilities, numbers, deployments, and a variety of worries that accompany such changes.
- Activities tangentially related to the treaties. In the case of CFE, military actions around the periphery of the reduction zone will raise questions about treaty compliance. The impact of air and naval movements and mobilization exercises on the treaty probably will be questioned.
- Conduct of military exercises and movements. Again in the case of CFE, those activities permitted within the zone of reductions will be watched closely and probably criticized. Training alerts, for example, and movements into and out of the zone will be liable to misinterpretation and dispute.
- Tit-for-tat behavior. If one country presses to the limits of what is permitted by the treaties—and perhaps a bit beyond—other countries will tend to follow suit. Such behavior almost certainly will occur from

time to time and will be a major source of noncompliance charges.
- Data disputes. Almost any list of data is open to question as to its authenticity or its conformity with prescribed requirements. In particular, data about manpower are extremely difficult to verify with great precision.
- Flaws in treaty drafting. Despite everyone's best efforts, there will be ambiguities, omissions, and loopholes in the treaties. The potential for tit-for-tat noncompliance in such situations is very high.

Are any of these issues presidential or prime ministerial business? Potentially any one of these could be and, in other arms-control treaties, some have been. The president's reports to Congress on noncompliance with arms-control agreements are full of such issues. The lesson is that in controversial matters—as arms control is—national leaders have not finished their work when they are authorized to ratify a treaty. Such treaties need almost constant high-level scrutiny by someone who can warn a national leader when issues are becoming politically sensitive. This, in turn, requires the kind of "tending" of agreements described by Flowerree: "some government officials must live with them full-time, all the time."[3]

Three basic principles should guide any U.S. administration in its management of arms-control treaties. First, the nation's political leadership should conduct the management process within the context of broad national objectives; single issue politics should not bias this process. Second, verification, in contrast to monitoring, should be recognized and accepted for what it is: judgment calls and reconciliation of conflicting opinions. It is not simply an intelligence function. Third, field operations, like onsite inspections, should not become the function of one of the interested policy agencies; the perception of tampering with the evidence must be excluded.

Organization Priorities

These principles have organizational consequences. Presidents and their most senior advisers must see to it that key management issues are evaluated at a level sufficiently close to the top of the executive branch so that decisions are not distorted by the limited responsibilities of subordinates in any one of the agencies. Essentially, this requirement means that the president's assistant for national security affairs should establish a treaty oversight unit within the White House staff.

Verification and monitoring are two different functions. Monitoring is the collection of data concerning a party's behavior relevant to treaty obligations. Such data may be ambiguous and subject to interpretation. Experts, whether intelligence, legal, or military, are, by themselves, inadequate interpreters of data and evaluators of treaty compliance. All of them together, under the leadership of someone entrusted with broad executive responsibilities, should participate in the judgment process that is the essence of verification.

Field operations are a relatively new part of arms control. There was not much of this, at least on an international basis, prior to 1987. The first onsite inspection in the Soviet Union took place in August of that year under the terms of the Stockholm document, which dealt with confidence- and security-building measures. Onsite inspections under the treaty on intermediate-range nuclear forces (INF) began in 1988 in the United States, the Soviet Union, and European countries where INF missiles were based. In the United States, an On-site Inspection Agency (OSIA) was established within the Department of Defense to deal with the INF treaty. It is headed by an army general, relies on military logistics, and reports to the undersecretary of defense for acquisitions. Policy guidance is provided by an interagency committee.

This agency is likely to assume responsibility for other field operations under new agreements. It is questionable whether the primary arms-control inspection service of the United States should be run indefinitely as an arm of the Department of Defense. This conclusion is *not* because the present arrangement has produced flawed results; indeed, OSIA has been doing an exemplary job in the first years of its life. It is clear, however, that the resources devoted to inspection activities are going to be very substantial in the future. To charge the expense of this activity against the defense budget and to use increasingly scarce defense manpower for inspection purposes is a questionable diversion of these resources. In addition, this procedure tends to obscure the true cost of the verification function.

OSIA should be established as an independent operating arm of the executive branch with its head a subcabinet civilian official subject to Senate confirmation. An alternative would be to establish a link between the Arms Control and Disarmament Agency (ACDA) and OSIA so that the director of ACDA also would supervise OSIA. This arrangement would recognize that ACDA's future is more connected with arms-control inspection operations than with negotiations or research. Negotiations inevitably become the domain of the secretary of state while research dollars are given to the Departments of Defense and Energy, not ACDA.

With the U.S. government organized and operating in accordance with the three principles outlined above, the president would have the tools and the information available to manage arms-control treaties in a manner that would secure maximum benefits for the United States.

Effective management of the CFE treaty also will be dependent upon an international staff. CFE will include provisions for a multilateral consultative forum, and because the actions of 23 different governments, rather than only 2, will be subject to microscopic scrutiny and second-guessing, its agenda will be a heavy one. To deal with it, members of the new institution will have to be in constant communication. Therefore, the forum will amount to a standing committee, quite possibly of the Conference on Security and Cooperation in Europe (CSCE). As such, it will take on considerable political importance going well beyond the "mere" administration of a treaty. It will be an instrument for managing what amounts to the beginning of a regime of cooperative security, embracing nearly all of Europe.

To deal with this within NATO, the secretary-general will need to organize the secretariat to provide support for these inspections and related efforts. The U.S. secretary of state has proposed that NATO should establish a verification staff, and that probably will be done. Perhaps NATO should go further, however, and organize itself to deal more effectively with other aspects of constructing the new Europe. More frequent meetings of CSCE ministers and conciliation machinery within the CSCE framework, as suggested by the United States, call for some supporting mechanism in NATO. The post of assistant secretary-general for cooperative security operations should be created as soon as possible because the amount of day-to-day work on verification and other matters relating to Europe whole and free soon will be more than the existing structure can handle. Unless NATO organizes itself properly to deal with these delicate matters, the management of the CFE treaty and other issues of cooperative security will deteriorate quickly into squabbling and chaos. This management function obviously is one at which NATO must succeed if it is to adapt to life in the new Europe.

Conclusion

Arms-control agreements could become a relic of the Cold War as other, seemingly more pressing issues pass it by. What to do with the so-called peace dividend is the only hot political issue that bears any remote resemblance to the peace issues that stirred voters in the early 1980s. The connection between the peace dividend and arms control is, in fact, tenuous, because reductions in defense spending will be only partly the result of arms-control agreements. Inevitably, arms control is sinking toward the bottom of the national and international agenda. Ironically, those who defend the importance of negotiated arms-control agreements in the new era will be deemed conservatives, nostalgic for the Cold War and intellectually frozen in time. Even in the field of arms control, the problems of missile and other high-tech proliferation are beginning to claim priority attention over the problems of negotiated build downs in nuclear and conventional forces.

In such an environment, arms-control-without-agreements might be the best and only answer to dismantling the tens of thousands of nuclear weapons and advanced conventional weapons that have not yet been touched by arms-control agreements. Coordinated restructuring of the military forces of the major powers is an attractive solution to the problem of bringing military potential into line with new political relationships, but the prospects for this solution are not very encouraging. Even to define stability in some form that several governments can accept and use as a guideline for restructuring their military forces has not so far been possible. The most interesting area of exploration lies in the proposal now before the Conference on Confidence- and Security-building Measures to share information about defense budgets. Further development of this approach could lead to useful results. Unfortunately, most nations are assigning higher priority to destroying old weapons than to coordinating mutual restraint in the building of new ones.

For better or worse, the START and CFE agreements are the last, best hope for establishing military relationships among the major powers based on firm understandings about how those relationships should develop in the future. If skillfully managed, those treaties could provide the infrastructure for much deeper, more far-reaching reductions and limitations than those now under consideration. Yet, the possibility that those treaties could fail through lack of proper management of their implementation is very real. If that were to happen, arms control would become one of the impediments to building the new era, not one of its most important tasks.

This article represents the views of the author and not necessarily those of his present or previous institutional connections.

Notes

1. The phrase originated with Kenneth Adelman, former director of the Arms Control and Disarmament Agency.

2. Charles Flowerree's excellent article, "On Tending Arms Control Agreements," *The Washington Quarterly* 13:1 (Winter 1990), is a welcome recent exception to this practice. The author stresses that "the means by which these agreements survive and adapt to changing conditions after they enter into force deserve as much attention as the negotiations that produced them in the first place." (p. 199)

3. *Ibid.*, p. 213.

U.S. Intelligence in an Age of Uncertainty: Refocusing to Meet the Challenge

Paula L. Scalingi

U.S. INTELLIGENCE, AFTER more than 40 years of evolution, is at a watershed. Created to counter the threats inherent in a bipolar world, today its mission is no longer relevant. The Union of Soviet Socialist Republics no longer exists. With the primary adversary gone, some national security experts are calling for draconian cuts in U.S. defense spending and for the United States to retreat from its international responsibilities. Among these voices are those who would substantially curtail the U.S. intelligence effort, even dismantle the Central Intelligence Agency (CIA). Most of the U.S. foreign policy establishment, however, with an eye to history, recognize that in an uncertain world a strong intelligence capability is a necessity. Thus, it is a matter of determining how best to strengthen and refocus U.S. intelligence to meet the challenges of a new era. Indeed, the extraordinary and unexpected events of the past two years—including the conflict in the Persian Gulf, the abortive coup in the Soviet Union, and their respective reverberations—underscore the need for accurate, forward-looking intelligence.

Even before the demise of the USSR, the end of the Cold War, budgetary constraints, and new international uncertainties had reinvigorated long-standing congressional interest in strengthening the individual and collective output of the dozen or so entities that comprise the intelligence community. There is currently an emerging consensus within the congressional committees that oversee intelligence that the community is not prepared to meet the challenges of the 1990s. The House and Senate Intelligence Committees and the Senate Armed Services Committee made suggestions on reorganization and the need to improve communitywide management in their respective reports on their fiscal year 1992 authorization bills.[1] The committees have indicated that they intend to take an even more activist approach to reform in calendar year 1992.

Community members, for their part, have undertaken their own internal reviews of programs and resources and have already taken some modest steps. The future role, structure, and,

---

Paula Scalingi is a professional staff member of the U.S. House of Representatives Permanent Select Committee on Intelligence. For 10 years she served in various analytical positions at the Central Intelligence Agency. She was most recently a strategic affairs specialist with the U.S. Arms Control and Disarmament Agency, where she served on the U.S. Delegation to the Strategic Arms Reduction Talks.

ultimately, effectiveness of U.S. intelligence will depend on how well Congress, the executive branch, and the community cooperate in undertaking the necessary initiatives.

Looking for a New World Order

What the international scene will look like in six months, a year, or five years from now is problematical. The post–World War II structure has been swept away and nearly three-quarters of a century of Communist rule in the USSR ended. Even the best intelligence analysts know better than to try to predict with any certainty trends and outcomes beyond the immediate.

The major impetus behind the genesis of the intelligence community was the Soviet threat—namely, the threat from the USSR, its allies and friends, Communist regimes, and radical political organizations. With the exception of the CIA, which was created by legislation, the other major community organizations were created by executive directive to cope with requirements generated by the Cold War. Also, unlike the independent CIA, they function as part of a parent agency. (The Defense Intelligence Agency [DIA], the National Security Agency [NSA], and the organization that handles U.S. national technical means systems are technically part of the Department of Defense; the Federal Bureau of Investigation [FBI] is part of the Justice Department, and the State Department's intelligence component is the Bureau of Intelligence and Research. The Departments of Energy and the Treasury and the military services have their own intelligence components.) Successive U.S. administrations have tinkered with the structure and mission of these organizations, often for political reasons, but have never considered a major restructuring.[2]

The CIA, alone among the members of the community, has a comprehensive mission. Its all-source collection and analytical efforts have traditionally covered all regions of the world and functional areas. The Soviet threat, however, until very recently, was the primary target within this broad, international context. Thus, CIA components tasked with covering, for example, Central America, the Middle East, or Africa tended to focus on Soviet machinations in those regions. Collection and analysis on technology transfer, emerging technologies, weapons development and monitoring, nonproliferation, and economic analysis were also skewed in that direction. Not unexpectedly, many top and mid-level CIA managers have made their reputation as Soviet experts or spent a portion of their career dealing with Soviet-related concerns. For example, both the current deputy director of Central Intelligence, Richard Kerr, and his predecessor, Robert Gates, are former Soviet analysts.

For the other community members involved in strategic intelligence—the DIA and the NSA—the Soviet threat has been the paramount focus chiefly because of these agencies' defense orientation. In the area of tactical intelligence, emphasis until very recently was on intelligence support in the event of an East–West conflict.

Through the decades, the amount of funds Congress has pumped into intelligence programs has ebbed and flowed, influenced by the public perception of the relative coolness of U.S.–Soviet relations. The biggest intelligence buildup, however, occurred in the 1980s. As a result of the revolution in Iran and direct or indirect Soviet interventionism in Afghanistan,

Poland, Central America, and Africa, there was a broad political consensus in the early Reagan years that intelligence needed to be strengthened with expanded covert action programs, personnel, and technical collection assets.

The community naturally greeted this new state of affairs with considerable enthusiasm, particularly the CIA, which had experienced personnel cuts and a diminished prestige during the Carter administration. The aura of optimism was best expressed by one top intelligence manager, who observed that in the "fat years" U.S. intelligence should move to "stack new officers like cordwood" to prepare for the inevitable belt-tightening in the post-Reagan era.

The result was an unprecedented, and at times uncoordinated, buildup of U.S. intelligence assets—collection and information-processing technologies, personnel, and infrastructure. Intelligence agencies hustled to hire and acquire and to secure more space to house their burgeoning resources. The DIA built a spacious flagship building at Bolling Air Force Base and immediately began lobbying to expand the facility. The CIA constructed a second behemoth building on its headquarters compound, ostensibly to consolidate its work force, which was dispersed in leased buildings throughout the Washington area. The additional space proved woefully inadequate by the time the structure was completed in 1987. The CIA now leases an even greater number of buildings to handle the overflow and in summer 1991 designated two sites on which it wants to construct large facilities.

In true bureaucratic fashion, the number and scope of intelligence requirements in the 1980s increased to accommodate the rapidly expanding work force. Within the CIA's Directorate of Intelligence, an analyst tasked with covering a particular country or issue was soon sharing this responsibility with two or more analysts, each now handling a subset of the same account. In certain cases, a branch (the Directorate's smallest organizational unit) of a few analysts tasked with a single topic mushroomed into a division several times its original size. Although some of this rapid growth was justified on the basis of new requirements, much of the increase was associated with the emphasis on Soviet and East–West issues. For example, in 1979, the Directorate had two analysts specifically tasked with covering the North Atlantic Treaty Organization (NATO) and associated European security issues. By 1988, there were two separate divisions within the Office of European Analysis working on such issues, as well as dozens of analysts in the sprawling Office of Soviet Analysis and other analytical components.

Consequently, turf battles became the norm—between analysts on the same account, within divisions in the same office, and between competing offices. Analysts increasingly found themselves forced to coordinate their work with several components and their many counterparts in different parts of the Directorate.

The agencies and organizations involved in defense intelligence also experienced unprecedented overall growth. The DIA, the NSA, and the military services substantially beefed up their collection and analytical capabilities.

By the late 1980s, the community was expanding its focus somewhat beyond the Soviet threat to meet new requirements. State-sponsored terrorism, high-profile espionage cases, and the international drug trade became major areas of concern, leading the Director of Central Intelligence (DCI) to create centers for counterterrorism, counterintelligence, and counternarcotics. The implementation of the Treaty to Eliminate Intermediate-Range Nuclear Forces and anticipated follow-on treaties on conventional and strategic nuclear forces resulted in the expansion of the small Arms Control Intelligence Staff, then part of the CIA's Directorate of Intelligence, into a communitywide body several times the original size and directly under the DCI.

Current and Future Requirements

The demands on the intelligence community today to isolate and assess pressing issues and predict future crises accurately are greater than ever before. The United States has had the luxury for half a century of knowing who its chief adversaries were. Now the world is experiencing one of its periodic eras of instability. The community in the 1990s must be able to cover a diverse array of regional and functional topics and have the personnel and technical resources, as well as management flexibility, necessary to fulfill this mission.

Today, the challenges facing the community are daunting. In the Middle East, the defeat of Iraq has left a power vacuum that its neighbors will move to fill. Third world countries continue to develop weapons of mass destruction with the help of armaments and technologies provided by industrialized nations. In the USSR, the moderate revolution begun by the Gorbachev regime in the mid-1980s has, in the wake of the August 1991 coup attempt, led to the demise of an empire and an uncertain future for its components. Once again, in Europe and elsewhere, ethnic and nationalist rivalries are threatening to undermine the status quo. It is useful to remember that since the mid-nineteenth century, these forces have helped cause several major and lesser conflicts, including two world wars. As history has shown, the United States can ill afford to take an ad hoc approach to national security planning and act only when the crisis is upon it. Desert Shield/Desert Storm and the subsequent belated discovery of Baghdad's advanced nuclear weapons program are grim reminders of this fact.

Intelligence managers, spurred by budget cutbacks and congressional concerns over the direction of the community in a post–cold war world, are reassessing and in some cases restructuring the way they do business. The CIA, the DIA, and the NSA have been reviewing their programs and requirements. For example, the CIA has reassigned a portion of its Soviet military and technical experts to other responsibilities and has been downsizing in other areas. The military services are consolidating and coordinating their collection and analytical operations. The Department of Defense (DOD) has adopted a plan that streamlines defense intelligence programs, promotes joint cooperation, and gives the Office of the Secretary of Defense greater coordination responsibilities.

Meanwhile, the congressional oversight committees are holding hearings and collecting data to better determine current and future intelligence needs. The committees have reacted positively to community efforts to strengthen intelligence but note that further initiatives are necessary. The committees also maintain that their own studies are in the early phase and that in the authorization legislation for fiscal year 1993 they intend to be ready to take more vigorous action if the community is reluctant to undertake the necessary steps.[3]

The committees have several areas under study that are of particular importance: creation of a director of National Intelligence, the devising of charters for certain community organizations established by executive directive, consolidation of duplicative programs, identification of the key intelligence requirements for the 1990s, and follow-up on the lessons learned from Operation Desert Shield/Desert Storm.

Reorganization Issues

Congressional interest in legislating changes in the leadership structure of the community and devising charters for individual agencies is not new but has fluctuated in concert with the perceived need to strengthen and reform intelligence.[4] This latest congressional push for restructuring and reorienting U.S. intelligence has stemmed, as noted previously, from budgetary constraints and the end of the Cold War. Other factors, however, have a role, including the continued fallout from the Iran–Contra investigation and the recognition that the intelligence community greatly needs consolidation, more cross-component cooperation, and overall better management.

Old ideas to rectify these shortcomings have been resurrected toward this end, including the creation of a cabinet-level director of National Intelligence. The rationale is that the CIA has long ceased to be the dominant player in U.S. intelligence while defense intelligence has become a major participant, and that the DCI has no real time or interest in the community as a whole because of his other "hat" as head of the CIA. Critics argue that creating a "DNI" would only add another layer to the intelligence management structure and that without a power base an intelligence czar would be a toothless tiger.

Another idea is to strengthen the coordination and oversight responsibilities of the Intelligence Community Staff, which has received strong criticism from both within and outside the community. Yet another recommendation is to create an assistant deputy of operations within the CIA to coordinate agency and DOD activities. The position would be filled by a top military officer recommended by the secretary of defense and appointed by the DCI.

Key Requirements

It is clear at this point that certain key issues will dominate U.S. interests in the 1990s, necessitating adjustments in the focus and scope of the analytical process and in human and technical collection.

Proliferation of Weapons of Mass Destruction. Already emerging as a key intelligence requirement for the 1990s, proliferation of nuclear, chemical, and biological weapons and ballistic missile delivery vehicles has become a top U.S. priority, especially in light of the collapse of the USSR and of the outcome of the United Nations inspections of Iraqi facilities. In the latter case, the failure of U.S. intelligence fully to gauge the magnitude of Baghdad's nuclear weapons program underscores that the community must find ways to improve its collection and analysis in this area.

Political and Economic Developments Associated with the Former Soviet Empire. For the foreseeable future, these developments will remain a number-one intelligence priority. How the map of this vast region will ultimately be redrawn will determine international stability throughout the world but especially in Europe.

The Strategic Nuclear Threat. Despite the end of the Cold War and the signing of the Strategic Arms Reduction Treaty (START) by the United States and the former Soviet government, the threat remains. Russia now has the lion's share of the USSR's strategic nuclear arsenal. Prior to the failed coup of August 1991, the Soviets had been modernizing their strategic nuclear forces, and it remains to be seen if this trend continues with Russia in the driver's seat. Whatever the case, the 30 to 35 percent force reductions mandated by the as-yet-unratified START treaty would still leave the United States vulnerable to nuclear attack.

Instability in Eastern Europe. Ethnic and nationalist antagonisms, unleashed by the collapse of Communist regimes in the region and the withdrawal of Soviet forces from the territory of the former Warsaw Pact members, have sparked civil war in Yugoslavia and have resurfaced in neighboring countries. Meanwhile, Germany continues to cope with the political and economic fallout from reunification. The impact of such forces on European Community (EC) cohesion and international stability overall must not be underestimated. Although progress toward European unity continues, movement will be slow, and economic problems, including growing unemployment and inflationary pressures, exacerbated by civil conflict, could derail or significantly set back further EC integration.

Potential Areas of Regional Conflict. Operation Desert Shield/Desert Storm starkly revealed the importance of intelligence contingency planning and the difficulty in assessing an adversary's intentions and predicting hostilities. U.S. intelligence needs to do significantly better in this area.

From the early years of its existence, the CIA in particular has periodically been taken to task for not providing adequate warning of impending crises. Unfortunately, Iraq has provided Congress and the media with yet another example of a perceived intelligence shortcoming. U.S. intelligence officials have publicly expressed satisfaction that the community indeed predicted that Saddam Hussein would invade Kuwait shortly before the invasion began and have blamed policymakers for not heeding mounting evidence of possible Iraqi military action. They also maintain that intelligence on Iraq's nuclear capability was good considering the paucity of information. The fact remains, however, that a primary responsibility of intelligence is to provide timely predictions of events that could affect U.S. security and warning of impending crisis or conflict.[5]

A way to improve the odds of timely forecasting of a conflict or crisis is to maintain constant vigilance over potential problem areas. Although the community already keeps watch on the world's trouble spots, it needs to have the capability to mobilize a coordinated response to support regional military operations when and where required (in effect, a movable regional joint intelligence center).

Such an approach would clearly place an additional burden on the intelligence community to create the kind of flexibility in analytical and collection operations that would allow the reassignment of personnel and technical assets to cover different and changing regional targets. It would also require improved dissemination and information-processing capabilities and the development of comprehensive data bases.

For personnel, this would mean training and maintaining language and area studies expertise in more than one country or region. This would be no easy feat, considering that the community currently lacks an adequate cadre of proficient linguists. To encourage the community to move aggressively on this problem, both the House and Senate Intelligence Committees have proposed initiatives in their respective reports on FY 1992 authorization legislation.

Arms-Control Monitoring and Support. In terms of support personnel and technical collection assets, monitoring the new conventional and strategic nuclear arms-control treaties will be a major drain on community resources. U.S. intelligence, by law, is required to monitor treaty compliance by other signatories. This includes all past and future agreements to which the United States is a party. Although the future direction of arms control has yet to emerge, it is likely that the United States will push to wrap up the multilateral chemical weapons agreement, to revitalize negotiations on defense and space systems, to move toward further limits on nuclear testing, and to initiate negotiations aimed at strengthening agreements on nonproliferation.

Economic Issues

In the last few years economic intelligence has been oversold as a major requirement both by top intelligence officials and the media. The traditional community focus on reporting international economic developments, emerging technologies, and technology transfer is an area in which U.S. intelligence has performed relatively well. More should be done, particularly on the latter two topics, and ongoing programs strengthened where possible.

The concept of economic intelligence, however, has lately expanded to mean something more than these traditional concerns. Although this "something" remains undefined, the idea is that the intelligence community should assist policymakers and business interests to make U.S. industry more competitive.[6]

Although this is an admirable goal, several factors militate against such a role for U.S. intelligence. Today, in an era of multinational corporations and international cooperation in research and development and operations, it is difficult to define what legally constitutes a U.S. company or a U.S. product. According to the deputy director of Central Intelligence, Richard Kerr, U.S. intelligence has no role in industrial espionage or the collection and dissemination of corporate secrets. Other current and former top intelligence officials have also pointed out that there is a problem in determining what business enterprises the intelligence community should target and what entities, apart from the U.S. government, should receive such information.

Environmental intelligence is yet another area that has been emphasized as a key focus for the 1990s. U.S. intelligence routinely covers natural and manmade disasters and the politics of international environmental issues. Although environmental issues are an increasingly important concern, they are not high priority compared to other more pressing intelligence requirements.

The Need for Flexibility

It should be kept in mind that the key issues noted previously are those that demand attention today. Within a matter of weeks, if not days, however, some of these requirements may have changed focus or new issues come to the fore. The community must constantly monitor intelligence requirements and should place greater emphasis on long-range predictions (i.e., a timeframe beyond six months). Unlike the media, which focuses only on the event of the moment, the community must always be looking ahead. Unfortunately, U.S. intelligence has increasingly been paying lip service to its responsibility to predict while in reality withstanding pressures to lean forward and postulate possible outcomes or assign percentage values to the likelihood of future developments. The community routinely produces National Intelligence Estimates that policymakers and intelligence officials agree offer scenarios in terms of broad generalities. Today, the intelligence that "really sells downtown" (at the National Security Council and White House) is analysis that is directly tailored to the immediate concerns of top U.S. policymakers. Typescript memos, situation reports, and other forms of current intelligence, unlike long-range analysis, often elicit positive feedback from policymakers. Although the community's responsibility is to support such efforts, it must not become so caught up in the psychic rewards of current intelligence that its long-range analytical capability suffers.

The recommended emphasis on the key issues outlined above does not mean that the community should curtail its fulfillment of traditional intelligence responsibilities. It is rather a matter of judiciously reallocating shrinking resources to maintain and enhance capabilities to deal with ongoing requirements while building up analytical and, particularly, human collection resources. Considering the duplicative and overlapping programs within the community today, there appears to be ample room for creative restructuring and reorientation.

Is More Better?

In light of these suggestions, the intelligence agencies need to take a hard look at their analytical output and determine whether the quantity produced is justified. The number of reports, memorandums, and studies the community generates daily has dramatically increased in the last 10 years, chiefly as a result of the great expansion of the analytical force and enhanced technical collection rather than the demands of consumers. In the mid-1980s, Robert Gates, then head of the CIA's Directorate of Intelligence, on a number of occasions publicly pointed to the jump in the number of longer analytical studies produced by the CIA as evidence of improvement in the quality of intelligence. Also, during this period, the number of pages of *The National Intelligence Daily*, the CIA's vehicle for current intelligence, doubled and a new special "in-brief" section provided abbreviated information on additional topics not deemed worthy of in-depth treatment. The idea was that any data of intelligence value should be duly noted, if only for the record.

Greater selectivity in choosing items for publication can free up shrinking analytical assets to focus on key areas. In addition, analysts covering low-priority accounts could handle two or more countries or functional issues.

Intelligence and Desert Shield/ Desert Storm

The war in the Persian Gulf is already significantly influencing intelligence requirements for the 1990s as the Department of Defense and the intelligence community assess the successes and shortcomings of the U.S. intelligence effort. Although these studies are not yet complete, there appears to be an emerging consensus that close cooperation among tactical and strategic intelligence organizations is crucial in wartime. According to a preliminary DOD study on the conflict, there was an unprecedented level of such cooperation, but there were also areas where the effort fell short.[7] The report observes that a month after the Iraqi invasion the Pentagon established a Joint Intelligence Center (JIC) in Washington to provide coordinated defense intelligence to send to the military theater. A similar center was established in Saudi Arabia to provide on-the-spot support to the theater commander in chief. The report points out that, overall, the advanced level of operational cooperation among U.S. military services was not reflected in a similar "jointness" on the part of intelligence agencies. In particular, the report cites the need to develop "compatible intelligence and communications systems" to provide timely data. The report also underscores the need for better imagery reconnaissance systems to provide tactical intelligence support and better ways to disseminate imagery to tactical intelligence consumers. The report, in addition, calls for the development of a broad area, all-weather search surveillance system to provide better intelligence to commanders in the field.[8]

The above shortcomings were first aired publicly by the U.S. central commander in chief, General Norman Schwarzkopf, in mid-June 1991. Schwarzkopf also pointed to battlefield damage assessment as "one of the major areas of confusion," claiming that the CIA and the DIA provided far more conservative estimates of damage to Iraqi forces by U.S. air operations and artillery than the Central Command.[9]

The general's charges were publicly countered by Kerr, who observed that the general's "complaints should be taken with a grain of salt," adding that intelligence support for the war was excellent and asking, "What more would you expect?"[10]

The DOD views, however, received a sympathetic audience on Capitol Hill, motivating the Senate Intelligence Committee and Senate Armed Services Committee to include in their reports on their FY 1992 authorization bills several recommendations and directives aimed at addressing the problem areas. For example, the committees mandated CIA participation in joint intelligence centers under DOD direction and recommended the creation of "a DOD imagery manager" to oversee and standardize all defense imagery systems.[11]

Outlook

It is unclear at this time whether the current impetus toward intelligence restructuring and reorientation will result in meaningful initiatives by Congress or the intelligence community. Although there are compelling factors behind the revitalized interest in intelligence reform, equally weighty factors could block any real progress. Not unexpectedly, many current and former intelligence leaders see no need to go beyond limited fine-tuning of priorities and programs. Sentiment within Congress has yet to coalesce around any particular major new courses of action. The continued fallout from the demise of the Soviet empire and other pressing international issues will demand constant congressional monitoring. Moreover, 1992 is a presidential election year, and domestic politics will be competing with international concerns for the attention of Congress and the executive branch.

Lastly, Congress will expect the new DCI to move vigorously to implement its recommendations and other initiatives and will be amenable to allowing sufficient time for a response. The DCI, more than any other single variable, will influence the future direction of U.S. intelligence. In the final analysis, the personality, goals, and vision of the new DCI will largely determine whether U.S. intelligence emerges stronger in the next administration or clings defensively to the status quo. Congress can recommend, direct, and legislate changes, but without a forward-looking individual to reshape the community for the future, U.S. intelligence will remain poorly prepared to meet the challenges of the 1990s and beyond.

The views expressed in this paper are those of the author and do not necessarily reflect those of the House Permanent Select Committee on Intelligence or the U.S. government.

Notes

1. U.S. House of Representatives, Permanent Select Committee on Intelligence, *Report on the Intelligence Authorization Act, Fiscal Year 1992*, May 15, 1991; also U.S. Senate, Select Committee on Intelligence, *Report on Authorizing Appropriations for Fiscal Year 1992 for Intelligence Activities of the U.S. Government*, July 24, 1991; in addition, U.S. Senate, Committee on Armed Services, *Report on the National Defense Authorization Act for Fiscal Years 1992 and 1993*, July 19, 1991. (The Senate Armed Services Committee has responsibility for defense intelligence matters. Thus it shares oversight responsibility with the Senate Select Committee on Intelligence. This distinct division of labor is not reflected in the House of Representatives, where the House Permanent Select Committee on Intelligence traditionally has had broad responsibility for intelligence oversight.)

2. For a synopsis of the history of intelligence reform, see Alfred B. Prado, *Intelligence Reform Issues* (Congressional Research Service, Washington, D.C., updated November 16, 1990).

3. U.S. House, *Report on the Intelligence Authorization Act*, and U.S. Senate, *Report on Authorizing Appropriations*.

4. Prado, *Intelligence Reform*, pp. 1–2.

5. For a discussion of warning intelligence, see Art Hulnick, "The Intelligence Producer-Policy Consumer Linkage: A Theoretical Approach," *Intelligence and National Security* 1 (May 1986), pp. 223–224; also U.S. House, *Report on the Intelligence Authorization Act*, pp. 17–18.

6. "The New Spy Wars," *U.S. News and World Report*, June 3, 1991, p. 22.

7. Department of Defense, *Conduct of the Persian Gulf Conflict: An Interim Report to Congress* (Washington, D.C., July 1991), pp. 14-1, 14-3.

8. *Ibid.*, p. 14-3.

9. *New York Times*, June 13, 1991, p. A–1.

10. *Oregonian*, July 16, 1991.

11. U.S. Senate, *Report on Authorizing Appropriations*, pp. 5–8; also U.S. Senate, *Report on the National Defense Authorization Act*, pp. 17–20.

Foreign Aid for a New World Order

John W. Sewell

THE MASSIVE POLITICAL, social, and economic changes that have occurred over the last two years in the world situation provide decision makers with an unprecedented opportunity to rethink and reorganize U.S. government policies, programs, and spending priorities in the field of international affairs. Although all programs in this field should be reviewed, the need is particularly urgent for those programs traditionally grouped under the heading of foreign aid.

Recognition of these changes is widespread in both Congress and the executive branch. President George Bush has spoken eloquently about the need for a "new world order," most recently in his address in March 1991 to a joint session of Congress. At the United Nations (UN) in October 1990, he called for a new partnership of nations that would transcend the Cold War. To promote our security and well-being we need, he said, "serious international cooperative efforts to make headway on threats to the environment, on terrorism, on managing the debt burden, on fighting the scourge of international drug trafficking and on refugees and peacekeeping around the world." Similarly, a number of influential members of Congress have called for rethinking U.S. global priorities.

John W. Sewell is president of the Overseas Development Council.

The need to consider new approaches and policies is particularly urgent now because in the next few years the administration and Congress will have a rare opportunity to contribute to a shaping of the world order that could last for the next several decades. Choices, however, are difficult because budget resources are not likely to increase. During the 1980s, new programs in the international affairs account were accommodated by increasing the overall budget, thus avoiding tough choices between competing priorities. For instance, the incoming Reagan administration was able to avoid reconsidering existing programs and any debate over trade-offs between economic and military aid by virtually doubling the aid budget.

That option is no longer available. Major expansion of the international affairs portion of the budget will be constrained by the continued pressures for deficit reduction. Policymakers in Congress and the executive branch now must reconcile the disparity between a radically changed global economic and political environment that has opened new opportunities to promote U.S. interests abroad and the persistence of long-standing programs in the existing budget designed for an era now past.

Unfortunately, these emerging perceptions of a changed world are not reflected in the proposed budget for fiscal year 1992. Instead, the administration's budget request for some $22 billion in discretionary budget authority for nondefense programs to "promote national security and advance America's interests abroad" continues many of the spending priorities and programs that in one form or another have existed for decades.

On the one hand, the overall proposed budget does contain funds for the innovative Enterprise for the Americas Initiative announced last year and for a major expansion in the capacities of the International Monetary Fund (IMF). It also accommodates congressional desires to increase the funding levels for the Development Fund for Africa. Nevertheless, the budget still allocates scarce budgetary resources for such cold war legacies as compensation to European countries for access to military bases, programs designed to transfer military equipment to those developing countries aligned with the United States, and broadcasting activities to Eastern Europe that now compete with Cable News Network (CNN) and other local and international news services. In addition, it contains funding for bilateral aid programs that were designed in the 1960s and 1970s and no longer reflect the changing nature of development cooperation.

Program allocations such as these are long overdue for serious reexamination. The conceptual basis for many of these programs was developed for the cold war era; they are to a great extent outmoded in the rapidly changing world of the 1990s. The unwillingness to end these programs means that resources are not available to respond adequately to new opportunities in regions such as Eastern Europe, to promote now-vital U.S. economic interests abroad, or to address the major interrelated global problems of poverty, environmental degradation, population growth, and political participation.

If the United States is to respond to opportunities inherent in the new post–cold war environment at a time when policymakers feel hard pressed to meet a variety of new needs, particularly on the domestic front, two steps are necessary. First, existing programs must be closely examined to see if they meet the challenges of the 1990s while still addressing important U.S. interests; if not, they should be phased out or canceled. Second, new programs must be developed to meet those new needs.

It's a Different World

Choices about U.S. international interests in the 1990s are made complex by three central new facts. First, there is no longer any single, all-encompassing U.S. international interest to replace the clearly defined goal of Communist bloc containment. In fact, the redefinition of U.S. interests in the world is one of the challenging tasks of this decade. Second, the boundaries between the great multicountry blocs that marked the post–World War II period have weakened considerably. Many of the factors that led to perceived common interests among the postwar groupings of nation-states now have been severely attenuated or have disappeared. Third, there is an emerging "global agenda" of new and old interrelated issues that could form the basis for a new set of international priorities. It includes the need to restart sustainable economic growth in the developing countries, to eliminate the absolute poverty that still scars the lives of 1 billion men, women, and children around the world, to sustain the earth's environment upon which both rich and poor countries depend, and to promote the open political systems that have emerged in recent years throughout the Third World and in Eastern Europe.

A number of major changes in the international environment that have important implications for redesigning the current international affairs budget have taken place over the past several decades. Seven of these developments merit special attention.

1. Although the conclusion of the Cold War has diminished superpower rivalries in the developing world, it will not end long-standing regional conflicts caused by ethnic, religious, and territorial differences, as the recent crisis in the Gulf demonstrated. These regional wars between and within countries will undoubtedly continue, making a renewal of attention to conflict resolution and peacekeeping mechanisms one of the policy priorities of the period ahead. Regional development arrangements and postconflict reconstruction can be part of these policies.

2. The developed world has changed. Economic developments over the last several decades have resulted in substantial alterations in the relative positions of nations and a blurring of the dividing lines between the economic groupings referred to as the First, Second, and Third Worlds. In the industrial world, three great centers of relatively coequal economic power are emerging—a unified Europe, Japan, and the United States. Japan has yet to come to grips with the policy implications of its global economic power; and Europe, now dominated by a unified Germany, remains preoccupied with its internal consolidation. As the current disagreements over trade liberalization (particularly in agriculture) and participation in the Persian Gulf force indicate, there is a greatly diminished sense of common purpose now that the threat of Soviet expansionism has ended.

3. The United States is now also in a different position. The U.S. economy is still the world's largest and wealthiest. The rise of other powers and U.S. economic mismanagement, however, have eroded the ability of the United States to pursue its interests unilaterally. The United States is now much more dependent on the outside world for investment capital and for export markets. Prior to the debt crisis, developing countries were major markets for those exports. Overseas Development Council (ODC) calculations show that in the second half of the 1980s, the debt crisis resulted in a loss of potential U.S. exports worth more than $60 billion each year, causing the loss of an estimated 1.5 million jobs by the end of the decade.

4. The countries of Eastern Europe, liberated from Soviet domination, are new players in the international arena. They face the very difficult tasks of instituting both market economies and open political systems. The position of the Soviet Union is also changing rapidly as it becomes clear that Soviet military strength has rested for a considerable period of time on very weak economic foundations. Indeed, both the countries of Eastern Europe and the Soviet Union now have become measurable *recipients* of economic aid, technical assistance, and even emergency relief.

5. The developing world has also undergone considerable change and is now much more diverse. From 1960 to 1980, rates of growth and social progress were remarkable. Per capita incomes increased, life expectancy jumped, and literacy became much more widespread. The industrializing countries of Asia and Latin America have been genuine success stories; they are now both major markets and

important competitors for the industrial countries. A number of other middle-income developing countries also did well, and giant countries like India and China now produce a variety of manufactures despite immense rural poverty. Many of the poor, low-income countries of sub-Saharan Africa and South Asia did not share in this success, however. Indeed, many African countries are worse off now than they were at independence 30 years ago. In addition, even within successful industrializing countries like Mexico or Brazil, poverty is widespread.

6. The relationships among aid donors have changed. Japan has overtaken the United States as the largest supplier of development assistance. The United States now provides only 16 percent of overall official development assistance (ODA), contrasted with 57 percent in the early 1960s. In addition, there are now many more donors, both public and private; and the locus of analysis of development problems and policies has shifted from the United States to multilateral development institutions, most notably the World Bank, and to the developing countries themselves.

7. Finally, the United States now sees that it needs the cooperation of a number of developing countries to deal with problems that directly affect it. For instance, the participation of major developing countries such as India and China is now seen as essential to international efforts to address the threat of global warming, and in the current trade talks the United States found it could make common cause with developing countries in seeking to liberalize global agricultural trade.

The implications of these changes for U.S. policies are considerable. Many developing countries no longer depend so heavily on foreign assistance to finance or manage their development programs. They earn their way through trade or borrow investment capital at market rates from private sources or international financial institutions. For them, the major threat to continued development is the international debt crisis and the restrictions it imposes on the willingness of international lenders to provide needed credits.

U.S. policies need to reflect these changes. In the future, U.S. policymakers who want to influence developments in other nations are going to have to rely far less on unilateral approaches, whether through military or development assistance. The premium will be on seeking to influence other donors to support initiatives and programs that address our mutual interests.

A New World Order Aid Budget

The annual debates of the foreign aid program in recent years have become almost a ritual. They revolve around whether particular countries or programs should get a few million dollars more or less than the previous year's level. In effect, the international affairs budget has become a series of "entitlements" for particular countries or programs. Strikingly absent from the debate is any serious discussion of whether or not current programs have outlived their time or of what new policy goals might lay claim to available resources.

An alternative foreign aid budget that is designed to make concrete the president's vision of a new world order but that stays within current budget constraints is quite possible. In the 1990s, however, marginal changes in existing programs are no longer adequate. Instead, the entire conceptual basis of U.S. bilateral and multilateral assistance needs to be recast into programs that reflect the new global interests of the United States in the post–cold war period.

Priorities for an international affairs budget designed to implement a new world order should address a series of pressing global problems and also promote this country's international economic, political, and social interests. The new budget should have four major objectives:

- promoting an open world economy;
- facilitating conflict resolution and regional reconstruction;
- expanding global cooperation for economic reform and development;
- modernizing bilateral development cooperation.

Promoting an Open World Economy. U.S. policymakers for decades have supported the concept that an open world economy was essential to meet the interests of both developed and developing countries. Free trade and free-market economies are seen as essential ingredients of any prescription for sustained growth in the developing world. Policymakers also now recognize that growth in the developing world could be a major factor in expanding markets for U.S. exports. This lesson was driven home by the contraction of Latin American export markets precipitated by the debt crisis of the early 1980s.

Restarting growth in the developing world on a more sustainable basis will require action in the areas of trade, investment, and debt. Interestingly, much of what has to be done will not require large amounts of budget resources. Continuing trade liberalization, for instance, will require mainly diplomatic and political efforts to complete the current multilateral trade negotiations.

Two areas that should command resources, however, are a major new effort on the part of the United States to address the problem of official debt and an expansion of credits to promote U.S. exports to the developing world and Eastern Europe.

The growing debt burden of the developing countries has been disastrous for those countries and their trading partners. The composite debt totals $1.2 trillion, of which some $520 billion is owed to commercial creditors. The remainder is official debt owed to governments and international institutions, of which some $60 billion is owed to the United States.

Budget limitations imposed by the ceilings for the international affairs account preclude the possibility of addressing the developing countries' commercial debt. It is, however, both possible and desirable to undertake a major effort to relieve the burden of servicing official debt.

The basic principle of bilateral official debt relief for low-income African countries was adopted by the leaders of the seven major industrial countries at the Toronto economic summit in June 1988. More significantly, the principle of bilateral official debt reduction for middle-income as well as low-income countries was accepted by the Bush administration when it announced its Enterprise for the Americas Initiative in June 1990. Last year the administration also proposed, and Congress approved, forgiving $7 billion of Egypt's military assistance debt.

In view of the critical economic situation in many other debtor nations, official debt relief initiatives need to be extended to a broader array of countries and the amount forgiven increased, particularly for the low-income countries. ODC calculations indicate that within the current ceilings it would be possible to increase the budget for official debt relief from the $600 million over three years proposed by the administration to as much as $6 billion over five years.

Export credit programs are controversial. Some view them as subsidies for U.S. exporters that are unnecessary either because the sales would be made in any event or because they represent government interference with the free play of market forces. Others feel export credit uses scarce funds better used for development assistance and, in any event, promotes patterns of industrialization that are antidevelopmental.

An increase in funds for direct credits for the Export-Import Bank is, however, in the U.S. economic interest. Such credits make an important contribution to the ability of U.S. exporters to compete in the growing markets of the middle-income developing countries, particularly in Asia. These countries have also reached a stage of development at which they can use these goods. Major U.S. competitors have access to a range of credit facilities provided by their own governments that often puts U.S. firms at a disadvantage.

Facilitating Conflict Resolution and Regional Reconstruction. The allied military success in the Persian Gulf is being followed by a major new effort at eliminating the roots of regional conflict in the Middle East. At the same time, a number of long-standing regional conflicts in the developing world are moving toward resolution.

The devastating and costly conflicts in Central America, Southern Africa, Afghanistan, and Cambodia had their origins in a diverse set of indigenous causes, but both the United States and the Soviet Union exacerbated the conflicts by making them part of the Cold War. With the end of the Cold War, however, the United States and the Soviet Union are cooperating in the settling of these disputes. There is now, accordingly, a major opportunity and indeed an obligation to repair the years of damage that resulted from these conflicts and to promote conditions conducive to the development of open, market-oriented societies. In addition, the recent events in Eastern Europe have underscored the need to ensure that the end of Soviet domination in those countries does not lead to economic and political collapse, civil unrest, and the return to repressive regimes from either the extreme right or left.

One of the high priorities for U.S. foreign policy in this decade should be the establishment of multilateral and regional mechanisms to resolve regional conflicts. Like trade liberalization, addressing regional conflicts consumes policy attention but not large budgetary resources. Postconflict regional development, however, may put a substantial claim on international development resources.

Postconflict reconstruction in these areas is not and cannot be the sole responsibility of the United States. Indeed, the interests and priorities of the major donor countries will vary considerably. A need for a new multilateral vehicle to support development in these areas and to maximize contributions from all donors would be a useful innovation. The United States should take the lead in establishing a Multilateral Reconstruction Fund specifically designed to meet the needs of those areas emerging from conflict.[1]

The advantages of an international approach to meet reconstruction needs would include the following:

- the leveraging effect of a modest U.S. contribution to prompt contributions from other donors;
- an opportunity for new players such as the Organization of Petroleum Exporting Countries (OPEC), Japan, and a unified Germany to make major contributions;
- the possibility of funding infrastructure investment and loan guarantee programs of sufficient magnitude to encourage private enterprises to invest in the areas.

This fund could be a part of the United Nations, or it might function as a special "window" of the World Bank, drawing upon the large reservoir of engineering and technical expertise the Bank offers. The U.S. contribution to such a fund could rise to $200 million a year, leveraging assets that could total $3 billion to $6 billion for use in that period (obviously depending on participation by other countries). Such a contribution to the problems of postconflict reconstruction, together with the debt relief mentioned earlier and expanded assistance for refugees, would have a major impact on the people affected by these conflicts and on priming the engines of economic development.

Finally, it is time to set up a specific Middle East peace account in the international affairs budget. Programs associated with the continuing U.S. effort to achieve a peaceful resolution of conflicts in the Middle East are crucial, but they are currently funded within the worldwide totals for U.S. development and security assistance accounts. The importance of these programs will increase in the post–Desert Storm period. Aid to the region must be used as an integral part of establishing an enduring peace in the region, however, and not just to maintain the status quo. A separate account would allow policymakers to focus on that issue and, as in the recent supplemental legislation, permit special increases without affecting overall budget ceilings.

Expanding Global Cooperation for Economic Reform and Development. Participation in the international development institutions, particularly the multilateral development banks, is a particularly important priority area in a decade when U.S. budgetary resources will continue to be constrained, and when leadership and agenda-setting should be an important strategy for U.S. policymakers.

The United States remains the dominant voice in the Bretton Woods institutions and to a degree in most of the regional development banks. (It is, however, a minority participant in the new European Bank for Reconstruction and Development or EBRD.) Some of the multilateral agencies are among the most effective development agencies. Their programs are targeted on the key sectors of developing countries; they encourage crucial policy reforms; and they are staffed with able and experienced specialists.

These institutions promote U.S. global interests in a variety of ways. The World Bank, in particular, is a major force for promoting market-oriented policy reforms and for alleviating poverty. The IMF, along with the World Bank and the EBRD, will be the major institutions supporting both economic and political liberalization in the emerging economies of Eastern Europe. In addition, all the banks act as catalysts for mobilizing financial flows from other donors and commercial investors. For these reasons, it is important for the United States, to the extent possible, to maintain a strong voice in their policies.

John W. Sewell

Modernizing Bilateral Development Cooperation: A New Sustainable Development Fund. There is no area of the budget more in need of attention than those programs currently designed to eliminate poverty, limit population growth, and sustain the environment. Each of these issues demands urgent attention. Already more than a billion men, women, and children are living under conditions of absolute poverty at a time when there are sufficient resources to help them change these abject conditions. Their number will grow unless major efforts are begun now. At the same time, both developed and developing countries face a new set of threats stemming from a physical environment that is deteriorating at both the global and the local level. Furthermore, both poverty and environmental degradation are exacerbated by population growth, which is persisting at a higher level than originally projected.

Current bilateral programs are no longer adequate to deal with these new challenges and the new policy environment. The Agency for International Development (AID), when it was established in 1961, reflected relationships between the United States and the developing countries that have now radically altered. AID was to be the lead agency for U.S. development policy, a task it no longer fulfills. U.S. policies toward the multilateral development banks are determined by the Treasury, and country allocations of aid are largely determined by the Department of State or, in the case of military aid, by the Department of Defense. In addition, AID does not have the clout to deal with decisions on trade and debt that have great impact on the developing countries.

There is skepticism in Congress and elsewhere about the continued effectiveness of AID as an institution. The agency has retained many good people, a valuable field organization, and some substantive strengths; but its technical capacities have diminished, and its overall policy direction is uninspired. It would be difficult to rebuild its old stature as a freestanding agency, and it no longer deserves to monopolize the distribution of U.S. bilateral assistance. A new bilateral initiative is needed to take its place, in accordance with which U.S. assistance would be aimed at priority purposes, not just (as now) at particular institutions, and the same kind of market competition that promotes private-sector efficiency would be brought to bear on the public sector.

These problems should be approached globally, through the establishment of a new Sustainable Development Fund (SDF), which would have as its charge specific global development challenges jointly chosen by Congress and the executive. In addition, it would subject public sector development programs and institutions to market competition. The SDF should concentrate on a few key global problems whose solutions would benefit great numbers of people. These would include poverty and employment, food security and rural development, human resource development, and the environment.

The SDF would provide innovative and catalytic funding for environmental programs that may cross national boundaries; large scale reforestation efforts that will require coordination with other bilateral and multilateral donors; multiyear support for a substantial effort to close the gap between the demand for family planning and the resources now available; and programs dealing with such urgent health problems as the growing AIDS epidemic.

The SDF would become the centerpiece of U.S. bilateral assistance. When it was in full operation, most of the bilateral aid budget would flow through it. It should, however, build its operational style slowly and carefully. It would take some time for the SDF to define its priorities, translate these into programs, and choose the implementors. At the same time, the Fund should have sufficient initial funding to be taken seriously and to plan for an expanding program.

As the scale of SDF operations increased, the discretionary resources available to other agencies such as AID would be reduced. AID could continue as a major delivery agency for development assistance but would have to compete for development contracts with other delivery organizations. These delivery organizations would include, for instance, other governmental agencies, international institutions, nongovernmental organizations in both developed and developing countries, and profit-making private firms.

After several years, therefore, the SDF would be the major vehicle for increases in bilateral development assistance. Existing development programs such as the Peace Corps and Inter-American and African Development Foundations, however, would continue and would be eligible to obtain increased resources through the SDF.

The Development Fund for Africa should also be continued. It was established by Congress in recognition of the urgent nature of Africa's problems and on the assumption that a program with fewer legislative restrictions and conditions would allow for a more innovative approach to those problems. Most observers now understand that Africa's development problems are unique and demand a long-term commitment. Sub-Saharan Africa is one of the few areas of the world in which the United States should maintain country aid missions.

The president's 1992 budget proposes to continue the Peace Corps at a level of slightly more than 5,000 volunteers, far below the level of 13,000 volunteers in the 1960s. In view of the low cost of the Peace Corps and its unquestionable benefits both for the host countries and for the U.S. volunteers, the number of volunteers should be augmented to 10,000 by the end of this decade, as proposed by Congress. The five-year cost of this buildup (still well below the levels of the 1960s) is estimated at only $330 million.

Can the United States Afford These Changes?

The United States cannot afford to reorder priorities and create new programs unless it subjects current programs now funded in the aid budget to reexamination. Fortunately, funds can be found to promote new interests, if Congress and the administration are willing to end programs that were driven essentially by the need to confront the Soviet Union.

Decisions to make major reductions in the defense budget have already been made. The administration's FY 1992 defense budget request, in keeping with the 1990 budget summit agreement, includes reductions that will result in savings of $322 billion over the next five years. Unless there is a major reversal of how the threat from the Soviet Union and the Warsaw Pact is viewed, it appears likely that even deeper reductions in defense funding will be possible over the next several years.

Congress and the administration have already agreed that the country's severe fiscal crisis makes it essential to allocate all of the initial savings achieved by the budget summit agreement to deficit reduction. If, as appears increasingly likely, the eventual five-year savings from defense reductions grow to levels more consistent with the diminished East–West threat, much of the savings can be used to deal with urgent domestic problems.

Although decisions to reduce future defense budgets have already been made, no parallel decisions have been made about the cold war–related programs now in the international affairs budget. The rationale for continuing a number of these programs at the levels proposed is no longer convincing. If Congress and the administration are willing to end those programs, funds could be made available to promote new U.S. interests *without* increasing the international affairs budget beyond the current level. If all of the recommendations that follow were adopted, the reductions in budget authority would be some $30 billion over the five fiscal years 1992–1996.

The cold war–related international programs that can be drastically cut back or eliminated with the savings used to meet new U.S. nonmilitary international interests cover at least three areas.

Base Rights and Burden Sharing. The United States has long maintained military bases in Portugal, Spain, Greece, Turkey, and the Philippines as part of a forward deployment strategy aimed at containing the Soviet Union. Although the host countries increased their own national security as a result of the U.S. presence, they have also received direct financial compensation. The need for U.S. bases in these countries was justified on the basis of a military threat to the free world from the Soviet Union and its allies. That threat either has been severely diminished or no longer exists. Consequently, the main justification for U.S. funding for these programs is now ended. If it is necessary to retain U.S. forces at some European bases in light of the continuing instability in the Persian Gulf region and Eastern Europe, then the costs associated with operations of those bases, as well as any "rent" payments made to the host country, should be borne by the European allies.

There may be occasions in the future, particularly in relation to the Middle East, when the United States will want to maintain bases or have access to military facilities in various parts of the world. Ultimately, it is up to the president and the Congress, who have the responsibility for the military security of the United States, to determine whether such facilities are necessary and whether they must be maintained even if the host countries refuse to contribute to their own defense either by forgoing rent or by reimbursing the United States for the costs it incurred. It would, however, be wise management to require that the costs of these bases, including "rent," be treated like the costs of other U.S. military facilities, whether in the United States or overseas. They should therefore be an integral part of the annual operating budget of the Department of Defense.

Transferring Foreign Military Financing (FMF) to the Department of Defense. At $4.7 billion, FMF is the single largest program in the president's FY 1992 international affairs request. Although much of this aid has been concentrated in areas of regional conflict and for the base rights countries, military assistance continues to some 40 other countries throughout the developing world.

With the end of the Cold War, these military programs also can be phased down. Such programs detract from the level of resources available to meet new opportunities to promote U.S. international interests. Also, however, the United States is contributing to the growing number of arms throughout the developing world. In the 1990s these programs need to be reevaluated to see whether they contribute to peace in the Persian Gulf, or to stability in Latin America, or to any other purpose that enhances the military security of the United States. Where they remain necessary, programs should be transferred to the defense budget, where they can be judged against other security programs. It is worth noting that adopting this recommendation could restore the pre-1970s practice of including military assistance in the defense budget.

Radio Broadcasting Activities. There are probably no nondefense programs more identified with the Cold War than the Board for International Broadcasting radio stations of Radio Free Europe and Radio Liberty and the United States Information Agency broadcasts of the Voice of America. Although these programs performed an essential service of providing news service to countries not having access to a free press, the world has changed. The peoples of Eastern Europe are free to listen to any radio broadcast they wish, and their own radio stations freely report the news. U.S. broadcasting activities can now be phased down and the remaining activities consolidated, under either the Board for International Broadcasting or the Voice of America.

The Time is Now

Until now, tough choices have been avoided by expanding the overall aid budget. Now, however, policymakers must use resources to stimulate trade and capital flows to those countries that should no longer receive concessional resources, must reallocate resources from security to economic programs, and must decide how to use existing funds more effectively to attack poverty, environmental, and population problems, as well as to support emerging democracies.

The recognition of changes in the international arena is widespread. New policies are needed to meet new realities. The successful effort to persuade countries from East and West, North and South, to join the multilateral effort to reverse Iraq's aggression in the Persian Gulf underscores the new opportunities to address the challenges of a post–cold war period. Creating a new foreign aid budget for the new world order would be a first step in seizing these opportunities.

This article was prepared with the help of Patrick Murphy, a research assistant at the Overseas Development Council. It draws heavily on John W. Sewell and Peter Storm, Promoting National Security and Advancing America's Interests Abroad: United States Budget for the New World Order *(Washington, D.C.: Overseas Development Council, 1991).*

Notes

1. This recommendation draws heavily on the research and findings in *After the Wars: Reconstruction in Afghanistan, Indochina, Central America, Southern Africa, and the Horn of Africa*, U.S.–Third World Policy Perspectives, no. 16 (Washington, D.C.: Overseas Development Council, 1990).

The Post–Cold War Public Diplomacy of the United States

Paul P. Blackburn

IN THE HALF century since its beginnings during World War II, the United States Information Agency (USIA)—the public diplomacy arm of the United States—has reached a comfortable, even complacent, maturity. Despite periodic reorganizations, critiques, budget traumas, and even occasional gaffes along the way, public diplomacy has at last taken root as a hardy perennial on the foreign policy landscape.

Now, in the aftermath of the Cold War, USIA must reexamine its purposes and chart a course appropriate to the present moment. Like other players in the foreign policy community, it suddenly faces a policy environment in which containment of the Soviet Union no longer provides a fundamental organizing principle of strategic thinking. However, in contrast to U.S. public diplomacy's pre–cold war crisis immediately following World War II, when government information programs were considered wartime relics, institutional ossification rather than oblivion is today's nightmare.

For more than four decades, public diplomatists have convincingly portrayed themselves to the U.S. public as strike forces in the Cold War's "war of ideas." The Voice of America (VOA)—charged with transmitting daily messages of freedom to the captive nations in the Communist world—embodied this simplistic but vivid image. Unfortunately, the image wrongly suggests that anticommunism has been USIA's primary stock-in-trade. Moreover, it does not adequately convey the responsibility of VOA (and USIA more generally) to present U.S. policies and society in an objective and balanced way. And it portrays USIA as an institution wedded to *monologue*, whereas two-way interaction, or *dialogue*, is its most prevalent (and frequently most effective) mode of communication.

A Record of Remarkable Success

USIA's futile, though dogged, efforts to gain a seat at the head table of U.S. foreign policy (i.e., the National Security Council) should not be used as a measure of its organizational accomplishments. In fact, its officers are today more deeply involved in lower-level policy deliberations than ever before. Even more strikingly, public affairs officers at U.S. missions overseas have earned recognition as skilled sub-

---

A career foreign service officer with the U.S. Information Agency since 1962, Paul Blackburn is currently a diplomatic associate at the Institute for the Study of Diplomacy, Georgetown University.

stantive and managerial professionals. They are, for example, increasingly called on by ambassadors to serve as acting deputy chief of mission or even as chargé d'affaires.

The agency's outstanding record of innovation, leadership, and service dates back to its World War II antecedents, the Office of War Information and the State Department's Office of Cultural Coordination. Although its accomplishments over the years have defied quantifiable "evidence of effectiveness," career public diplomatists have long known that their work is central to the fundamental processes of the contemporary world—a belief vividly reaffirmed by the popularly based movements toward free institutions that have swept the Soviet Union, Eastern Europe, South Africa, China, and elsewhere. This sea change in the intellectual environment for public diplomacy is the culmination of decades of cross-border (and cross-cultural) communication in which USIA—its officers and its programs—has been intimately involved.

From its earliest days, USIA has been an agency of ideas, discourse, and interchange. It has stood for intelligent dialogue with the nation's overseas audiences, for imaginative use of new media of communication—for example, its Worldnet television service—and for the widest possible exchange of persons. If its tone has been less strident than some conservative well-wishers and funding sources might have desired, USIA's measured approach has bought valuable credibility that has paid off handsomely when the agency has sought to refute Soviet disinformation and other misrepresentations of U.S. policies.

The U.S. wartime experience and its immediate aftermath gave impetus to the four most prominent dimensions of U.S. public diplomacy: strong advocacy of U.S. policies, international broadcasting, educational exchanges, and the showcasing of U.S. institutions, values, and cultural achievements.

Policy Advocacy. Careful, authoritative articulation of policy positions has been at the heart of U.S. public diplomacy since its earliest days. The United States is not alone in this respect because advances in communications and popular participation in governance have made public advocacy an indispensable ingredient of virtually every nation's foreign policy. As USIA has gained in maturity this function has included, but gone far beyond, press spokesmanship. The agency's advocacy strategies have, moreover, become much more sophisticated—and respectful of the intelligence of its audiences—than the cold war–era "Campaign of Truth" and "People's Capitalism" campaigns of the early 1950s. For example, as part of USIA's all-out efforts during the Persian Gulf crisis, agency officers effectively used the full gamut of print and electronic media, as well as their assiduously cultivated personal relationships, to impart U.S. policy positions and to counter Iraqi disinformation.

The Voice of America. Since its first broadcasts in March 1942, and most recently during the Gulf War, the VOA has demonstrated its exceptional value as a timely and credible source of news and official policy. Its commitment to objectivity has been challenged by those who would inject a propagandistic tilt into its programming, but VOA has successfully maintained news and features autonomy as called for in the VOA charter. Unfortunately, the VOA editorials that are intended to fulfill the charter's mandate for policy articulation too often receive neither the policy vetting nor the editorial hand of radio professionals that would maximize their efficacy.

Fulbright Exchanges. By funding unprecedented numbers of carefully chosen exchange students and professors for intensive educational experiences in the United States and other countries, the Fulbright Act of 1946 launched one of history's single greatest contributions to global understanding. Now the flagship of all U.S. government supported exchanges, the Fulbright program has attracted numerous imitators, and the overseas binational commissions have drawn support from foreign governments that in many cases matches (or even surpasses) contributions by the United States itself. For 45 years the Fulbright exchanges have served broad U.S. interests while bringing fundamental, overwhelmingly positive change to the lives of hundreds of thousands of students, scholars, and their families. Perhaps most remarkably, neither the program itself nor its management by USIA (and, earlier, by the State Department's Bureau of Educational and Cultural Affairs, or CU), the Board of Foreign Scholarships, and the overseas posts and binational commissions has drawn more than the barest whiff of criticism.

American Studies. U.S. public diplomatists have consistently given high priority to the serious portrayal of U.S. thought and institutions. This long-term effort makes intensive use of such instruments as libraries and cultural centers, academic linkages, programs that teach English, student advisory services, speakers (via telephone and video hookups as well as in person), the export of high-quality U.S. cultural products, and the universally respected International Visitor program. Efforts to project American core values began in earnest with the reeducation and democratization programs in postwar Germany and Japan. The open-shelf libraries and cultural centers set up throughout both countries, the legions of speakers from the United States who met with school groups, parents' associations, town councils, and labor unions, and the thousands of exchange visitors brought to U.S. shores all contributed fundamentally to shaping modern-day Germany and Japan and to establishing the formal alliances and personal bonds of friendship that give texture to their relations with the United States.

The Price of Success

Although it can look back on many successes, USIA cannot afford to rest on its laurels. It must instead seek to set its own agenda. Lacking a clear articulation of its basic purposes and capabilities, the agency has in recent years been on the defensive—to the point that it has begun to resemble a pond stocked with fattened trout. Not surprisingly, members of Congress, senior administration officials, ambassadors, and entrepreneurial USIA staffers have learned how to fish the resources in that pond to secure agency backing for favored individuals and programs. In setting new directions, the agency's leadership must overcome three stultifying trends: a tightening budgetary squeeze, the conceptual and fixed-cost constraints of USIA's traditional activities, and ever-increasing congressional micromanagement.

USIA employees are forced to carry out existing programs with diminishing resources, the result of multiplying congressional earmarks combined with a steady six-year decline in USIA's roughly billion-dollar budget in real terms. Congress has increased its funding of agency exchanges per se but has forced cuts in the "salaries and expenses" account used to pay for staff to run those same exchange programs. Perhaps inevitably, agency managers have chosen to take cuts in precisely those areas that lack strong political support, among them exhibits (including the multimillion dollar exhibitions sent to Eastern Europe and the Soviet Union), agency publications such as *Economic Impact,* youth exchanges (a heavily publicized Reagan administration initiative in the early 1980s), and programs in Africa. Deplorably hard hit have been the books, periodicals, on-line reference services, and staff support necessary to maintain the 210 U.S. Information Service (USIS) overseas libraries and cultural centers. Clearly, the agency needs more money—the U.S. Advisory Commission on Public Diplomacy puts the shortfall at $50 to $100 million.[1]

Actions that severely constrain the flexibility of agency management are equally serious. Part of USIA's current dilemma stems, ironically, from a reputation for competence it has gained with the Congress, the White House, and its private-sector exchanges constituency. Recognition that the organization can effectively administer whatever is sent its way has made it the "agency of choice" for awkward public diplomacy endeavors.

The Seville World Fair. When the Reagan administration decided that the United States should take part in the high-profile 1992 Seville World Fair, the State Department and the Department of Commerce reluctantly agreed to join USIA in an equal sharing of the $15 million price tag for the official U.S. contribution. Subsequently, both State and Commerce, pleading lack of funds, dropped out of the project. Recognizing the important public affairs impact of the fair (and the even more serious implications of staying out), USIA was left to foot the additional expenditures from its own funds.

Radio Martí. When the United States decided to establish "surrogate" radio broadcasts to Cuba in the mid-1980s, most observers assumed the new element would be placed under the Board for International Broadcasting, the umbrella organization for Radio Free Europe and Radio Liberty. However, opposition to that arrangement by a key senator caused Radio Martí to be placed under the Voice of America, where, it was argued, it would enjoy greater credibility and be more resistant to political pressures. Despite Radio Martí's apparent effectiveness prior to Castro's initiation of jamming in mid-1990, few would argue that its mandate is consistent with that of VOA, or that it receives any significant level of direction from its nominal parent.

TV Martí. When the Reagan and Bush administrations and the Florida congressional delegation wanted to start a television counterpart to Radio Martí, they decided it should be put under the same organizational structure. Commencing operations in 1990 and heavily jammed by Cuba, TV Martí now costs $16 million annually. Although it is housed in the same building as USIA's Worldnet TV operation, it has no direct institutional ties with other USIA elements. Nor do they share a common program philosophy. In its 1991 report, the U.S. Advisory Commission on Public Diplomacy, noting that all other television activities of USIA are funded at only $31 million, delicately stated the obvious conclusion that "TV Martí is not cost-effective at the present time when compared with other public diplomacy programs of proven value."[2]

The "au pair" Program. USIA has become the reluctant—and inappropriate—overseer for the "au pair" child care programs carried out by the U.S. private sector that bring European women to the United States to provide live-in household help to affluent U.S. families. This responsibility was shoehorned into the agency under its J-Visa authority (which enables foreigners to enter the United States to participate in educational and cultural activities), using the questionable argument that child care is embraced within the broad purposes of the 1961 Mutual Educational and Cultural Exchange (Fulbright-Hays) Act. A General Accounting Office (GAO) study completed in 1990 found it, to no one's surprise, to be essentially a work program that entails full-time employment and no significant study outside the home or structured interaction with the local community. Thus, said the study, au pair programs are "not compatible with the original intent" of the 1961 legislation.[3] Nonetheless, in the intervening months, USIA has encountered stiff resistance from the exchange community and its congressional allies to its efforts to comply with the GAO report and transfer the program out of the agency.

In addition to activities that fall to USIA because there appears to be no alternative organizational sponsor, its managers have found it difficult to cut programs that have significant political clout (i.e., most of its activities in the broadcasting and exchanges areas). The agency therefore finds itself today with significantly less flexibility than heretofore (a problem admittedly not unknown to other elements of the federal government).

Citizen Exchanges. When in 1989 USIA's leadership sought, for budgetary reasons, to reduce funding for citizen exchange programs such as the American Council of Young Political Leaders and Sister Cities International, these organizations mounted such a strong counterattack that the agency withdrew its plan and agreed there would be no cutbacks. This contretemps confirmed that USIA's funding levels for such organizations more closely resemble "entitlements" than discretionary grants whose recipients and amounts are to be determined by USIA management.

VOA Language Services. In early 1990 USIA and VOA management determined to save money at VOA by eliminating six lower-priority language services from among the 44 then being broadcast. The vociferous complaints of affected employees and their congressional allies, however, produced such a firestorm that the agency's director reversed the decision and the services remain on the air.

Labor Programs. USIA's cooperation with the George Meany Center of the AFL/CIO represents an especially vivid example of an "entitlement" relationship. For decades that organization has maintained nearly total control over labor programming under the International Visitor program. This influence has continued without abatement under Republican and Democratic administrations.

Congressional earmarks, a familiar fact of life in bureaucratic politics, severely reduce management flexibility, except in instances when new money accompanies the earmark. That is rarely the case, however. Specific language in USIA's authorization and appropriation bills contains many requirements that establish policy and tie the hands of agency leaders. Some examples:

- Under the 1990 and 1991 authorization acts USIA must broadcast in Chinese for at least 12 hours a day. In addition, it must establish a Tibetan service and broadcast in it for at least 2 hours a day.
- Under the same act, Fulbright scholarships must be given to not fewer than 30 Tibetans and 15 Burmese who live outside their countries.
- Sometimes the earmarked amounts are minuscule, but they show up in the legislation because of dissatisfaction over internal management decisions. For example, the Maine congressional delegation, reflecting concerns within the VOA training office, inserted in the 1991 legislation a requirement that $200,000 be spent on programs for French-speaking African and Caribbean journalists at the University of Maine. The money was to be dispensed by VOA but to come from the exchanges account of the Bureau of Educational and Cultural Affairs (an agency element that might have chosen to spend such funds for other purposes, or at other institutions).
- Following a pattern set by earlier earmarks for the Goodwill Games in Seattle, the 1992 authorization act for USIA is expected to require that $2 million be spent on "cultural and exchange related activities associated with the 1993 World University Games" in Buffalo.
- The same bill requires other expenditures that respond to particular congressional interests. For instance, the Florida delegation put in $1 million for "the Claude and Mildred Pepper Scholarship Program of the Washington Workshops Foundation" and $10 million for "an educational institution in Florida known as the North-South Center" (presumably to be modeled on the East-West Center in Hawaii). The congressional leaders themselves inserted $2 million to be spent on "Soviet-American interparliamentary meetings and visits in the United States approved by the joint leadership of the Congress."

The Senate-passed version of the 1992 authorization mandates $24 million additional spending (the money to come out of existing "salaries and expenses") for new East European and Soviet Union exchanges at the high school, undergraduate, and graduate levels.

Among these examples, no single earmark is without merit. Some, like the Soviet and East European exchanges, represent obviously desirable goals. Each is feasible, and none would cripple the agency if carried out as directed. In combination, however, they graphically illustrate the difficulty of managing an agency that is being systematically "fished" by those who would set its agenda.

USIA's Mission for the 1990s

In August 1991 USIA's recently appointed director, Ambassador Henry E. Catto, issued a "Strategic Goals Statement" that updates the 1978 articulation that accompanied the reorganization of USIA and State's CU Bureau. The new statement helpfully clarifies many aspects of current agency policy and notably includes a forthright assertion of USIA's pivotal role in fostering "democracy-building." It does not, however, attempt to set priorities among countries and regions; nor does it refer to one controversial goal stated in the 1978 memorandum, namely, USIA's responsibility to "assist individual Americans and institutions in learning about other nations and their cultures" (the so-called "second mandate").[4] Although many exchange professionals in and out of USIA consider this goal almost sacrosanct, top management has not explicitly endorsed it as a discrete objective for more than a decade.[5]

Executive and congressional attention to the broader issues facing USIA currently focuses almost exclusively on the Task Force on Government International Broadcasting, which is charged with recommending ways in which VOA, Radio Free Europe, and Radio Liberty might be consolidated. How such a combined entity, if one is to be achieved at all, might relate to USIA and to the State Department is unclear at this writing. The accelerating trend toward VOA autonomy from the rest of USIA has, however, become so strong in recent years that its retention as part of the overall structure of the agency appears less urgent than in previous eras—particularly because USIA no longer looks to VOA as its "stalking horse" in securing congressional funding.

In setting the agency's new course, USIA's leadership should consider six urgent priorities.

1. Expand USIA's Involvement in the Policy Community. Although the argument is sometimes made that USIA's job is to explicate and help implement policy but not to involve itself in its substance, Director Catto has rightly asserted that the agency "should play a central role" in U.S. policy formulation. Similarly, the Advisory Commission's 1991 report noted "a historic pattern of insufficient commitment to public diplomacy at the highest levels of the Executive Branch. Attention to public diplomacy has been episodic, crisis-related, and tied largely to communication of high profile policies."[6]

For public diplomacy professionals it is axiomatic that decisions on policy substance cannot be divorced from decisions regarding policy implementation. USIA, too often denied access to the formulation process, has thus been impeded in its efforts to advance U.S. policy objectives. It must help craft the policies that, by deed as well as word, advance U.S. interests in a competitive global milieu, whether these policies involve U.S. security and commercial objectives, environmental and narcotics issues, or the long-range goals of promoting democracy, human rights, and the rule of law.

Besides seeking representation at the highest echelons of foreign policy making, USIA should deepen its contacts with substantive specialists in and outside the State Department. Integration of USIA's policy arm into the Department of State, as Gifford Malone has advocated,[7] would not improve such access; rather, it would drastically limit the agency's freedom of action by involving USIA too directly in State's battles over "policy lead" issues with other parts of the government.

In addition to advocating the substance of policy as enunciated by the State Department, USIA has an ongoing responsibility to help overseas audiences understand the roles and views of other players in the foreign policy process. It should therefore strengthen its day-to-day involvement with such executive branch elements as the Departments of Defense, Commerce, and the Treasury, the Office of the U.S. Trade Representative, the Drug Enforcement Agency, and the Environmental Protection Agency, as well as with the key congressional committees dealing with these issues.

At a minimum, the agency should insist on participation in decisions that deal with its areas of expertise and responsibility. Regrettably, no USIA personnel had a hand in President George Bush's agreement with President Mikhail Gorbachev at the Malta Summit to increase exchanges of university students in each direction by 1,000 by 1991. Although that goal is undeniably attractive, the specific time frame was clearly impractical. USIA, the inevitable action office for the U.S. side of the project, had to play catch-up to develop a realistic plan for carrying it out, including establishing a more feasible time frame than the one originally set. And, equally inevitably, USIA was not and has not yet been given specific additional funding to pay for it.

2. Critique Current Operations. USIA must use its capacity for self-examination to resist the natural impulses of bureaucratic turf-protection. Fixed installations (e.g., VOA facilities), traditional USIA-administered exchanges (e.g., the Fulbright program), and "entitlement" grants to underwrite the administrative costs of private-sector organizations all represent commitments of overhead that foster such protectiveness.

Although subjected to scores of studies, investigations, and outright attacks during its formative years, the agency's operations have not been given a comprehensive assessment since the Stanton Committee Report that preceded (but was largely disregarded by) the 1978 reorganization.[8] The annual reports of the USIA Advisory Commission, although valuable in providing a broad perspective on current programs and issues, have not represented systematic analyses of operations. And the investigations carried out by the Office of the Inspector General have applied an auditor's narrow focus to procedural and accounting inadequacies. Moreover, the overseas posts themselves do very little self-critical introspection of the kind practiced during the former era of regular overseas inspections.

Clearly, some delineation of priorities among both countries and activities must be established. It is time for a systematic, searching reassessment of major USIA programs to determine how specific agency activities can be made more effective, or if they should be reduced in size or even eliminated. Is USIA holding on to a given program for its own sake? Is it overly attached to "time-tested" ideas, individuals, and institutions? Does it shy away from short-term grant relationships and sunset clauses? Is it so wedded to its own programs that it is passing up chances to advance U.S. interests by playing a background role as catalyst, networker, ground-breaker, or temporary niche-filler (areas where it has achieved many of its greatest successes in years past)? Does it give adequate attention to opportunities for consultation, joint programs, and shared funding with, for example, U.S. universities, foundations, corporations, media organizations, arts institutions, municipalities, and citizen exchange organizations that share its objectives?

The university affiliation program, by which USIA gives three-year grants of approximately $70,000 each to fund linkages between U.S. and foreign universities, exemplifies how the catalyst role can be handled imaginatively (although that program itself is overdue for a full-scale evaluation).

3. Strengthen Relations with Germany and Japan. In the competitive, multipolar 1990s the United States must foster the best possible communication with the world's other two economic powerhouses and regional leaders, Germany and Japan. Although this interaction will at times produce frictions, it affords exceptional opportunities for cooperation as well.

With its past record of deep involvement in both countries, USIA is in an excellent position to assist this effort. It can, for example, capitalize on the increasingly important role played by public diplomacy in the foreign relations of both Germany and Japan and the position the United States holds as the primary "target" for each—a fortuitous, possibly transitory condition. The agency must track what the Germans and Japanese are doing in this country (and in third countries) and make even greater use of bilateral mechanisms that already exist, such as the U.S.-German cultural talks and the U.S.-Japan Cultural Conference. Where mutual interests intersect, there will be many occasions to share program planning and funding, as is present practice in the bilateral Fulbright commissions in each country.

4. Contribute to Positive Change in Eastern Europe and the Soviet Union. Stepping up its expanded operations in the region under the broad rubric of President Bush's "Eastern European Initiative," USIA must take all possible steps to ensure a full reintegration of Eastern and Central Europe (and the Soviet Union) into the great intellectual and cultural tradition of the West. Drawing on its vast—but insufficiently recognized—experience in promoting democracy around the world, USIA can help those nations build the institutions of democracy and open markets, including respect for the rule of law, unfettered media, and free labor movements, that constitute the basic underpinnings of liberal society.

In consolidating the new U.S. relationships with Eastern Europe and the Soviet Union, a considerable capital outlay will be necessary. Such funds should be used to establish high-quality facilities (such as cultural centers, student advising offices, and English-teaching classrooms), to expand officially supported efforts such as the Fulbright program, and to help launch private exchange efforts that offer promise of becoming long-term, self-sufficient interchanges. English teaching itself deserves special priority because it can help establish the infrastructure of communications upon which future U.S. relations with the region will depend. The United States must act quickly, recognizing that the pendulum may soon carry these countries toward reaction against the Western-style political, economic, and social institutions that today seem both attractive and achievable.

Eastern Europe is likely to occupy its current priority for at most another decade, during which U.S. informational and cultural programs can be expected to normalize at levels comparable to those of middle-sized West European states. The turbulent and disintegrating Soviet Union presents a very different picture. Because of its size, complexity, nuclear arsenal, and darker ideological and political currents, it must be a prime focus of U.S. public diplomacy for the indefinite future. How USIA will find the necessary additional resources to carry out such a mandate is a major unanswered question.

5. Reduce the Chasm of Misunderstanding Between the United States and the Islamic World. USIA must concentrate considerable resources on trying to bridge the tremendous gulf of prejudice and misunderstanding between the United States and the Islamic world, especially its masses in the Middle East.

Emphasizing American values of tolerance and democracy, while stressing that the United States (and the West more generally) is not an implacable foe of Islam, the United States must seek avenues of communication with those who believe themselves embroiled in fundamental, irreconcilable conflict with "America the great Satan." Success in the cold war ideological competition should not lead to the conclusion that U.S. ideals will carry a similar grass-roots resonance in Islamic societies.

Besides increasing USIA's presence in the Middle East and the Gulf states, the agency should significantly expand its Arabic language translations of the basic works of U.S. political thought. At the same time, it should move beyond the relatively good relations developed with Western-educated technocrats and intellectuals and promote exchanges with those of more modest horizons. Special attention should be given to interchange among the young, including high school and university students, young artists, and second-echelon activists in voluntary organizations.

U.S. ignorance of the region is as pervasive and insidious as is the reverse. USIA must look for creative ways to expose Americans to the traditions, arts, and lifestyles of the Islamic world. Although the agency's "second mandate" responsibilities for furthering "the American learning experience" are all too often honored in the breach, they are especially relevant to this urgent national issue.

6. Multilateralize USIA's Thinking. USIA has for far too many years been mired in the mindset of bilateralism (a condition fostered by the otherwise admirable practice of giving field posts a major say in agency resource allocations). In adopting a globalist perspective, it should not shrink from addressing the complex dimensions of contemporary international diplomacy and the country groupings and multilateral institutions that have become major participants in the global arena.

No other U.S. agency, and no private-sector institution, can match USIA's demonstrated capacity for fostering broad international attention to the great issues of the day. It has a well-deserved reputation for providing authoritative information on the U.S. experience with a given issue, organizing the exchange of unsung as well as prominent subject-area experts, and arranging the venues for interchange (whether the format is one of formal seminars, VOA discussions, or Worldnet "inter-actives"). Heretofore, these talents have appropriately been put to furthering USIA's primary mission of "telling America's story." Now it is time to apply the agency's capabilities more directly to the international agenda of the 1990s.

Although articulation of U.S. policies must always be central to the agency's purposes, that task represents only part of public diplomacy's potential. The new international agenda, in which the United States will increasingly seek to accomplish its objectives in a multilateral context, implies a public diplomacy in which issue analysis, consensus building, and the fostering of constructive communications processes are often as important as the forceful advocacy of clearly drawn U.S. positions.

Among the many global problems for which the international community is groping for solutions, some naturally lend themselves more than others to multilateral public diplomacy. A preliminary agenda of international issues deserving the agency's attention in the 1990s might include: human rights violations, the painful consequences (as well as benefits) of political and economic reform, environmental degradation, endemic third world poverty, emerging fault lines in the structure of the world economy, the AIDS pandemic, the scourge of narcotics, the destruction of cultural patrimonies, and insidious ethnocentrism in the curricula of the world's secondary schools and universities.

USIA should adapt its operations to the inescapable reality that the major global issues are of particular importance to certain groups of countries and dominant regional powers, as well as to established multilateral organizations. Concentrating effort on the most influential players concerned with a given problem area will ensure maximum efficiency and impact. To supplement bilateral "Country Plans" for each nation in the world, the agency should develop planning documents that encompass natural groupings, for example, the European Community, the Association of Southeast Asian Nations, Eastern Europe, the Arab countries, Central America, and francophone Africa. Special attention should be given to those giants of the developing world whose cooperation is essential for addressing the international agenda, among them China, India, Nigeria, Egypt, Brazil, and Mexico.

By "multilateralizing" its approach, U.S. public diplomacy can productively join hands with selected information and exchange programs of existing international institutions to which it has heretofore given only peripheral attention—for example, the World Bank, the International Monetary Fund, the United Nations Development Programme, the United Nations Fund for Drug Abuse Control, the United Nations Environment Programme, the World Health Organization, and the United Nations Educational, Scientific and Cultural Organization.

Only with strong leadership that focuses USIA on the essential tasks of the future and not on the more limited objectives of the bipolar past will the public diplomacy of the United States finally cast off its image as a handmaiden of the Cold War. With such direction from the top levels of the agency, and with the broad support of the White House, Congress, and colleagues in the academic and citizen exchange communities, USIA can over the coming decades make a profound contribution to the national agenda.

The views expressed are the author's own and not necessarily those of the U.S. Information Agency.

Notes

1. U.S. Advisory Commission on Public Diplomacy, *1991 Report* (Washington, D.C., 1991), p. 18.
2. *Ibid.*, p. 42.
3. U.S. General Accounting Office, *United States Information Agency: Inappropriate Uses of Educational and Cultural Exchange Visas* (Washington, D.C., February 1990), p. 20.
4. The White House, "Memorandum for Director, International Communication Agency," March 13, 1978.
5. Some agency leaders have expressed active hostility to the concept itself. See, for example, the remarks of Deputy Director Gilbert A. Robinson in "The Telling of America: U.S. Public Diplomacy in the Reagan Years," *The Washington Quarterly* 5 (Winter 1982), p. 132.

6. U.S. Advisory Commission on Public Diplomacy, *1991 Report*, p. 13.
7. Gifford D. Malone, "Managing Public Diplomacy," *The Washington Quarterly* 8 (Summer 1985), pp. 199–213.
8. A Panel on International Information, Education, and Cultural Relations, established in 1973, and headed by Dr. Frank Stanton, former president of CBS. Its findings are contained in Frank Stanton et al., *International Information, Education and Cultural Relations: Recommendations for the Future* (Washington, D.C.: Center for Strategic and International Studies, 1975).

V. A More Complex Agenda

The Security Challenges of Global Environmental Change

Ian Rowlands

TODAY, THE WORLD'S states are faced with a new threat to security. Encompassing the problems of depletion of the ozone layer and global warming, the issue of global environmental change is quickly accelerating toward the top of the international political agenda. National leaders are beginning to recognize and acknowledge the links that exist between the natural earth and the anthropocentric world. Thus, they are compelled to take account of the impact that their decisions will have upon the environment—and vice versa. In this way, the political consequences of global environmental change are beginning to be felt. To place this discussion of the security challenges of global environmental change into a broader context, I would like first briefly to review some other threats to state security.

Traditional Interpretations of Security

Traditionally, "security" was considered to be synonymous with "military security" because most challenges to a state's normal way of life seemed to come from external violence—perhaps also coupled with internal insurgent

Ian Rowlands is lecturer in Environment and Development at the London School of Economics and Political Science. He is a former editor of *Millennium: Journal of International Studies*.

violence. Logic dictated, therefore, that a state's quest for security would involve the buildup of similar force in order to resist an attack or deter a would-be attacker.

But due to the rapid changes that the world experienced after the end of World War II, such a restrictive interpretation of security soon became outdated. Indeed, a number of nonmilitary challenges to states' vital interests have arisen in an increasingly interdependent world. The economic threats to state security are perhaps most vivid. In a liberal international economic order—characterized by free trade and specialization—a country's well-being may be threatened by external economic activity. There is little doubt that national leaders regard sanctions, trade "wars," and other instruments of economic statecraft as potentially threatening. Thus, when examining state security, decision makers must account for such possible hostile action.

Additionally, technological advances in communications have meant that a state's values can be more easily attacked. Although these challenges are less tangible than economic or military considerations, it is recognized that external social forces can contribute to the destabilization of a state. For example, propaganda—in the form of radio transmissions, newspaper and magazine distribution, or carefully orchestrated photo opportuni-

207

ties—can be used as an effective weapon by one state against another. Once again, a relevant concept of state security must be broad enough to encompass such challenges.

There also have been environmental threats to state security. The most vivid example of an environmental challenge to a state's way of life and, in fact, to its integrity, involves "transboundary material flow." This category includes all of those international issues that result from the flow of unwanted natural material from one state to another. After crossing international boundaries (by either air or water), these materials can incite degradation in another country's physical environment. The degradation can take a variety of forms—the substances may, for example, contaminate drinking water, affect agricultural output, or reduce forestry yields. These developments can destabilize the political structure by disrupting the normal way of life and so threaten the security of the state.

It is evident, therefore, that a number of threats to state security exist. However, I have made no effort to distinguish between the challenges to state security that are intentional (e.g., a trade embargo directed against a particular state) and the challenges that are unintentional (e.g., emissions from a factory smokestack that cause acid precipitation in a neighboring state) because an identification of the actor's intent is not necessary for the argument. Instead, this brief review has simply been presented in order to illuminate the distinguishing features of the new challenges.

Global Environmental Change and Security

The security challenges being posed by global environmental change are unprecedented. Unlike any previous challenge, they are genuinely global in scope. Moreover, they are systemic in origin.

The global character of the problem is amply demonstrated by the fact that the two phenomena of current major concern, ozone layer depletion and global warming, constitute natural processes whose effects cannot be limited to any single geographical region. The depletion of stratospheric ozone or a change in the global climate will be the concern of every national leader. Thus, although all of the other identified threats to security usually play themselves out on a regional stage, no country will be immune from the security challenges posed by global environmental change.

The assertion that global environmental change is systemic in origin has important implications for the discussion of security. First, it should be noted that these two phenomena represent traditional "Tragedy of the Commons" scenarios[1]—in other words, any attempt to address the situation fully would be dependent upon the behavior of all other involved players. This characteristic alone, however, does not make these two issues distinct. Indeed, our initial discussion of security identified two other issues that have been modeled constructively as "collective goods": military alliances and international trade. What distinguishes the ozone layer depletion and global warming issues, however, is that they have significant inertial forces propelling them. In other words, any policy action taken on these two issues will not have immediate effect. Instead, owing to the significant lifetime of many gases in the atmosphere, an appropriate strategy will have to acknowledge the lag-times involved. This unique characteristic of these natural systems has important implications for state security.

Normally, threats to state security—both military and nonmilitary—are initiated by foreign actors. Further, these actors usually retain control while the threat is being posed and therefore have the ability to withdraw their challenge at any time. The withdrawal might take any of a variety of forms: recalling troops, lifting sanctions, ceasing radio transmissions, or shutting a factory. Similarly, the threats posed by global environmental change have also been initiated by foreign actors: states' citizens have discharged gases and chemicals into the atmosphere. The situation is no longer, however, in the control of a decision maker. Instead the circumstances are being regulated by the earth's natural systems, and therefore no one individual or group of individuals has the ability immediately to withdraw this security challenge. This is the key distinguishing feature of the new security threats.

In order to address these new challenges, new techniques are required. Just as we saw our understanding of security break loose of its military shackles after World War II, so too must we today seek another monumental shift in the manner in which states strive for adequate security. National leaders can no longer be solely reactive in their security policies; they instead must also be preventative. For in these times of global environmental change, full faith and confidence cannot be placed in our traditional understandings of crisis management and brinkmanship. Instead, in light of these new systemic threats, thinking about security must be forward-looking in order to account for the lagtimes at work in the earth's natural systems. Thus global responses are essential. Before I examine the world community's response to the challenges of global environmental change, I would like first to consider the implications that ozone layer depletion and global warming could have for state security.

The Security Challenges of Ozone Layer Depletion

The ozone layer, located 15 to 50 km above the earth's surface, absorbs most of the incoming ultraviolet radiation. The natural equilibria of the gases in this layer have been disrupted recently by a number of human-made substances that have been destroying ozone. If these chemicals (the major one being chlorofluorocarbons [CFCs]) continue to be emitted and the world experiences a depletion of its protective ozone layer, then more ultraviolet radiation will be able to penetrate the troposphere and hit the earth's surface. This increase in ultraviolet radiation would have devastating effects upon humans, animals, material objects, and the natural environment.

The U.S. Environmental Protection Agency (EPA) recently completed a study that examined the implications of increased ultraviolet radiation (i.e., if nothing were done to save the ozone layer) for the U.S. population. The report found that among those people alive today and born by 2075, there would be an additional 163 million to 308 million cases of skin cancer, of which 3.5 million to 6.5 million would be fatal.[2] It has also been shown that there would be an increase in the incidence of cataracts and a general weakening of the immune system, making all people more susceptible to illness and disease. Further, similar health ailments would affect animals. With greater amounts of ultraviolet radiation, therefore, the productivity of raising farm animals would decrease.

Perhaps more significantly, preliminary studies suggest that the DNA of phytoplankton—the tiny sea-organisms that photosynthesize light and form the basis of the food chain—would be damaged. Declining stocks of phytoplankton would place the existence of their predators in doubt and, like dominoes, endanger the whole food chain. Additionally, research has indicated that some plants would be harmed by greater doses of ultraviolet radiation, and crop yields would decline. Nor would non-living things be immune from the effects of a thinner ozone layer. A variety of manufacturing materials would be weakened by greater ultraviolet flux and therefore would have to be replaced more frequently. Finally, since the CFCs are also "greenhouse gases," they would not only deplete the ozone layer, but they would also accelerate the rate of climatic change. This last observation—which illustrates the link between ozone layer depletion and global warming—provides us with an appropriate starting point for an examination of the security implications of this second aspect of global environmental change.

The Security Challenges of Global Warming

The earth's atmosphere is constituted so that it allows most sunlight to stream in uninterrupted. After striking the earth's surface, this solar energy is reflected as longer-wavelength infrared radiation. Some of this radiation is subsequently trapped in the atmosphere by clouds and greenhouse gases (which include carbon dioxide [CO_2], methane, nitrous oxide, and CFCs). Without this greenhouse effect, the surface of the earth would be about 33°C cooler than it presently is and thus the phenomenon is necessary for life, as we know it, on the planet. But since the Industrial Revolution, humankind has pumped more gases into the atmosphere and has, in effect, "thickened" the greenhouse blanket that surrounds the earth, therefore trapping more heat near the surface. The Intergovernmental Panel on Climate Change (IPCC) has estimated that average global temperatures may rise by 1°C by 2025 and by 3°C by the end of the twenty-first century. This increase in average global temperature would induce a number of natural changes that would have significant consequences for the world's population.

One major outcome of higher temperatures would be a rise in sea levels. Given that warmer water occupies more volume, it has been estimated that the world's oceans could rise by between 10 cm and 30 cm by 2030 and by between 30 cm and 100 cm by 2100. Flooding in coastal areas would cause a recession of shorelands and wetlands, displace low-lying urban infrastructure, and increase the intrusion of salt into freshwater supplies. A shortage of fresh water—for both agricultural activities and human consumption—would result.

In a warmer world, the resulting shift in climatic change would also have a significant impact. First, with different climatic characteristics for a given geographical location, agricultural patterns would be forced to change. With human intervention, some degree of adaptation may be feasible on private lands, but changes in the wild would have significant ecological consequences. Researchers suggest that not only would certain species vanish, but entire specific ecotypes could also be lost. Further, forest areas would shrink since trees would not be able to migrate quickly enough to keep up with the shifting climatic zones. Those living things that would prosper in a warmer world would be weeds and insect pests—thus causing more havoc for human settlements and other living creatures. Additionally, all regions of the world would experience a harsher and more unpredictable climate with greater incidence of storms, floods, and droughts. Considering all of these developments, the IPCC Working Group 2 report emphasizes that the regions that appear to be at greatest risk for "sustaining the population" are those that are already arid and marginal,[3] suggesting that the world's poor would be hardest hit. There is little doubt that climatic change would give rise to a greater number of environmental refugees—people driven off their land by direct or indirect environmental change.

New Thinking about Security

The natural transformations that would be brought about by global environmental change would have a profound effect upon the world's population. Viewed with traditional concepts, any force that had the power to inflict such harm upon a state—kill some of its citizens and displace others, reduce its agricultural output, threaten its water supply, and destabilize its ecological balance—would be received with considerable attention. Today, therefore, just because these particular challenges are not being issued and controlled by a national leader does not mean that they should be ignored. Indeed, the fact that they are beyond such control makes them all the more threatening and ominous. New approaches to state security must, in consequence, be considered.

As I have argued in this paper, in order to address the security challenges of global environmental change, worldwide agreements must be realized. The extent to which states will be secure in the coming years will be directly proportional to their ability to formulate a common global response. Before I consider some of the possible obstacles and openings that may lie ahead in the drive to achieve this objective, let me first review the historical experience of these two international issues.

The International Politics of the Ozone Layer

Although ozone was first detected late in the nineteenth century, the presence of ozone in the stratosphere was not discovered until 1917. Speculation about the formation and destruction of ozone prompted British chemist Sydney Chapman to investigate the substance. In 1930 he proposed that the amount of ozone present was dictated only by the concentrations of atomic oxygen, molecular oxygen, and ozone. His work became the accepted foundation of this branch of atmospheric chemistry for many years.

Following an investigation of new data collected after the International Geophysical Year (1957–1958), however, scientists learned that other atmospheric trace gases also affect the ozone balance. The discovery that both hydrogen compounds and nitrogen compounds influence ozone levels helped to launch the public debate about the ozone layer.

This new scientific information was used by environmentalists (and others) in order to challenge the supersonic transport (SST) project, which was being developed in the late 1960s. They claimed that the substances released by the airplanes while in flight would threaten the ozone layer. One estimate suggested that there could be 500 SSTs flying by 1985, leading them to argue that the damage could be significant. Although at the time most of the development of the SST was being undertaken by Boeing in the United States, the Soviets were also building a prototype (Tupolev 144), and the French and the British were collaborating on the Concorde. In light of the scientific allegations, the U.S. government decided to investigate further the possible dangers of SST flights, and the U.S. Congress ordered a report in 1971. This report, initiated by the U.S. Department of Transport and undertaken by the Climate Impact Assessment Program, was completed in 1974 at a total cost of $40 million. The final report concluded that a 500-plane fleet of Boeing SSTs would have caused a 16 percent depletion of ozone in the northern hemisphere and an 8 percent depletion in the southern hemisphere.[4] But by this time Boeing's program had been discontinued. (The Senate, in 1971, had canceled the plan. Not only was the environmental impact of its operation being questioned, but the SST"s economic nonviability also played a major role in the final decision.) The Soviet program was also eventually canceled. Further, the commercial viability of the Concorde never materialized, and today there are only about a dozen Concordes in operation. The SST controversy marked the first time that the issue of stratospheric ozone depletion had come up on the agenda of any national government. And indeed the ensuing debate about U.S. landing rights for the Concorde demonstrates that this issue also had international dimensions.

With the waning of the SST issue, public interest in the ozone layer subsided. However, the issue once again started to occupy a part of the public's consciousness after the 1974 publication of a paper in the scientific journal *Nature*.[5] In this paper, it was hypothesized that the chlorine present in CFCs had the potential to destroy significant amounts of stratospheric ozone. With this supposition, the international ozone debate entered a new dimension.

The scientific community was in an uproar as controversy over the validity of the theory ensued. But since it was such a serious assertion, with significant implications, it was not taken lightly. A major international conference was convened in Washington, D.C., in March 1977. Its delegates produced a World Plan of Action on Ozone that called for greater monitoring and research into both technical and social issues in the problem area.

The worldwide political response was varied, and by the late 1970s, two blocs had formed. On the one hand, the United States (soon to be joined by Sweden, Norway, and Canada) had outlawed the use of CFCs in nonessential aerosols and was calling for a global ban. On the other hand, the major states of the European Community (EC), along with Japan, had refused to impose stringent controls. Citing uncertainties in the theory and the lack of empirical evidence, the EC only called upon member states to reduce nonessential aerosol usage voluntarily by 30 percent of their 1976 production figure by 1982.

Neither side wavered from its position, and during the early 1980s little political movement took place. Further, governments' interest in the issue diminished during the early 1980s for four major reasons. First, in 1981 the new Reagan administration appointed Anne Gorsuch to head the EPA. She did not pursue the issue vigorously because she dismissed ozone depletion as just another environmental scare. Second, the international scientific group that was studying the issue was steadily revising its calculation of ozone depletion—downward. It estimated eventual ozone depletion to be 15 percent in 1979, but only 10 percent in 1980, and down to between 5 and 10 percent in 1981. Third, the world was experiencing a recession, and environmental matters took a back seat to economic issues. Finally, owing mainly to the U.S. "can ban," the use of CFCs was declining worldwide.

Nevertheless, under the auspices of the United Nations Environment Programme (UNEP), international negotiations toward a convention and protocol commenced in January 1982. Just over a year into the process, international interest in the issue was revived: there was a change in the EPA leadership; there was increased growth in the use of CFCs; and the chemicals' potential link to global climatic change was firmly established. The friction between the two groupings of countries, however, endured.

Although negotiations for a convention were proceeding satisfactorily, conflict inhibited the prospects for an accompanying protocol. The Americans, the Scandinavians, and the Canadians demanded that an aerosol ban be written into the ozone convention. The Europeans, for their part, did not want to focus solely on aerosols because they believed that this approach would be beneficial only in the short term. They proposed a production cap on all CFCs. The dispute persisted.

On March 22, 1985, the Vienna Convention for the Protection of the Ozone Layer was signed by 20 countries. There were no specific obligations upon the parties to the convention. Rather, it created a framework for international cooperation on research, monitoring, and information exchange with respect to the ozone layer, potential modification of the ozone layer, and the potentially adverse health, environmental, and climatic effects of such modification. Nevertheless, this was a very historic document because, for the first time, states agreed in principle to tackle a global environmental problem before its effects were felt or its scientific foundations firmly proved. With the convention signed, the next step was to try to achieve a protocol.

In the middle of 1985 the international efforts were given a further sense of urgency by two developments. First, the discovery of a significant "crater" in the ozone layer above the Antarctic was reported by the British Antarctic Survey.[6] Second, a report was jointly released by the U.S. National Aeronautics and Space Administration (NASA) and UNEP in July of 1985. In this report, 150 scientists from 11 countries concluded that the ozone layer had already been damaged. However, they also stated that they had too little information to predict what the future might hold.

By the summer of 1986, a consensus had been reached upon a number of issues: that substitutes were limited by price, not chemistry; that production rates were rising; that the concentration of the chemicals in the atmosphere was increasing; and that emissions must be cut by 85 percent to keep chlorine levels from growing.

Negotiations toward a protocol continued fervidly during 1986 and 1987. Finally, on September 16, 1987, 27 countries signed the Montreal Protocol on Substances that Deplete the Ozone Layer. The significance of this document is that it committed signatories to reduce their consumption of certain CFCs by 50 percent of their 1986 figure by 1999. The wording of the final document reflects the delicacy of the negotiations because it contains a number of clauses to cover the special circumstances of several states. For example, the Europeans insisted that the limits be placed on consumption—not production—and thus still allow for exports. Further, concessions were made to allow existing industrial producers in the United States, the EC, and Japan to produce up to 10 percent more if the incremental production went to developing countries. (This was to discourage developing countries from constructing their own CFC-production facilities.) The Soviet Union was also allowed to complete two CFC plants then under construction and to increase per capita consumption (to 0.5 kg/capita) so as to account for the implementation of its five-year plans. Finally, states of the developing world were given a 10-year period of grace to implement the controls. These facts should not, however, diminish the significance of the document.

Just as the ink was drying on the Montreal Protocol, an important scientific expedition set off from Punta Arenas in Chile. With 150 scientists and support staff from 19 organizations, this NASA-sponsored expedition traveled to the Antarctic in order to investigate ozone depletion. The group's discoveries demonstrated "an undoubted chemical cause in the destruction of ozone by atmospheric chlorine."[7] These results, which implicated CFCs, not only highlighted the significance of the just-signed protocol but also suggested that its controls were perhaps not strong enough.

During the entire 14-year history of the CFC debate, the chemical industry had been adamant in its belief that there was not enough scientific evidence to warrant international controls. Thus DuPont's announcement, in March of 1988, that it planned to phase out CFCs was quite notable. It is generally agreed that this decision was motivated by the results of a NASA-sponsored study, released in the same month. Following upon the fall expedition to the Antarctic, the NASA-sponsored group (which had over 100 scientists from 10 countries) had scrutinized a large amount of ozone data and found ozone depletion in excess of what had been predicted by computer models.

In 1988, such mounting evidence of ozone depletion prompted a number of national governments, including Norway, Finland, and the Netherlands, to take unilateral control action beyond their obligations as outlined in the Montreal Protocol. Further, in March 1989, the environment ministers of the EC agreed to phase out CFC use by 85 percent as soon as possible and to seek a total ban by the end of the century. The next day, President George Bush stated that the United States would join the ban. Thus, in a space of two days, 13 countries, among them producing over two-thirds of the world's CFCs, had agreed to a total phaseout of the chemicals. An unprecedented agreement about the severity of the problem was emerging among the industrialized states. This consensus was one of the two dominant themes that emerged at major international conferences in London in March 1989 and in Helsinki in May 1989.

At these meetings, a general sense of urgency prevailed as delegates recognized that the provisions contained in the Montreal Protocol would not adequately address the ozone layer problem. A feeling was emerging that the Protocol would have to be amended and that the timetable for reducing and eventually eliminating CFCs would have to be brought forward.

But delegates were also accepting the fact that the Montreal Protocol would have to be altered in another manner. At these two meetings, the issue of global equity became dominant. Politicians from developing states, led by the Chinese and Indian representatives, demanded assistance in order to meet the obligations of the Montreal Protocol. They argued that since the industrialized world had caused most of the destruction of stratospheric ozone, the developed countries should be primarily responsible for paying the costs of repair. The developing states' leaders made it clear that they did not want to jeopardize their prospects for a higher level of development by forgoing the use of these chemicals. They called for technology and financial resources to be transferred—free of charge—from the North to the South. This would allow their citizens to leapfrog the use of CFCs and immediately use substitute chemicals. Decision makers from the North recognized that Southern participation in the Protocol was essential to its success. Although the developing world produces a relatively small amount of CFCs, it was accepted that it could easily expand its capacity for production. Thus, these demands became a primary issue in the international politics of the ozone layer.

In London in June 1990, the parties to the Montreal Protocol met in order to amend the agreement legally. After three days of intense negotiations at the ministerial level, the delegates agreed to phase out CFCs completely by 2000. Further, controls on halons were strengthened and controls on carbon tetrachloride and methyl chloroform were introduced. Additionally, a $240 million fund was established. This money, to cover an initial three-year period, would be used to assist developing countries to switch from CFCs. In this way, less than three years after the Montreal Protocol had been written, the terms of the groundbreaking document were considerably tightened.

The International Politics of Global Warming

The greenhouse effect was first described by the French mathematician Baron Jean Baptiste Fourier in 1827. In 1896, Svante Arrhenius, a Swedish scientist, published a paper that postulated that an effective doubling of the amount of CO_2 in the atmosphere would cause the average global temperature to rise by 5°C. Subsequent work in the area has effectively borne out his conclusions.

Yet the question of global warming did not reach international headlines until the 1980s. Instead, during much of the post–World War II period, the international community—if interested in climatic change at all—was concerned with global cooling. Average global temperatures had decreased from 1945 to 1970, and this had initiated a spate of investigations into the prospect of a coming ice age.

One of the first serious inquiries into the possibility of global warming was held at the Massachusetts Institute of Technology (MIT) in July 1970. Researchers attending a conference on "The Study of Critical Environmental Problems" concluded that the likelihood of climatic change during the twentieth century was small. However, they did "not discount the possibility of such consequences in the longer term, and [they] recommended continuous measurement of the CO_2 content of the atmosphere."[8]

The World Meteorological Organization (WMO) convened the First World Climate Conference in Geneva in February 1979. Much of the discussion centered around the debate between the ice-age prophets and those who saw global warming as being more important in the medium term. It seemed that a consensus was slowly building in favor of the latter view. The final declaration agreed that

> we can say with some confidence that the burning of fossil fuels, deforestation, and changes of land use have increased the amount of carbon dioxide in the atmosphere . . . and it appears plausible that [this] can contribute to a gradual warming of the lower atmosphere, especially at high latitudes. . . . It is possible that some effects on a regional and global scale may . . . become significant before the middle of the next century.[9]

Thus, only 11 years ago, it seemed that global warming would not become a political issue before the twenty-first century.

Following two workshops on the issue in Villach, Austria, and Bellagio, Italy, in 1987, the question of global warming entered the international agenda in 1988. In June 1988, the Toronto conference on "The Changing Atmosphere" was held. With over 300 participants from 46 countries, it was the first major international gathering to focus on global warming. The final conference declaration stressed the need for a comprehensive global convention as a framework for protocols on the protection of the atmosphere. The delegates also proposed a World Atmosphere Fund as a financial mechanism to assist the developing states. More concretely, they also called for a 20 percent reduction from 1988 levels of CO_2 emissions by 2005.

In North America, the summer of 1988 will also be remembered as one of the hottest on record. The drought conditions, although not necessarily manifestations of global warming, galvanized interest in the issue for both policymakers and the general public. Additionally, an influential statement was delivered on June 23, 1988: James Hansen of NASA's Goddard Institute for Space Studies in New York appeared before the U.S. Senate Energy Committee and declared that he was 99 percent certain that the warming of the 1980s was not a chance event. He went on to argue that it was time to stop stalling on the basis of scientific uncertainty and time to start taking action to address global warming. This statement attracted widespread attention and illuminated the importance of the issue.

On December 6, 1988, the UN General Assembly, at the initiative of the government of Malta, passed a resolution (43/53) that formally requested the UNEP and the WMO, through the IPCC, "immediately to initiate action leading, as soon as possible to a comprehensive review and recommendations with respect to . . . [e]lements for inclusion in a possible future convention on climate."[10] The assembly also recognized that climate change was the common heritage of humankind. Thus, with two international organizations committed to the issue, climate change became the subject of global debate.

During 1989 and 1990 there were numerous international conferences on the issue. Let me just refer to a couple of the most significant meetings. In March 1989, the governments of the Netherlands, France, and Norway hosted an international conference in The Hague. Representatives from 24 countries attended and issued a declaration that emphasized the use of legal instruments in trying to stabilize the atmosphere. The participants also envisaged an important role for the International Court of Justice, namely that of dispute resolution.

At the World Economic Summit

(G–7) meeting in Paris that July, the leaders of the world's largest industrialized states addressed "green" issues for the first time as a group. Their final communiqué recognized that "[d]ecisive action is urgently needed to understand and protect the Earth's ecological balance."

Meanwhile, at the other end of the economic spectrum, Rajiv Gandhi (Indian prime minister at the time) called for a huge transfer of resources from the North to the South. Making the proposition at a meeting of the Non-Aligned Movement in Belgrade in September 1989, Gandhi outlined his plan for a Planet Protection Fund, putting the price at $18 billion.

A major ministerial conference on atmospheric pollution and climate change was held in Noordwijk, the Netherlands, in November 1989. Although environment ministers from 68 countries were unanimous in their call for a climate convention as soon as possible, more specific agreement could not be reached. The United States, supported by Japan and the Soviet Union, proved to be the most resistant to any further declarations. They refused to agree to a Dutch proposal that would limit current levels of CO_2 emissions by the turn of the century. Thus, the battle lines in this international debate were, at the time, firmly established.

This confrontation continued at a conference hosted by the United States in April 1990. Following George Bush's election promise to implement the "White House Effect," the president gathered international decision makers and experts on the global warming issue. But once again, emphasis was placed upon further research and upon, in the meantime, a business-as-usual approach. The meeting ended in disappointment because delegates resented the Bush administration's attempts to recruit their governments to this passive position.

The United States continued to occupy the role of chief antagonist at a meeting in Sundsvall, Sweden, in August 1990. At this conference, representatives from 75 countries drew up the final report of the IPCC. Throughout the proceedings, U.S. representatives frequently tried to tone down statements by citing scientific uncertainty. This notwithstanding, the delegates finalized the report, which was scheduled to be presented at the Second World Climate Conference in Geneva in November 1990. At this conference, delegates were scheduled to prepare a framework agreement for global action on climate change. The international process would then enter its next dimension because formal negotiations on the drafting of a framework convention would be allowed to begin. (These talks are now scheduled to get under way in Washington, D.C., in February 1991.)

Politicians hope that this convention will be ready for signing by June 1992. At this time national leaders from around the world will attend the UN Conference on Environment and Development in Brazil. Celebrating the twentieth anniversary of the landmark UN Stockholm Conference on the Human Environment (a meeting that continues to be the single most important event in international environmental politics), the 1992 conference hopes to have, as its centerpiece, the signing of a global convention on climatic change. If this can be achieved, then the 1992 Brazil conference may be considered just as significant as its predecessor because a tangible, worldwide response to global warming would thus be finally evident.

Recent years have thus witnessed a great flurry of international activity on issues of global environmental change.

But is the world successfully responding to these international threats to security? Will the earth experience profound natural changes, or has international action managed to slow the processes and thereby dampen the ensuing challenges to security? The experience cited here shows that the answer is mixed. There has been (relatively) considerable success at addressing the issue of ozone depletion, yet most of the significant hurdles of climatic change have yet to be cleared.

Toward the Future

Though I point to the success of protecting the ozone layer, we should not assume that the case is by any means closed. As of August 1990, India and China, despite signs of interest, had yet to join the procedure. Thus, as was noted before, any chance for a truly global effort to combat the issue would be defeated if these two huge countries, with their great potential to produce ozone-destroying chemicals, were to remain outside the Protocol.

Further, a number of scientists and pressure groups argue that the enhanced regulations agreed in London do not go far enough. Even with the new controls, scientists say that the rate of ozone layer depletion will continue to rise until at least 2000, and that the Antarctic ozone hole will not be fully repaired until well into the second half of the twenty-first century. Thus it is apparent that they believe that ozone layer depletion could still threaten state security. As a result, numerous scientists and policy analysts have called for even stricter controls and an accelerated timetable.

Third, the substances that are replacing the CFCs are quickly becoming topics of debate. It has been argued that the hydrochlorofluorocarbons (HCFCs, the most significant substitute chemicals), though more benign than CFCs, will nevertheless destroy some stratospheric ozone. Because chemical companies estimate that these second generation ozone depletors will replace about 30 percent of the CFC market, pressures are building for restrictions to be imposed. In London, however, no legal controls were placed upon HCFCs, although a declaration that they should be used carefully by industry and phased out by between 2020 and 2040 was agreed. With such a long time horizon, the international political dimensions of the issue may well persist.

Finally, just as Thomas Midgely had no idea in 1930 that the new cooling agent he had just invented would deplete ozone, there may be other substances, presently being used, that could do the same. Therefore, if the international community is to curtail the security threats being posed by ozone layer depletion, its members must remain vigilant.

As the empirical description has illustrated, progress on the global warming issue is not as advanced. Although international negotiators state that they recognize the severity of the problem, and although work is under way on an international convention, little concrete action has thus far taken place. As of August 1990, only two countries (West Germany and the Netherlands) had committed themselves unilaterally to cut the amount of CO_2 that they emit.

Many commentators have argued that the experience in international cooperation on the ozone issue can serve as something of a dry run for the issue of global climatic change. Regardless of the validity of this assertion, it is clear that the two phenomena—each being an example of global environmental change—share many characteristics. Therefore, by occasionally recalling the international experience in the ozone layer negotiations, I would now like briefly to suggest what the future may hold for the international negotiations on global climatic change.

One of the major hurdles impeding the implementation of any global convention on climate change is the perception that any actions will be expensive. Figures in the billions and trillions of U.S. dollars are often mentioned when the costs of adjusting energy consumption are calculated. Although there are those who challenge this assertion—some argue that it will actually result in a net economic benefit—the popular perception in many states is that both restructuring domestic society and assisting those in the developing world will cost dearly, far in excess of the cost of eliminating ozone-depleting chemicals. Further, with a global economic recession perhaps just around the corner, the priority of environmental issues may be downgraded.

To continue with an economic perspective, it is evident that interest groups will continue to occupy a major place in discussions of this issue. Many energy producers (oil and coal companies among them) believe that they are primary targets in the global warming campaign. Perceiving this threat, they are ensuring that their interests are protected and preserved. Likewise, in the ozone layer depletion case, a large sector (the chemical industry) was portrayed as the wrongdoer. However, an important difference between the two cases must be highlighted. Despite international agreement, DuPont, ICI, and the other chemical giants will not lose significant markets because these same businesses are manufacturing the substitute chemicals. In contrast, much of the energy industry—unless they venture radically into new areas—will simply lose business. Apart from some investment in alternative technologies, the primary prescriptions to combat global warming do not involve replacement (as in the CFC case), but rather reduction. Thus, certain powerful organizations will have little incentive to advance the global commitment to slow climatic change.

Because of the global nature of the problem, states continue to be reluctant to enter into any action unilaterally, lest others take a free ride. Thus decision makers reasonably expect that any global agreement reached will be entered into, and honored by, all states of the world. Some sort of verification process may be needed. The ozone experience does set down a precedent of sorts—Article 7 of the Montreal Protocol obliges countries to report consumption data. However, the ozone case is small in scope compared to the global warming situation. There are only a small number of firms that produce, import, or export the chemicals, and these businesses operate in a relatively small number of states. Thus, although still a challenge, recording activity in the industry is feasible. In contrast, greenhouse gases are produced by every state in the world and are discharged from a wide variety of sources. Given the breadth of production, increasing the respect for international agreements on global warming will be a far greater challenge. Not only will reporting be required, but on-site audits and remote sensing may also be necessary. These procedures would obviously entail the collection of large amounts of physical data from all states of the world. Some national leaders would be reluctant to let others, even international organizations, undertake such a compilation because they might suspect the motives behind the act. Knowledge is power, and the command of information can be of strategic importance: national leaders may not let it be collected so easily. "Data sovereignty" may, therefore, hamper efforts to address this issue.

Scientific uncertainty has played a role in the international politics of each of these two issues, albeit in different ways. In the ozone-CFC case, the 1974 theory that implicated CFCs was not generally accepted until the second NASA expedition to the Antarctic (fall 1987). Until that journey, three different theories about ozone depletion—the CFC or chemical theory, the natural or dynamic theory, and the solar cycle or "odd-nitrogen" theory—each had respected proponents and large followings. However, even while the theoretical debate was continuing, there was adequate evidence of ozone depletion. The stunning time-series computer plots of Dobson measurements taken over the Antarctic were repeatedly shown on television programs. The multicolor graphics vividly displayed the ozone crater opening in the Antarctic spring.

In the global warming issue, the situation is reversed because the theory has far greater credibility than the evidence. The underlying theory of the greenhouse effect is generally accepted, but the magnitude of the effects and the severity of the impacts are still being debated. There is no irrefutable and tangible evidence that the earth's atmosphere is warming. Indeed, because of the large noise-to-signal ratios, scientists have stated that it will be at least a decade before they can unequivocally say whether or not the world is experiencing global warming.

Thus it is clear that scientific disputes will remain part of the political debate for a number of years to come. No one knows how the long-term climate will unfold, and thus no one can foretell how it will threaten security; scientists can only provide us with probabilities for different scenarios. Hence, as long as there is scientific uncertainty, it will be left to the politicians whom we empower to assess evidence, make value judgments, and implement appropriate policies. Obviously, since different leaders make different interpretations and hold different values, their decisions may not concur. And in light of the uncertainties, who can judge what is right or wrong? Thus the key observation to make is that a disagreement with the prevailing scientific consensus will continue to play a role in political decisions on global warming. In this way, the extent to which empirical evidence is evident will affect the prospects for a worldwide response. It is interesting to recall that while the scientific jury was still out on the ozone layer case during the early 1980s, decision makers in France and Britain stalled the negotiations on the basis of scientific uncertainty. In the end, it was shown that this action was inappropriate. Today, the United States (and occasionally others) is employing the same reasoning in the climate debate. Only time will tell if this policy decision is also ill-advised.

But there are also reasons for optimism. One of the most important factors creating a more promising prospect involves the visibility that environmental issues now have in the public consciousness. Opinion polls show that an unprecedented number of people are concerned with the natural environment, and national leaders accept that it is now a primary matter on the agenda. Not wanting to provoke the ire of important political constituencies, leaders are now eager to display and enhance their "green" credentials. This has been especially true on the international (rather than domestic) stage because it seems that rhetoric can be sustained at that level for a longer time. British Prime Minister Margaret Thatcher personifies this new breed of political eco-entrepreneur. After identifying environmentalists as the "enemy within" in 1985,[11] she began to adopt green causes in September 1988, and since then has become a major figure on the international environmental scene. We can expect more leaders to become engaged in the issue and thus increase the prospects for an international response.

Additionally, the emergence of various international institutions and other nonstate actors is another reason for optimism. The UNEP, under the dynamic leadership of Mostafa Tolba, achieved one of its greatest successes with the signing of the ozone agreements. The experience that the organization's members gained in those negotiations can now be used in the global warming case. Further, a large number of environmental pressure groups are also now active in the negotiations. These organizations perform a variety of functions. First, they create channels of communication that can later be used by states' representatives in order to conduct intergovernmental negotiations. Second, they inform national and international public opinion in order to pressure governments to take national and international actions on the environment. This also helps to create new international norms and thereby stimulate "bottom-up" pressure from the grass roots. And third, they contribute to the scientific debate and therefore help to achieve common scientific understanding on the technical aspects of environmental matters.[12] Thus, their presence—in greater numbers, but more importantly, with greater effectiveness—will be beneficial.

Finally, the revolutionary changes in the broader international political system improve the prospects for future common actions. The unprecedented reply to Iraqi aggression in the late summer of 1990 bodes well for future common responses to other threats to security, notably global environmental change. In this way, the cooling of the traditionally hot East–West relationship may allow the global community to slow the warming of the earth.

Conclusion

The physical transformations induced by global environmental change are spilling over into the social world. This unprecedented link is compelling the world's leaders to supplement their traditional understanding of security with a broader interpretation. New preventative worldwide arrangements are required. The response of the international community to the challenge of global environmental change has thus far been mixed: considerable progress on the ozone layer case but little of tangible value coming out of the global warming negotiations. The future is unclear. Although there are reasons for guarded optimism, a number of factors are still thwarting progress. It is, nevertheless, evident that global environmental change has propelled the security debate into a new phase.

The research for this paper was supported by the Commonwealth Scholarship Commission in the United Kingdom. The author is grateful to this organization for its generous support. The views stated here are the author's and are not necessarily those of any organizations with which he is affiliated.

221

Notes

1. Garrett Hardin, "The Tragedy of the Commons," *Science* 162 (December 13, 1968), pp. 1243–1248.
2. EPA report entitled *Costs and Benefits of Phasing Out Production of CFCs and Halons in the United States*, cited in testimony of David D. Doniger before the Subcommittee on Health and the Environment, Committee on Energy and Commerce, U.S. House of Representatives, January 25, 1990.
3. Cited in George M. Woodwell, "The Effects of Global Warming," in *Global Warming: The Greenpeace Report*, Jeremy Leggett, ed. (Oxford: Oxford University Press, 1990), p. 127.
4. *WMO Bulletin* 25 (January 1976).
5. Mario J. Molina and F. S. Rowland, "Stratospheric Sink for Chlorofluoromethanes: Chlorine Atom-catalysed Destruction of Ozone," *Nature* 249 (June 28, 1974), pp. 810–812.
6. J. C. Farman et al., "Large Losses of Total Ozone in Antarctica Reveal CLOx/NOx Interaction," *Nature* 315 (May 16, 1985), pp. 207–210.
7. David Lindly, "Ozone Hole Deeper Than Ever," *Nature* 329 (October 8, 1987), p. 473.
8. Luther J. Carter, "The Global Environment: MIT Study Looks for Danger Signs," *Science* 169 (August 14, 1970), p. 661.
9. W. W. Kellogg, "Prediction of a Global Cooling," *Nature* 280 (August 16, 1979), p. 615.
10. UN General Assembly, *Resolutions and Decisions Adopted by the General Assembly During Its Forty-Third Session* (New York: United Nations, 1989).
11. Cited in Larry Tye, "All Environmental Talk, No Action," *The Citizen* (Ottawa, Canada), July 22, 1989.
12. Some of the most sophisticated technical research is now being undertaken by nongovernmental organizations. (This is a point that is often overlooked.)

The Future of the International Trading System

Peter M. Ludlow

ANY DISCUSSION OF the future of the international trading system must sooner or later deal with a paradox. International trade continues to grow at rates that are both surprising and comforting. At the same time, however, many insiders or well-informed observers believe that the system is under threat, that the days of nondiscriminatory free trade are already past, and that the world is moving inexorably toward an era of protectionism, managed trade, and regional blocs. How does one explain this pessimism in the midst of plenty, particularly when strong evidence supports both pessimists and optimists?

Take the negative side first. The evolution over the past 20 years, "from a trading order characterized by general rules, to one characterized by permanent negotiation over market access"[1] is a fact that can scarcely be denied. David Henderson of the Organization of Economic Cooperation and Development (OECD) recently marshaled an impressive array of examples to demonstrate the European Community's (EC) resort to less-than-liberal devices, including variable import levies and subsidies within the Common Agricultural Policy (CAP), selective import restrictions, specific subsidies to exports and problem sectors, and the use of countervailing and antidumping duties linked occasionally to regulations concerning local content. Furthermore, increasing discrimination has accompanied the use of these new instruments of trade policy. The EC has a vast number of special arrangements of different kinds with almost all countries on the globe. According to a World Bank study, the community has 11 different types of preferential arrangement with developing countries alone.[2]

The evidence concerning the EC can be matched by an equally impressive list of deviations by the United States from the pure doctrine of multilateralism and nondiscrimination in the General Agreement on Tariffs and Trade (GATT). The Omnibus Trade and Competitiveness Act of 1988 is not exactly a model of consistent legislation, but one can see it in some ways as a monument to the new era in which Americans find themselves and which the orthodox can only deplore. The concepts and political forces that brought it into being are totally different from those that prevailed in forming the postwar system. If the act does not guarantee illiberal behavior, it will certainly facilitate it.

Section 301, particularly the "super" 301 provisions, is a case in point. Unilateral decisions by the U.S. trade representative (USTR) on what constitutes unfair trade and the related U.S.-imposed time limits for negotiations and retaliatory action regardless

---

Peter M. Ludlow is director of the Centre for European Policy Studies in Brussels.

of GATT authorization are inconsistent with GATT rules. So, too, are the provisions concerning telecommunications, the escape clause in Section 201, the unilateral character of the Buy America provision, and others. Recent statements by Carla Hills, the new USTR, concerning the apparent review by the new administration of its relations with Japan and particularly the suggestion that the United States will negotiate with Japan "appropriate" levels of Japanese imports, properly reflecting "the international competitiveness of U.S. suppliers," suggest that the United States will use opportunities offered by the act to go further in the direction of managed trade.

These examples of illiberal practices or tendencies in the two largest economies are only part of the story. Parallels abound elsewhere: in the continuing barriers to trade maintained by Japan, Korea, and Taiwan, not to mention by the developing world. More generally, the fact that GATT participants skate on the brink of a possible breakdown of the Uruguay Round suggests that consciousness of the importance of a multilateral trading regime is far from being an *acquis communautaire* or *internationale*.

Yet, trade continues to grow. The recent GATT report on world trade in 1988 provides the clearest possible evidence. The volume of world merchandise trade grew by 8.5 percent in 1988, the fourth consecutive year of accelerating growth. Once again trade growth exceeded the increase in world output, which implies that economic linkages between countries continued to grow.

Furthermore, trade growth was broadly spread across products and across countries. The 1984 situation, in which a massive increase in U.S. imports more or less explained the story, no longer obtains. On the contrary, the United States' 6.5 percent increase in import volume was well below the overall increase in world trade. The growth of intra–West Pacific trade has been particularly notable throughout the 1980s. As the following table shows, however, trans-Pacific and Euro-Pacific trade have also grown significantly faster than intra–North American, intra–West European, or transatlantic trade. Nor is this simply a reflection of a low starting point. Trans-Pacific trade in merchandise now counts for 11 percent of world merchandise trade while intra–West Pacific trade is still only 9 percent. Even Euro-Pacific trade, with a 6.5 percent share of total world trade, is more significant than the 5.5 percent share represented by intra–North American trade. For all the talk (and reality) of regional blocs, a genuine global economy continues to emerge.

How then does one explain the coexistence of good and bad, and what relevance does it have to reflections on the future of international trade?

First, facile optimism is clearly misplaced, particularly at a moment when the future of the Uruguay Round hangs in the balance. It is nevertheless important to recognize that a great deal of conceptual confusion surrounding discussion of international trade stems from a failure to appreciate the importance of major changes in the international political economy in the last 15 to 20 years.

Second, in trying to arrive at a coherent understanding of what is happening, it is essential to pay due regard not only to economic developments but also to changes in the political order in the West and in the world as a whole. It would be futile to pretend that nation-states have muddled through to a new, well-balanced system. The emergence of new actors, both in the community of states and regions and in the international private sector, however, has introduced new checks and balances in the system that have increased our defenses against complete breakdown and that can be integrated into a more coherent global order over the coming decades.

Third, in facing the future, policymakers must admit that a tidy global system of the kind that more or less existed in the heyday of the GATT is not realizable in the short or medium term. Strategies must include proposals at several different levels—global, regional, and bilateral—if some order is to be brought to a process that defies simple solutions.

This does not indicate a retreat from the GATT. On the contrary, as the final section urges, completion of the Uruguay Round and an adequate follow-up to it remain of central importance. Yet, by itself, the GATT is not enough. Other steps are also essential, if only to avoid undue reliance on, and therefore subsequent disillusionment with, the multilateral regime.

A New International Political Economy

The crisis of the GATT is not an isolated event. Nor is it simply a result of bad policies. It is more a consequence of changes in the structure and functioning of the international economy and the international political order. The former are more familiar and remain, of course, extremely important. The political dimension is more easily overlooked, however, due partly to the fiction of equality of sovereign states that underlies all intergovernmental organizations and partly to the persistent tendency among even the most knowledgeable to treat trade re-

Table 1.
Volume of World Merchandise
Trade and Output, 1980–1988
(Percent change over preceding year)

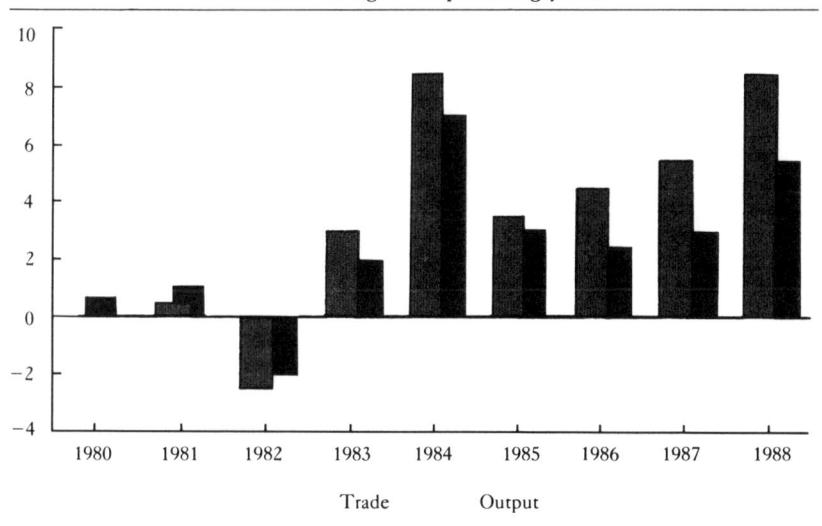

lations as unrelated to political and security issues.

The fortunes of the GATT cannot be treated apart from the evolution of the international political system in general. The world in which it was born was very different from the one that exists today. Outside the Soviet Union and its immediate sphere of influence, it was characterized chiefly by U.S. predominance—in the military sphere, in the international monetary system, and in the distribution of energy resources, through U.S. control of the principal sources of European and Japanese supplies.

The decisive influence of the United States over the rules and conventions governing international trade was therefore only one element in the system and depended to a great extent on the maintenance of the system as a whole. The original signatories to the GATT were all to a greater or lesser extent client states, as were the two most notable newcomers of the 1950s, the Federal Republic of Germany and Japan, not to mention the European Community, whose agenda and function were influenced by the prior existence and primacy of the alliance.

American hegemony was neither harsh nor particularly demanding. Client states within the system could and did develop different priorities in economic and security policy and argue with one another and with the alliance leader. There was nevertheless a uniform system in which U.S. standards defined the limits of maneuver, and dependence upon U.S. protection prevented even the most powerful among them from straying beyond those limits. The dominance of the dollar in the international monetary system made European economic and monetary union not so much impossible as superfluous. By the same token, the central role of the United States in international trade ensured EC conformity with Article 24 of the GATT. The provisions of the GATT depended more on all-pervasive United States predominance than on the enforcement powers invested in the GATT itself.

In the late 1960s and early 1970s, this relatively simple system began to dissolve. Twenty years later, its dissolution is not yet complete. From 1970 onward, there was no way back to the comfortable stability of the old regime. A new international political economy was in the making.

Four themes are particularly noteworthy.

The Altered Role of the United States in the Western System. It would be foolish to exaggerate, as many commentators have in the last 20 years, the extent to which the United States has become an ordinary country. It is still the most powerful and richest country on the globe. Nonetheless, as a consequence of economic changes and political crises in Vietnam and elsewhere, the United States has over the last 20 years become increasingly subject to the constraints of the international regime rather than its architect or arbiter.

The New Centers of Economic and Political Power. From the early 1970s onward, the debate about the management of the international economy became increasingly trilateral. The decision to hold a major new round of GATT negotiations in Tokyo in 1973 was a clear acknowledgment of this fact. So too was the endless discussion of the need for coordinated growth policies, in which Japan and West Germany, even more than the United States, would act as locomotives to drag the world out of recession. Tokyo and Bonn remain the most important targets of United States' criticisms, but the process has been complicated by the advance of regional integration in Western Europe and in the Western Pacific.

The Increase in the Number of Political Actors. Signatories to the original GATT included a number of countries, such as Burma, Ceylon, India, Lebanon, Pakistan, Southern Rhodesia, Syria, Brazil, and the Republic of China, which did not belong to the First World. However, the situation 40 years ago was still different from the one that has emerged over the last 20 to 30 years, in the wake of decolonization, the creation of the United Nations Conference on Trade and Development (UNCTAD), and a series of experiments in developing world cooperation. More recently, the picture has been complicated by the emergence of Communist countries, China and Hungary, within the framework of the GATT.

The End of International Monetary Stability. The collapse of the Bretton Woods system and the end of U.S. hegemony are integrally linked, but responsibility for monetary instability in the 1970s and 1980s cannot simply be attributed to the United States. On the contrary, the instability points to the emergence of a more complex international economy. The principal motor has been technological innovation, which has transformed both manufacturing industry and the financial markets.

The initial impact of the dissolution of the old order and the partial emergence of the new was not comfortable. Discipline snapped in monetary matters, in trade, and even in security policies. From the early 1970s, protectionism became a theme of international economic reports. Nor was it an imaginary threat. Various bad practices, such as the introduction of nontariff barriers, special exemptions, and quotas, were real and damaging. They cannot be understood apart from the disorder that stemmed from the end of the hegemony. It can be seen also in international monetary instability, the divergence of economic priorities, and the proliferation of regional conflicts, in which neither superpower would intervene effectively.

Disorder and instability are not the principal hallmarks of the new era, however. In the crisis of the 1970s, important elements of a new international economic political order began to take shape. As time passed, their features became clearer and their significance greater. Three features of the story are particularly relevant to the discussion of the future of international trade: the multilayered character of the new order, altered conceptual underpinnings, and the role of business in the new political economy.

The Character of the New Order

In any account of efforts to manage the international economy since the disorder of the 1970s, initiatives at the global level still merit serious attention. One need only mention the inauguration of the global economic summits in 1975, the related development of the machinery for international economic and monetary policy coordination in the Group of Seven, the completion of the Tokyo Round and the launching of the Uruguay Round itself. These are all important developments and point toward a global regime which may replace the one that crumbled in the late 1960s and early 1970s.

It is, however, important to recognize the limitations of these efforts at the global level. In the monetary and

Table 2.
Growth in the Volume of World Merchandise Trade
by Selected Countries and Groups of Countries,
1984, 1987, and 1988
(Percentage change over preceding year)

	Imports			Exports		
	1984	1987	1988	1984	1987	1988
United States	24	6½	6½	7½	15	21½
West Germany	5	5½	6½	9	3	7½
Japan	10½	9½	16½	15½	½	4
Other developed countries	6½	6½	9	9½	5½	8
Organization of Petroleum Exporting Countries	−6	−13½	−1½	½	−2	8½
Other developing economies	6½	8	12	11	10½	10
World merchandise trade	9	5½	9	8½	5½	8½

macroeconomic sphere, it is true that international cooperation has achieved some successes, notably in the aftermath of the 1987 stock market crisis. Yet, 15 years of experience, backed up by empirical and theoretical studies, suggest that the actual importance of global coordination of policies is profoundly limited. A similar reserve must be expressed in relation to the Uruguay Round itself. In its scope and ambitions, it represents a major step toward a more effective international trade regime. Despite the progress that has been made in enlarging the agenda of the GATT negotiations and the eventual achievement of a midterm agreement, however, it is clear that the provisions eventually agreed to within GATT will not bring order to the complex realities of international trade in goods and services in the last part of the twentieth century.

The principal grounds for adopting this skeptical position are political rather than economic. In the absence of a hegemonic power, it is difficult to see how any global trade (or monetary) regime can acquire the authority that is essential if consistently liberal rules are to be applied.

An indication of the difficulties involved in developing an enforceable system may be found in the intra-European debate about the Single Market. As the 1985 White Paper shows, a modern international trade regime, capable of regulating "new" obstacles to trade, such as technical barriers, fiscal barriers, or rules covering government procurement, involves such deep incursions into national sovereignty that agreement is difficult even among a group of nations such as the European Community. It is barely conceivable that the contracting parties to the GATT, which are more numerous and more widely dispersed in terms of political power, tradition, and economic performance, could agree on any regime comparable in strength.

This is said to put the development of regional groups and even bilateral agreements in their proper perspective. Although there is always the danger that they could become instruments of protectionism, regional and bilateral initiatives can be seen as legitimate responses to a situation in which the old global order has disappeared, and a new one cannot be adequately fashioned overnight. Far from being negative features of the new world scene, regional agreements can and ought to be seen as building blocks on the way to a new world order.

It ought also to be stressed that the new regional regimes are not simply trading arrangements. These latter are part of a political reorganization which finds expression in monetary and even security initiatives. The European Monetary System is an obvious case. Conceived of as a European response to the dethroning of the dollar, it has helped the Europeans to create a zone of stability. As such it has made an important contribution to the maintenance of monetary order in general. In the strictly trade sphere, the point already made in relation to the Single Market could be developed through a discussion of the evolution of relations between the European Community and the European Free Trade Association. In terms of the GATT, the regime that has emerged, particularly since the Luxembourg Declaration of 1984, is undoubtedly, as David Henderson recently observed, preferential and discriminatory.[3] One could even agree with him that one of the main constituent elements of a liberal trading system has thus been explicitly set aside.

If, however, one stops comparing this regional agreement with some abstract model of multilateral trade, and looks at the implications of organizing a genuine free trade regime, the lesser regime, in geographical terms, becomes not an obstacle to international order, but an important contribution to international stability. The same might be said of the Canada-United States Free Trade Agreement, notably in its procedures for dispute management which go far beyond anything that could be contemplated at the global level.

In short, in the new political economy, a multilayered regime is not a sad improvisation or compromise, but an essential feature of the global order.

Altered Conceptual Underpinnings

The world after 1971 may have lost some of the simplicity that characterized the so-called American system at its peak, but this loss has been offset by a remarkable shift in attitudes toward economic management. This shift began to emerge in the second half of the 1970s and created a new environment for governments in the 1980s. In brief, some of its main elements include the following:

The priority given to anti-inflationary policies. The acceptance of the West German model in the late 1970s by France and other European nations that became members of the European Monetary System was matched at the global level by the shift in U.S. policies during the last years of the Carter administration, partly in response to pressure from the Europeans. The initial consequences were painful in Europe, the United States, and the developing world. As the most recent GATT Report on World Trade shows, however, the success in restraining inflation is among the most important explanations of the continuing growth of world trade.

The reduced role of government in economic management. Politicians have not always been consistent in applying the new principles, and there is still covert demand management through fiscal policies and subsidies to industry, agriculture, and other sectors and groups. In general, however, there is little doubt that the consensus is now more minimalist than it was 10–15 years ago.

The vogue for deregulation and increased competition. An obvious example is to be found in the financial mar-

**Table 3.
Interregional and Intraregional
Merchandise Trade, 1980–1988
(Average annual percentage change in value)**

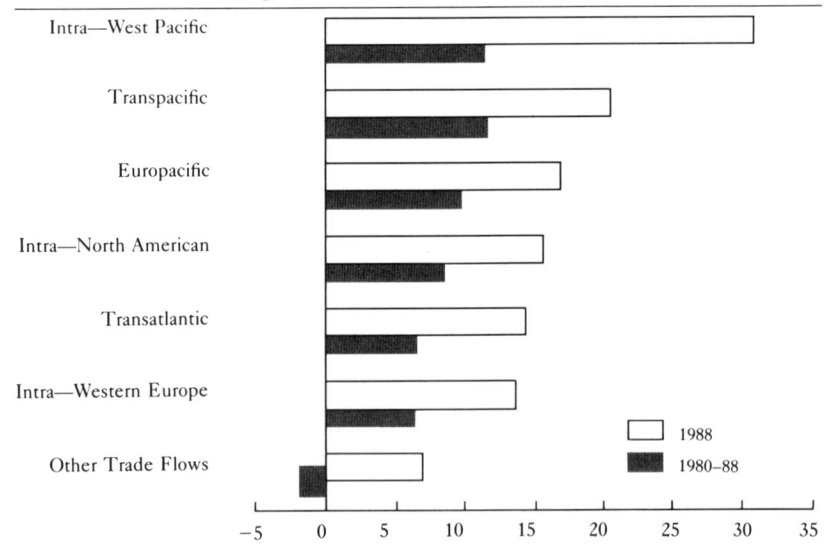

Category	1988	1980–88
Intra—West Pacific	~31	~12
Transpacific	~21	~12
Europacific	~17	~10
Intra—North American	~16	~9
Transatlantic	~15	~7
Intra—Western Europe	~14	~7
Other Trade Flows	~7	~-2

kets, both within countries and regions and at the global level. By releasing a vast quantity of financial assets, they have altered the method by which current account imbalances are financed and created the possibility of an orderly unwinding of the U.S. trade deficits, which many professional economists and market operators still believed improbable a short time ago.

The changes in the ideological climate that have occurred in the last 10 years are among the more important factors making this phase of regional bloc building and reorganization at the bilateral or national level so much less menacing than the oft-cited interwar experiments. The fact that those in high places, not only in the Western world but in the Third World and in the East, have now come to accept the need for sound, noninflationary economic management and the primacy of market forces is of considerable importance for the future of international trade.

The Role of Business in the New Political Economy

In more market-oriented economies, those active in the market are bound to assume a more important role in determining the conditions under which the international economy develops. The important political role of business at the international level can be seen most clearly in Western Europe, where the coalition between the leaders of major European companies and the Commission, which emerged in the early 1980s, has significantly affected both the formulation and implementation of community policy. Both the new generation of industrial policies that were launched during the

Thorn Commission and the Single Market plan itself owe a great deal to the input of the European business sector.

The role of business, however, in altering intra–Community relations goes much further. Acting on the assumption that a single market is now more or less bound to emerge, their strategic planning and their investment decisions, mergers, and acquisitions are already restructuring the European economy and guaranteeing that 1992 becomes a reality.

The role of business at the global level is by definition more diffuse. It is, however, no accident that in explaining the unexpectedly fast growth of world trade in 1988, the GATT secretariat singled out, among the more significant influences, the part played by business investment. In the OECD area, the volume of private nonresidential investment increased by an estimated 11 percent in 1988, a rate of growth matched only twice since the beginning of the 1970s. In an era of global manufacturing and intra–firm trade, the decisions of companies can fundamentally alter the environment with which an international regime must cope. They also constitute another check against foolish policies and global recession.

Policy Priorities in the New International Political Economy

The analysis offered in the preceding section should help explain the paradox posed at the beginning of this paper. It would be wrong to dismiss all jeremiad predictions of gloom as entirely misplaced or suggest that there is nothing dangerous about the present situation. On closer examination, however, the disquiet of many insiders about current developments can be traced back to a tendency to judge contemporary policies by yesterday's standards, in the absence of yesterday's rulers and yesterday's international economy. Nostalgia for the world that existed before 1970 does not provide a basis for policy.

What then are the priorities? The central theme is the need for a multilayered strategy. The thesis can be summarized under the following headings.

Successful Conclusion of the Uruguay Round

Nothing that has been said is intended to suggest that the GATT is irrelevant or that failure in the Uruguay Round would not be disastrous. On the contrary, it is highly undesirable and could be politically dangerous. In order to establish a convincing case about what the GATT can and should do, however, it is extremely important to be mindful of what it cannot do.

It is useful first to distinguish between GATT's functions as the custodian of certain norms of international trade and its role in surveillance and disputes settlement. The GATT has always had a contradictory character: it is the embodiment of the highest universal ideals while also being a down-to-earth reflection of the compromises that its contracting parties could arrive at through negotiation. The principles of free, nondiscriminatory trade embodied in the preamble and Article 1 will (or should) endure forever. The exceptions allowed in Article 11 dealing with agriculture are monuments to human frailty and political wheeling and dealing.

Both types of norm, the permanent and the transitory, are essential to the regime. The former represents the ultimate aspiration while the latter testifies to the continuous and only partially successful effort to bring a widening number of parties and products within the scope of international agreement. In the gap between the universal and the particular, however, there is not only scope but also need for intermediary regimes that go beyond the lowest common denominator. A minimum of international agreement is good in itself: zones where higher standards still can be agreed and enforced do not diminish its utility but complement it.

A similar point emerges in connection with the more practical role of the GATT in surveillance and dispute settlement. To the extent that it can perform either function efficiently, the international economy is bound to be healthier. Its various procedures need, however, to be ranked according to their desirability as well as to their effectiveness. For this reason, the discussion of ways in which GATT's surveillance role could be enhanced are particularly important. Without supernational powers of the kind that are vested in the European Commission or the European Court, there are obvious limits to the ability of the GATT to impose order. It could become, however, a much more important focus for international pressure on wrongdoers than it currently is. Although there has been a great deal of hysteria in non-European discussion of Fortress Europe within the past 12 months, it is difficult to deny the utility of external pressure in persuading European policymakers that the external implications of their policies were of vital importance. If the GATT surveillance machinery were radically reorganized and its decisions communicated and advertised, it could institutionalize external pressure in a highly constructive manner.

Such institutionalization would be, however, a big step. Successive GATT director generals and many of the representatives of member governments have taken pride in the smallness of the secretariat, and the strong emphasis on quiet, patient consensus building. The first director general, Sir Eric Wyndham White, noted that "unlike many other international organizations—and in large part because of its origin—GATT is unencumbered by elaborate administrative or procedural trappings; these are often the antithesis of efficiency."[4] Others contrast the consensus-building record of the cozy club on the edge of Lake Geneva with the more hysterical conduct of trade disputes and wars over matters of lesser significance between the United States and the EC. Yet, if the more regrettable consequences of the emergence of intermediary, less-than-comprehensive regional or bilateral agreements are to be avoided, and a genuine and efficient multilayered regime is to be established, the global layer will need greater authority and a higher profile. This must mean that the GATT secretariat is capable of producing independent analyses of the quality associated with the OECD and the International Monetary Fund. It will also have to develop a capacity to communicate its views, not only to a small number of insiders but through the media, the parliament, and public opinion. These developments would represent a major departure from existing staffing levels and organizational practices. They also go further than measures under discussion in the working party on the functioning of the GATT system. The price is, however, a small one to pay if the principles on which international trade ought to be based are better understood and the intermediary authorities pressured to behave in a more responsible manner.

There are other initiatives which could be taken to underpin the global system. The first would involve the negotiation of some kind of agreement with the Soviet Union and other Eastern bloc countries. It is obvious that in present circumstances full participation in the GATT on anything like normal terms is inconceivable. There is, however, a great deal to be said for involving the USSR even if it is only on an observer basis. Such a move could have educational value for the Soviets and add an element of durability to the liberalization process. It would also be useful to the West, since the issues raised by trade and investment in and with the East seem certain to become important, not only for Western countries, but also as a source of tension and misunderstanding between them.

A second initiative would be the involvement of the private sector in the process. European experience in the 1980s has shown how fruitful a coalition between an international agency (the Commission) and business leaders can be. A deepening of links between business and the GATT secretariat and associated missions could be highly beneficial.

The Development of Regional and Bilateral Initiatives

Stronger regional groupings and even bilateral agreements should be seen primarily as a natural response to the dissolution of the international political economy of the 1950s and 1960s and secondly as complementary to world order. Anybody who doubts this point should consider whether it is conceivable that a legislative program of the dimensions required by the EC White Paper of 1985 could be negotiated within the GATT. If the answer is negative, the necessity of intermediary structures becomes apparent. The danger that these intermediary authorities may establish new types of protectionism does not invalidate the point. It simply reinforces the argument that only a multilayered approach can be effective.

Against this background, there is no reason why any of the countries of the OECD should object to: (1) the negotiation of a comprehensive agreement between the EC and the European Free Trade Association (EFTA) giving reality to the pledge made at Luxembourg in April 1984 by all 18 member states to create a dynamic European Economic Space; (2) the development of a more systematic regime covering EC-EFTA relations with the Mediterranean economies; (3) the intensification of U.S.-Mexico negotiations; (4) the development of Australian-New Zealand cooperation; (5) the creation of a Pacific OECD, with a role not dissimilar to that of the original OEEC in Western Europe; (6) further strengthening of the Association of Southeast Asian Nations (ASEAN) group; and (7) the realization of long cherished but unrealized plans for regional cooperation in Latin America.

The list could be extended indefinitely. In so doing it would become apparent that no one type of regional regime is universally applicable, and that overlaps, the coexistence of special arrangements, and an air of untidiness seem certain to characterize moves in this direction.

Coordinated Western Policies Toward the Developing World

This idea is already implicit in the call for strengthening the global system. It should be considered in its own right, however, because of its intrinsic importance and its long-term benefit to Western countries. It would be a highly visible and effective demonstration of the fact that regional blocs and bilateral agreements are not incompatible with the responsibilities of global citizenship. Changes in the ideological climate referred to above have created a widespread consensus that those who help themselves will flourish best. The recent performance of certain developing countries, with or without IMF tutelage, lends weight to this thesis. There should not be any reversion to the ineffective and expensive paternalism of the immediate postcolonial era. Conditionality should go hand-in-hand with liberality.

In any balanced plan, financial measures will be of paramount importance. Trade policies also have a role. What is needed is a mixture of market-opening measures in the industrialized world, coupled with hard negotiation on the dismantling of tariff and other barriers to trade in the developing world itself. Within the Uruguay Round, the Western countries should agree to abandon the Multi-Fiber Agreement and move further toward the liberalization of trade in agriculture than either the EC or the United States is ready to do.

It would, be dangerous, however, for the developing countries if measures were taken unilaterally by the West. The developing world has its inefficient agricultural producers and textile manufacturers, and any regime that allowed the governments to evade the restructuring of their own economies would do a disservice not only to international trade, but also to the countries themselves. What is required is the consistent application of liberal principles on both sides.

Political Cooperation in the West

This may appear a strange proposal in a paper concerned with the evolution of international trade. During the first 25 years of the postwar alliance the member states have operated a double-track strategy, separating trade policy from more general political and security considerations. The separation could be justified by the asymmetry of the alliance itself, and by the character of East-West relations, in which the military balance was the principal concern and commercial contacts were of much less significance.

In the new international political economy, however, maintenance of a double-track strategy is inappropriate. Those responsible for trade policy or economic policy exercise a vital influence on relations between East and West. One of the most important diplomatic challenges facing the West will be management of change in the Soviet Union and Eastern Europe. Armies will be less exposed than banks and the European Community, which, through its common commercial policy, will be as deeply involved as the NATO Council. Compartmentalized policy formulation, in which security experts talk only to security experts and trade negotiators feed on each others' prejudices, could be dangerous not only for the development of East-West relations but also for the maintenance of cordial West-West relations. Political leadership will be increasingly necessary. Various practical initiatives could be recommended, including the revival of a long-standing proposal to create a transatlantic institution ensuring a regular dialogue on political as well as specific Community concerns between the EC and the United States. A similar mechanism might be devised involving the EC and the Japanese or a more durable trilateral structure.

Acknowledgment: An earlier version of this paper was presented at the March 31–April 2, 1989 conference on "The 1990s: Critical Change" at the Palais d'Egmont in Brussels, Belgium, cosponsored by the Center for Strategic and International Studies and the Centre for European Policy Studies.

Notes

1. Martin Wolf, "The European Community's Trade Policy," *Britain and the EEC*, Roy Jenkins, ed. (London: MacMillan, 1983).

2. David Henderson, "1992: The External Dimension," Group of Thirty, Occasional Paper 25, 1989.

3. *Ibid*.

4. "Trade Policies for a Better Future," the Leutwiler Report (Nijoff, 1987), p. 169.

A Capital-Starved New World Order: Geopolitical Implications of a Global Capital Shortage in the 1990s

Penelope Hartland-Thunberg

FEARS ARE MOUNTING that George Bush's New World Order may founder on a much-bruited global capital shortage. Indeed, the international community is very likely to be starved of capital to varying degrees in the decade ahead. But at the core of the issue is a fundamental paradox: the New World Order is threatened less by what happens to capital availability than by the circumstances that would prevent the emergence of a capital shortage. These circumstances include principally the failed development of the conditions necessary for peace, prosperity, and cooperation in the world, especially in key areas such as Europe and the Middle East. The consequences would be political instability within countries, political tensions between countries, and a slower growth of the world economy. Thus whether or not the shortage materializes, its implications for geopolitical relations in the world arena are serious and merit attention. In what follows the outlook for the supply-demand balance in international capital mar-

kets is examined first and then the geopolitical implications of a relative shortage or plenty of global capital.

In an economic sense a shortage of capital is important because of its significance for interest rates and inflation. Excess demand will either force real interest rates to rise, thereby dampening economic growth, or, if interest rates are kept artificially low through monetary policy, will result in inflation—or both. These consequences of course are important for the outlook for world economic growth and development. But because of the nature and direction of the anticipated excess demand for capital, the consequences of a global shortage during the 1990s are also important to geopolitical relations.

Evidence adduced in support of the capital shortage thesis rests on shifts in international capital flows first observed in the late 1980s and expected to continue during most of the 1990s. These shifts involve a change in the position of some areas of the world from that of a net capital exporter to a net importer (e.g., Europe and Latin America). They also involve a shift from a position of balanced capital flows (or very small net movements) to a net import status (the Middle

---

Penelope Hartland-Thunberg is a senior associate at CSIS. Her most recent book is *China, Hong Kong, Taiwan and the World Trading System* (New York: St. Martin's Press, 1990).

East); a shift from a net import position to an even larger net import position (Asia, excluding Japan); and a shift from a sizable net export flow to a significantly smaller export surplus (Japan). The United States is likely to remain a major capital importer, although during the first half of the decade the decline in the net import position of the United States that commenced in 1988 may counterbalance these movements to some degree.

The Outlook in International Capital Markets: Near Term

Since the mid-1980s global capital markets have been dominated by the dramatic shift in the position of the United States from a net capital exporter to a net importer of unprecedented amounts of foreign capital. Where previously the United States had typically invested abroad a few billion dollars more than foreigners had invested in the United States, in 1985 that position was reversed. Between 1985 and 1990 the United States imported on average every year nearly $125 billion more of capital than it exported.

Foreign individuals and institutions worldwide increased their purchases of dollar assets. On balance, however, most other countries were in the same position as the United States; they were net capital importers. Only a handful exported capital on balance. Chief among these were Japan, Germany, Switzerland, and Kuwait. For the last five years of the 1980s, according to the International Monetary Fund (IMF), their net capital export averaged, respectively, $72 billion, $42 billion, $7 billion, and $5.5 billion.[1] Among others exporting smaller amounts were the Netherlands, Belgium, Korea, and South Africa. Despite data inadequacies, it is clear that the United States hogged the market for international capital because, for good reasons or bad, it was perceived as more credit-worthy than its competitors.

From the evidence available today, it appears likely that the United States will continue as a net capital importer through the 1990s and that it will confront increasing competition in its demand for foreign capital. Demand increases are likely in traditional importing areas like Asia, Latin America, and the Middle East, and also in the shift of traditional export areas to the net import list—notably in Europe.

Economists generally agree that for the United States to eliminate its dependence on foreign capital it must drastically reduce the government budget deficit (federal, state, and local combined). To make the United States self-sufficient in capital requires an increase in national saving; recently savings in the private sector from individuals and corporations have been increasingly offset by negative savings (excess expenditure) in the public sector. Even in the late 1980s when the federal deficit dropped, that improvement was offset by a declining budget surplus at the state and local level with the consequence that government saving remained constant at −2 percent of gross national product (GNP).[2] A recent probing study by the Federal Reserve Bank of New York concludes that even if the budget were balanced by 1995, the net inflow of capital into the United States would continue through the end of the decade, although at a declining rate. Even if the national savings rate by mid-decade were to increase by 5 percentage points (as a share of GNP), either through a decrease in the public deficit or an increase in private savings (a scenario that appears lacking in feasibility), the dependence on foreign capital would continue through the end of the century.[3] In other words, even on the basis of highly optimistic assumptions about the requirement for public-sector borrowing during the 1990s, the United States will continue to rely on foreign capital; the amounts will depend on the national savings rate,[4] and private domestic investment.

During the second half of the 1980s competition for international capital confronting the United States was subdued because various potential claimants were perceived as relatively poor credit risks compared with the United States. The experience of creditors with many of the debt-impacted developing countries had previously been so disastrous that new funds were almost totally unavailable. The consequence was that developing countries as a group became net capital exporters as interest and amortization payments exceeded new inflows. In addition, EC '92, the concerted effort by the European Community to develop community-wide free movement in goods, services, people, and capital (hopefully by 1992 but realistically by the turn of the century), only began to capture the attention of investors at the end of the decade. As it did so, international capital increasingly turned toward Europe. Similarly the attraction of the "Little Tigers" in Asia (Thailand, Malaysia, Indonesia) grew into boom proportions only late in the decade, as did the Japanese investment boom at home.

Meanwhile, the Middle East was a capital deficit area. Despite popular perceptions to the contrary, the larger oil exporters of the region rapidly increased their expenditures abroad after oil price rises but were slow to reduce expenditures following price declines. Only Kuwait and the United Arab Emirates (UAE) sustained net capital exports in every year of the last five years of the 1980s.[5] The Communist countries as a group were capital importers, the largest importer being China. "The poorest of the poor," namely most of the developing world, of course were small capital importers.

Although a global capital shortage is not imminent, international capital markets may become increasingly tight as the 1990s progress. In the immediate future (i.e., for the next 12 to 15 months or so) demand may be sluggish; two factors account for the near-term outlook. First, relatively low economic growth in the industrial countries, a consequence of recession in the United States, Canada, Britain, and Australia, and tight monetary policies in Europe and Japan, will continue to affect investment into next year. Slow growth in the Organization for Economic Cooperation and Development (OECD) is reflected in less buoyant exports from the developing countries with the consequence that even growth rates in the lively industrializing economies of Asia are relatively depressed.

Second, although the total capital requirements implicit in converting Eastern Europe to a free private market system from one of central planning and government ownership and in raising its productivity to the levels of the West are immense, certain basic legal and functional institutions and practices must be replaced before recovery there can take hold. Revising laws in a democracy and dramatically altering such functions as banking practices and accounting definitions inevitably take time. The essential institutional changes are currently in train, although to differing degrees in each country, but it will take more

239

time for practices to change effectively and for the region to be perceived as credit-worthy by investors.

Similarly the total capital requirements implicit in restoring the economies of Kuwait and Iraq to their prewar levels are huge. The same is true of those implicit in even moderately raising growth rates and living standards in the many poor Middle Eastern countries. Only in Kuwait is it likely that much progress will be made in the next year or two. Meanwhile, with the threat of political instability deterring foreign private investors, war-related costs in the Gulf area will remain sufficiently high that the region will be in capital deficit for at least the first half of the decade.

Outlook for International Capital Markets: Long Term

By the end of 1992 or thereabouts world economic activity is likely to quicken and with it the global demand for capital. Although growth in the United States is likely to be close to the bottom of the list of OECD countries, U.S. reliance on international capital will rise because of governmental funding requirements and low private savings rates. U.S. recovery will be retarded until about mid-decade by the high level of corporate and personal debt, by excess capacity in the financial sectors, by the huge overhang of empty commercial buildings on the real estate market, and by the just-in-time inventory policy of business. In the public sector it will be retarded by constraints on state and local governments forced to reduce expenditures and by the federal government's need to finance off-budget items like the savings and loan rescue (which will add to its borrowing requirements but provide no fiscal stimulus), the war, recession, and such. In addition, the low deficits forecast by the budget accord of 1990 were based on several optimistic assumptions that are unlikely to be realized. All of this suggests that unemployment will fall only moderately until later in the decade, private sector savings will remain substantially below their level of the 1970s, and relatively high interest rates and slowly dwindling excess capacity will depress private investment until mid-decade. The one buoyant sector in the U.S. economic outlook for the entire decade of the 1990s will be the export industries that will benefit from more vigorous growth in the rest of the world. Private investment should recover around 1995, resulting in a larger inflow of capital in the second half of the decade.

Europe will be increasingly energized as the EC '92 program moves toward completion in the next century both by rising foreign investment as U.S., Japanese, and Asian businesses seek to benefit from positions inside the Community, and by rising consumption and investment in the new Germany, which will make the Federal Republic an engine of growth for Europe.

Also, as institution-building in Eastern Europe is completed and as training programs become increasingly effective in the area, Poland, Czechoslovakia, and Hungary will offer more and more attractive opportunities for foreign investors. When the USSR will be able to attract foreign investment will depend on when its political crisis is resolved and when the warring internal factions come to agree on what kind of economic system will replace their current chaos. The country's potential for absorbing foreign capital later in the decade is significant. Meanwhile, the European Bank for Reconstruction and Development (EBRD), which opened its doors on

April 15, 1991, will be increasingly able to provide financing to the area and to find projects worthy of support. Although the Bank's annual transfer of capital through the end of the decade may not amount to more than one or two billion dollars, its activities are likely to encourage and support (through market research, joint investments, and such) investment in the area by others from Eastern Europe, Western Europe, and the rest of the world. As the decade continues, Europe's credit-worthiness is likely to be perceived as brighter and brighter and its ability to absorb international capital will expand.

How much capital investment the East will attract will of course depend crucially on developments within the Soviet Union. Bloodshed in the USSR with or without a return to a centralized authoritarian regime would depress investment in Eastern Europe and probably in Western Europe too. On the other hand, higher defense spending that would follow such a contingency would compensate to some degree for the otherwise recessionary consequences. One should not forget that the New World Order assumes that the Cold War will not return, but that assumption has not yet been proven valid.

If during the 1990s Eastern Europe successfully initiates and makes progress on the transition to free private enterprise and the market system while the USSR is unable to do so (or vice versa), global capital markets would still be tight but the capital shortage would not be as acute as if both parts of the East were competing for capital. Estimates of the amount of Western capital "required" are almost as varied as the people making them. In 1991, a year when the "trickle" of Western capital into Eastern Europe was only beginning, it has been estimated at $15 to $20 billion (excluding the former East Germany). It seems reasonable to assume that as the transition moves forward that sum will increase by 50 percent or more, a significant amount when combined with other potential sources of demand. In addition, it has been estimated that in 1991 the German government will spend about $80 billion on the eastern sector, an awesome figure suggesting the magnitude of the task all of these countries are undertaking.

Whether the Middle East remains a capital-deficient area throughout the decade will depend primarily on the course of oil prices, which in the past have been notoriously difficult to forecast. A consensus of informed observers foresees a tightening of oil markets through the 1990s, how tight depending on a variety of factors. IMF forecasts assume that world oil consumption will increase at 1 to 2 percent annually, that real oil prices will remain roughly constant until middecade (as production is resumed in Kuwait and Iraq, it will be reduced elsewhere in the region) and then will increase at about 3 percent a year. Assuming a small current account deficit for Iraq (with funds primarily provided by international institutions), larger deficits for Iran and Saudi Arabia, and a rough balance for Kuwait after middecade implies at best only a negligible capital surplus for the region in the second half of the 1990s. Moreover, as Iran rejoins the world community and undertakes reconstruction after its decade of war and destruction, opportunities for foreign investment there could boom. Saudi Arabia's appetite for arms and industrial construction is likely to be expansive; indeed, the entire area appears addicted to arms that the Chinese and North Koreans at least are willing to provide.[6] The commitment of Saudi Arabia (and the other countries of the Gulf Cooperation Council) to those countries in the region and elsewhere that supported its war effort together with its interest in moderate oil prices seem likely to insure that the Saudi balance of payments will show little surplus for investment elsewhere. If, moreover, political developments within Iraq appear favorable to foreign investors, public and private capital could flow to that country in sizable amounts. All oil-producing countries in the region (and elsewhere) are seeking to expand or upgrade their facilities for production and refining, both highly capital-intensive operations. In short, from the vantage point of the present, the Middle East is unlikely to be a net supplier of any significant amounts of capital during the 1990s and could be a significant absorber.

In contrast to the other traditional sources of capital, only Japan seems likely to continue as a substantial net capital exporter during the 1990s. The pattern of Japan's capital exports, however, has been shifting and these shifts are likely to be maintained during the forthcoming decade. Other countries in Asia like Taiwan, Singapore, and Korea are likely to export more capital on balance as the decade advances; also the rapidly growing emerging countries will save more as their incomes increase and will be able to provide a larger share of their own capital requirements as the next century gets closer.

Until the late 1980s, Japan's appetite for U.S. assets appeared insatiable—indeed, in the United States the complacent rhetorical question was often repeated, "Where else are they going to put their money?" The answer came in earnest in 1990, although the shift began in the previous year. An investment boom at home caused Japan's private domestic fixed investment as a share of GNP to jump by 3 percentage points between 1988 and 1990, while capital exports declined by nearly 40 percent. At the same time, East Asia's economic growth and the imminence of EC '92 made investment in those areas more attractive than in the United States. The consequence was disinvestment by the Japanese in U.S. securities at the turn of the decade and a shrinking of its purchases of U.S. real estate.

The outlook for the 1990s is controversial only in regard to the size of Japan's international capital availabilities, not in regard to the greater diversification of its geographic destinations. The greater attraction of potential yields in Europe and Asia will continue to be strengthened by Japanese concerns over protectionism in North America and the desire to make up for lost time by investing in Europe. Although to date Japanese businesses have been highly cautious about investing in Eastern Europe, they have monitored events there carefully. When they consider the time to be ripe they will be ready to invest. This is not to say that Japanese institutions and businesses are likely to withdraw from U.S. investment activity, but the annual volume is likely to be significantly below the average of the mid-1980s.

There are reasons to expect that Japan's net capital outflows may decline in volume during the decade. Demographic trends indicate that the labor shortage that has recently plagued Japanese industry will continue, thereby stimulating high domestic investment in Japan in labor-saving equipment and techniques. In addition, personal savings in Japan are in a long-term decline, a movement that will be furthered by demographics. Moreover, ongoing institutional changes in the country's financial sector, in raising the level of interest rates internally to international levels, will lessen the attraction of lending abroad.

Competitors for Japanese international capital will include, in addition to the emerging countries of Asia, Western and Eastern Europe, and the United States (probably in that order of credit-worthiness in Japanese perceptions), China, and a few Latin American countries. Total foreign investment in the People's Republic of China will remain subdued until a new regime once again embracing economic reform is installed in Beijing. That may not be until the twenty-first century. Meanwhile, new market-oriented regimes in Mexico, Chile, Venezuela, and possibly Argentina and Brazil will offer more and more attractive opportunities for foreign investors. Israel, which has a moral claim on the investable funds of Jews and Jewish institutions around the world, is overwhelmed by an influx of Soviet immigrants and anticipates foreign borrowing requirements for the next five years at $20 billion. Even Vietnam and the rest of Indochina are likely to be in the market for capital in the 1990s. Beyond a select few, however, the developing countries will find private capital mostly beyond their reach.

Demands on public aid funds and on the facilities of the international financial institutions, the World Bank Group—the International Bank for Reconstruction and Development (IBRD) and its associated agencies—and the IMF, are mounting as are proposals for new institutions or facilities within or outside of the existing ones. The Gulf Cooperation Council (comprising Saudi Arabia, Oman, Qatar, Bahrain, Kuwait, and the United Arab Emirates) has already established its own $10 billion development program to aid war-affected countries and other supporters of the Gulf War effort and is urging developed countries to contribute. The EBRD has only $12.4 billion in capital provided by 39 industrial countries, but its president hopes that its activities will stimulate with a multiplier effect more than $100 billion in new public and private capital for Eastern Europe and the USSR. The Bush administration has proposed a five-year "Enterprise for the Americas" plan of $1.5 billion, urging Japan and the EC to join as equal partners, again with the hope that the plan will stimulate private investment in the area. The World Bank is seeking an increase of $1.3 billion in the capital of its private sector affiliate, the International Finance Corporation. Although during the late 1980s both the IBRD and the IMF became net receivers of funds because repayments exceeded new loans, their lending activities have recently been increasing, especially to Eastern Europe. Indeed an Asian Development Bank (ADB) report in April 1991 worried that new demands from Eastern Europe and the Gulf could drain funds from Asia and increase the cost of capital to the region. The loan activities of the ADB have also been slowing and budget constraints on its donors will probably result in no real growth in ADB resources through the first half of the 1990s.[7] The British meanwhile have been pushing for international support for a plan, known as the "Trinidad Terms," to ease the debt burden of the poorest developing countries by a cancellation of their debts to creditor governments.

Together these plans, hopes, and prayers rest on a shrunken base of capital availabilities compared with the salad days of the 1970s. Many are bound to be disappointed, all will find the costs high. The potential for world inflation is significant as all parts of the world in aggregate strive to consume

243

and invest more than the world as a whole is producing; the Bundesbank, the Bank of Japan, and the Federal Reserve Board will have their work cut out for them.

Geopolitical Implications

It is useful to speculate about the factors that might forestall the development of a global capital shortage. This expectation rests heavily on the conversion of Europe to the status of a net capital importer, which in turn depends primarily on a mounting flow of funds, public and private, into Eastern Europe and the Soviet Union from Western Europe and the rest of the world. It also rests on the assumption that oil prices will remain moderate. The capital inflow will fail to develop to any significant degree if political stability in the East is viewed as precarious or if rising costs there make the bottom-line calculus unattractive. Either would be bad news. Investment would be discouraged by the danger of the political instability that would probably be the consequence of a strong internal faction's advocacy of political independence. Such instability would hamper the fashioning of national economic policies (e.g., in the USSR or Czechoslovakia). In addition the retention of extensive government ownership of business would similarly delay the formation of new market-oriented policies. Neither of these contingencies would cause investment to cease, but it would delay and diminish the flow of capital and the recovery of the economies of Eastern Europe.

The very fact that the word *balkanization* has become part of the West's lexicon suggests that the danger of political fragmentation has strong historical precedent in Eastern Europe. Long-suppressed nationalistic forces can quickly resurface after the removal of authoritarianism and may lead to the creation of sovereign states too small to be viable economic entities.

The strength of liberal and conservative political factions internally varies from country to country. Either, moreover, can wane, surge, split, or recombine as has recently happened in the USSR and Hungary. Investment shrinks as uncertainty rises.

The greatest unknown in Eastern Europe lies in the degree of political patience that the citizenry can summon in the face of the austerity and unemployment that temporarily must accompany the wrenching experience of shifting from a planned, widely subsidized economy to one based on individual initiative, profit, and bankruptcy. What is involved is essentially a shift from a secure, riskless society to an environment offering the opportunity for individual betterment but at relatively high risk. The more severe and prolonged the period of austerity, the more the enthusiasm for the new system is likely to wane and the more comfortable the old will appear.[8] An articulate, populist leader claiming that he can solve the problems of unemployment and living standards without austerity may have great appeal.[9] This, however, is the Latin American solution that has often resulted in authoritarian regimes as well as hyperinflation and general economic deterioration as the countries struggle in vain to consume more than they produce.

The danger of insufficient patience to stay the course toward a new society will be enhanced if the European Community is niggardly in admitting exports from the East to its protected market. In this regard EC agricultural policies are of special importance because of the large role of agriculture in the economies of Poland and Hungary as well as Rumania, Bulgaria, and Albania. Thus far the Community has not been forthcoming in response to appeals from the East for some kind of associate membership. If the EC's reluctance persists, capital investment in the East can be seriously retarded.

Political instability in Eastern Europe and/or the USSR, whether the result of economic or political causes, would be likely to lead to increased defense spending in both the East and West. In the East, defense spending could be a tool of economic policy (to help solve unemployment problems) and security policy (to help maintain the existing regime in power). In Western Europe it would follow from the perception of heightened dangers on the eastern borders. In either case rising defense expenditures would be likely to retard the flow of investment resources to Eastern Europe as national savings rates declined.

Slow growth and prolonged austerity in Eastern Europe and the USSR would undoubtedly be accompanied by a rising volume of migration from East to West, legal and illegal. Since the collapse of the iron curtain, European Community members have been agitated by the danger of a mounting flood of foreign workers seeking employment in the EC and the political dissension and internal resentment in the West that could follow. This potential has made the EC '92 goal of a free flow of labor within the Community vastly more difficult to implement. By the same token the immigration potential is an important factor in EC reluctance to admit East European countries to associate membership.

Foreign capital alone cannot ensure a successful transformation within the decade of Eastern Europe and the USSR into growth economies with a rising standard of living because the capital requirements are beyond the capacities of the West to provide. At the margin, however, a rising inflow of foreign investment can buoy the hope and sustain the confidence of the East, encouraging the citizenry to stay the course of sacrifice and hard work that is essential to the transformation. Western capital, moreover, cannot compensate for political or geographic fragmentation in the area, for the failure of the EC to open its markets, for the failure to establish institutions that provide the foundation of a successful market economy, or for the unwillingness of a majority to sustain the declining living standards and great insecurities involved in the early years of the transformation process.

Thus if Europe as a whole does not become a net capital importer during the 1990s, the consequences are likely to entail enhanced political instability in the entire area. The New World Order, with its hope for peace, justice, and prosperity, could be aborted. For Eastern Europe the lost opportunity could be irreplaceable. If much of Eastern Europe or the USSR should follow the Latin American option, they would slip yet farther behind the West, thereby making the task of catching up even more difficult. If a diaspora of East Europeans were to follow and become concentrated in Western Europe, it could delay or obliterate the completion of EC '92. In addition, it could divert Europe's attention from larger, worldwide issues to solely Eurocentric concerns. The world as a whole would have lost an opportunity for growth and amity unequaled in the century.

The appearance of a global capital shortage in the 1990s could also be forestalled by the development of a sizable and sustained net capital export from the Middle East. Such an eventuality would be most likely to

245

occur as a result of a large increase in the real price of oil (e.g., above $30/barrel in today's prices). A sustained oil price hike would come about only if the Saudi Arabian regime were to initiate a dramatic shift in its long-term oil price policy. Since the early 1970s the Saudis have argued for a moderate oil price policy in order to avoid the stimulus to conservation and the development of oil substitutes that high real oil prices induce. Saudi petroleum reserves are so immense that such a pricing policy maximizes the aggregate long-term revenue attainable from them. Although the House of Saud may change its price policy temporarily for political reasons, a long-term sustained high oil price policy seems improbable during their tenure.

Any sustained change would imply the replacement of the royal family by a regime committed to maximizing present, not long-term, oil revenues. Such a regime would probably have different geopolitical goals than those of the Saud family. If the new regime represented a radical Arab group, higher current oil revenues could be desired for welfare payments to the poorer Arab states, for economic development in those states, for war preparations (including nuclear and missile capabilities) against perceived external enemies, for subversion, propaganda, and espionage abroad, or any combination of the above. The geopolitical map of the world would be vastly altered; growth rates in the oil-importing countries would collapse, at least temporarily; the effects on Eastern Europe could be disastrous; even with oil prices in the moderate range, East Europeans have been struggling to find the convertible currency now required for their oil imports from the USSR. The USSR would benefit, but unless the leadership of that country had committed itself to economic reform, the higher foreign exchange earnings would probably be squandered.

High oil prices (above $30/barrel in 1991 prices) if sustained for a number of years would almost certainly obliterate the New World Order. Resentment in oil importing countries against the regime instituting such a policy could become virulent. The danger of another armed conflict in the Gulf would be high. This danger in fact would be likely to give pause to any regime contemplating such a pricing policy shift.

Although from a rational viewpoint a sustained high oil price policy in the Middle East appears unlikely, the many long-standing enmities lacerating the region endure; its commitment to violence and retribution appears little altered. Bitterness between the haves and the have-nots can only be heightened by the policy of the rich Gulf states to aid solely those who offered support in the war. While Saddam Hussein remains in power, political instability will be rife, and if Iran should engineer his replacement by one of its supporters, nascent cooperation between Iran and Saudi Arabia would return to competition. A coup in Saudi Arabia cannot be ruled out, nor can the chance of high oil prices.

The appearance of a global capital shortage could also be forestalled if investment opportunities in Asia cease to be attractive. Once again the most likely cause of such an eventuality is political; potential economic causes do not have a high probability. For example, a sharp spike in real oil prices in the first half of the decade could have such an effect, but oil-consuming countries have had a good bit of experience in learning how—and how not—to cope successfully with high real oil prices. Moreover, Asia is an oil producer and thus would benefit somewhat from higher prices. Although temporary high oil prices would reduce the volume of world trade and redirect it, the competitive strength of the Asian economies implies that they would suffer less than other parts of the world. Investment, except in the oil producers, would decline and the global capital shortage would at least be postponed but less because of the decline in the demand for capital in Asia than from its decline elsewhere.

Whether a collapse in the U.S. market for Asian exports would by itself be sufficient to reduce Asia's growth and demand for international capital is not clear. Japan and the rest of the Pacific Rim could remain prosperous and growth in South and East Asia could continue, although at a slower pace, if policy changes in Japan successfully encouraged a large increase in Japanese consumption. Such a drastic change in Japanese policy appears improbable but not impossible.

A collapse in the U.S. demand for Asian goods could flow from virulent protectionism introduced in the United States. Such a development would affect world trade in the aggregate and could effectively eliminate the possibility not only of a global capital shortage but of the continuing U.S. role as the world leader. The New World Order would have no hope of surviving.

Investment in South and East Asia could be depressed by political developments in the area, perhaps in the form of renewed Chinese or Soviet threats to the stability of the region. A military crackdown by the People's Republic of China (PRC) in Hong Kong (to suppress alleged subversion there) or an attack on Taiwan (because of a declaration of independence there) would probably be highly destabilizing because, rightly or wrongly, it would be perceived as an expansionary move on the part of the PRC. The return of an authoritarian regime in the USSR, especially if it resulted in enhanced Soviet influence in Indochina, would also be threatening. None of these now appears to present a threat to Asia in the 1990s. The most likely source of political instability seems to lie in the Korean peninsula, where an aging leader in the North will in due course move on. Events in North Korea after Kim Il-Sung are unpredictable, but rumors of a nuclear capability there are rife. A nuclear-armed North Korea under Kim or his successor could be highly destabilizing, not only to the area, but also to the entire world.

In summary, a global capital shortage in the sense defined above would reflect successful reconstruction and development in parts of the world mostly untouched by economic growth since World War II. As such it should be welcomed. The high interest rates that are implicit would allocate private capital to the most credit worthy; bilateral and multilateral foreign aid could ensure that countries of greater perceived risk are not totally excluded.

Dangers of inflation could be awesome. Pressures on governments to provide more help to eminently worthy countries, groups, and institutions may be irresistible. Efforts to expand the abilities of the multinational institutions to offer aid to the poorest of the poor as well as emerging economies will mount. In any year, however, the resources of the world are limited; the world cannot consume and invest more than it produces. World inflation would redistribute income toward rentier classes, further impoverishing the poor and contributing to political instability all over the world.

Inflationary dangers could be managed by appropriate monetary and fiscal policies. Such management would by no means be easy but it is not impossible. If, however, the worldwide demand for resources does seriously outstrip increases in world output—whether or not because of policy mismanagement in one important area—bitter recriminations over policy are likely. In these the United States will certainly be called to task for competing ("unfairly" will be implicit if not explicit) with struggling young democracies valiantly attempting to change their ways in the face of a greedy, recalcitrant, arrogant behemoth.

For the United States, a global capital shortage in the 1990s implies increasing competition for U.S. goods, services, and companies around the world. Trade will follow capital flows; thus although U.S. exports will benefit from growth in Asia and Eastern Europe, exports from Japan and Western Europe (respectively) will benefit most. More rapid growth in Europe and Japan implies that U.S. economic leadership will steadily diminish. It is not inconceivable that the Japanese economy could equal the U.S. economy in size at the turn of the century. By the twenty-first century the United States may be the world leader—a world leader or an also-ran.

Implications for the New World Order and the United States

The New World Order has been defined in summary as post–cold war responsibility-sharing. President George Bush defined it more fully during a speech in Alabama in April 1991. He spoke of his vision of new ways to achieve peace and prosperity in the world based on "a responsibility imposed by our successes." He based his hopes on commitments shared by large and small nations to four principles: peaceful settlement of disputes; solidarity against aggression; reduced and controlled arsenals; and just treatment of all peoples. He took the occasion to warn that in an interdependent world "no industrialized nation can maintain membership in the global community without assuming its fair share of responsibility for peace and security."

The leadership of the New World Order, however, remains ambiguous. The United States has seized the leadership role in this, as in the Gulf War, by default. U.S. military strength and its commitment to international agreements were put to the test and proven in that war (although some would doubt the accuracy of this statement). Unlike its ability to lead by example in the military realm, however, U.S. ability to set an example in the economic realm has been emasculated by a decade of economic excess. Not only does the United States lack the resources necessary to support its vision of the New World Order, but it is competing for those resources with the very nations it wants to help. The United States seeks to lead by exhortation, but with little or no leverage. Its geopolitical priorities are not necessarily those of Europe and Japan, for whom "responsibility-sharing" equates to "burden-sharing." Many in Europe and Japan resent what they see as a U.S. demand that they foot the bill for U.S. initiatives in which they have no voice. Disputes over priorities are simmering; the resolution of the burden-sharing versus the responsibility-sharing issue is not in sight. To a large degree this resolution awaits a definition by both Japan and Europe of what their proper role in the post–cold war world should be and whether it should be regional or global. In the past each has been content to confine its world role to international commerce, leaving leadership in geopolitical decisions to the United States. Now they are being asked to dilute their pursuit of profit by the broader interests of world peace and political stability. The ambiguity of their responses to the Gulf War indicates that they are not yet committed to a world role.

The opportunity for constructive harmony in geopolitical relations has never been so great since World War I when sharp ideological differences first began to shape the world. Today the degree of consensus on the principles of a market economy, democracy, and pluralism is truly astonishing, embraced not only by the industrialized democracies but by most of the developing world and the formerly centralized, one-party authoritarian states. This consensus developed Topsy-like during the 1980s as the failure of communism was acknowledged by its practitioners and while the rapid growth of export-based Asian economies, most of whom claimed without justification to be free markets, attracted attention in the import-replacement, closed economies in most of the developing world. The awesome victory of the United Nations coalition during the Gulf War served to consolidate the consensus. That consensus encouraged the industrialized countries to believe that fledgling market economies and emerging democracies merited financial help.

Just as the opportunities contained in this new consensus are immense, so are its hazards. The terms *democracy* and *market-mechanism* have been grasped by citizens of failing systems as an incantation, often without any real comprehension of what is entailed or what sacrifices will be necessary to make the shift to the newly embraced system. There is the danger that the amulet can be discarded as quickly as it was grasped.

The greatest contribution that the United States can make during the 1990s toward the success of the New World Order lies in strengthening its own economy. Only by increasing the productivity of its own resources can it once again raise its own standard of living, eliminate its dependence on foreign capital, and generate the resources necessary to support its foreign policy by example rather than exhortation. If the promise of the New World Order fails to materialize, the blame will fall in large measure on the United States.

Notes

1. Data on international capital flows are ambiguous and unreliable. They are statistically hard to measure because they exist in such magnitude, because of exchange rate changes and other valuation problems, because of the desire for secrecy on the part of many borrowers or lenders, and because statistical techniques employed in many countries leave much to be desired. As a consequence of the resulting errors and omissions, IMF data show aggregate payments of international capital exceed receipts, which for the world cannot happen. Figures cited in the text should be viewed only as rough orders of magnitude, even for the United States and other developed countries. It should be noted that the consistent direction of the errors gives a bias toward gloom in the IMF data.

2. Federal Reserve Bank of Boston, *New England Economic Review*, September–October 1990, p. 44.

3. Ethan S. Harris and Charles Steindel, "The Decline in U.S. Savings and Its Implications for Economic Growth," Federal Reserve Bank of New York, *Quarterly Review* 15, no. 3–4 (Winter 1991), p. 14.

4. It is interesting to note that in most industrial countries private savings (as a share of GNP) are relatively constant with changes in corporate savings moving in the opposite direction from changes in personal savings. "Savings Trends and Behav-

ior in OECD Countries," *OECD Working Paper No. 67* (Paris, 1989).

5. Robert Mabro, "Surplus Economies: Middle East Oil Producers," *International Economic Insight* 2 (March/April 1991), p. 4.

6. *Far Eastern Economic Review*, May 23, 1991, p. 16.

7. *Financial Times* (London), April 24, 1991, p. 4; *Far Eastern Economic Review*, April 25, 1991, p. 51.

8. See "Old Regime Comforts Many East Germans," *Financial Times* (London), May 24, 1991, p. 3.

9. In Poland after only about six months of austerity following the shift to a market system an astonishing number of Poles voted for a Canadian businessman (for president) who was promising such wonders.

Global Demographic Trends to the Year 2010: Implications for U.S. Security

Gregory D. Foster et al

ON JULY 18, 1969, in proposing the creation of a National Commission on Population Growth and the American Future, president Richard M. Nixon observed:

> One of the most serious challenges to human destiny in the last third of this century will be the growth of the population. Whether man's response to that challenge will be a cause for pride or for despair in the year 2000 will depend very much on what we do today. If we now begin our work in an appropriate manner, and if we continue to devote a considerable amount of attention and energy to this problem, then mankind will be able to surmount this challenge as it has surmounted so many during the long march of civilization.

These words are, if anything, even more salient today than in 1969 for, although people are two decades closer to the end of the century, they

---

Gregory D. Foster is professor of sociology at the Industrial College of the Armed Forces, National Defense University. He, Alan Ned Sabrosky, and William J. Taylor, Jr., coedited *The Strategic Dimension of Military Manpower* (Cambridge, Mass.: Ballinger, 1987). This article is derived from a report prepared for the Commission on Integrated Long-Term Strategy.

remain woefully unappreciative of the demographic dimension of international relations. Largely, this is because both the causes and the effects of complex social phenomena continue, as always, to elude scientific understanding. Circumstances do not permit Americans the luxury of ignoring events until they occur simply because the tools of prognosis at their disposal are so ill developed. In fact, looming resource constraints demand heightened levels of prescience by the United States in its handling of global affairs. It is appropriate, therefore, even if somewhat daunting, to look once again into the future—perhaps to the end of the first decade of the next century—to ascertain how important population matters might be to the security interests of the United States.

Generally speaking, demographic developments promise to have a material effect on the general complexion of the world over the next two decades. The world's population, which now stands at 4.9 billion (almost double the 1950 level of 2.5 billion), is increasing at an annual rate of 1.7 percent. If this rate were to continue, global population would double again in 41 years. However, the rate of growth has been declining since the late 1960s, when it peaked at 2.1 percent. It is expected to fall to 1.4–1.5

percent by the year 2000, then to zero toward the end of the twenty-first century.

Despite declining growth rates, the absolute size of the world's population will continue to grow dramatically. According to UN estimates, annual additions to world population will average 86 million between 1990 and 1995, will peak at 89 million between 1995 and 2000, then gradually taper. By 2010 roughly 7 billion people will live on this planet. Ninety-three percent of the growth between now and then will be in the less developed countries (LDCs). Whereas LDCs represent slightly less than 76 percent of current world population (nine percentage points higher than in 1950), fully 81 percent of the population two decades from now will reside in the Third World.

One of the most important issues in the years ahead will be the extent to which demographic developments are likely to affect the size and composition of military establishments around the world. On the whole, demographic factors will produce completely different concerns in the developed world than in the developing world. Declining fertility rates will make it increasingly difficult for the United States and its North Atlantic Treaty Organization (NATO) allies and the Soviet Union and its Warsaw Pact allies alike to maintain military forces at current levels. In contrast, exceptionally high fertility rates in most LDCs, if not matched by a commensurate growth of jobs, could lead to expanded military establishments in affected countries as a productive alternative to unemployment. In other words, where labor forces are significantly underemployed, military establishments may have a built-in momentum to capitalize on unused manpower for purposes of both internal and external security.

The distribution of population change may or may not produce shifts in the international balance of power over the next two decades. To the extent that the types of conflicts likely to predominate in the years ahead are manpower-intensive regional conflicts, developing states may indeed accrue added power and influence. Nonetheless, increased population in and of itself will not increase national power. National power will be enhanced only where a solid economic base, a stable political system, and adequate educational resources are present as well.

Another significant demographic fact affecting the world today is the general aging of the population, a condition brought on by the decline of previously high fertility rates and increases in life expectancy since 1950. The number of elderly persons has grown and, for the next 50 years, will continue to grow, more rapidly than the total population in most countries. At present, more than 286 million people in the world are 65 years of age or older, a figure that will increase to 418 million by 2000. The situation is especially pronounced in the developed world, where the median age by the year 2025 will be almost 39. In contrast, the median age in the developing world by that time will stand at about 30 (with some regions, such as Africa, appreciably lower).

The significance of this pattern lies in the fact that aging implies a reduction in productivity and the possibility of economic stagnation. It produces a high ratio of retirees to workers and thus increased taxes and social security expenditures. Armed forces must compete for both money and people, but less overall money exists because the productive population base has shrunk. Such conditions seem likely to have their most demonstrable effect in the years ahead among NATO nations and in Japan, all of which have sizable welfare spending programs.

An altogether different type of spending burden will manifest itself in the developing world, where rapid population growth already has produced a situation in which sizable proportions of the population are under normal working age. Thus, whereas in the developed world resources may have to be diverted to support elderly nonworkers, in the developing world resource diversion may be necessary to support youthful nonworkers. In Africa, for example, 43 percent of the population will be under the age of 15 in 2010.

A particularly critical issue that will continue to spark heated debate concerns the economic and resource implications of rapid population growth. Neo-Malthusians contend that rapid population growth slows down the growth of per capita income and further depletes an already burdened world resource base. Critics counter that such assumptions ignore the role of markets in bringing population, resources, and the environment back into balance. They see population growth to be a stimulus, rather than a deterrent, to economic advancement. The truth seems to lie somewhere between these two positions. Although slower population growth promises to enhance economic development, expanded population size may produce such positive effects as greater conservation. The real bottom line is that rapid population growth will continue to aggravate the ill effects of policy failures, such as an overemphasis on urban areas at the expense of rural areas, food subsidies that distort agricultural markets, and inadequate management of common property, such as air and water. Consequently, where such rapid growth occurs, special attention must be paid to social organization, technological exploitation, and the general governing capacity of the regimes in power.

Urbanization seems certain to remain a major source of problems that could produce political and social instability in various parts of the world. In 1950 29 percent of the world's population lived in urban areas. By 1985 that figure had risen to 42 percent. Whereas only four cities in the world at the start of this century had more than 2 million people, there were 85 such cities in 1985. By 2000 there will be an additional 85 cities of that size. Nearly half of the world's population is expected then to be living in urban areas: 40 percent in developing countries and 78 percent in developed countries.

If there be any cause for alarm over the level of urbanization in the developed world, it concerns the potential vulnerabilities of such population concentrations to acts of terrorism. More discernible are the seeds of social unrest that have accompanied, and will continue to accompany, rapid urbanization in the developing world: crowded living conditions, the spread of contagious diseases, lack of sanitation, severe unemployment, environmental pollution, high crime rates, and heightened demands on local and national governments for services that already have been overextended by dwindling tax bases. Unless such conditions are alleviated, the potential for violent upheaval will be considerable. Considering the extent to which rapid population growth in LDCs is likely to continue being absorbed by cities, no developing region seems immune. By 2010 the percentage of urban population may be as high as 75 percent in Latin America, 73 percent in the Middle East, 46 percent in Africa, and 43–44 percent in South and Southeast Asia.

Given what are likely to be increasing disparities between have and have-not countries and regions of the world, international migration also promises to assume ever greater proportions. Perhaps the most critical movements of humanity will occur where low-growth areas lie in close proximity to high-growth areas: the United States with the Caribbean Basin and Europe with the Middle East and North Africa. Where immigrants cannot be assimilated readily due to cultural differences and where they are perceived to be taking jobs from host-country citizens, political instability may ensue.

Such generalized developments and others as well assume meaningful and actionable policy dimensions only when viewed in terms of their expected nature and magnitude in various countries and regions of the world. Accordingly, it is useful to look at those demographic trends and developments around the globe that may have implications for U.S. security in the years ahead.

The United States

Today the United States is the fourth most populous country in the world with a population of roughly 244 million. That population will grow another 40 million by 2010. The population is expected to begin declining seven years later. The United States' percentage of total world population has declined from 6 percent in 1950 to 5 percent in 1988 and will drop to 4 percent by 2010.

The population 18 to 24 years of age peaked in 1981 at 30.5 million—a total that may not be surpassed for at least the next 100 years. This military-age group will decline by about 7 million through 1996, then gradually increase again to peak at around 27.7 million in 2010 (comparable to the population level in 1987).

The U.S. population is aging: the median age nationwide was 31.5 years in 1985; in 2010 it is expected to be more than five years older. The elderly (65 and over) now number almost 29 million in the United States (12 percent of the population), twice what it was in 1955. The figure is likely to double again by the mid-2020s and by 2050 will approach 70 million (accounting for more than 20 percent of all Americans). In 2010 the figure will be about 39 million.

Immigration may account for approximately one-fifth or more of U.S. population growth in future years. During the period 1980–1985, net immigration represented over 28 percent of total population growth in the United States, the highest rate in this country since the 1901–1910 period. Forty-eight percent of the immigrants admitted during this most recent period were Asians and 35 percent Latins.

In 1985 persons of Spanish origin represented about 7 percent of the population. This figure is likely to increase to 11 percent by 2010, with a higher proportion in younger age groups (for instance, 13 percent of all 19-year-olds). Under varying assumptions, Hispanic persons could account for between 20 and 54 percent of U.S. population growth over the next 25 years.

By 2010 white non-Hispanic persons will represent 68–73 percent of the population, compared with 78 percent in 1985, as the proportion of blacks, Hispanics, and Asians increases. The fastest growing minority group—Asian-Americans—is expected to increase from around 1.6 percent of the population to just over 3 percent by 2010.

In 1985 studies showed that 71 percent of women 18 to 44 years old were in the labor force. About 48 percent of new mothers (with a child 12 months or younger) were working, compared with 31 percent in 1971. By 1990 65 percent of all new job applicants may be women.

Educational attainment levels have increased among persons 25 years of age and over, and proportionately more for blacks than for whites. At the same time, scores on widely used tests of aptitude and scholastic achievement have declined remarkably. Yet, other researchers report massive IQ (intelligence quotient) gains that have occurred over a single generation in 14 nations (including the United States).

Finally, the U.S. Centers for Disease Control expect 324,000 diagnosed cases of acquired immune deficiency syndrome (AIDS) by the end of 1991, compared with about 35,000 cases in May 1987. Other experts forecast 400,000 or more diagnosed cases over the next four or five years. In 1987 about 1 of 30 young to middle-aged men were reported to be infected with the virus.

One of the most important questions facing the U.S. military in the years ahead under all-volunteer conditions will be not whether it can recruit the required quantity of manpower but whether it can entice the required quantity with the required qualities to join. Given the increasing technological complexity of the U.S. military today, most jobs in the armed forces call for aptitude-test scores that exceed minimum eligibility scores. Aptitude requirements in certain high-tech jobs currently would disqualify as many as 70 percent of the male population and almost 90 percent of all otherwise eligible women. By the early 1990s some authorities believe 55 percent of all qualified and available men under the age of 23 would have to volunteer for service if the military is to fulfill its requirements (assuming no changes in current military policy and standards).

As the population continues to shrink, competition to fill vacancies undoubtedly will intensify between the military, colleges, and civilian employers. As this competition intensifies, recruiting costs seem likely to escalate, and pay levels will have to be increased to keep pace with the civilian job market. Pumped-up pay or bonuses for enlistment and reenlistment, when combined with other defense expenditures, could seriously squeeze the federal budget.

Demands for increased social spending also are likely to increase pressures to trim defense. A good deal of the pressure will emanate from the needs of the aging U.S. society. The nation's elderly currently receive 28 percent of the federal budget (almost double the share 25 years earlier) and nearly half of all domestic program spending. Most of the money goes to Social Security (received by 93 percent of the elderly), and about 23 percent of the total is spent on Medicare. The number of people requiring formal or informal long-term care is expected at least to double by 2020.

One of the most notable changes that has taken place in the U.S. military in recent years and that will continue to have a telling impact is the appreciable increase in married personnel. One survey conducted in 1985 showed that 60 percent of enlisted personnel were married, with higher proportions in the upper pay grades.

Approximately 70 percent of the officers surveyed were married. Because married service members and their families are heavy consumers of services and benefits, costs will probably expand.

Whatever impact AIDS may have on military and social cohesion and the depletion of manpower, its most likely immediate effect will be the rising costs of the disease to the nation as a whole. A recent study, endorsed by the Office of Technology Assessment, predicts that medical costs alone will grow eightfold, totaling $8.5 billion by 1991. Research, education, and blood screening costs are expected to quadruple to $2.3 billion. In addition, indirect costs from the lost wages and productivity of working-age people could reach $55.6 billion. These costs add up to $66.4 billion—a staggering increase over the total economic cost of $5 billion in 1985 and $10 billion in 1987. These developments and others will set discernible bounds on how the United States interprets and responds to situations around the world over the next two decades and beyond.

The Soviet Union

The Soviet Union, with a population of 284 million, is the third most populous nation in the world. By the year 2010 the Soviet population is expected to be 334 million. Similar to the United States, the Soviet Union's share of the world's population has declined from 7.2 percent in 1950 to 5.8 percent in 1988 and will decline further to 4.8 percent by 2010. As with other areas of demographic concern, tremendous disparities exist among the Soviet republics with respect to their contributions to overall population growth. Among the most striking examples is Uzbekistan, which constitutes 7 percent of the Soviet population but currently contributes 30–40 percent of net Soviet growth.

Crude birth rates (births per 1,000 population) and fertility rates (number of children born per woman) both reflect similar disparities among republics. The overall crude birth rate, which was roughly 30 in 1950 and dropped to 17.4 in 1970, was 19.6 in 1986. Whereas the rate in the Russian republic and the Baltic republics is 13 to 15, it ranges from 30 to 40 in the Central Asian republics. Overall fertility rates, in turn, dropped from 2.8 in 1958–1959 to 2.4 in 1984–1985 and are expected to be roughly 2.3 in the year 2000. Among Russians, the fertility rate is roughly 2; among Slavs and Baltic peoples 1.6; and among Central Asians 4.5–6. Pronatalist policies adopted by the Soviet leadership in 1981 to stimulate fertility, especially among Slavs and Baltic peoples, have brought western republics close to a rate of 2.1 (replacement level).

Since 1979 morbidity rates have increased radically. A major cause is diphtheria, a sickness which averaged 1,500 new cases a year during the 1983–1985 period (compared with 0 to 2 cases a year in the United States). The incidence of diphtheria is high because about 50 percent of the people in the Russian republic and several other republics do not receive vaccinations. Typhoid and hepatitis are two further sources of high morbidity rates. In contrast with the United States, which may have 100–500 new cases of typhoid a year, the Soviet Union reported 18,900 new cases in 1984 and 17,600 new cases in 1985. Similarly, an estimate of 1.4 million cases of hepatitis in the Soviet Union in 1981–1982 compares with a recent figure of 65,000 new cases in the United States. Other leading causes of death in the USSR include cardiovascular diseases, respiratory diseases, and cancer. More conscripts reportedly are being rejected due to poor health. Nonetheless, health expenditures, after falling in recent years, appear again to be rising at least slightly. Consequently, life expectancy in the Soviet Union in 1988 is up to 64 for males, reattaining the 1959 level after two decades of decline.

Some estimates indicate that the Soviets draft 80–85 percent of available 18-year-old males each year. In 1985 the cohort of 18-year-old males was estimated to be 2.1 million—half a million smaller than in 1979. This trend may have bottomed out and started to rebound. Nonetheless, the U.S. Census Bureau projects that by the year 2000 the cohort will number only 2.5 million, still less than in 1979. If Mikhail Gorbachev's economic reforms work or if arms-control agreements alleviate military pressures, the available manpower pool is likely to continue to suffice. However, if the economic reforms fail, the Soviets may have to return to a more extensive approach to economic growth. This could exert pressure for military manpower reductions because conscripting most of the available young men could have disruptive effects on the civilian labor market. During 1970–1985, there was a net growth in the Soviet workforce (the 20–59 age cohort) of 30 million persons. Between 1986 and 2000, though, the net growth in that age group is expected to be only 6 million, mostly from the southern tier. Two factors will continue to restrain military manpower reductions. First, the Soviet leadership still views service in the armed forces as a major instrument of political socialization. Second, the republics, especially in Central Asia, have been unwilling to accept the greater economic burden that goes with increased preinduction training needed to offset reductions in the armed forces. Thus, the Soviets may have to resort to other measures: 3-year rather than 2-year terms of service, more widespread use of women, and even weapon cutbacks.

The potentially more troublesome problem for the Soviets will be the ethnic composition of the force. By 2010 the USSR will be a completely different country due to ethnic reconfiguration. Although Russians will remain the dominant nationality, low fertility and a relatively high death rate will reduce their share of total population from 52 percent in 1979 to a projected 47 percent in 2000 to a mere 32 percent in 2050. In 1970 19 percent of potential draftees came from Moslem republics; by 2000 their share is projected to be 33 percent. Some authorities see the rising dependence on non-Slavic minorities for military recruitment as a threat to the efficiency of the Soviet armed forces. Other experts, however, present convincing evidence that the Soviets will keep the problem within manageable bounds by continuing efforts to increase the numbers of minority officers and to provide accelerated Russian-language training programs.

Demographic problems will strain the Soviet system increasingly. However, these problems seem unlikely to challenge the system as a whole. Demographic developments typically do not generate immediate crises. Instead, they tend to present long-term problems that allow the Soviet government to work out long-term solutions. Even though it is not entirely clear either that the Soviet leadership fully understands the USSR's demographic problems or that government intervention will have the desired effects, the situation seems manageable and not subject to U.S. manipulation.

Western Europe

Europe as a whole is the slowest growing region. Between 1950–1955 and 1980–1985 the average annual growth rate for the region declined from about 0.8 percent to 0.3 percent, passing through a peak of 0.9 percent in 1960–1965. The decline is expected to continue, falling below 0.2 percent around 2000 and close to zero by 2025. By 2025 four important West European states now among the 16 most populous nations in the world—West Germany, Italy, the United Kingdom, and France—will plummet in the rankings. France is expected to rank twenty-fifth in total population by that time; the others will rank yet lower.

West Germany represents the most notable example of such population decline; Turkey represents the opposite extreme. West Germany's total fertility rate dropped below replacement level (2.1) in 1970 and has fallen since to virtually unprecedented levels. The average for 1980–1984 was 1.38, and the figure for 1984 was lower at 1.27—35–40 percent below replacement level. West Germany's overall population will decline by over 2 million between 1989 and 2010, and its 18–22-year-old male cohort will drop from 2.6 million to 1.6 million.

A marked decline in the number of 18–22-year-olds will bottom out in most countries within the region some time between 1995 and 2000, but by 2010 the size of each nation's eligible cohort will remain well below current levels. Declining, but still positive, population growth rates will characterize other countries of the region, such as Ireland, Portugal, and Spain.

The most significant counterexample to this pattern, though, will be Turkey. Turkey's overall population will increase 54 percent (to 80.5 million) and its 18–22-year-old cohort alone 34 percent between 1988 and 2010. Considering that Turkey's population growth rate of 2.2 percent compares with a per capita gross national product (GNP) growth rate of 1.1 percent, the generally lower standard of living may provide a breeding ground for increasing internal unrest. As disturbing as that prospect may be, NATO authorities will have to face the more fundamental question of whether an expanded role for Turkish (and Spanish and Portuguese) troops within NATO's defensive alignment would be feasible and viable.

Western Europe's aging population is another issue of considerable concern. For the 12 European Community countries combined, the proportion of their population over 65 years of age is projected to rise from 14 percent in 1988 to 20 percent by 2010. This could place extraordinary demands on the welfare state. For example, old-age pensions and medical insurance account for about two-thirds of West Germany's total welfare spending, which has ballooned within three decades to more than $250 billion, or about one-third of the nation's total economic output. Roughly 18 percent of a German worker's taxes now go toward social welfare. In a decade that figure will rise to 24 percent. By 2030 almost one-third of those taxes will be so expended. This increase is because at present the ratio of workers to retirees is 4:1, by 2010 the ratio will be 3:1, and by 2030 it will be less than 2:1. These figures become gloomier if the under-20-year-old age group is added to the over-60-year-old group. The ratio of workers to nonworkers will be 3:2 by 2000. By 2030 nonworkers will outnumber workers. Similarly, in both France and the United Kingdom, which devote nearly a quarter of their GNPs to welfare spending, the proportion of the elderly to overall population will be roughly 22 percent by 2010.

What do such trends portend? Among other things, the labor force will decline, a condition that can have both positive and negative consequences. On one hand, as the labor force declines, unemployment may decline, labor productivity may rise, and more people may opt to stay in the labor force longer, thus easing pressures on social programs. On the other hand, if the economy does not expand, fewer taxpayers will foot the enormous costs of the welfare state, and tensions between defense spending and social spending will be exacerbated.

Militarily, there seems little doubt but that West Germany will find it virtually impossible to field the size force it does today—that is, unless it and other NATO allies are willing to institute internal policy changes. So many factors intervene between the changing size of the 18–22-year-old cohort and the output of any defense establishment that numerous alternative policy levers deserve more serious consideration: capturing more of the relevant age cohort through enhanced recruitment efforts, conscription, and the restriction of exemptions; extending terms of military service; improving reenlistment rates; achieving greater labor efficiency through reduced combat-to-support ratios; expanding roles for women, civilians, and outside contractors; relying more heavily on reservists; accelerating the speed of mobilization; substituting firepower and defensive barriers for manpower where possible; and automating selected human functions. Absent a willingness to undertake such measures, NATO members are likely to feel increased tension over conventional burden sharing, countervailing pressures against denuclearization and associated conventional force build-ups, and even a heightened possibility that the alliance's forward defense posture will unravel.

Eastern Europe

Demographic developments among the Soviet Union's East European allies will have little measurable effect on the military posture of the Warsaw Pact. Population growth rates in the region, though low and declining, still will be higher than those in Western Europe over the next two decades. Nonetheless, because East European countries draft about 50 percent of the available military-age cohort each year, they will have limited flexibility in overcoming sizable productivity problems in the civilian economy.

With the exception of Romania and to a lesser extent Poland, the East European countries have moved to a pattern of low birth and low death rates with slow population growth and a gradually aging population. This, of course, has happened all across Europe, although the enormous flow of *Gastarbeiter* (guest workers) from the south has forestalled some of the more negative effects of this development in Western Europe. Some aspects of the labor force participation patterns (comprehensive involvement of women in the external workforce) and development patterns (leading to the elimination of unemployment as conventionally understood) make adjustment to slower labor force growth quite difficult.

Observers believe East European policymakers would prefer more rapid population growth, but with the collapse of West European fertility in the 1970s and some revival in Eastern Europe, the situation is not seen as a crisis requiring strong pronatalist measures (Romania's highly coercive approach being the exception). Pronatalist measures in the region have had modest positive effects, and fertility patterns have become a source of greatest immediate concern in terms of their future labor force and economic growth ramifications. All in all, although the future will likely witness increasing competition for manpower between the military and other sectors of East European economies, the ultimate problem will continue to be labor force productivity rather than availability.

Political and economic frictions between the Soviet Union and the member nations of the Warsaw Pact will continue to be a source of unrest nurtured by but not caused by demographic developments. Unrest also may develop from various ethnic divisions throughout the region: Romania's large Hungarian population, Bulgaria's significant Turkish segment, and Yugoslavia's (not a Pact member) Macedonian issue vis-à-vis Bulgaria and its increasingly restive Albanian population in Kosovo. In the final analysis, although many of the social, political, and cultural issues that will affect Eastern Europe in the years ahead will have demographic dimensions, the latter are not likely to be primary causes or determinants.

China

The People's Republic of China (PRC) reported a population of 1.06 billion at the end of 1986. With another 20 million in Taiwan, 5 million in Hong Kong, and 0.4 million in Macau, the combined population of the China region was just shy of 1.1 billion, between a fifth and a quarter of total global population. Due principally to the country's stringent 1-child policy, the PRC's rate of population growth just exceeds 1 percent, one of the lowest in Asia. If present trends continue, China's population may be smaller than India's some time after the turn of the century.

The male population in the prime military ages (18–21) will decline from a maximum of 55 million in 1990 to a low point around 2030 or 2035. If China strictly enforces the 1-child policy and the total fertility rate falls to about 1.1 in the near future, the numbers of males in the prime ages could drop as low as 16 million by 2035. For two reasons, therefore, the military may have to step up its recruiting efforts. First, the upgrading of the technical capability of the Chinese military will create a greater need for skilled manpower. Second, recent policies have encouraged spontaneous urban enterprises, which provide alternative employment more attractive to educated youth. Counterbalancing these factors, however, is the PRC's move to a smaller, more modernized standing army. The military's force structure has been cut roughly 2 million personnel since 1982, when it totaled 4.2 million.

One of the most significant demographic developments likely to affect China in the future is its aging population. China's population has been extremely youthful in recent years, with over 50 percent of the total under 21 years of age. In 1982 only 4.9 percent of the population was 65 years old and over. The proportion will rise only very slowly to 6.5–7.5 percent by the end of the century. Thereafter, the growth of the elderly population will be extremely rapid. Between 2010 and 2040 the number of elderly will increase 1.9–4.5 percent a year as the population in the productive ages declines. The peak of aging will come between 2030 and 2050, when the population aged 65 and over probably will exceed 20 percent. If China adheres to its 1-child policy until the turn of the century, 27.5 percent of the population could reach these ages by 2050. Dependency ratios (the numbers of persons under 15 and those 65 and over per 100 persons aged 15 to 64) could range from 60 to almost 75, a formidable burden. The number of working persons per retiree could fall from 13 in 1982 to only 2 in 2050. It remains to be seen how the PRC will finance this state of affairs.

As of 1982 the Chinese labor force totaled 546 million, of whom 26 million were unemployed. Although the number of unemployed seems staggering, it is less than 5 percent of the labor force. A primary concern on the part of Chinese authorities is whether the country will have difficulty finding useful employment for this still growing labor force, which is expected to increase another 100 million by 1990. According to Chinese sources, state-run enterprises across the country presently have about 1.5 million surplus workers, and 30–40 percent of the rural workforce is surplus. Because the reduced birth cohort born in the early 1970s reaches age 16, the official age for entry into the labor force, in 1988–1989, there should be a measure of relief for urban authorities responsible for creating jobs for new entrants and a reduction in rural underemployment.

The urban population alone of the PRC—330 million—is larger than the total population of any country except India. Due to restrictive policies, the proportion of the Chinese population that was urban remained essentially unchanged at 17–18 percent from the early 1960s to the late 1970s. Recently, the government has modified its policies and permitted fairly rapid urbanization. As of 1985 the proportion of the Chinese population living in cities stood at 36.6 percent. Best-guess estimates by the U.S. Census Bureau put that figure at roughly 50 percent by 2000. Because so much depends on how tightly the government tries to control the pattern of urban growth, the long-range prospects for urbanization remain unclear. The idea of restricting the growth of large cities has two dimensions: the necessity of providing transportation, water, sanitation, power, and other essential services at a much higher standard than is currently provided for the rural population and a pervasive fear that a highly urbanized population may be difficult to control politically and socially.

Chinese authorities evince more than a little concern about the socialization process itself. The disbanding of collective controls in agriculture and the loosening of some controls on urban enterprises have encouraged the exercise of individual initiative and sparked an increase in the productivity of labor. Deng Xiaoping's policy of opening to the outside world and of sending the brightest and best-educated youth abroad for advanced studies is bound to have a political leavening effect and could lead to more civil disturbances. The 1-child family has also prompted fears, namely that only children, doted on by parents and grandparents, favored by school teachers, and given preferential treatment in health and other matters, are becoming spoiled and selfish. On one hand, when a generation consisting of a majority of only children raised in an atmosphere of overindulgence has replaced past generations who grew up within extended families that required deference to authority, the relationship of people toward political authority could change profoundly. On the other hand, if the PRC is to develop a modern technical economy, it may require personnel who are capable of independent initiative and innovation and who are not too deferential. For China's neighbors and the world at large, this could have both positive and negative ramifications.

In the final analysis, the keys to social and political stability in the future are likely to be political and economic rather than demographic. Preoccupied with domestic needs and problems, the PRC is unlikely to constitute a threat to its neighbors. The exception is Taiwan, but China probably would not be militarily aggressive unless political initiatives proved hopeless and the Taiwanese seemed increasingly attracted to a separatist view of the island's future.

Western Pacific

The importance of the Western Pacific region to U.S. interests cannot be gainsaid, and demographic factors seem highly likely to play a continuing role in U.S. security relations with that part of the world. East and Southeast Asia alone contain some of the most densely populated areas of the world—southern Japan, South Korea, eastern China, most of the Philippines, the Red River Valley and Bac Po Plain of North Vietnam, Java and Bali, and the crowded city-states of Singapore and Hong Kong. The population factors in the region that are most likely to affect sociopolitical stability and governmental policy over the next two decades concern the high percentage of youth and their attendant political attitudes; the high rate of urbanization; pressures of population growth on land, water, and other resources; differential rates of growth and general differences between racial and ethnic groups; the availability of suitable employment; and the quality of living conditions.

Population growth rates in the region are generally lower than the world average of 2.4 percent for developing nations (excluding China) and close to the average for all nations including the more developed. These rates range from 0.6 in Japan, 0.8 in Australia and New Zealand, and 0.9 in Hong Kong to 2.6 for Vietnam and 2.8 for the Philippines, to 3.3 for Vanuatu and 3.6 for the Solomon Islands. Thirty-nine percent of the population of Southeast Asia and South Korea is under the age of 15, slightly higher than the average of 37 percent for all developing countries. This youth bulge has important implications for stability in the region as urban and international influences intrude on traditional mores. In contrast, Japan, Australia, and New Zealand all are experiencing graying populations.

Urbanization rates in East and Southeast Asia currently are estimated at 25 percent of total population, compared with 34 percent for all developing countries. By 2020 50 percent of East and Southeast Asia are expected to be urbanized, versus 57 percent for all developing countries.

Perhaps Japan's most serious demographic problem is the aging of the society, which will be accomplished with unprecedented speed. Over the next several decades, the elderly proportion of Japan's population will more than double, with those 65 years old and above composing nearly one-quarter of the population by 2020. Japan's elderly population is expected to surpass that of the United States in the 1990s and to maintain that lead through the first several decades of the next century. The ratio of pensioners to contributors in social security programs is projected to increase from less than 14 percent in 1980 to over 40 percent by 2025. Such developments could have a measurable impact on Japan's competitiveness in the international marketplace.

South Korea has one of the highest population densities in the world—over 400 people per square mile—with most of the country unsuitable for agriculture. Sixty-four percent of the population lives in cities—40 percent in and around Seoul alone, only 25 miles from the demilitarized zone. Overly rapid urbanization continues to plague South Korea and provide a seedbed of dissent among the youthful population. In addition, economic inequalities, though not as pronounced as in other developing countries, are politically explosive. Nonetheless, the country has strong ethnic unity, cultural homogeneity, and economic dynamism—all stabilizing factors.

The population of the Philippines has more than doubled in the last 25 years to 61.5 million in 1988 and is projected to be almost 107 million by 2010. Population pressures have helped aggravate nationwide conditions of landlessness, unemployment, and poverty (70 percent of the population lives in poverty). Unemployment and underemployment, already at levels of 15 and 40 percent respectively, are expected to rise as automation spreads in modern industry and the work force is swollen with millions of new entrants into the job market. Unless these population pressures are alleviated, they seem almost certain to threaten the Philippine economy and the country's social institutions.

Vietnam's population is expected to double to over 121 million people by the year 2020. This high rate of growth aggravates chronic shortages of food and arable land. It also impedes economic development in terms of high dependency ratios and infrastructure allocations. Prospects for improvement are tied to the government's ability and willingness to adopt practical policies and efficient management practices.

Thailand's principal demographic problem is the growth of Bangkok. Currently increasing by more than 5 percent per year, Bangkok is doubling in population every 15 to 20 years. This has entailed gross overcrowding, pollution, inadequate public services, and traffic jams and has aggravated such social disorders as prostitution, drugs, and crime. Contributing to potential unrest in Bangkok are its high proportion of young unmarried males, the concentration of Chinese ethnics in urban enclaves, considerable unemployment and underemployment, and the breakdown of traditional family life.

Indonesia, though pursuing one of the world's most enlightened population programs, nonetheless will add over 100 million people between 1988 and 2020. This will intensify many of the problems it already faces: oppressive population concentrations, an oversized labor force, high rates of unemployment for educated youth, and exceptionally high dependency ratios (40 percent of the population under the age of 15).

Despite such imposing problems, the western Pacific region is generally favored with pragmatic leadership, an absence of religious conflict, cohesive and hard-working cultures, high rates of literacy, and economic vitality. Such attributes will help mitigate at least some of the problems that can be expected to arise.

South Asia

South Asia, which includes 3 of the 10 most populous countries in the world

(India, Bangladesh, and Pakistan), accounts for and will continue to account for about 23 percent of the world's total population. The combined population of the region is over 1 billion. Although growth rates, which now are less than 2 percent a year, have been declining steadily since the late 1960s, the region will grow by more than half between 1988 and 2010, an addition of 536 million people.

Apart from South India and Sri Lanka, the region has been fairly resistent to demographic change over the past 20 years or so. Birth rates have declined somewhat, but, because death rates also have declined, growth rates have decreased only moderately. The two countries most favored by U.S. population assistance, Bangladesh and Pakistan, have turned in the poorest performances.

The outlook throughout the region is for continued urban growth, although great uncertainty exists over the pace of that growth and its causes. Projections of city growth in India indicate an increase of 80–100 million by the end of the century. Cities everywhere in South Asia already are pressing the limits of tolerance in the living conditions they afford their populations, especially new arrivals. Consequently, managing the transition from a predominantly agrarian economy to one based increasingly on urban activities will entail enormous costs.

The conjunction of rapid population growth and urbanization certainly may breed the seeds of political instability, but it also may have the positive effect of reducing fertility rates, which in turn will further change the age distribution of populations throughout the region. The ratio of persons under age 15 to those of ages 15–64 (the youth dependency ratio) is slowly falling. In India today, the number of young dependents is nearly two-thirds as large as the adult population on whom they depend. By 2000, assuming that fertility will have fallen to 3.5 children, the ratio will be close to one-half. This would mean nearly 90 million fewer young persons under the age of 15 by the turn of the century.

Other South Asian countries will experience similar trends, depending on how much birth rates decline. Sri Lanka, with a current ratio of 0.6, may reach 0.4 by 2000. In contrast, Bangladesh, which has 8 young persons for every 10 adults, is expected to end the century with an age distribution similar to India's today (that is, with about two-thirds as many young people as adults). Pakistan's present age structure differs little from that of Bangladesh. However, considering the bleak prospects of Pakistan reducing its birth rate, its dependency ratio is unlikely to change appreciably by the turn of the century.

Over the next 15 years the working age population in South Asia is expected to grow by more than a quarter of a billion persons. India alone may experience an increase of 187 million. Whether this expanded labor force will find jobs or be unemployed or underemployed will depend principally on the level of economic growth. Regrettably, full, productive employment is likely to remain a distant goal and poverty a slowly receding condition for many South Asians. As in most developing countries, the major bottlenecks to increased production and employment are to be found on the supply side: shortages of capital, raw materials, intermediate products, and skilled human resources; inefficient commodity and loan markets; poor transport and communications; foreign exchange shortages. Add a rapidly growing, urbanizing population, a degrading habitat, and the political turmoil deriving from the collapse of old systems and the scramble for advantage in the new order, and the perils of the next two decades become palpable.

Latin America

Latin America is an extraordinarily diverse region—physically, socially, politically, economically, and demographically. The demographic heterogeneity is especially noteworthy. In terms of population size, the two regional giants, Brazil and Mexico, have populations of 142 million and 82 million respectively. At the other extreme are 18 countries with populations of 3 million or less. The regional population increased from 165 million in 1950 to 405 million in 1985. It is projected to rise to 546 million by the end of the century and to approximately 778 million by 2025.

Mexico and Brazil alone are responsible for about half of the region's population, jointly accounting for 80 million people in 1950 and a projected 400 million by 2025. By the turn of the century, Brazil's population should approach 180 million; Mexico's, 110 million. By then the U.S. population is expected to be less than twice as large as Brazil's and less than three times Mexico's. Whereas in 1950 the U.S. population almost equaled that of all of Latin America and the Caribbean, by the end of the century Latin America will have twice as many people as the United States.

Because of differential fertility rates that range from as low as two in some countries to as high as six in others, the percentage of the population below 15 years of age can be substantially different in various parts of the region. In temperate South America and some Caribbean countries, 30 percent or less of the population is below that age, and in parts of Central America and tropical South America, nearly half of the population is 15 or younger.

Latin America is one of the most urbanized regions in the world, but major intraregional differences are evident. The least urbanized countries tend to cluster in Central America and the Caribbean, although Cuba, Mexico, and Venezuela have high percentages of their populations—over 70 percent—living in cities. Only Argentina, Chile, and Uruguay—each with 80 percent of its population living in cities—are more urban. Many of these countries are approaching the upper bounds of urbanization, and, in a few, the absolute size of the rural population is on the decline.

Rapid population growth has led to very large increases in the size of the economically active population (EAP). This has been especially true in cities where rural to urban migration has combined with natural urban increase to push labor force growth rates well above national population growth rates. The International Labour Office estimates that the regional EAP rose from 58 million in 1950 to 140 million in 1985. The EAP is projected to reach almost 200 million by the end of the century and 307 million by 2025. Between 1950–1960 and 1970–1980 the annual growth rate of the EAP increased from 2.1 to 3.1 percent. Henceforth, the rate is expected to decline gradually, approaching 2.4 percent by 1990–2000 and 1.3 percent by 2020–2025. Latin America must create about 4 million jobs a year for the remainder of this decade and well into the twenty-first century just to provide employment for young persons entering the job market for the first time. Reputable estimates put combined unemployment and underemployment in the region at 40 percent of the working-age population.

Migration patterns in the region are

and will continue to be significant. All Latin American countries are sources of emigrants, but some also are recipients of large flows of regional migrants. Although the majority of Latin American and Caribbean migrants seek the United States, Argentina and Venezuela also have received sizable influxes. Although economic considerations motivate most migrations, political reasons stemming from violence throughout the region have increased in recent years. Aside from Mexico, major sources of emigrants are Bolivia, Chile, Colombia, Cuba, Haiti, and Paraguay, as well as some of the English-speaking Caribbean island nations. Forced migration as a weapon seems likely to become more prevalent.

Competition for land, fed by rapid population growth, could serve as a continuing source of conflict, particularly between large landholders and poor peasants. Land scarcity in the region is likely to result not from physical constraints but from such factors as the misuse of political and economic power in the dominant classes, the excessive exploitation of available land by poor subsistence farmers, and the unavailability of frontier lands caused by a dearth of roads and other infrastructure. Moreover, the commercialization of agriculture has produced a greater concentration of land holdings and the erosion of traditional forms of rural patronage that in the past contributed to the maintenance of the status quo.

To an extent, rapid population growth may limit the options Latin American nations have for dealing with many of their problems. Population growth places demands on scarce resources. There is little evidence, however, that resource constraints exist in Latin America. Resources generally are considered plentiful in the region though perhaps largely untapped and unevenly distributed. More evident is the misuse of and wanton disregard for resources, whether through misguided economic policies, discriminatory access, or mismanagement. Population growth merely exacerbates and illuminates such problems.

Middle East–North Africa

The Middle East is perhaps distinctive in the extent to which population pressures and endemic propensities for violent conflict interact to produce great potential for instability. Total population for the region stood at 233 million in 1987. That figure is expected to increase to 323 million by 2000 and 418 million by 2010. Egypt and Iran, the two largest states, will add 35 million and 49 million respectively by 2010. These projections actually could be low because they are based on U.S. Census Bureau assumptions that the fertility in all countries of the region will decline. Annual growth rates rose from 2.4 percent in 1950–1955 to 3.6 percent in 1975–1980 and will remain above 3 percent until after the turn of the century. If the current growth rate of 3.1 percent is sustained (a reasonable possibility), the population of the region could reach 466 million by 2010.

Rates of population growth and perceptions of those rates vary widely throughout the region. At one extreme are those countries (or peoples)—Iran, Iraq, Kuwait, Libya, Qatar, Saudi Arabia, the United Arab Emirates, Bahrain to some extent, and the Palestinians—that tend to prefer high growth rates. The average growth rate of this group currently is 3.7 percent per year with a doubling time of 19 years. Members of the Organization of Petroleum Exporting Countries desire rapid population growth in order to provide necessary manpower for service and development tasks now carried out by imported labor. The Palestinians want to keep their growth rates high to compensate for losses of life and to outnumber the Israelis in the occupied territories. At the other extreme is Israel, which stands essentially alone with a low natural growth rate of 1.7 percent that fluctuates from year to year based on net migration. Israel's growth rate may be as low as 1.4 percent by 2010.

Because virtually all states in the region have mixed ethnic-cultural composition, the potential for communal conflict will remain high. Israel and Lebanon are especially noteworthy in this regard. In Israel, aside from growing tensions between Ashkenazic and Sephardic Jews, the position of the Palestinians will remain a central concern. The Arab minority in Israel has grown since 1948 to constitute 16.3 percent of the 3.7 million population of the country. Palestinians number 1.4 million in the occupied territories. The Arabs have a birth rate of 40–45 per 1,000 compared with 23 per 1,000 for Jews. By the mid-1990s the total Israeli population will approximate 5 million, of which the Jews will constitute 78 percent (compared with 84 percent currently).

With the exception of Israel, the age composition of all countries in the region is predominantly young, with 40–45 percent of the population under the age of 15. Within 10 to 20 years today's children will be in their prime reproductive years and will far outnumber those who have completed their reproductive years. Even with the institution of fertility control measures, this young age structure will have a delaying effect on population decline. It also will produce a large pool of youth who could be recruited into political activism or fundamentalism. Finally, the attendant high dependency ratio (85 percent throughout the region) will force a diversion of economic resources from investment to consumption.

Urbanization, increasing at an unplanned, unregulated rate of 6 percent per year, is a growing problem throughout the region. Countries with high proportions of their populations residing in cities include Libya (76 percent), Iraq (70 percent), Saudi Arabia (69 percent), Tunisia (54 percent), Iran (52 percent), Egypt (45 percent), and Morocco (43 percent). Cairo's population, for example, currently is 8 million, compared with 2 million in 1950. By 2000 the city's population may exceed 20 million. Cairo is merely one example of many; most of the major cities of the region will triple or quadruple in size by 2000. (Kuwait City is expected to grow eightfold.)

Sub-Saharan Africa

Africa is far and away the fastest growing region of the world. It is the only major area in which the rate of population growth has increased almost continuously since 1950. The growth rate is expected to increase further, exceeding 3 percent a year during 1990–1995, before it starts to fall again. Between 1988 and 2010 Africa's population will more than double to 1.2 billion, about 16.6 percent of the global total. Between 1985–2030 the total increase will be 1.1 billion. Nigeria, with an estimated 103 million people in 1988, is expected to double in size by 2009, triple by 2024, and quadruple by 2035, adding 312 million people to the world's population in 50 years. By 2035 Nigeria is expected to surpass both the United States and the Soviet Union to become the third largest country in the world. Kenya, with a growth rate of 4.1 percent for the 1980–1985 period, is the fastest growing country in the world (excluding those countries whose growth is due to substantial immigration). Kenya's population of slightly over 20 million is expected to double in approximately 17 years. Four other states in the region—Ethiopia, Zaire, Tanzania, and South Africa—are likely to be among the top 25 nations in population by the year 2025.

Although population specialists generally assume that fertility in Africa will decline relatively rapidly over the next 50 years, the rate of decline between 1988 and 2010 is likely to be rather modest (say, from seven to five children per woman). Given the young age structure and the momentum built into it, the addition of huge numbers of persons to the region's population in a relatively short time is virtually inevitable.

Per capita food production in Africa has been declining since the 1960s due to a combination of land degradation, political upheavals, government policies that give short shift to farmers, and rapid population growth. One key to Africa's ability to feed itself is the availability of unused arable land. In the aggregate and by comparison with other parts of the developing world, sub-Saharan Africa is land rich. The World Bank estimates that as much as a third of the region's land is potentially cultivable, yet less than 6 percent was in use in the late 1970s. In Asia, by contrast, only about 20 percent of the land area is cultivable and already 16 percent of the total is being planted.

Although all nations in the region except South Africa are still overwhelmingly rural, the increase since 1970 in the proportion of their populations residing in urban areas outstrips all but that of Middle Eastern oil-producing countries such as Saudi Arabia. The urban population of the region grew from 21 million in 1950 to 93 million in 1980, a 450 percent increase in 30 years. The proportion of the population living in urban areas is projected to grow from 24 percent in 1980 to 45 percent in 2010.

The gap between jobs and workers in sub-Saharan Africa is growing. The labor force of the region will increase by 111 million workers between 1980 and 2000. If current trends continue, underemployment alone will increase to 71 percent of the rural labor force, or 203 million workers, by 2008.

AIDS, of course, which is so prevalent in East and Central Africa, is the greatest unknown that could invalidate any population projections for the region. The World Health Organization has estimated that 1–2 million people are infected in Africa and that a minimum of 10,000 cases annually may be occurring there. Other reports have noted anywhere from 50,000 to several hundred thousand AIDS-related deaths in the region. Because even these current estimates are based on such tenuous data, realistic projections for the future are virtually impossible. Nonetheless, it is not unreasonable to conclude that, although AIDS has the potential to slow down the growth rate of the African population by the year 2010, the total size of the population still will grow substantially. It would take a much higher incidence of the disease than can reasonably be predicted for such a large population to alter this conclusion appreciably. The real importance of AIDS to the future population prospects of Africa may lie less in the direct attribution of numbers than in the more indirect effects on customs and institutions. The epidemic has the potential to change sexual behavior and marriage customs, to affect the balance of population distribution between cities and rural areas, and to redirect public investments away from primary health and prevention to crisis management.

Confronting the Challenge

It almost borders on the inane to suggest that demographic developments will be important in the future of the United States and the world more generally. So self-evident is this shibboleth that one is inclined too readily to overlook the extent to which such developments may assert themselves. Even if one pays more attention to population change, the implications for U.S. security would remain frustratingly, perhaps irrevocably, unclear. The relationship between demographic variables and security-related variables is exceedingly complex and not fully understood even by those who profess expertise in such matters. Do rapid population growth and rapid urbanization, for example, produce political and social instability, or is the reverse more likely to be true? Demographic developments do not occur in isolation. Rather, they must be viewed in the context of their economic, political, and social concomitants. As political scientist Myron Weiner observed:

> There is no evidence to suggest that population growth alone as an independent variable can explain instability, violence, aggressive behavior, and the rise of radical movements of the left and right. . . . The effects of population growth are bound to be different in highly developed societies, in densely populated countries with high economic growth, and in countries with low densities. The level of technological development, the existing population density, and the rate and pattern of economic growth will determine the effects of rapid population growth.

Demography, like its parent discipline economics, can be seductively misleading because it involves the manipulation of readily quantifiable—and thus presumably hard—data. The quality of demographic data, however, is highly variable. Many parts of the Third World, for example, may have very poorly developed collection and transmission mechanisms. Furthermore, because demographic reporting typically emanates from official government sources, political and ideological motives frequently bias the data in desired directions.

AIDS represents the most telling contemporary example of limitations in this regard. Although embryonic efforts are underway to forecast the future prevalence and effects of AIDS, it remains an ill-understood phenomenon of pandemic proportions that could easily invalidate all existing population projections. According to the World Health Organization, more than 71,000 cases of AIDS have been reported worldwide by 129 countries. However, because of incomplete surveillance and reporting (China reports two cases, the Soviet Union and East Germany four each, and Cuba six, for example), the true count probably is closer to 150,000. Thus, Stephen Peter Rosen, in a recent issue of *The National Interest*, noted, "Hard evidence on which to make definite predictions about the eventual impact of AIDS on national security issues is not available."

The World Health Organization estimates that 5–10 million people are infected with the virus worldwide, a count that could reach as high as 100 million by 1991. Some analysts argue that if 100 million people, or 2 percent of the world's population, were infected, total deaths from AIDS in the 1990s could be 50 million. The number infected then could double several more times after that and wipe out some countries in 10 to 20 years. If the number infected increased to 20 percent of the world's population, the delayed deaths could begin to cancel rapid global population growth.

As difficult and uncertain as the task may be, policymakers and strategic planners in this country have little choice in the coming decades but to pay serious attention to population trends, their causes, and their effects. Already the United States has embarked on an era of constrained resources. It thus becomes more important than ever to do those things that will provide more bang for every buck spent on national security. To claim that decreased defense spending must lead to strategic debilitation is fatuous. Rather, policymakers must anticipate events and conditions before they occur. They must employ all the instruments of statecraft at their disposal (development assistance and population planning every bit as much as new weapon systems). Furthermore, instead of relying on the canard that the threat dictates one's posture, they must attempt to influence the form that threat assumes.

Ben Wattenberg argued, with considerable alarm, that "the geopolitical security and potency of America and its Western allies are likely to be threatened by a variety of population trends now under way around the world." He may or may not be correct. The surest and most dangerous way to find out, though, is to ignore the links that exist between population variables and security variables—even if the nature and direction of those links elude current capacity for understanding.

Acknowledgement: This analysis is drawn, sometimes verbatim, from commissioned papers prepared by Mark J. Eitelberg, Naval Postgraduate School (United States); Murray Feshbach, Georgetown University (Soviet Union); Michael S. Teitelbaum, Alfred P. Sloan Foundation (Western Europe); Robert J. McIntyre, Bates College (Eastern Europe); John S. Aird, consultant (China); Ambassador Marshall Green, consultant (Western Pacific); John F. Kantner, The Johns Hopkins University (South Asia); Sergio Diaz-Briquets, Commission for the Study of International Migration and Cooperative International Development (Latin America); Abdel R. Omran, University of Maryland (Middle East–North Africa); and Etienne Van De Walle, University of Pennsylvania (sub-Saharan Africa); and from additional insights provided by Michael J. Deane, Booz-Allen & Hamilton (Soviet Union); Susan L. Clark, Institute for Defense Analyses (Western Europe); and Thomas J. Goliber, The Futures Group (sub-Saharan Africa).

Democracy, Conflict, and Development in the Third World

Robert L. Rothstein

A POWERFUL TREND toward democratization, or at least political liberalization, seems to be continuing in much of the Third World. A concomitant trend toward a market economy, which some analysts see as a necessary prerequisite for stable democracy, also seems to be continuing, if largely because of the failure of closed economic strategies and the pressures of international financial institutions. Moreover, the Western world seems to have definitively won the Cold War. Indeed, even Iraq's brutal aggression against Kuwait, which obviously has the potential to alter some of the previous trends and to create entirely or partially different trends, may have the ironic result of generating much greater pressures for democratization in the one region in the world that has resisted such pressures—a bizarre testimonial to the actions of an evil thug.

It is hardly necessary to add that caution is imperative. Any or all of these trends could be derailed or reversed, any or all might produce unanticipated or perverse results, and—should they continue—likely consequences are exceedingly unclear. Yet these very consequences are of critical

Robert L. Rothstein is Harvey Picker professor of international relations at Colgate University.

importance, and not least to those in government who have made the support of democratization a central tenet of U.S. policy to nurture the emergence of a post–cold war world order.

Policymakers and a variety of commentators have argued that the United States should support transitions to democracy because that policy will lead to a more peaceful world, a world more compatible with U.S. values, a world in which support for the free market will enhance the prospects for prosperity, a world in which citizens of third world democracies will be treated more equitably and have more of their basic rights protected, and a world in which the likelihood of political stability will increase. This essay focuses on the two central propositions: that democracy will produce peace, and that it will produce prosperity.[1]

This discussion will not deal with the arguments, frequently enunciated by the left, that U.S. support is a cynical disguise for continued bolstering of autocrats said to be tied to the United States or useful propaganda against domestic political opponents. This may well have been true in the past in some cases, and it might still be true for some individuals in the present, but current support for democracy is genuine, which is not to say that it is carefully analyzed or articulated.[2]

Policy arguments in support of democracy are especially difficult to make because democracy is only an intermediary goal. That is, the United States supports democracy largely because there is a presumption that the creation of more democratic regimes will lead to other results that are considered beneficial. What is generally missing in most of the policy arguments is any very clear statement of how or why democracy will produce these other results. Instead, statements of faith and pious platitudes are issued about the benefits of faith. It is probably unfair to expect extraordinarily busy policymakers to be skeptical about a goal that has so much emotional resonance in the U.S. political system.

In any case, the policy arguments have not usually been very sophisticated. Support for democracy is presumed to be in the "enlightened self-interest" (undefined) of the United States, or it is asserted that it is or will be easier for the United States to deal with democratic regimes (despite some evidence to the contrary).[3] Others in the policy community have argued that an order based on force is fragile (but so will be an order based on weak democracies) or that U.S. support for authoritarian regimes increases popular dislike for the United States and popular support for radicals (which is true but what the alternatives imply is not always discussed). More recently, arguments have been made that democratic regimes will be more peaceful and more likely to support free market policies, important points to be discussed below.[4]

Samuel Huntington has provided a more sophisticated set of arguments to justify U.S. support for third world democracy, despite the fact that he is pessimistic about the prospects for democracy and about U.S. ability to have much impact on its emergence.[5] He argues that democracy has a strong association with the future of freedom and that the latter is clearly in the U.S. interest. In a general way this is certainly true, but it is less clear that support for weak democracy, which will require continuing financial and other aid, will lead to more freedom—or more stability. He also argues that with increased interdependence the importance of establishing a more congenial environment for U.S. policy is growing. If the new democracies are more peaceful, and if they are likely to deal with the socioeconomic problems that arise from interdependence and an unstable international economy in a more cooperative fashion, support for democratic regimes would be eminently sensible. However, neither proposition is self-evidently true.[6] Huntington also argues that a house divided against itself cannot stand; consequently, the stability of the international system will be precarious without some movement toward ideological compatibility. The international system has changed markedly since 1984 when Huntington wrote, and the decline in the Cold War presumably implies less likelihood of major war. By the same token, however, division and conflict in other parts of the international order may have intensified, the creation of new states and new democracies may generate new patterns of internal and external violence, and there is as yet little sign of a "house unified." Finally, Huntington notes the potentially beneficial impact an increase in democratic regimes might have on other goals such as economic development, equity, and political stability. Democratic regimes may indeed have some effect on the prospects for achieving other goals, but the effects might be minimal, negative, or unclear. Moreover, the specific linkages between democracy and the other goals need to be more carefully specified.

Many of the justifications for supporting democracy are essentially "milieu" goals that seek to affect "the shape of the environment in which the nation operates." Such goals are likely to become more prominent in an interdependent system in which the need for cooperation increases.[7] It should not be assumed that milieu goals are not in the national interest. Nevertheless, the potential conflict with other, more immediate goals can be quite sharp, and it may be difficult to generate much more than rhetorical support for them. In addition, it is usually even more difficult to develop international support for goals that seem abstract and long run, which increases the likelihood of free riding. The problems are obviously exacerbated when the goals themselves are ambiguous.

There is, however, an even greater problem with the arguments discussed above. Milieu goals are essentially goals pursued by the United States. They are important to specify in the context of the U.S. foreign policy system just because that system tends to undervalue or ignore such goals—another version in its own way of the declining U.S. willingness to pay the costs of producing international public goods. But these kinds of goals do not connect very well with the policy process—or the justification of choice—in the Third World. U.S. support for democracy is very important but, whatever the United States does, democracy will not be stable or beneficial in the Third World unless third world elites and publics see it as supporting their needs and reflecting their interests. Arguments about the future of freedom, or the consequences of interdependence, or the dangers of a house divided are not likely to generate much practical support in the Third World. Put differently, U.S. observers need to try to understand why the Third World should support democracy, especially weak democracy, not why the United States should support democracy.

Such arguments are difficult to make not only because some of the benefits of democracy are unclear or long term but also because elites and masses in the Third World may want things other than democracy or have different patterns of expectations about its potential benefits. Thus the elites may only want a very limited form of democracy that does not threaten their own power but that suffices to pacify internal dissent and to deflect international pressures. The masses, conversely, are likely to want democracy primarily as a means of changing the status quo and improving—relatively quickly—their standard of living. The potential internal conflicts are obvious. In any case, any discussion of the potential benefits of democracy for the Third World must take account of the fact that the Third World itself is internally divided and some benefits (for example, increased equity) may appear threatening to some groups.

Are there nonetheless some potential benefits of democracy that seem likely to justify or garner widespread support—if the benefits can be earned? This essay looks first at the currently fashionable notion that a democratic world will also be a more peaceful world. It then considers the relationship between democracy, capitalism, and economic growth. There is a vast, controversial, and frequently inconclusive literature on these topics. What follows is an abbreviated and

273

personal comment on these issues, not the kind of detailed analysis they require.

Democracy and Conflict

Conflict has been endemic in the Third World. Most of the wars that have taken place since 1945 have been between third world countries and much of the internal conflict has also been in the Third and "Fourth" Worlds. Given unsettled boundaries (especially in Africa and the Middle East), declining economic performance, ethnic and communal divisions, and the widespread availability of arms, perhaps the most interesting question is why more conflict has not occurred. This may be especially true now as interdependence increases inequalities within and between regions and as the decline of the Cold War increases fears of marginalization, of being left behind forever. Perhaps the elite focus on internal survival (and enrichment) and the lack of a capacity to project power effectively (except against one's own citizens) provide part of the explanation for the relatively limited amount of external warfare.

What impact will increased democratization have on the prospects for international conflict? Until recently, most analysts argued that the likelihood of war involvement did not vary greatly with regime-type: democracies were as likely to be involved in war as nondemocracies.[8] However, Rudolph Rummel has generated a scholarly debate by arguing that democratic (or relatively freer) states do not fight each other, that more free states means less war in the system, and that this holds whether the definition of the "more free" is political or also includes economic freedom and whether one is discussing the frequency or the intensity of war.[9]

What sort of empirical support is there for Rummel's arguments? At best, findings on the relationship between democracy and conflict involvement are mixed or inconclusive; at worst, some studies completely contradict Rummel. The disagreements are no surprise not only because of significant differences in defining and operationalizing key concepts (democracy and conflict) but also because of important differences in the kinds of conflict being studied and the time period under examination. And it is worth emphasizing that relatively small shifts in how concepts are defined or measured can have relatively large effects on the results obtained. These empirical and conceptual disagreements among highly intelligent and methodologically sophisticated analysts are something of a warning about coming to any definitive conclusions about the impact of democracy on conflict.

One study by Steve Chan has concluded that "contrary to the view that freedom discourages war, the evidence points in the direction that it is associated with more war."[10] In addition, although he does not find convincing evidence that freer countries are less likely to start wars, he finds empirical support for the proposition that democracies fight nondemocracies as much as nondemocracies fight each other. Chan finds some partial support for Rummel in the years since 1973, with the freer countries apparently less war-prone in recent years than in the more distant past.[11] Weede also concludes that democratic states were as frequently involved in war as other states in the 1960s and 1970s but confirms Rummel's finding that the democratic states were less involved in war in the very narrow period that Rummel studied (1975–1980).¹² A more recent study by Zeev Maoz and Nasrin Abdolali concludes that freer states are neither more nor less conflict prone than nonfree states, that democracies are disproportionately likely to initiate disputes against autocracies, and that the proportion of democracies in the international system *positively* affects the number of disputes begun and under way.¹³ Thus Rummel's argument that a system with more free or democratic states will also be more peaceful has not received much support from other researchers; perhaps we can rest with that well-known Scottish verdict, not proven.¹⁴

The one argument that all the analysts agree on is that democracies do not fight other democracies. This argument, which has a long intellectual history, has attracted a great deal of attention. Before discussing it, however, another issue requires very brief attention. If the empirical evidence seemed to imply that a world of more democracies would be a world with less conflict, why should democracies be inherently more peaceful than other states? The answer to this question is important because, unless the peaceableness of democracies toward each other can be related to specific characteristics of democracy, the argument itself will be inconclusive: the pacific qualities might be related to other characteristics that have little to do with democracy itself.

There are a variety of answers to this question, none conclusive, but—taken together—at least plausible. Analysts have thus suggested that the very diversity of values and interests in a democracy, all of which can be freely expressed, make it difficult to get a consensus on warlike actions (especially the initiation of such actions) and that the citizens of a democracy do not want to risk death or pay the costs of war, especially when they are enjoying the fruits of prosperity. In effect, having more to lose, citizens are more risk-averse. Presumably a government intent on war may also find it more difficult to create sufficient hatred against the target if it does not control the media or the legislature.¹⁵ Secrecy and the suppression of dissent are inevitably harder to achieve when the procedures of democracy are operating effectively. Democracies may also be reluctant to intervene in other regimes that meet the same standard of legitimacy. It should also be noted, of course, that some of the same characteristics that militate against initiating warlike actions (e.g., reluctance to pay the costs of war or to spend heavily on arms) may also increase the likelihood that enemies will attack what seems a tempting target.¹⁶

If these are the reasons why democracies are more peaceful, one further important point ought to be noted. Very few of these reasons are likely to hold in the Third World. In the more limited and restricted forms of democracy that are likely to prevail in the Third World, with greater restrictions on individual freedoms and perhaps greater power for the ruling elite, the procedures that inhibit an "easy" choice of war are likely to be less powerful, the diversity of interests and values may not be expressed, and the aversion to risk may not be as high. The last point reflects the obvious fact that many in the Third World feel that they have little to lose in using violence (Mueller in fact suggests a continuing romanticism about violence in the Third World), they are not getting richer, and they are certainly getting more dissatisfied with the status quo.¹⁷ A possible response is that most of the genuine third world democracies do not spend heavily on the military, thus suggesting that first inclinations are not likely to be toward a military solution, but even this is not very persuasive: the democracies that face threats, such as India or Sri Lanka, spend about as much on arms as their enemies do.[18] In short, we cannot assume that because one group of democracies has been relatively pacific, subsequent democracies will also be pacific.

There has been much rummaging through history and much definitional conflict to try to find cases where democracies have fought each other. Quibbling aside, the absence of direct conflict is impressive and intriguing. Surely at some point conflicts of interest, or miscalculations, or misperceptions would presumably have produced a war of the democracies. But there only seem to be close calls. Still, the message here is caution. As with the point just made, it is not possible to extrapolate in any simple fashion from the historical record. Indeed, to do so might actually produce an increase in conflict.

In the first place, the implicit message of the democracies-do-not-fight-democracies school might seem to be that existing democracies ought to use violence against nondemocracies in order to end the scourge of war—violence to achieve nonviolence. Much more is known now about transitions than in the past, but not nearly enough to even contemplate a jihad for democracy. The moral dilemmas are massive and the consequences unforeseeable. The need to get rid of brutal murderers like Saddam Hussein should not be used as justification for a crusade.[19] In the second place, although more democracies seem to be emerging, most of the states in the system are not democratic. And, as noted, there does not seem to be much evidence that democracies fight nondemocracies with less frequency than authoritarian regimes fight each other. Since the international system seems likely to remain in this mixed and constantly shifting posture, it would seem that this is the conflict situation that ought to be of central concern.

Two other reasons for caution ought to be noted. The basis of conflict may be shifting increasingly to economic and resource issues. There is no inherent reason why these conflicts should end in violence and, in the abstract, it might be assumed that they are more easily resolved by compromise. Two points, however, are worth noting here. First, international (and perhaps domestic) economic conflicts are coming increasingly to resemble classic "security dilemma" conflicts in that the stakes have risen greatly, defensive actions to protect national interests can have negative external effects, and the perception of zero-sum outcomes seems more prevalent. Second, it is reasonable to ask whether democratic regimes, to the extent that participation is high and leaders must compete for the popular vote, are more likely to adopt nationalistic, short-run policy stances that exacerbate conflict and make it more difficult to resolve. Thus democracies might (or might not) diminish the frequency of external wars, but they *might* also increase the amount of economic conflict in potentially dangerous ways. This is an issue that requires much more research.

The most important reason for caution, especially in a third world context, concerns the possibility that democracy in deeply divided societies may actually increase the likelihood of internal conflict. On one level, this raises the question of whether democracies perform badly (or worse than authoritarian regimes) in economic terms, thus generating greater discontent, increased arms spending, and the prospects of military intervention (see the next section). On another level, the issue is whether democratic procedures may actually exacerbate domestic conflicts if the procedures encourage politicians to manipulate ethnic and communal conflicts for their own benefit, if they increase the likelihood that ethnic or other groups will organize to pursue their own interests, and if therefore the democratic process itself undermines national unity and makes effective and impartial governance more difficult. This is again a problematic issue because it is unclear that authoritarian regimes deal with these conflicts more effectively or that the power-sharing approach of consociational democracy can or will be a reasonable compromise between democracy and authoritarianism.[20]

None of these arguments should be taken to imply the superiority of nondemocratic regimes or the necessity of opposing democratic transitions. Rather, the point is cautionary: it is a mistake to jump too easily from the point that democracies do not fight each other to the notion that a world of mostly democracies (many of them weak and potentially unstable) will necessarily be more peaceful, either internally or internationally.

Two other issues must be discussed, if very briefly, in this section. The first concerns the immensely troubling fact that the continuing deterioration of the resource base in many third world countries and regions may be undermining the possibility that *any* form of government can effectively meet the needs of its citizens. The linked and escalating problems of excessive population growth, declining agricultural productivity, deforestation, desertification, and increasing water shortages are familiar, but the questions of how to deal with them and whether democratic or authoriarian regimes are likely to handle these issues relatively better are unresolved. Further, resource constraints can generate either or both internal and external conflicts and, for the poor countries, even an effective strategy to begin dealing with these issues will require substantial external aid and a great deal of regional cooperation. With economic conditions deteriorating everywhere and with the familiar tendency of political systems to focus on the short run in full swing, the prospects for either aid or cooperation are probably not very high.

Fears about resource shortages have already had negative effects on growth rates and quality-of-life indices. They have also had some negative effects on military spending. For example, sharply increased military expenditures in Asia have been attributed not only to internal conflicts but also to fears about future conflicts over oil and fishing rights in the ocean.[21] And there has been much talk in the Middle East about future "water wars," which will probably diminish the possibilities of significant reductions in military spending. Fears that the West Bank and Gaza will not be economically viable because of population pressures, agricultural decline, and water shortages have also played a small part in raising Israeli doubts about the stability of a Palestinian state.

As Janet Welsh Brown indicates, all of the policies that might begin to diminish these problems create serious internal threats: cutting subsidies, changing agricultural practices, enforcing pollution controls, conserving water, and preserving the forests all threaten the livelihood of some groups.[22] It is unclear, however, whether democratic or authoritarian governments will be relatively more effective in imposing necessary but painful policies. For example, reducing population growth rates would ease the number of young and low-income people and thus may be the most important link in the syndrome of deterioration, but there is disagreement about which form of government is more effective on this issue or indeed whether forms of government make much difference at all.[23] Conversely, there is some evidence that the democracies that have given their citizens some socioeconomic rights (such as Costa Rica and Sri Lanka) also have better foodgrain output and lower birthrates.[24] In any case, whether or how or when the deterioration of the resource base is likely to lead to increased conflict is unclear. Many different patterns of response are possible both internally and externally, in part because factors other than resource shortages affect the decision to use violence, but it does seem plausible to suggest that elite perceptions of rising demands and diminishing means to meet them will lead, sooner or later, to new justifications for authoritarianism and war against neighbors. One doubts that these responses will diminish the problem, not least because there is little evidence to suggest that authoritarian regimes (bar the "good" or paternalistic East Asian regimes) will make the right policy choices or elicit sufficient support for necessary sacrifices by the citizenry. On the margin, democratic regimes, if they receive enough external support, may be more effective because greater legitimacy may give them somewhat more time to deal with the issues; there is some evidence that citizens of a democracy may be more willing (up to a point) to sacrifice immediate material benefits for a greater say in choosing their rulers and having more protected rights; and there is also some evidence that in some cases democratic policymaking can be more flexible and more able to correct mistakes quickly. But it is also clear that unless necessary policies are adopted quickly, and unless the international response to what is a shared problem is rapid and generous, resource deterioration could become irreversible.

Finally, what impact will the decline of the Cold War have on third world conflicts? To begin with the obvious: the decline of the Cold War will not have a single, clear effect because it intersects with a variety of other factors that will be perceived differently by different actors. Whatever the effects are, they will probably shift over time and place, and response patterns are likely to reflect a prolonged learning process that may well produce some surprising or unanticipated results. Note also that the decline of the Cold War and the accelerating process of democratization are separate and only partially linked phenomena. The process of democratization, outside what used to be called the Soviet bloc, is a response to a variety of autonomous factors, although the process might be energized by a "demonstration effect" from Eastern Europe or, conversely, partially derailed by a shift of aid and investment funds away from the Third World. The Cold War, whether in decline or resurgence, has also obviously followed its own imperatives. The linkage of importance here is whether cold war developments are likely to encourage or inhibit conflicts elsewhere.

Most wars in the Third World have begun from largely local causes and the superpowers have been dragged in, frequently reluctantly, in pursuit of their own goals. The local causes for either internal or external conflict are hardly diminishing and may be accelerating if economic and resource problems lead to conflict. This presumably implies that the amount of third world conflict is unlikely to decline. It also implies that the major effect of the decline of the Cold War is likely to be on the character of war (intensity, scope, duration) rather than its frequency.[25] But nothing in this complex world is simple. It is possible, for example, that the decline of the Cold War could indeed have an effect on the incidence of war by removing the restraining effect of the superpowers and the implicit rules of conduct that developed within the Cold War; by generating even greater pressures to build local arms industries, to acquire the most destabilizing kind of arms, and to establish ties with even more exporters of arms; and perhaps by changing the calculus of choice for third world decisionmakers, who will have to make their own decisions on the likelihood of winning a conflict—presumably with less information than before and with increasing domestic pressure to "do something" to deal with problems.[26] In short, whether the decline of the Cold War leads to more or less conflict cannot be easily predicted because conflict decisions will reflect many factors and many perceptions.

Presuming that third world democracies are as likely as authoritarian regimes to be involved in conflict, perhaps some other *possible* effects are discernible. As the superpowers lose a direct or strong interest in most third world conflicts—bar the Middle East and perhaps South Africa—the third world countries may have to increase arms spending to provide security. This will also mean that very scarce resources will have to be diverted from other needs, which will increase discontent. As aid diminishes and as the costs of using force increase, there may be an increasing tendency to strike "out of the blue" or to use the most horrific weapons quickly in order to win quickly. Moreover, as the superpowers lose interest in most of these conflicts, and as the ideological battle lines crumble, the superpowers are likely to be much more indifferent to domestic transformations in the Third World. In the third world democracies, this might mean less U.S. opposition to leftist or radical or religious parties, who will be energized by economic decline and protected by democratic procedures. Note, for example, the possibility that fundamentalist religious groups might come to power by democratic means and then seek to thwart or turn back pressures for continued democratization. Thus, perversely, the survival of even weak democracy in the Third World might be undermined by the protection granted to radical left (or right) groups and the indifference of the strongest external supporter of democracy. U.S. support for democracy *ought* to be less ambivalent or ambiguous now because the justification for supporting most authoritarian regimes has sharply diminished but, in the complexity of pursuing multiple goals in a complex environment, the United States may not be able or willing to sacrifice all of its authoritarian "friends."

The effects of the decline of the Cold War are indeterminate—or perhaps it is merely too early to forecast them. But the need to provide for security in a deteriorating domestic and international environment, and without the support of a rich patron, does imply continuing problems for new democracies in terms of rising military expenditures and domestic turmoil. Perhaps the much discussed revival of the United Nations may lead to the creation of a new security order in which the implied promise of support against aggression will diminish the burden. But it seems inherently unlikely that many third world conflicts will generate so rapid and powerful an international response as has Iraq's annexation of Kuwait.

Apart from the rather special case of democracies not fighting other democracies, strong conclusions about the relationship between democracy and conflict are premature. This is not surprising because so many other factors can and do influence choices about conflict and because the democratic regimes themselves are a complex mixture of democratic and nondemocratic characteristics. Moreover, generalizations drawn from macrostatistical analyses, even when they manage to agree on something, tell little about specific cases or even small groups of cases. Nor are they very useful in attempting to understand whether changes that are occurring are likely to invalidate generalizations drawn from an earlier period or a different set of circumstances.

It is, nevertheless, clear that the democratic variable is likely to have different effects in different contexts. More democratic (or "relatively freer") regimes do not guarantee less international conflict. Nor do they guarantee less spending on arms in a situation where cold war patronage is on the decline, potential enemies are arming rapidly, and economic conditions are worsening. Democratic regimes in deeply divided countries may also exacerbate ethnic conflict or make it more difficult to resolve. And they may make international economic conflicts relatively more difficult to compromise. Conversely, in terms of the resource problematic, democratic regimes, at least those with a reasonable degree of legitimacy, may be somewhat better at establishing effective policies and persuading the populace that sacrifices are necessary and will be shared equitably. But all of these judgments are, at best, tentative, and firmer judgments will require detailed analysis on a case-by-case basis. However, it can at least be said that the judgment that a world with more democratic states in it will be a more peaceful world is unproven—as the economists say, it all depends. Because authoritarian regimes do not, in general, have a better record on conflict, the uncertainties about the relationship between democracy and conflict do not imply that support for democratic transitions is mistaken. Rather, the point is that other reasons for supporting (weak) democracies should also be examined.

Democracy and Development

Many analysts once argued that there is a positive linear relationship between levels of socioeconomic development and the development of democracy. This necessarily implied that the achievement of democracy before some stipulated level of socioeconomic development must be "premature" (and thus "false" or unstable) and might indeed slow or derail socioeconomic development itself. In both the Third World and the First World it became fashionable to denounce democracy as an inappropriate short-run goal for poor countries, a form of government and a system of values imposed on the former colonial areas by the West. That attitude still persists in many third world countries where democracy is resisted not only because of fears that it will impede development but also because of fears that it will exacerbate internal divisions—and, of course, threaten elite prerogatives. The potential disabilities of democracy, any or all of which might force a sharp trade-off between democracy and economic growth, are quite familiar. The gravamen of the indictment is that democracies, to the extent that courting the vote or the support of the masses becomes necessary, are compelled to sacrifice economic growth for consumption (e.g., reducing investment, increasing subsidies, raising wages faster than productivity, indulging in deficit financing). Democracies are also accused of generating runaway inflation, of being unable to change inherited class structures, and of a failure to control the self-interested behavior of interest groups or the very rich. There is also some evidence that democratic regimes in Latin America have not been successful at implementing stabilization programs, perhaps because the necessary compromises of democratic politics prevent the adoption of tough policies that sacrifice consumption and prevent efforts to shift problems to the future.[27] It is not without interest, incidentally, that conservatives who insist that capitalism is a necessary prerequisite for democracy share many of these fears about runaway democracy. They insist that capitalism, which is a defense of property and privilege, can survive only if the powers of democracy are sharply limited.[28]

More recent analytical work has undermined the notion of a simple linear relationship between increased levels of development and increased levels of democracy. For example, an empirical analysis by Zehra Arat found that only 8 out of 120 developing countries fit the linear model and that there were widely varied relationships between levels of development and democracy.[29] Erich Weede, analyzing four studies on the relationship between growth and democracy, reports that three of the studies conclude that democracy retards growth and one concludes quite the opposite. Weede also notes, however, that the effects in all the studies are quite weak and that the data analysis is crude.[30] Once again, regime-type is not a very strong variable, not only because of the difficulties in conceptualizing regimes whose characteristics are mixed and shifting but also because so many other factors affect both the growth process and the democratization process. Systematic relationships between levels of development and political regimes, or between political regimes and the rate of economic growth, are thus hard to discern—and are to be treated cautiously when (apparently) found.

"Casual empiricism" is not much more helpful in terms of understanding this crucial relationship. India, Sri Lanka, Jamaica, and Costa Rica, third world democracies of long (and continuous) standing, have rarely had high growth rates and many of the recent democratic transitions in Latin America have come in a period of slow growth and economic turbulence (which suggests democracy by default, not achievement). In any case, just as high growth does not guarantee a democratic outcome, low growth does not mean that the establishment of a democracy is precluded. Nevertheless, it is not unreasonable to presume intuitively that a democracy established in a period of low growth must gradually improve its record—support moral legitimacy with performance legitimacy—or become increasingly unstable, as recent evidence from Trinidad and Tobago, Venezuela, and Sri Lanka suggests. It is not without interest, for example, that the three or four *continuous* democracies in Africa (Mauritius, Botswana, Gambia, perhaps Zimbabwe) have all been quite prosperous in African terms, and that Costa Rica also performed very well until its debt crisis began eroding prosperity. Yet India, Sri Lanka, and Jamaica have remained relatively stable despite poor economic performance over long periods of time. Economic orientations were also mixed: the African democracies were mostly capitalist or state-capitalist; Costa Rica was capitalist with strong elements of state intervention to protect the poor; India and Sri Lanka were a curious mixture of socialism and the market. In short, in some cases the disabilities of democracy do seem to impede or slow the achievement of economic goals, although they are not the only factors that reduce performance; in other cases the disabilities do not seem decisive and democratic governments can perform acceptably—not as well as the "good" authoritarians but as well or better than the rest. This is at least a start: democracy may, but need not, impede the achievement of economic goals.

One study has produced unusually interesting results. In it Weede argues that the presumed negative effect of democracy on growth does not hold when the analysis is limited to developing countries—in effect, good news for supporters of democracy. But Weede also tested independently for the effects of strong government involvement in the economy. His results show that democracy is a major barrier to growth only in countries where state intervention is high, thus seeming to confirm the arguments of many conservative economists.[31] The real trade-off seems not to be between democracy and growth but between state involvement and growth.

These are impressive and interesting results, but they are not entirely persuasive. Almost *all* the genuine third world democracies have had high levels of government involvement in the economy (India, Sri Lanka, Costa Rica, Jamaica, Mauritius, Botswana) and some have done reasonably well economically, at least in comparison to neighbors. Moreover, the conservative version of limited democracy, in which the state functions largely to protect property and limit participatory "excesses," contains its own long-run dangers. In many third world countries, only the state has the power to control the ugly face of capitalism, to limit corruption, and to protect the poor—and unless the latter is done by some means, the long-run stability of democracy cannot be guaranteed. Note the negative effects of uncontrolled capitalism and corruption on Nigeria's democracy: a *popular* military coup against an elected government. Conservative fears about populism are not irrational, but if they lead to policies that make a mockery of the egalitarian basis of democracy—by weakening one institution that can (although it often does not) help the poor—a popular revolt against democracy is inevitable. Short-run gains in wealth and income for the rich are not a sensible strategy for democrats, even rich democrats. In short, to revise Weede's revision of the traditional trade-off between growth and democracy, perhaps the real trade-off is between short-run prosperity with limited government and long-run prosperity with a government committed to both growth and equity. Or perhaps one should say that it is not necessarily government that is the problem but government that is corrupt, biased, and inept.

The quest for grand generalizations about the relationship between democracy and development has yielded only inconclusive results. Perhaps it will be useful to concentrate on more detailed case studies and compare results only with similarly situated neighbors: say, India with Pakistan or China, Costa Rica with its Central American neighbors, Jamaica with other Caribbean states. This will yield not only a sense of context but also a more realistic pattern of comparison. This kind of analysis is too extensive to be attempted here, but the results of one such analysis are suffiently interesting to warrant discussion.

John Sloan compares the economic performance of three Latin American democratic regimes with the performance of four modernizing authoritarian regimes.[32] In terms of per capita GDP growth, the democratic regimes were not as successful as the most effective authoritarian regimes but were more effective than the less efficient authoritarians. The democratic regimes were more effective in holding down the inflation rate but neither set of regimes was effective in dealing with the problems created by large external debts.

These comparisons do not prove anything, but they are at least suggestive. The most damaging disabilities of democracies need not apparently operate everywhere, and the presumed economic advantages of authoritarian regimes also cannot be taken for granted. Of course, there are also democracies that seem to embody the worst fears of the antidemocracy school. Jamaica under Michael Manley in the 1970s is a case in point because Manley's populist and socialist policies generated a disastrous period of negative growth. And South Korea, as it moves toward democracy, may also be illustrating some of the potential dangers: consumption expenditures are up, wages are increasing faster than productivity, and social discipline may be on the decline. However, it must also be said that the continued imposition of authoritarian policies on an increasingly educated and prosperous populace might result in even greater economic and political turmoil. Perhaps the safest conclusion is that the mixed performance record of *both* authoritarian and democratic regimes suggests that generalized descriptions of the presumed costs and benefits of different types of regime are not very useful. Other considerations need to be added before a judgment can be reached: elite and governmental commitments to growth and equity; economic resources and the level of development; the presence or absence of internal conflicts; and the state of the world economy.

Lack of space precludes a detailed discussion of the relationship between capitalism and democracy. Democracy and capitalism work well together, especially in the advanced Western countries, largely because a capitalist market economy helps to provide the autonomous structures (pluralist groups and associations) that support and sustain a democratic political system. The political struggle does not need to degenerate into a zero-sum struggle for the control of the state; prosperity and the enjoyment of economic and political rights are not dependent on a life-or-death conflict over which group controls the government. Whether economic liberty is a prerequisite for political liberty, or whether there is a conflict between the two that cannot easily be resolved is unclear, but surely both realms work better when they are complementary. Andrew Schmookler seems to have it right when he says that both systems rest on a similar psychological structure or set of internalized virtues: "a capacity for compromise, a degree of geniality and empathy in interpersonal dealings, a sense of responsibility."[33]

The difficulty once again comes from extrapolating these arguments to the Third World. There are obvious dangers that capitalism may increase already severe inequalities, that the needs of the poor and the unorganized will be ignored, that corruption will increase, that the losers will resort to violence, and that Schmookler's internalized virtues will never develop. In these circumstances, the need for a strong state to protect the weak and to provide stability is imperative. This implies the need for a third option between a limited state that provides prosperity for a few and a powerful state that yields to populist impulses or is used by one group for its own benefit, but whether such an option can be devised is unclear.

Conclusions

Practitioners want from academics what academics cannot provide: grounded theories that generate precise predictions and focus on variables that the policymaker can control or at least influence. But the academics have—at best—produced only weak theories that require judgment in application, "essentially contested" concepts, interminable definitional disputes, and a data base that is not always adequate or reliable. Still, at a more modest level, they are better at challenging the conventional wisdom, asking awkward (if sometimes unanswerable) questions, and *perhaps* suggesting a different framework for debate and discussion. Something of the first two tasks has been attempted in the preceding pages. Some very tentative and preliminary steps toward accomplishing the latter task follow.

There are no perfect democracies and all democracies are a matter of degree, falling somewhere along a complex spectrum. This necessitates a nuanced and discriminating view of the world as well as great caution in attributing specific patterns of behavior to regime-types that exist only analytically. Of course, none of this has inhibited numberless comments and generalizations about the virtues and vices of democracies, authoritarians, or totalitarians. Still, the more important question in the present context is whether the differences in degree between advanced and developing democracies (or even different generations of third world democracies) are profound enough to be or to become differences in kind or whether the differences merely mark way stations along the road to a relatively more complete democracy. There is no clear answer to this question since everything depends on the interaction of an extraordinary number of factors now and in the future. Moreover, there is no a priori reason to assume that one answer or even a few answers will suffice; shifting and at least partially contradictory patterns are probably as likely as anything else. Nevertheless, this issue must be faced as directly as possible because it affects the very crucial question of what can or should be expected from a world with a continually growing number of (weak) democracies.

In making their case for U.S. support of democracy, policymakers and commentators extrapolate too readily from the history of Western democracies. There is, of course, some possibility that each of their propositions about democracy's benefits will prove to be true to some degree in some circumstances. It is perhaps equally probable, however, that weak democracies in a difficult environment may generate more domestic and international conflict, that they may not produce greater prosperity or greater equity or greater support for U.S. values or interests, and that they may or may not be more stable—at worst, they may be travesties of the democratic ideal, at best pale and uncertain imitations of the real thing. A good deal of the uncertainty about likely results has to do with the obvious fact that regime-type is only one factor among many that affect behavior. Nevertheless, it is worth reemphasizing that the failures of (most) authoritarian regimes have become so apparent that support for weak democracies that produce uncertain outcomes may still be justified or preferable—if done cautiously with a sense of the risks *and* the responsibilities.

Sorting through these complexities will never be easy but it is helpful to keep in mind what needs to be compared with what. It is obvious that comparisons with advanced Western democracies are usually misleading, although Westerners find it hard to avoid this trap—the pictures in their heads about democracy can only reflect what they know and have experienced. At the same time, comparisons with brutal and inept authoritarian regimes in the Third World are not very illuminating: even weak, imperfect, and limited democracies with a moderate record of success and unclear prospects for the future are preferable to the regimes of Saddam Hussein, Idi Amin, the "Emperor" Bokassa, "Baby Doc," and all the rest. The more relevant or important comparison may be between the weak democracies and the small number of "good" authoritarians who have achieved some degree of growth, equity, and stability. One has here democracies with an important degree of normative legitimacy and a much lower degree of performance legitimacy matched against authoritarians with a substantial degree of performance legitimacy and a marginal degree of normative legitimacy. There is no abstract way at any particular moment to choose which of these regimes is preferable because each fulfills important public needs. But over time, in a policy sense, the tilt—where it does not require the sacrifice of other important goals or interests—clearly should be toward the democracies: the longer the democracies survive, the more likely they are to achieve an acceptable or improving level of performance. The authoritarians are likely to be increasingly unstable if they do badly or if they succeed and create demands for the kind of legitimacy they cannot provide.

The other comparisons that make sense, as noted earlier, are with regional neighbors at roughly the same level of development. And here the democracies seem to do relatively well, especially in a composite index that weights a variety of factors. These democracies seem "premature," at least if empirical theories of democracy are taken seriously, because they lack the required socioeconomic prerequisites, they do not always have a political culture that supports democratic values and procedures, and their elites frequently fear the potential "excesses" of democracy. But even weak democracies can survive if the government has sufficient resources and leadership to meet citizens' needs and expectations, if ethnic conflicts have not reached a zero-sum stage, and if the international economic environment stabilizes or the Western powers are farsighted enough to provide additional resources during the difficult transition period—and after. The "ifs" suggest the problem: demands for democracy may continue to escalate; the results in some cases may be beneficial for the country and the international system; but the fundamental issue is not (or not only) the creation of more democracies but the creation of conditions in which the new regimes can survive and prosper. Without these conditions, the potential for a backlash against democracy (and perhaps for radical and/or irrational alternatives) may increase, nostalgia for "our SOBs" may return to the United States, and the prospects for conflict and economic decline will escalate.

In short, it is a mistake to expect too much from third world democracy; imperfect democracy produces imperfect outcomes. But two factors seem to justify a continuing tilt toward democracy in U.S. policy choices—justifications that go beyond the fact that, from a sufficiently elongated perspective, authoritarianism is an anachronism. These factors are not entirely obvious; they are a step away from detailed analysis of the relationship between democracy and the other variables already discussed; and they are likely to be most significant in cases where they are bolstered by substantial external support.

As many social scientists have emphasized, one of the key factors in establishing stable democracy is the institutionalization of autonomous groups, associations, and processes, an institutionalization that helps to create a democratic culture and that supports and supplements the democratic political system itself. In this sense, one of the greatest costs of authoritarianism is that it prevents and inhibits—usually out of fear—the emergence of an institutional base that can help a new democracy to survive, especially if the authoritarian regime has failed economically and has not generated relatively autonomous economic structures. Weak democracies can at least begin the learning process that creates attitudes, structures, and procedures that, joined to an acceptable level of performance, stabilize even premature democracies. As in so many cases now in the Third World and Eastern Europe, departed authoritarian regimes tend to leave behind (apart from the consequences of their failures) a political vacuum, which means that the new democratic regime must cope with a difficult policy environment while teaching its own citizens what democracy means. Perhaps also even a weak democracy that has permitted or facilitated the development of autonomous institutions will consider or perceive a different range of options than an authoritarian regime when a crisis develops or hard trade-offs have to be made between different but equally valued goals.

Presumably democracies, even weak democracies, are relatively better at learning from their mistakes and correcting failing policies because of the presence of an active opposition, a free press, and an involved citizenry. Obviously not all democracies are good at learning, perhaps because the disabilities of democracy may be more powerful than the benefits in particular cases. After all, sharply limiting participation also limits feedback and the growth of trust about government intentions. Nevertheless, most of the stable democracies have demonstrated some ability to learn and adjust, if less than perfectly at least enough to survive. There is no single reason for this but the one common thread that runs through these cases, to which insufficient attention is paid, is a pattern of reasonable expectations among the citizenry—expectations about how well and how fairly the government will perform.

It may be useful in trying to understand this issue to think about the problem of expectations in the context of failed democracies—or failed authoritarian regimes. What most citizens of most third world countries have learned to expect from their governments is failure: empty rhetoric, biased and corrupt implementation, and policies that achieve few goals. Whether the government is democratic or authoritarian, most citizens have learned to expect little, to assume that failure is likely, and to take protective actions that are reasonable but that also generate a negative self-fulfilling prophecy about government policies. The usual outcome is in the form of a pendulum with left and right governments succeeding each other and failing in turn. This has generated an interesting literature on the need to break out of this cycle by devising a third model of development, although what the content of this model ought to be and how it is going to be accepted and implemented is never entirely clear.[34]

The central question is why citizens who have quite rationally (and accurately) expected failure should expect anything different from a third—or fourth or fifth—model. One answer is that they will learn from experience not to expect instant gratification from the political system and/or they will be frightened into a new set of expectations by a sense of crisis. It is not clear whether this learning process is more likely to occur in democratic or authoritarian regimes. Many factors will affect the process, not all of them within the control of the regime in power. It seems reasonable to assume that a democracy that manages to survive and perform relatively well over a period of time will be more effective in this regard than an authoritarian regime, for reasons already noted. But this begs the question of how a weak democracy can manage to survive long enough or to perform well enough for citizens to establish a pattern of reasonable expectations. There are, however, some actions that a democratic government can take that might facilitate the learning process, although space permits no detailed discussion of them here.[35] Rather, what actions could external powers, especially the United States, take that could help the regime convince its citizens that what they can reasonably expect from an imperfect democracy is likely to be better than what they can reasonably expect from an imperfect authoritarian regime?

The United States in the past has supported many authoritarian regimes, largely because they professed to be anti-Communist or because it assumed that economic development would lead to political development and that the authoritarians would be better at enforcing the necessary sacrifices for development. Neither rationale any longer makes much sense, and the United States has now shifted (bar the Middle East) to direct support for the institutionalization of democracy and a redefinition of U.S. interests in the Third World toward milieu goals. As already noted, even if these goals are sound, achieving them will be difficult, U.S. support may rest on some unrealistic assumptions about how the new democracies will behave, and there are many difficult and unresolved questions about the trade-offs between different values and interests. Nor has the United States thought through very carefully what kind of democracy it is supporting in the Third World and whether political democracy in the context of great economic inequality will be stable or just. In addition, the United States has not considered the moral implications of supporting transitions to democracy if it is not also willing to provide substantial financial resources to the weak and heavily burdened democracies that emerge. Offering lectures on the virtues of the market will not suffice.

The United States could do a variety of obvious things to increase the chances that new democracies will survive and prosper. For example, it could and must work with U.S. allies to reestablish a stable international economic environment—no third world regime is likely to be able to deal effectively with a world economy that is volatile, beset by crises and shocks, and increasingly operating outside the principles and rules of the Bretton Woods system. The United States could also seek to establish an international fund to support new democracies, if largely to increase the pool of available resources and to deflect charges of interventionism (if the United States alone supports the new regime). Perhaps also, in a longer term perspective, the United States could invest more in educating third world elites about the attitudes and beliefs—and the value system—that are crucial supports for stable democracy.

The United States may do none of these things, or may do them badly, or may do them well but still be surprised, if not dismayed, at the results. Creating more democracies in the world that now exists, or that all hope may be emerging, will not guarantee a utopia of peace and prosperity. Still, even if the uncertainties are vast, and even if the United States has been wrong in the past about the imminent arrival of a democratic world, the movement toward democracy is likely to continue: the failures of authoritarianism are too salient, the normative superiority of democracy is too evident, and the spread of communications has been too profound to assume that people will continue to accept rule by corrupt and inept dictators. Nevertheless, it would be prudent and wise for the U.S. government to lower its rhetorical posture on the democracy issue. Making support for democracy (or any single goal) the center of a policy approach to the Third World may lead to charges of cynicism if the United States does not resolve the questions noted above or if it decides in some cases that other interests must take precedence. Moreover, as an issue rises in political importance, it may become badly politicized and raise doubts about whether succeeding administrations will support earlier decisions.[36] The most important point, however, is that lowering the rhetoric of support will reduce the assumption that the United States will provide financial aid for all democratic transitions and might also make a small but important contribution to lowering internal and external expectations about the immediate benefits of democratization. Implying that the best is achievable may make the good less achievable.[37] None of this should be taken as an argument against supporting democracy; rather, it is a warning that U.S. support needs to be nuanced and differentiated, hopeful but not naive.

A longer version of this article will appear in Conflict Resolution in the Post–Cold War Third World *(Washington, D.C.: United States Institute of Peace, forthcoming). Used by permission of the publisher.*

Notes

1. For a thorough review of all of these propositions, see the author's "Weak Democracy and the Prospects for Peace and Prosperity in the Third World" in *Conflict Resolution in the Post–Cold War Third World.*

2. This essay will also not deal with the argument that the United States has no moral right to attempt to establish democracy because it is ethnocentric. In fact, democracy has been widely accepted as an international norm. In any event, the United States has an effect on the democracy issue whatever it does because of its power and influence, and there is not much point in supporting inept authoritarian regimes. A better argument against support is that the United States lacks the knowledge to do it wisely or the willingness to follow through on its support—but both conditions may be changing.

3. See, for example, various official comments in *Authoritarianism and the Return of Democracy in Latin America*, Hearings Before the Subcommittee on Western Hemispheric Affairs of the House Committee on Foreign Affairs, 98th Cong., 2nd sess., June 6, 1984.

4. See the interesting "Statement of Hon. Stephen J. Solarz," in "The National Endowment for Democracy in 1990," Hearing Before the Subcommittee on International Operations of the House Committee on Foreign Affairs, 101st Cong., 1st sess., September 28, 1989. Congressman Solarz makes many of the standard points about supporting democracy, among them that it will foster stability in U.S. allies and make it easier to muster support for U.S. objectives.

5. Samuel P. Huntington, "Will More Countries Become Democratic?" *Political Science Quarterly* 99 (Summer 1984), pp. 193ff.

6. Note that democracies may find it relatively more difficult to establish policies or to move away from a centrist position because of the need to consult and to compromise diverse interests and because of the tendency to establish catchall political parties. It may also be harder to gain support as the Cold War declines and the need for unified positions seems less pressing. Perhaps more important, note that one possible implication of the emergence of more democracies in an interdependent world is that international political and economic relations may become even more domesticated—which may make international agreements even harder to negotiate.

7. See Arnold Wolfers, *Discord and Collaboration* (Baltimore: Johns Hopkins Press, 1962), p. 73.

8. Erich Weede, "Democracy and War Involvement," *Journal of Conflict Resolution* 28 (December 1984), p. 649.

9. See R. J. Rummel, "Libertarianism and International Violence," *Journal of Conflict Resolution* 27 (March 1983), pp. 27–71.

10. Steve Chan, "Mirror, Mirror on the Wall—Are the Freer Countries More Pacific?" *Journal of Conflict Resolution* 28 (December 1984), p. 632. Chan also notes that the four countries with highest war-per-years scores are democracies: Israel, India, France, and Great Britain (pp. 626–627).

11. *Ibid.*, pp. 632–633.

12. Weede, "Democracy and War Involvement," p. 657; Jack Vincent, "Freedom and International Conflict: Another Look," *International Studies Quarterly* 31 (March 1987), pp. 103–112, also disagrees with Rummel's findings.

13. Zeev Maoz and Nasrin Abdolali, "Regime Types and International Conflict, 1816–1976," *Journal of Conflict Resolution* 33 (March 1989), pp. 3–35.

14. Note that the uncertainties about democracy and conflict involvement in no way imply a better record for authoritarian regimes.

15. John Mueller, *Retreat From Doomsday—The Obsolescence of Major War* (New York: Basic Books, 1989) argues that it is a change in attitude or patterns of thought that has prevented war in the liberal community (p. 24). He also discusses the aversion to war as citizens become richer and have more to lose (p. 252).

16. This is obviously suggestive about why the war involvement of democracies is high.

17. Mueller, *Retreat from Doomsday*, p. 255.

18. For a discussion of the relationship between arms spending and threat perception, see Robert L. Rothstein, "The 'Security Dilemma' and the 'Poverty Trap' in the Third World," *Jerusalem Journal of International Relations* 8, no. 4 (1986), pp. 1–38.

19. One should also note that the freer countries have always been a minority and that they have frequently been too distant or too different in size to make armed conflict a sensible or likely choice.

20. On consociational democracy as a means for dealing with sharp internal divisions, see Arend Lijphart, *Democracy in Plural Societies* (New Haven: Yale University Press, 1977). One problem with consociational democracy is that the initial agreement may be increasingly undermined by patterns of change (e.g., population growth rates and differential economic performance) that the agreement ignores. Thus short-run success can be bought at the price of greater long-run conflicts.

21. See the *New York Times*, May 2, 1990, for

some of the details on rising arms spending.

22. Janet Welsh Brown, "Why Should We Care?" in Brown, ed., *In the U.S. Interest* (Boulder, Colo.: Westview, 1990), pp. 1–18, has interesting comments on these matters. The pattern of response to resource deterioration could vary greatly from irrational acts of violence (terrorism, assassination) to desperate attempts to emigrate or wars against neighbors—or perhaps just despair and resignation.

23. For example, Vaman Rao, "Democracy and Economic Development," *Studies in Comparative International Development* 19 (Winter 1984–85), p. 76, insists that only nondemocratic states have succeeded in controlling population growth rates. But recent World Bank figures show a much more mixed record on this issue.

24. Edgar Owens, *The Future of Freedom in the Developing World* (New York: Pergamon Press, 1987), pp. 52–63.

25. This is also the position of Mueller, *Retreat from Doomsday*, p. 254.

26. Note also that the superpowers and many others may continue to sell arms because of the economic benefits. Perhaps the foolishness of this policy has become more apparent in the wake of Iraq's aggression against Kuwait, but doubts remain. Still, it is possible at least to say that the reaction against Iraq makes the judgment that small states can now act with impunity when they take military action seem simplistic.

27. See Rao, "Democracy and Economic Development," pp. 73–78, on the first points and Robert Kaufman, "Democratic and Authoritarian Responses to the Debt Issue," *International Organization* 39 (Summer 1985), p. 473, on the last point. It should be noted that the performance of authoritarian regimes has been only marginally better on this issue.

28. See especially Dan Usher, *The Economic Prerequisites to Democracy* (Oxford: Basil Blackwell, 1981).

29. Zehra F. Arat, "Democracy and Economic Development," *Comparative Politics* 21 (October 1988), p. 30. Arat also found much shifting back and forth between regimes in individual countries.

30. Erich Weede, "The Impact of Democracy on Economic Growth: Some Evidence from Cross-National Analysis," *Kyklos* 36 (1983), p. 25.

31. *Ibid.*, pp. 28–32.

32. See Table 1 in his article "The Policy Capabilities of Democratic Regimes," *Latin America Research Review* 24, no. 2 (1989), pp. 118–120.

33. Andrew Bard Schmookler, *The Parable of the Tribes* (Boston: Houghton Mifflin, 1984), p. 190.

34. For an exceptionally interesting article on this issue, see Marcelo Diamond, "Overcoming Argentina's Stop-and-Go Economic Cycles," in Jonathan Hartlyn and Samuel A. Morley, eds., *Latin American Political Economy* (Boulder, Colo.: Westview, 1986), pp. 129–164. One problem with the third model is that it tends to be a selection of policies that worked from each extreme and amalgamating these into a new model is not easy.

35. One advantage that some of the developing countries may have over the Soviet Union and perhaps Eastern Europe as they democratize is that third world expectations do not include the kind of social services net that has existed in the socialist countries. There people have suffered badly but at least have been provided with a wide variety of low-level benefits: guaranteed employment, cheap housing, and health care, for instance. The people fear losing these benefits more than they expect to benefit from democracy and the market. And the new or not-so-new regimes lack the resources to continue subsidizing these services, at least if they want to grow. The dilemma has no obvious resolution.

36. One 1986 study listed support for democracy as the *last* of 14 goals for U.S. foreign policy among both the U.S. public and elites—which suggests that lowering U.S. rhetoric will not necessarily lead to large protests.

37. One possible alternative to a central focus on democracy is a refocusing of the debate on the idea of legitimacy. Briefly, in a situation of profound questions about the meaning of democracy and of hybrid regimes, a focus on legitimacy may be useful

Weak Democracy and the Third World

because it incorporates and evaluates *all* regimes according to a common standard, namely, whether citizens are complying voluntarily with regime policies and whether the regime thus seems to be meeting their needs.

Democracy and World Order

Brad Roberts

ARCHITECTS OF A post–cold war world order would do well to reflect on the precarious tilt of the campanile of the cathedral in Pisa, Italy: whatever the merits of structural integrity and aesthetic appeal, a durable construct must rest on a stable foundation. Speculation about the emerging post–cold war world order tends to focus on the redistribution of military and economic power in an international system wrought by an ascendant Germany and Japan, a descendant Soviet Union, and a United States showing signs of both. Too little attention has been paid to the foundations of this emerging structure—those factors of politics and values that determine to a significant degree the parameters of statecraft. The collapse of totalitarianism and the reinvigoration of the liberal ideal in the 1990s mark the end of a century-long competition between two opposing views of economics, politics, and humanity. Democracy's resurgence is profound. This trend will help determine the limits and extend the possibilities of the post–cold war era.

A Democratic Revolution

For most observers, the fall of the Berlin Wall in November 1989 symbolized the democratic renewal. It brought unity to a democratic Germany, set in motion a chain of events that helped Central Europe escape its authoritarian and totalitarian straitjacket, and met Ronald Reagan's key test of Mikhail Gorbachev's sincerity as a reformer. But the collapse of communism in Europe and the gripping rollercoaster of reform in the Soviet Union have distracted observers from what is in fact a much broader trend. In 1989 alone, democracy enjoyed remarkable successes. Countries as diverse as Taiwan, Nicaragua, and Namibia underwent significant political openings that year, while the two largest democracies in the world—India and Brazil—conducted sharply contested elections that resulted in the peaceful transfer of power to new civilian governments.

But 1989 was only the most dramatic year in a decade of rapid, broad-based movement toward democracy. Outside Europe, this movement was perhaps most dramatic in Latin America, where country after country cast out dictatorships of the right (and later of the left) in favor of elected leaders. In Asia, the decade brought significant democratic successes in Korea, Pakistan, and the Philippines, among others. Even in Africa, the authoritarian alternative and single-party politics seemed to play themselves out, with 1990 bringing widespread expectations of democracy's rebirth from Algeria to South Africa. In broader historical terms, these transitions should

---

Brad Roberts is editor of *The Washington Quarterly*.

be seen as part of a series of events that began on the Iberian peninsula in the mid-1970s, when authoritarian rulers were swept out of Portugal and Spain by broad-based social movements.

This quick survey suggests that the democratic movement of recent years has been a movement of governments and states. In fact, it is both broader and deeper. It is broader in the sense that the process of democratization means different things in different societies. In some, such as former East Germany or Nicaragua, it means decisive rejection of an anti-democratic state and its replacement by a wholly different system. In others, such as South Africa and Mexico, it means a partial opening of the system. In yet others, such as the Soviet Union and China, democratization may occur fundamentally as a social factor, but not (yet) as a matter of state structure.

The democratic movement is deeper in that it touches on more than questions of political organization. Underlying the regime transitions is a social revolution of values and expectations with as yet incomplete political implications. The losers of the last decade were not merely isolated dictators, but also the totalitarian and authoritarian ideal itself. As an ideal embodying high human aspirations and an inherent skepticism of state power, democracy has an appeal across divisions of culture and history that could hardly have been anticipated as recently as the 1970s, when it seemed an isolated notion in a beleaguered set of industrial states. This is genuinely a revolution in both form and substance.

There are of course many factors driving political change around the world, and it is difficult to generalize about democratic transitions or openings when each is obviously rooted in the history of discrete societies. But there are several factors that seem to coalesce in one way or another in most cases.

One is the failure of communism. Lauded by some as a totalitarian solution to problems of development and justice, communism's failure has accelerated the delegitimization of nondemocratic forms of government of both left and right. The abject state of the Soviet Union and China has revealed just how far-reaching is the collapse of communism. Indeed, these societies are in crisis, not just of governance and prosperity, but of health, environment, and moral fabric as well.

The second factor is the success of the democracies in competing with totalitarian and authoritarian states. That competition is in part economic: democracies by and large have provided an environment for growth that is both stable and relatively equitable. But it is also much more than economic: democracies provide other basic social goods, principal among them domestic justice and individual liberty, in greater proportion than non-democracies.

A third factor is the success of democrats in founding their movements on indigenous philosophies, histories, institutions, and aspirations. Democracy previously made false starts in many countries where it has made a new start in recent years. Those earlier attempts often failed because of the lack of legitimate local roots of democratization. Throughout the post-colonial world in the 1960s and 1970s, the facade of democracy collapsed because democratic institutions were the vestiges of a political life imposed from the outside. In the 1980s and 1990s, democratic movements seem to have reconnected themselves to long-standing domestic social forces. Democracy is no longer rejected by intellectuals in non-Western countries as something narrowly Western or modern; instead, it is accepted by many as something relevant to human communities everywhere. In the words of the Senegalese scholar Jacques Mariel Nzouankeu, "Human rights have no frontiers and are indivisible; there is no liberty that is good for the West and bad for Africa."[1]

A fourth factor in the democratic transition is the communications revolution. So far, at least, it appears that George Orwell's apocalyptic view of the human future spelled out in *1984* had it completely wrong—modern technology has been used in the service of the individual, not the state. Television, telephones, photocopy machines, personal computers, and now fax machines and data links have worked to pry loose the grip of the state on the individual.[2] The communications revolution has empowered ordinary people as consumers and distributors of information, encouraging them to take control of their own lives. It has propelled economic integration on an unprecedented scale while raising expectations about the right to life, liberty, and the pursuit of happiness.

A fifth major factor is the collapse of ideology as a dominating political force and the concomitant prominence of pragmatism. Ideology's moment has passed as a force able to command broad public activism on questions of national organization. Political communities around the world are today struggling to cope with the demands of political and economic empowerment. Democracy is defended by many in these communities as the best tool available to meet this pragmatic need.

A sixth factor is an international environment decidedly conducive to democratization. Dictators have been unable to argue that the tide of history is moving with them. Democrats have taken courage and ideas from the successes of like-minded individuals in other societies. Moreover, the dominant events of early 1991—war in the Persian Gulf and retrenchment in the Soviet Union—seem not to have dampened the expectation that democratization will continue to be a fundamental international political force in the decade ahead.

To be sure, these factors have not operated equally in every society. Communism's collapse is not complete in the Soviet Union and China. The established democracies are not universally admired, especially in some parts of the Muslim world. In places like Latin America, democracy has emerged more by default than design, and the collapse of old anti-democratic regimes cannot universally be seen as a triumph of indigenous democratic forces. The communications revolution has reached more people in the developed world than in the developing one. Anti-democratic ideologies remain relevant, especially among elites who still command the instruments of state repression in closed societies such as Iran or China. And external factors that were so important to democratization in Eastern Europe have so far had considerably less impact in Africa.

Moreover, democracy is not, of course, uncontested. Some democratic transitions will fail, while others will no doubt suffer setbacks. In countries such as the Soviet Union there has been a reassertion of the old authority as the reform effort has ground to a halt. But even in the Soviet Union a return to rigid totalitarianism seems less likely than a blend of authoritarianism, limited political expression, and anarchy in the coming years. Elsewhere, such as in some countries in

Latin America, democratization may proceed only on the surface and not in the distribution of power and participation in political life. In quite a few places, fragile new democracies must contend with destabilizing social forces. The Soviet Union provides the most powerful example of what is in fact a quite common problem: social chaos arising from resurgent ethnic divisions and a general rising tide of expectations. And in quite a few states of the developing world, thuggery still passes for governance.

Given the numerous challenges confronting societies navigating democratic transitions, it is prudent to expect that the immediate future may breed less optimism about the prospects for democracy than the recent past. It is possible that, like the pendulum of a clock, societies will swing back from opening to closure. Indeed, this is likely in some. But a wholesale reversal of the democratic openings of recent years appears unlikely. Eastern Europe will not quickly return to totalitarian rule. The authoritarian alternative in Latin America is discredited as never before. Rising prosperity in Asia has brought with it the new political demands of emerging middle classes. In short, analysts should be careful not to dismiss too quickly the power of the pro-democracy forces described above.

Most skeptics of the democratic prospect point to economic performance as the basic determinant of the sustainability of new democracies. Noting fascism's emergence from the decay of weak capitalist democracies in the 1920s, they assert that economic decay spells political instability. But this gives undue emphasis to economic performance. As argued above, it is not economic factors alone that have contributed to democracy's resurgence. In fact, history includes many examples of even fragile democracies surviving economic turmoil because of public commitment to democratic values and institutions, such as Israel, India, and Costa Rica. The priority accorded economic performance undoubtedly varies from society to society, but even in those countries where it is accorded a high priority, voter dissatisfaction may prove more costly to specific governments than to democratic instruments and institutions. Poland's democratic credentials remain intact even after continuing economic turmoil caused the voters to cast out a government widely admired internationally.

To be sure, democracy is no guarantee of economic prosperity. Nondemocracies have sometimes outperformed democracies in generating increases in gross national product. In Korea and Taiwan, for example, economic growth occurred in societies with a narrowly constrained political life. In general, however, democracies seem to make possible stable, long-term, and broad-based growth, as demonstrated by the members of the Organization for Economic Cooperation and Development and many of the newly industrializing countries. They do this by making possible the improvement of market efficiency. Nondemocratic governments have on the whole shown themselves incapable of providing the framework necessary for economic adaptation to changing domestic and international circumstances. Providing a possibility does not ensure a result, however, and democracy certainly is not an economic panacea. But in that possibility is the superiority of the democratic alternative.

The central challenge confronting the new democracies is not economic performance but the broader issue of governance. Most new democracies face a crisis of governance much deeper and broader than is understood in the United States. While few societies today seem willing to choose the route backward to nondemocracy, few seem to know the way ahead clearly either. They look to the established democracies for valuable experience and lessons, but recognize that the leisurely development of democracy in the transatlantic community over the last three centuries stands in sharp contrast to their own urgency. They must compress in time what the developed democracies took centuries to learn in building the cultural, ethical, educational, and legal infrastructures of democracy. Moreover, they must do so against a rising tide of demographic and environmental constraints. Because these are societies in crisis, their leaders are hungry for ideas that work. This helps the door stay firmly shut on the discredited ideologies of the nineteenth century. The world of the next century will put demands on the state that would have been unimaginable in the last; this helps concentrate the public and political mind on democracy's strengths in meeting the crisis of governance.

One of the basic determinants of the new democracies' ability to navigate the crisis of governance and secure their transition to stable democracy is the weight of the past. This is measured in terms of the inheritance of institutions, values, and expectations. Each new democracy is located at a different point along a continuum, stretching at one extreme from states where democratic rule had been interrupted only temporarily, to those roughly in the middle with some, but limited, democratic experience, to the other extreme where the detritus of nondemocratic government litters a political, social, and economic wasteland. For example, Turkey has quickly regained relatively stable democracy after a period of authoritarian rule in the 1970s and 1980s. The middle of the continuum is perhaps best demonstrated in Central Europe, where many countries bring to their democratic transitions the vestiges of civil society and a democratic tradition carefully nurtured under the shadow of totalitarianism. The struggling Soviet Union and China perhaps best exemplify the other extreme, confronting the challenges of democratization across a yawning abyss.

This historical legacy is important because it conditions the capacity of a society to undertake the tasks of democratization. These extend well beyond the construction of a democratic state, as defined in terms of a competitive electoral system and institutions of government operating according to democratic norms, to include the creation of a democratic society. In the absence of a democratic society, a democratic state will not long survive. But building a democratic society is a daunting, long-term challenge. It is also a responsibility that extends well beyond the state and political leaders. Czechoslovak President Václav Havel has spoken persuasively of the challenge of nurturing citizenship: imbuing an electorate with a commitment to both freedom *and* responsibility. A democratic society entails some appreciation of the virtue of compromise, protection of minority as well as individual rights, and a military establishment committed to democratic norms.

The capacity of societies to democratize seems to be a function of the extent to which the state has historically dominated society. In those countries where a private sector has been permitted to exist, where myriad private associations have come into existence that compete with the state for allegiance and public energy, and where religious conviction and worship are tolerated, the prospects for successful democratization appear decidedly bright. Countries lacking these assets will measure progress toward a democratic society only in their piecemeal accumulation. In societies where old totalitarian structures were not brought down in war or revolution, reformers have found it easier to dismantle the old than to start with the new. But even in these societies, hope can be found in the rapid expansion of the independent sector. In the Soviet Union, for example, there are many thousands of new institutions and associations, to say nothing of a sizable religious revival, that constitute the hope for a brighter future.

If each society brings a different capacity to the challenges of democratization, the leaders they choose are similarly varied. The best will work wonders in the face of seemingly insoluble problems, while the worst will squander what opportunities come their way. Leadership is measured not just by commitment to democratic processes and nonviolence, but also in terms of the ability to generate public consensus and understanding, and (as Solidarity leaders in Poland have often put it) to use the power of the truth to confront the challenges of governance. The best leaders will recognize and avoid steps leading to populist or majoritarian democracy. They will also educate elites enjoying inherited roles in society to be more open to change and to learn to see politics in a democracy as more than zero-sum. The salience of skillful democratic leadership has been well demonstrated in the USSR, where many democratic politicians have learned how to score points with constituents and how to say "no," but have not learned those other skills expected of democratic leaders: the ability to compromise, build consensus, and achieve governmental results.

It follows that similar leadership should also be expected of political figures in opposition. The fragile democracies of countries such as Pakistan have foundered in part because of the willingness of the leaders of political parties in opposition to join with anti-democratic forces to bring down governments led by their political competitors. Also, since democratization is a process extending well beyond the state, leadership is something society needs not only in politics but also in the intellectual, media, religious, business, labor, and military communities. Political leaders who encourage and accommodate the emergence of leaders in other sectors of society are contributing to the health of new democracies.

World Order Politics in a Democratic Era

What are the implications of the democratic revolution for the way the world works and for the kind of world order emerging in the post–cold war era? Will increased democratization ease chronic international conflict or will international security grow more precarious because of the fragility of the new democracies?

Democratization is not a panacea for the problem of international conflict. The view that it might be has enjoyed growing currency of late, with proponents arguing that history shows that democracies are less warlike than non-democracies. In fact, the empirical evidence in support of this proposition is murky.[3] Although one could debate definitions of democracy and war endlessly, the historical record does seem to indicate that democracies have gone to war just about as frequently as nondemocracies. But the historical record is unequivocal that democracies do not war with one another.

What is it about democracy that accounts for its pacific orientation if not predilection? Because they depend on popular consent for their legitimacy, democracies can only make wars that are perceived by the public as just. Wars of aggression or punitive wars waged by or among democracies are rarities in the modern era. Similarly, given that democracies are based on the domestic exercise of public principle, their leaders are less apt to look at the world in Machiavellian terms than the leaders of states whose primary domestic concern is the use of coercive power. And by permitting free inquiry and a reasoned consideration of the costs and benefits of national actions, democracies are also less likely than nondemocracies to stumble into war unwittingly.

Moreover, democracies lend themselves to the evolution of a community of like-minded neighbors. As Immanuel Kant observed two centuries ago in his *Prolegomena to a Perpetual Peace*, there is something qualitatively different about an international system in which states share rather than compete over basic values. Kant argued that states disposed to respect the rights of individuals would respect the legitimacy of other countries similarly governed and would encourage rather than restrict mutually satisfying trade relations, leading to the gradual emergence of what he termed "zones of peace."

Even at this abstract level, however, some notes of caution are in order about the possible effects of democratization on international security. To begin with, democratic governance may have certain drawbacks with regard to foreign policy. As Alexis de Tocqueville argued,

Foreign politics demand scarcely any of those qualities which are peculiar to a democracy; they require, on the contrary, the perfect use of almost all those in which it is deficient. . . . [A] democracy can only with great difficulty regulate the details of an important undertaking, persevere in a fixed design, and work out its execution in spite of obstacles. It cannot combine its measures with secrecy or await their consequences with patience.[4]

Furthermore, democracies are prone to populist policies, bouts of nationalism, and demands for policy success in the short term. This calls into question their ability to consistently manage the demands of interdependence and complexity, challenges that are emerging as buzzwords in the post–cold war era.

Second, the pacific orientation of democracies toward one another may have as much to do with their relative political stability and development as with their democratic character, meaning that the new, fragile, and unstable democracies may be less secure in their international relations. Weak democratic institutions will be slow to overcome the tradition of personalized politics in the developing world and may be exploited by outside powers. Incomplete democratization of society may exacerbate the problems of populism, nationalism, and emphasis on the short term. Many new democracies suffer from the hangover left by their predecessors, a hangover measured not just in economic collapse but social chaos.[5]

Third, the wave of democratization has brought a few international insecurities of its own. The power imbalance wrought by the Communist collapse in Europe has sown the seeds of instability. The power vacuum in the USSR is especially worrisome, raising the specter of the Union splintering into a plethora of weak, unstable, and perhaps nuclear-armed states; or, at the other extreme, of an attempt by a right-wing military government to resurrect Soviet state power through domestic repression and renewed claims to superpower status, based on its only remaining superpower credential—military power.

Lastly, the wave of democratization has not diminished the significance of remaining nondemocracies. If anything, the anti-democratic states of the developing world are growing more important to the future world order because of their steady accumulation of advanced military power, including sophisticated high-technology weapons and weapons of mass destruction. Heavily armed renegade states are multiplying in the developing world. Iraq has not been the only state interested in testing the international rules of the post–cold war era.

Despite these cautionary notes, if one probes beyond generalizations about democracy and peace to test specific hypotheses in specific conflicts, democracy emerges as centrally relevant to peace and world order. Retrospectively, the propensity of democracies to peace has been a significant factor in the post–World War II era. To be sure, there have been other factors: the geostrategic coincidence of Western and Asian democracies mutually confronted by a powerful Soviet Union, technological change that has brought both the nuclear bomb and far-reaching economic interdependence, and shared transatlantic cultural traditions. But shared democratic values and shared interests emanating from extensive peaceful political and economic interaction have made war among the developed democracies obsolete. They also provided the foundations of a common response to the Soviet threat.

Looking to the world order challenges of the 1990s, how exactly are democracy and further democratization relevant?

In Europe, the establishment of democracy has helped to create considerable optimism about the durability of the new European peace order embodied in the historic agreements signed in Paris in November 1990.[6] The sense of promise and expectation attached to a united Germany, an integrated European Community in 1992, and a security architecture designed around the Conference on Security and Cooperation in Europe (CSCE) has its foundation in the democratic character of the states involved.

In the Middle East, the movement toward more participatory forms of government is seen by many as critical to the achievement of a relatively durable peace. The absence of legitimate governments in some countries and the power of existing elites to block the negotiating process in others are stumbling blocks to the kinds of compromises and risks that will be necessary if negotiated security measures are to have any chance of succeeding. Also, the absence of democracy in Iraq helped precipitate the war in the Persian Gulf. Saddam Hussein's isolation from political debate contributed to his series of strategic miscalculations, and his capacity to repress popular dissent effectively robbed economic sanctions of any significant political effect. Some experts have advised that regional, cultural, and historical factors make full democratization unlikely or even unnecessary, and that instead local political communities may only grow more open and participatory in the coming years, but not truly democratic. Whether local publics will see it that way is another question. As experience in so many other parts of the world demonstrates, supposed cultural barriers to democracy are quickly swept aside by restive publics unhappy with the limits inherent in a participatory but only quasi-democratic regime.

In Asia as well, democratization is relevant to the major questions of peace. On the Korean peninsula, expectations about the achievement of a breakthrough are shaped fundamentally by the process of liberalization in the South and the anticipated decay of the autocratic regime in the North. Among the member nations of the Association of Southeast Asian Nations, economic prosperity continues to create new demands for political participation. In Taiwan, Hong Kong, and Singapore, long-term prospects are directly tied to democracy's durability. Looked at in historical perspective, Japan's emergence as a stable democracy is a force for regional and international stability.

In Latin America, the challenge of (re)building democracy in Panama and Nicaragua and encouraging political openings in El Salvador and Mexico is the key to whether the region will return to endemic turmoil. Moreover, some regional leaders see the broadening of democratic institutions and rules as directly relevant to their ability to cope with the problems of insurgency, drugs, and immigration.

Conversely, the failure of democratization in China and to a lesser extent the Soviet Union underscores starkly the flip side of the issue. The pursuit of a global post–cold war agenda is held hostage to the faltering reform process in the USSR. The apparent collapse of the reform movement and its replacement by hard-line government has dampened hopes for further progress on the East–West arms-control and diplomatic agendas and might spell the return of global ideological and possibly military competition.

Democratization also seems relevant to the kinds of international priorities emerging in the post–cold war era. That era is rich in opportunities presented by economic interdependence, but it is also burdened with problems compelling new forms of collective responses. These include the environment, where new regimes are under negotiation to limit pollution; collective security, where the principles and mechanisms embodied in the United Nations are enjoying a revival; multilateral arms control, where regional and global negotiations to reduce or eliminate armaments are gaining momentum; changing trade relations; and perhaps even drugs. To reap the benefits of interdependence and cope effectively with emerging problems requires above all a capacity for cooperation, which is more likely in a system dominated by states with shared values than in one dominated by ideological competition.

If democratization creates incentives for cooperation in the new era, it may also help diminish the domestic sources of international conflict. Democracy can help societies cope with the demands of change. It does this by providing mechanisms for articulating the necessity of change, establishing agreed rules to proceed with change, and legitimizing shared sacrifice. There is no guarantee that the new democracies will choose to employ these mechanisms or will succeed in doing so. But their success will be directly relevant to their ability to deal with structural economic adjustment, resource problems, and the social dislocations of modernizing societies.

The democratic revolution in world politics may have two additional virtues for international security. The first is that it may provide an anchor for the United States in global affairs at a time when the nation is trying to define its proper role post–Cold War and post–Persian Gulf War. The success and further trial of democratic values abroad may serve as a useful corrective to the cynicism that periodically grips Americans about the world and to the isolationist impulse.

The second possible virtue stems from the fact that the support of democracy abroad is not a project for the United States alone. The democratic revolution holds the promise of a stronger sense of international community, a larger set of common projects, and a shared set of values that transcend realpolitik considerations of national interest and cold war ties. Democratization can help to provide a sense of direction and purpose in global affairs at a time when both are subject to international debate. The end of the Cold War will have many implications—the passing of the superpower era, the advent of multipolarity, the growth of military power outside of the East–West framework, and possibly prolonged instability in the formerly Communist world. With the passing of the old structures, there is a distinct risk that anarchy and not order will emerge. The sense of direction and purpose afforded by democratization may provide just the boundary markers necessary to navigate the choices about foreign policy, trade, arms proliferation, and freedom that to a large extent will define the world order politics of the 1990s.

It is too early to predict with certainty whether either of these last two virtues will emerge as a cornerstone of the foundation of world order in the years ahead. But given the reaction of the United States and the world community to Iraq's annexation of Kuwait, and George Bush's active promulgation of a world order politics, there are reasons for optimism. In any case, these are but two parts of a much larger picture of a world order building on the benefits of democratization.

United States Policy Responses

What are the appropriate means and ends of U.S. policy with regard to the democratic revolution, and where do they fit in the overall foreign policy priorities of the country in the years ahead?

At the height of euphoria about "the end of history" and the fall of the Berlin Wall, it was common to hear the argument that support for democracy abroad should be enshrined as the central pillar of a post-containment grand strategy for the United States. But the abrupt eruption of the war in the Gulf and the retreat of reform in the Soviet Union have provided a useful corrective to the notion that the United States could lead a kind of *jihad* for democracy and that this would be enough to define the full range of U.S. global strategy.

To make the democracy revolution the centerpiece of U.S. grand strategy in the post–cold war era is neither possible nor desirable. As Americans and their leaders search for an understanding of the world and their nation's place in it, the political orientation of states overseas is an important part of the overall picture. But it is only a part. The United States will be called upon to exercise leadership on many issues other than political development, including not least security, trade, and arms control, where U.S. interests will sometimes compel diplomatic efforts to build coalitions among ideologically diverse states.

This compulsion will cut directly across an effort to foster democracy in other states as the United States' first priority.

Moreover, the U.S. commitment to democracy abroad is hardly a novelty of the post–cold war era, something that the United States would do well to perceive and articulate. Although it has been implemented in different ways in different eras, that commitment predates the rather felicitous international environment of the 1990s and is evident throughout U.S. history. American political, intellectual, and moral leaders have always spoken about American ideals as ideals for the world as a whole, even if they have been inconsistent in implementing that commitment. Cold war containment ought be seen at least in part as one manifestation of that fundamental national orientation to the world.

The U.S. commitment to democracy can take a variety of shapes in the 1990s. President Bush's commitment to a new world order based on the rule of law enforced by collective security represents one possible avenue. The use of U.S. military power in Panama and the Persian Gulf suggests another potential role, that of global policeman. The historical predilection of the American public for the more modest role of honest broker suggests a possible compromise route. Noteworthy for their relative isolation in the public debate so far are those pundits who have argued that democratization abroad is an excuse for the United States to pack its bags and come home to a more nationalist, isolationist set of policies.[7]

The key foreign policy question for the United States is not so much where America stands on democracy as what can America do to help. One focus might be proactive—to give priority in bilateral diplomacy to efforts to unseat remaining nondemocratic governments. With the passing of a bipolar world order the interest of the United States in promoting the democratic domestic order of other states need no longer be held hostage to strategic competition with the Soviet Union. Certainly, the United States has learned a great deal over the last decade about how to facilitate rather than obstruct democratic transitions in other countries. But the American public would not long support a foreign policy based on intervention to destabilize other countries. In any case, such a strategy ignores the fact that democracy must spring from indigenous roots if it is to survive, and democratic regimes installed under U.S. pressure would likely be perceived as illegitimate and thus short-lived.

A second possible focus of U.S. policy is human rights. The protection of human rights abroad has been a cornerstone of U.S. foreign policy under the last three U.S. presidents and remains a priority in a world where democratization is still incomplete. Diplomatic measures that give political power to that commitment, such as the CSCE, should be continued; indeed, their applicability to other regions of the world might be considered. But the traditional human rights agenda has been transformed by democratization. The selective defense of specific human rights must be implemented in a more comprehensive framework that recognizes the new, larger possibilities for a stable national politics based on democratic principles.

A third possible focus is consolidating transitions in the new democracies. This is the most all-encompassing option, and therefore probably also the most difficult. Responding to myriad political changes in scores of countries overseas will require of U.S. diplomacy an unprecedented degree of flexibility, wisdom, and historical sensitivity. Moreover, although the United States has learned something in recent years about how to encourage transitions *from* authoritarianism and totalitarianism, it has learned less about how to complete the transition *to* democracy. This reflects in part an inability to discern and articulate the lessons of democracy-building in America's own society. It also reflects the fact that outside powers can play at best a limited, secondary role in assisting societies to democratize.

In fact, no single policy focus will suffice. American resources and power must be used judiciously at different times and in different ways to nudge closed societies toward political openings, to help new democracies to secure their transitions, and occasionally to cut deals with regimes whose principles it finds abhorrent. United States support may make a difference in those countries where its influence has historically been strong. Its ability to work collaboratively, especially in regions or countries where the U.S. role has not been strong, will also be relevant to the course of democracy.

Damage to the democratic movement abroad can also result from U.S. actions. A wavering American commitment to democracy abroad would undermine the democratic prospect both where U.S. leverage might make a difference and where democrats take inspiration from principled U.S. leadership. In fact, U.S. policy has not been consistent in its support of democracy abroad. American diplomacy toward Angola and Zaire, for example, continues to be driven by old cold war priorities rather than democratic ones. Similarly, Latin America appears to have receded once again from the list of U.S. policy priorities, with democracy in Nicaragua and Panama suffering the consequences. Only with improved consistency will U.S. policy become more credible and effective.

As usual in Washington, the debate about the commitment to democracy abroad turns into a debate about money, with critics of foreign assistance generally fearing that the democracy theme is little more than the latest gimmick to leverage a bit more money out of the U.S. taxpayer. But the American proclivity for throwing money at problems obscures the fact that supporting democracy is not fundamentally a question of money. Democracy abroad will not rise or fall in direct relation to the spending abilities of the U.S. federal budget. Western aid can facilitate but cannot itself ensure the restructuring of the societies or economies of fledgling or potential democracies.

This is not to argue that U.S. aid is without consequence. On the contrary, the United States can do much to help new and emerging democracies. At a basic political level, American aid is important as a signal of the U.S. intent to be a player in world affairs and promote those values that animate its domestic political life. Some second and third world democrats look at the United States and see a state intent on being the world's policeman and one often on the wrong side of questions of political reform; others see a country sympathetic to their cause but incapable of being anything more than an impotent bystander. Even if not effective at generating high economic growth rates or dramatically opening closed societies abroad, a modicum of aid would earn the United States substantial political capital.

In implementing an aid strategy for democracy, the most decisive steps are probably those at the macroeconomic level. In Eastern Europe and Latin America particularly, the debt burden left by departed dictators poses a daunting impediment to fragile new governments seeking to jumpstart broken economies. Debt relief would provide a window of opportunity for these states to begin the business of rebuilding their economies. Toward this end, the commercial banks must go further in writing off their debt in these countries. Also, the failure to halt the slide toward a less open international trading system would have serious long-term ramifications for the governability of new democracies.

At the bilateral level, U.S. aid can play a role in nurturing pluralistic institutions, encouraging economic empowerment, providing a safety net during periods of transition, and easing the burdens inherited from the past. Clearly, these roles are not for the United States alone; other prosperous democracies are playing an increasingly important part in this process. The coordination of aid efforts is important. This suggests the desirability of emphasizing multilateral rather than bilateral approaches in collecting and distributing resources to the new democracies.

Sometimes Western and U.S. aid may be critical in a society's movement to democracy. Aid that has focused on building institutions of pluralism—political parties, independent media, legalized opposition, human rights organizations, legal training programs, and so forth—has been important in countries as varied as Chile, Poland, and the Philippines. More money should be directed to projects that build the infrastructure of democracy (electoral materials and supervisors, for example) as well as projects to promote citizenship. This implies that more money should flow to the U.S. National Endowment for Democracy and to the democracy initiatives of the Agency for International Development.

Where economic aid is employed, it must work not to prop up the old ways but to facilitate the transformation of economic structures and to address the rising political and economic aspirations of the electorate. In most weak democracies struggling with problems of governance, this means that aid should focus on undoing the dictatorship of the bureaucracy. These states struggle with huge and entrenched inherited bureaucracies that are accustomed to operating without the inhibiting forces of effective legislative, public, or even executive oversight. This is a problem shared by new democracies in both the developing and post-Communist worlds. Western aid can be used to encourage bureaucratic simplification and accountability, transparency, predictability, and the rule of law in government.[8] Without such reform at the nexus of economic and political life, stagnation is likely to persist.

Recognizing that U.S. and Western aid can be both carrot and stick, there is an important question about the extent to which such aid should be conditioned on democratic reforms of the political and economic structures. Donors should consider to what extent they would be willing to cut off aid to long-standing friends when democratization slows or halts. This proved easy for the United States in regard to Pakistan once the strategic rationale of the Afghan conflict passed, but has proven more difficult in the case of Western aid to the Soviet Union or U.S. aid to long-standing recipients in Africa. Conditionality poses tough choices for U.S. policymakers, although at least a few of those tradeoffs will have been made less difficult by the passing of the Cold War.[9] Moreover, the threat to cut off U.S. aid may either be taken as hollow by the target regime, or as a price worth paying to achieve certain domestic objectives.

Aiding democracy abroad is not a task for government alone. The nongovernmental sector has an especially important and currently underutilized contribution to make to the consolidation of democratic transitions abroad. As argued above, the crisis of governance facing many newly democratic societies is largely intellectual—learning how to manage complex and rapidly changing societies without much room for trial and error. Private institutions and individuals are better suited than government to articulate the lessons of their experiences and to help like-minded individuals abroad build and manage effective institutions. Self-help organizations, nonprofit institutions, environmental protection groups, etc., all have a role to play in nurturing the emergence of civil society in new democracies. Defining the necessary and proper function of the state in a developing democratic society is a challenge underappreciated in the developed world.[10]

Arguably, the most important thing that the United States can do for democracy abroad is to look after the health of its own democracy. Foreign policy experts sometimes seem not to recognize that the debate between democratic and anti-democratic forces abroad is shaped to a significant degree by the successes and failures of American society. Perceptions of American democracy as successful, particularly in terms of its ability to manage with relative fairness the challenges of a multicultural society and to provide opportunity for all, pay significant international political dividends. Today, the continued success of that experiment is in some doubt overseas as U.S. society confronts increasingly hostile race relations, worsening crime rates, a drug epidemic, a widening of income differentials, the emergence of a chronic underclass, and seeming federal paralysis on budgetary questions. If democracy in the United States is seen to weaken, democratic forces around the world will be weakened as well.

Conclusion

Neither the United States nor the world is likely to come to terms quickly with the endings and beginnings of 1989–1991. Although dramatic events in the Persian Gulf and the Soviet Union punctuate the transition from the old era, what follows will emerge slowly from the cumulative actions and decisions of states and individuals. Policymakers should anticipate that the wave of democratization of recent years will continue to be a driving factor in international politics. The need to secure recent democratic transitions and encourage such transitions in as yet nondemocratic states will remain a priority. U.S. policy will ignore these trends at its own peril, but it will enshrine them as the centerpiece of U.S. grand strategy only at some risk.

The broad global movement toward democracy does not eliminate the many problems of war and peace confronting the international community in the 1990s. But it does ameliorate some of them. And it creates the preconditions for a more cooperative approach to common international problems. This cooperation may well yet prove to be the foundation of a new world order politics.

Notes

1. See Jacques Mariel Nzouankeu, "African Democracy," *Vision* 2, no. 3 (December

1990), newsletter of the Center for Strategic and International Studies, Washington, D.C. See also his journal, *Alternative Démocratique dans le Tiers Monde,* published by the Centre d'Etudes et de Recherches sur la Démocratie Pluraliste dans le Tiers Monde, Dakar, Senegal, especially vol. 1, no. 1 (January-June 1990).

2. See Gladys D. Ganley, "Power to the People via Personal Electronic Media," *The Washington Quarterly* 14 (Spring 1991), pp. 5–22.

3. For a thorough review of that empirical evidence and the debate about the relationship between democracy and peace, see Robert L. Rothstein, *Conflict Resolution in the Post–Cold War Third World* (Washington, D.C.: United States Institute of Peace, forthcoming); and Rothstein, "Democracy, Conflict, and Development in the Third World," *The Washington Quarterly* 14 (Spring 1991), pp. 43–63.

4. Alexis de Tocqueville, *Democracy in America,* vol. 1 (New York: Vintage Books, 1945), pp. 243–244.

5. See Rothstein, *Conflict Resolution* and "Democracy, Conflict, and Development."

6. W. R. Smyser, "Vienna, Versailles, and Now Paris: Third Time Lucky?" *The Washington Quarterly* 14 (Summer 1991), pp. 61–70.

7. Alan Tonelson, "On Democrats," *The National Interest* 16 (Summer 1989). Patrick Buchanan, "Messianic Globaloney," *The Defense Democrat* (November 1989). See also George Weigel, "That New, Improved Ready-for-Prime-Time Isolationism," *American Purpose* 3 (October 1989), pp. 60–61.

8. See Hernando de Soto, *The Other Path: The Invisible Revolution in the Third World* (New York: Harper and Row, 1989) and the regular newsletter of his Institute for Liberty and Democracy in Lima, Peru, for analysis and policy recommendations.

9. Carol Lancaster, "The New Politics of U.S. Aid to Africa," *CSIS Africa Notes,* no. 120 (January 28, 1991).

10. The work of the institutions affiliated with the International Center for Economic Growth headquartered in Panama is a benchmark in this regard. See the article by its general director, Nicolás Ardito-Barletta, "Democracy and Development," *The Washington Quarterly* 13 (Summer 1990), pp. 165–175.

VI. Domestic Politics and U.S. Leadership

The Quest for Bipartisanship: A New Beginning for a New World Order

Jay Winik

WITH THE COLLAPSE of the Cold War as we have known it and the assumption by the United States of a leading role in forging a successful coalition to undo Saddam Hussein's invasion of Kuwait, a great debate is quietly—but still only quietly—beginning. President George Bush has introduced it in calling for a "new world order." But the debate really concerns something far more fundamental and, indeed, quintessentially American. Put simply, it is this: What ought to be the nature of U.S. participation in the world arena? This is a far from theoretical question, and the answer will dictate whether the United States will adhere to the internationalist tradition of actively playing a role in constructing a freer, more democratic and stable international system, or conversely, will return to neo-isolationism and focus almost exclusively on economic and social problems at home.[1]

At the very core of the debate, however, lies an even more fundamental issue. Can the spirit and practice of bipartisanship that enabled this country to lead the Western democracies

---

Jay Winik is a senior research fellow at the National Defense University Foundation and was the deputy director of Defense Secretary Frank Carlucci's Bipartisan Blue-Ribbon Commission on Base Realignment and Closure.

with coherence and unity of purpose for four decades be recaptured? If not, and if the continuing breakdown of bipartisanship goes on unchecked, the creative U.S. international achievements that have culminated in the demise of the Soviet empire may well be sacrificed. Equally important, the opportunities available not just to end the Cold War but to win the peace may be squandered at this remarkable, perhaps even defining, point in world history.

Indeed, it can be argued that the need for a sense of rededication of effort is no less urgent today than when the wise men of both political parties assembled with a sense of dire urgency in the aftermath of World War II to create a bipartisan foreign policy and rally the nation behind the burdens of global leadership. It is true that there is scarcely a U.S. policymaker or legislator who does not pay lip service to or believe that the restoration of bipartisanship is a priority. Yet for all this sentiment, success in forging bipartisanship in all likelihood will be far more elusive than it was in the wake of the world war, when the fate of the industrialized democracies literally hung in the balance. This point has largely been overlooked by policy analysts or drowned out by the din of world events in the last year.

It is crucial, then, to understand the nature of the domestic divisions—the breakdown of executive–legislative relations, the philosophical chasm between the two political parties, and the absence of firm political leadership—that are fracturing the country and have reduced bipartisanship to the lowest common denominator. Only then can the United States move on to create a bipartisan policy that will enable it to provide the leadership and purpose made necessary by the opportunities and pitfalls that lie ahead on the international scene.

The U.S. stake in speaking and acting with one voice is enormous. Two former secretaries of state, themselves of different political parties and holding different political ideologies, have warned:

> The American national purpose must at some point be fixed. If it is redefined—or even subject to redefinition—with every change in Administration in Washington, the United States risks becoming a factor of inconstancy in the world. . . . Other nations—friend or adversary—unable to gear their policies to American steadiness will go their own way, dooming the United States to growing irrelevancy.[2]

The Need for Bipartisanship in the New World Order

The urgent need for creating a new bipartisanship is also an acknowledgment of the changed international system. In the early 1950s, the United States produced 52 percent of the world's gross national product. It enjoyed a nuclear monopoly and was without question the world's preponderant power militarily. The past 40 years, however, have witnessed a relative decline in U.S. wealth, dictating that the United States can no longer simply overwhelm any problem with its vast national resources. Economic realities have also changed domestic political realities, forcing the country to make very real choices between guns and butter and to establish its priorities. Indeed, in the absence of a bipartisan consensus on the role of the United States in the world, public sentiment—including among certain foreign policy elites—is already calling for the United States to turn inward.

The fact is, however, that the twilight of the Cold War actually creates a greater need for bipartisanship as the United States confronts a more anarchical international system. The transition of the postwar blocs from East–West bipolarity to multipolarity will significantly alter the structure of the international arena, making conflict more, not less, likely.

With the passage of time, Japan and a reunited Germany will almost certainly emerge as more assertive and independent actors pursuing their own national interests. China will continue to be a major player on the world stage and will have great sway over world events. Furthermore, as the two superpowers continue on the path of arms control and scale down their military efforts, as anticipated, the gap between their capabilities and those of rising powers will diminish significantly. Additionally, by the year 2000, at least a handful of new countries will possess long-range delivery systems and weapons of mass destruction, and greater numbers of countries, including rogue states that do not adhere to or respect traditional standards of deterrence, will possess crude but nonetheless similarly daunting weapons. These countries will be capable of terrorizing other states or of sowing general chaos in the international system.

The result will be a new international system characterized by highly dynamic interaction and, over time, shifting alliances and interests more akin to the strife-ridden European balance of power system than the twentieth-century system, in which peace has been enforced by the nuclear balance of terror between the two superpowers. Although the risk of cataclysmic nuclear war between the United States and the Soviet Union is at its lowest point in history and is likely to remain so, it is far from certain that this new international structure will be more stable than the one it replaces. Fixed lines between allies and adversaries will blur, and alliances will shift with greater regularity across different issues.

At the same time, these changes will occur against the backdrop of a Soviet Union in decay, itself a potential cause of vast instability; the existence of nuclear weapons; and rising nationalistic, religious, and ethnic strife stretching from Europe to the Middle East to Southeast Asia. To use Kaiser Wilhelm's words, the world may once again be made safe for "jolly little wars," the difference this time being the existence of weapons of mass destruction. There are few—and really no—parallels in history to serve as a model or paradigm for guiding U.S. policymakers in an international setting of this kind. Thus, at a time when bipartisanship is at its lowest ebb, U.S. policymakers are now being challenged in more ways intellectually, politically, diplomatically, and militarily than during the past 40 years.

The United States does have the resources to continue to play a major world role and to deal with its domestic problems at the same time, although admittedly those resources are now constrained. In addition, when one looks at military, economic, and even cultural factors, the United States has no challenger to its position as the preeminent world power should it choose this role. The problem for the United States is clearly not that epitomized by the apocalyptic cries of the "decline school" as portrayed by Paul Kennedy—that is, decline following upon "imperial overstretch."[3] Rather, the problem the United States faces is an international system in flux, characterized by the diffusion of military capabilities and power abroad, all of which will create far more complex, nuanced, and unpredictable challenges. In the future, deterrence of conflict will be more difficult, and U.S. defense planners and diplomats will have to address the capabilities and intentions of a wide array of actors far beyond that of the Soviet Union alone. Threats to U.S. interests and those of its allies will often appear ambiguous, falling in the greyer areas of "not war, not peace." Rather than following the well-defined and clearly understood rules of the road that largely governed U.S.–Soviet relations, the U.S. political system will have to react to the varied crises of the new world order. Even when working at its smoothest, it will have difficulty doing so effectively. Small-scale Sarajevos and Munichs may well be the norm, and their prevention or containment will require a cohesive nation, acting with a clear and consistent voice in the international arena, which will only happen if a new bipartisanship is forged.

Thus, it is demonstrably clear that, in the absence of bipartisanship, dealing with the new international system will be difficult at best and at times next to impossible. Friends and foes alike, watching U.S. indecision at home, will not see the United States as a credible negotiating partner, ally, or deterrent against wanton aggression. This is a recipe for increased chaos, anarchy, and strife on the world scene. The appeal, then, to recreate anew as the hallmark of U.S. efforts abroad the predictability and resolve that can only come from bipartisanship at home is as critical as during the perilous days following World War II.

Bipartisanship in Context

The ease of constructing bipartisanship, however, should not be overstated. Its halcyon years are often idealized. People forget that the golden years from Pearl Harbor to the Tet offensive were the exception rather than the rule. Consensus was not a prevailing characteristic in the first 170 years of the Republic. Critics have noted with justification that it was the clear lack of purpose regarding vigorous U.S. involvement in world affairs that led to the U.S. rejection of membership in the League of Nations. In no small measure, this rejection led to the 20-year crisis that resulted in the rise of Hitler.

Proponents of bipartisanship point out its crowning achievements. Unprecedented unity between the two political parties made it possible for President Harry S. Truman and a Republican senator, Arthur H. Vandenberg (R–Mich.), to join forces and create such monumental achievements as the Marshall Plan, the Truman Doctrine, the North Atlantic Alliance, and the United Nations Charter. Despite strains between the two parties over the Korean War and China, to name but two issues, that unity held firm and enabled the United States to act with continuity and consistency. Allies saw that the United States was strong and reliable, and the unmistakable message to adversaries was that the United States would abide by its commitments.

Some argue that it was the foreign policy consensus prevalent during the Cold War that made possible the tragic U.S. involvement in the Vietnam War. But this argument in no way invalidates the benefits of bipartisanship and, in the case of Vietnam, represents an oversimplification of the facts. The failure of U.S. involvement in Southeast Asia had as much to do with the unique circumstances of the war itself, which were exacerbated by the then current theories of limited war fighting. These factors, in conjunction with the profound domestic turmoil on both domestic and foreign policy that was tearing at the U.S. political fabric, made a complicated and protracted war abroad virtually impossible to prosecute.

More generally, the fact remains that the perception of strength resting on bipartisan unity has been crucial to the United States in times of crisis. This principle was most vividly displayed by the bipartisan support for President John F. Kennedy during the Cuban missile crisis. Had the Soviets felt the United States was divided, the situation might have ended in tragic defeat or quite possibly in a devastating war. Although history will be the final judge, it could be argued that in the recent Gulf crisis it was precisely the vast chasm that separated the Republicans from the Democrats over whether to use force or to employ sanctions in order to reverse Saddam Hussein's aggression that led him to calculate that the United States would never actually employ significant military power. This encouraged him to ignore the resolutions passed by the United Nations (UN) and wait for the United States to seek a watered-down diplomatic compromise. Certainly Hussein's statements that the American people would have to "face rows of coffins" if there were a war, echoing statements emanating from lengthy Senate hearings and floor debate, were designed to play into the antiwar sentiment that wanted to "give sanctions a chance." Tragically, the perception of division and weakness at home made the necessity for a military solution almost inevitable.

Executive–Legislative Relations: The Search for Balance

The foundation of sustainable bipartisanship is effective executive–legislative relations. After the Vietnam War, however, the cold war foreign policy consensus, supported by harmonious executive–legislative relations and by both parties in Congress in a manner that minimized conflict over foreign affairs, was rudely shattered. Although it was not completely undone, as is often claimed by the pundits, and central elements of the postwar consensus enjoyed a fair degree of support, it was severely frayed. As a result, a slide began down a slippery slope leading to the balkanization of the U.S. approach to national security, and today this threatens to inject chaos into the foreign policy process. Congress lies at the heart of the issue.

In his inaugural address, President George Bush underscored that bipartisanship remains blemished by the Vietnam War and stressed his commitment to rejuvenating the traditional postwar pattern of foreign policy making. Bush said: "We need a new engagement . . . between the executive and the congress . . . our great parties have too often been far apart and untrusting of each other. It's been that way since Vietnam. That war cleaves us still . . . and the old bipartisanship must be made new again." What the Bush administration appears never fully to have appreciated—a point to which we shall return—is the extent of the fragmentation of executive–legislative cooperation that is accounting for the increasing breakdown of bipartisanship. It thus underestimates the difficulty of mending it.

On its face, the problem of workable executive–legislative relations should not be intractable. The separation of these two branches of government is an indispensable element at the heart of U.S. constitutional democracy. As Justice Louis Brandeis put it:

> The doctrine of the separation of powers was adopted by the Convention of 1787, not to promote efficiency but to preclude the exercise of arbitrary power. The purpose was not to avoid friction, but, by means of the inevitable friction incident to the distribution of the governmental powers . . . to save the people from autocracy.[4]

Over the past 20 years, however, the pattern has altered dramatically. The constructive tension between Congress and the president is no longer the product of a natural tug-of-war between a legislature and an executive operating as partners within an understood framework. Instead, the balance between Congress and the president has so radically shifted that the "inevitable friction" Justice Brandeis welcomed has devolved into something quite different—a real war marked by episodes of great rancor and a virtual battle over who controls foreign policy. Rather than becoming another stage in the natural push and pull between the Congress and the president it has reached crisis proportions, prompting fears that an "imperial congress," not an "imperial presidency," is the real problem. This has led one longtime policymaker, Eugene V. Rostow, to assert that the president is being transformed "into a ceremonial figure graciously presiding over the activities of an omnipotent congress."[5]

Although Rostow may somewhat overstate the case, particularly given Bush's efforts to restore the balance in favor of the presidency, his portrayal aptly illustrates the tendency against which Madison so powerfully warned us in *The Federalist Papers*. Madison cautioned against "the dangers from legislative usurpation" that would lead to "tyranny." In prescient words that could easily describe today's process, he warned:

> [The legislative body's] constitutional power being at once more extensive, and less susceptible of precise limits, it can, with the greater facility, mask under complicated and indirect measures, the encroachments it makes on co-ordinate departments.[6]

It is quite true, as defenders of interbranch conflict point out, that the increasingly divided government of the United States is preferable to the wild swings or complete paralysis that afflict various parliamentary systems. It is also certainly preferable to dictatorship, which is anathema to the U.S. tradition. But these comparisons constitute a straw man that obscures the real issue. The question is not whether the U.S. system is better than others (it is), but rather is it suitable in its present state for a superpower expected to bear the burdens of global leadership? Moreover, is the process less effective than it has been in the past?

The framers of the Constitution made the president commander-in-chief and the executive agent of Congress in negotiating treaties, while the Senate gives its advice and consent to treaties and the appointment of ambassadors. But in words reminiscent of Madison's caveats, two prominent senators, David L. Boren (D–Okla.) and John C. Danforth (R–Mo.), have written that partisanship in the Senate has "increased alarmingly"; they have gone so far as to assert that "Congress has confused [its] shared responsibilities for foreign affairs" with "incessant and irrelevant meddling."[7] Coming from such consummately moderate senators, these words are not to be taken lightly. In point of fact, they understate the case: the "incessant meddling" is often highly relevant and has great impact on U.S. policy. Through amendments to routine authorization and appropriations bills, Congress takes advantage of almost unlimited opportunities to revise the administration's foreign policy. In doing so, it is aided by the breakdown of the congressional seniority system, the proliferation of subcommittees and congressionally mandated reporting requirements, and the expansion of staff (now numbering some 35,000 people) since the congressional reforms of the late 1960s. These factors enable individual members to pursue their own foreign policy and not only to increase Congress's authority and oversight of the administration's actions but also to constrain and block outright the president's initiatives as well.

Although Congress is not empowered by the Constitution to recognize or to negotiate independently with foreign governments, it has sought to do so, thereby illustrating the magnitude of the problem. Congressional discussions with the former Sandinista regime were but one notable example. More recently, Congress has tried through the appropriations process to legislate official discussions and relations between the United States and the Vietnamese-installed Hun Sen government in Cambodia with little regard for its effect on the UN-mediated peace process already under way. As a general practice, few of these congressional bills or amendments receive any serious consideration in the appropriate committees and often little if any debate on the Senate floor. Indeed, it has become common to slip cleverly worded and seemingly obscure amendments onto the floor late at night or early in the morning during the waning hours of the appropriations process, when few senators or staff are present to debate the issue.[8]

The practical effect of these actions, often overlooked by even the most serious observers of congressional behavior, is to give power to Congress beyond what the founding fathers intended, making it tantamount to a shadow government and vesting it with de facto powers that are prohibited by the Constitution.

The argument is often made in support of congressional activism that Congress can actually strengthen the hand of the president through a "good cop, bad cop routine," an idea that has existed for some time. With Congress acting as the bad cop, threatening to undo a particular set of negotiations, whether on trade, human rights, or other issues, the president can then extract concessions that it may otherwise be unable to obtain. In theory this approach has merit, and on occasion it has worked, such as in buttressing the president's hand in negotiating with the Japanese on trade or in exacting human rights concessions from the Soviet Union. But on the whole, this approach assumes far more support by one branch of government for the other than actually exists. Benefits that do occur are usually more the result of accident and random behavior than of design.

As a practical reality, congressional activity is freewheeling, and everything is left open to debate or amendment, whether it be on aid to friendly governments, negotiations on arms control, tactics of war fighting, or U.S. involvement in regional conflicts to combat antidemocratic regimes. The result is that the U.S. government all too often sets out in one direction, only to change its policy abruptly in midstream. Quite frequently, this leads adversaries and allies alike to realize that they must hedge their bets in relations with the United States, and, even more, that they must negotiate with two partners: the administration and the Congress. In the face of this, it is little wonder that many feel Congress has exceeded its brief.

The gravity of executive–legislative disputes is exacerbated by the modern political habit of electing a Democratic congress and a Republican president. The Republicans, now embracing a philosophy based on internationalism and a balance of power view of the world, have won five of the last six presidential elections. In contrast, the Democratic party, more readily embracing a neo-isolationist and "peace through diplomacy" philosophy, has controlled Congress following 18 of the last 21 congressional elections. A stark statistic noted in *The Washington Quarterly* by two political scientists amply illustrates the effect of this "divided government."[9] Pointing out that ideological disputes between the two parties have increased in recent years, they show that Truman received bipartisan support for his foreign policy roughly two-thirds of the time during the 80th Congress, whereas in the 99th Congress, President Ronald Reagan received support on only one of every seven issues he supported. Given the nature of the electoral situation, there is little incentive for either party to engage in political compromise or seek to bridge their differences.

Furthermore, these statistics only partially indicate the magnitude of the crisis created by this divided government. Having lost the White House from 1967 to 1988, save for the one-term presidency of Jimmy Carter, the Democrats have become entrenched in an opposition mentality. Put more concretely, unable to govern from the White House, they seek to do so from the Congress. Notwithstanding the proliferation of staff and research resources, however, Congress still lacks the expertise to deal with the myriad of complicated issues the executive must face. Moreover, in view of the fact that Congress must also represent narrow parochial interests, it does not have the political space or mandate to represent the higher U.S. international interest on its own. Finally, it should not be lost on observers that Congress, in effect, undertakes to set policy from Capitol Hill, meanwhile enjoying the luxury of not being accountable for such major issues as war and peace as the president is—and must be. This gridlock only diminishes, rather than increases, U.S. influence abroad, precisely at a time when greater coherence and flexibility is needed by the executive to address the highly fluid and ever changing international system.

Congress, nevertheless, has an important role to play, and it would be wrong to conclude that congressional opposition in and of itself is unwarranted, new, or deleterious. Senate opposition led to the outright rejection of more than 100 treaties in the first 200 years of the Republic. The Senate's rejection of the Treaty of Versailles is to this day portrayed as a major foreign policy disaster for President Woodrow Wilson. It was also a sign of the legitimate, and powerful, influence Congress can have over decision making. Indeed, virtually every president has suffered a significant foreign policy setback in the face of congressional opposition. Congress did not act on the Threshold Test Ban Treaty negotiated by President Richard M. Nixon. It shelved the treaty on peaceful nuclear explosions negotiated by President Gerald Ford. So great was congressional opposition that President Carter did not even seek congressional ratification of the Strategic Arms Limitation (SALT) II treaty after the Soviet invasion of Afghanistan.

In the wake of the experience in Vietnam and the free-wheeling activities of the White House evidenced in the Iran-contra revelations, it is unreasonable for Congress to confer upon any administration a blank check reminiscent of the Tonkin Gulf resolution. Madison was equally cogent on this issue, reminding his readers that the accumulation of all power in the executive would amount to "the very definition of tyranny" no less than if it were concentrated in the legislative branch. It is also important to assert that bipartisanship should not mean an absence of healthy policy debate. Debate is the essence of a democratic society, and calls to stifle open discussion demean the spirit of bipartisanship and run contrary to the ethos of the United States. When executive–legislative relations are in proper balance, Congress can, as Alton Frye has thoughtfully noted, "affect policies at the margin." In doing so, he continues, Congress plays a crucial role in helping the administration fine-tune its policies. When the administration is wedded to outmoded or futile policies, Congress can "de-constrain" the executive branch and allow it to make necessary policy adjustments.[10] When adversaries believe U.S. resolve to be weak, Congress can demonstrate support that sends an unmistakable signal of the country's unity.

But the problem is not one of congressional participation, oversight, or comment. Rather, it is that the scales have tipped too far. More than at any time in recent memory, Congress is entrenched in an institutional, partisan, and ideological approach to national security that is at odds with the executive, and there is little indication that this downward-spiraling trend will be reversed. For all practical purposes, the spirit and practice of bipartisanship as it guided this country after World War II is dead, and the looming question is how to resuscitate it.

Bush and Bipartisanship

From the outset of his administration, President Bush sought to pursue a bipartisan approach to foreign policy. The preeminent examples cited to demonstrate his commitment were, first, his choice of a pragmatic foreign policy team and, second, the bipartisan accord on Central America that Secretary of State James A. Baker III negotiated with the congressional leadership in March 1989. Eschewing the potentially divisive policy that would have resulted if the administration had sought additional military assistance for the Nicaraguan resistance, the accord allowed for humanitarian aid to the resistance until the Nicaraguan elections of February 25, 1990. The executive–legislative agreement was negotiated in what amounted to extensive shuttle diplomacy between the administration and the congressional leadership, almost reminiscent of Baker's efforts in the Middle East. Once a pact was attained, Nicaragua was removed from the political arena as a source of contention.

This pact presaged later efforts that, upon closer scrutiny, were often geared as much toward avoiding domestic friction as toward achieving policy goals abroad. A careful look at the agreement on Nicaragua is revealing. The fact that Violeta Barrios de Chamorro would ultimately defeat the Sandinistas was in no way to be predicted upon the conclusion of the bipartisan accord. Indeed, many participants in the executive–legislative branch discussions, including seasoned Central America hands in the administration, felt the Sandinistas would win the election under the new arrangement. Many saw the endgame less as one of ending Sandinista rule than of putting an end to the bitter executive–legislative disagreements. In short, pursuing policy abroad took a backseat to domestic policy at home.

After eight years of deep division between President Reagan and the Democratic Congress over Nicaraguan policy, it may have been unrealistic to have expected President Bush's foreign policy team to seek renewed military support for the resistance. For that matter, a close reading of the bipartisan accord shows that even asking only for humanitarian aid still met stiff resistance from the House Democrats. However, this agreement set the tone for an administration style that was often founded less on securing acceptance on difficult issues than on reaching domestic agreements.

In its present form, the Bush administration style of resurrecting bipartisanship is premised primarily on bureaucratic and procedural mechanisms for consultation rather than on defining shared principles and philosophy. Much of this is surely because the administration recognizes the highly politicized way the Democrats approach foreign policy and the vastly different philosophy that separates the two parties. As it stands, the administration's approach is an important first step, but only a first step, toward rejuvenating bipartisanship in the sense that President Bush called for in his inaugural address. Left in its present form, it will fall short of achieving the president's goals.

Consultation Is No Substitute for Consensus

In many ways, the Bush administration style is reminiscent of Dwight D. Eisenhower's Republican administration. Eisenhower knew that ignoring Congress was a sure recipe for exacerbating any existing lack of consensus. Although he sought congressional deference to the administration, he actively cultivated Congress, often employing what he referred to as "the personal touch." He ensured that Congress was there at the takeoff, the ride, and the landing. He saw to it that his secretary of state, John Foster Dulles, consulted Congress extensively, providing it with a continuous say in the development and execution of foreign policy. Dulles had 160 meetings with congressional groups from 1954 to 1957, among them a series of informal breakfasts and lunches. The Bush administration has replicated this style by significantly expanding the Office of Legislative Affairs in the State Department, which is charged with ensuring greater frequency of consultation with the Congress and more generally keeping its finger on the congressional pulse. Almost no major policy initiative is undertaken without input from this office. The idea behind this arrangement is largely to enable members of Congress to understand the rationale behind proposed policies better, to moderate initial partisan reactions, and to reduce mutual misunderstanding.

This procedure has been successful in reducing the discord of the past eight years between the two branches of government. But it has proved inadequate as a replacement for genuine bipartisanship based on shared goals and philosophy. Several examples illustrate this inadequacy. Congress cut in half military assistance to the democratically elected government of El Salvador, thereby weakening the efforts of its democratic center to achieve a negotiated settlement with the Farabundo Martí National Liberation Front (FMLN) and reducing the incentive of the FMLN to abide by a UN-sponsored cease-fire. This was done in spite of the FMLN's massive offensive that threatened to topple the Salvadoran government itself and in which civilians, including Americans in the Hotel Sheraton, were used as hostages. The FMLN's violence continued unabated up until the Senate vote; indeed, on the very day before the October 19, 1990, vote, the FMLN actually launched yet another attack on the government and so undermined the view that they were committed to a peaceful political settlement. Congressional sensitivities about the murder of the Salvadoran Jesuit priests on November 16, 1989, were rightly intense, but this does not explain Congress's willingness at the time to ignore the ongoing pattern of violence by the FMLN that belied their claims of wanting to take part in El Salvador's political process and be serious partners in the UN-mediated peace talks over a cease-fire.

In a second area, the Congress extensively debated giving the administration the authority to seek limited lethal aid for the non-Communist resistance forces in Cambodia as an inducement to help bring about a peacefully negotiated solution in the Paris peace talks on Cambodia. Even after prolonged Senate floor debate, during which a unique coalition of Republicans and southern conservative and northern liberal Democrats provided an overwhelming vote in support of aid for the non-Communists, the Democratic leadership and Democrat-controlled Senate Appropriations Committee nonetheless all but ignored the will of the Senate as expressed by the floor vote and sent the message to the administration that they remained strongly opposed to such aid. Consequently, the aid was never formally requested. In a third area, Congress all but unilaterally restructured the architecture of the Strategic Defense Initiative (SDI), depriving some of the program's more promising technologies of funding. In each of these instances of congressional micromanagement the philosophy of the Democrats prevailed.

Each time the president has taken a personal interest in an issue, however, he has managed to get his way by exerting executive leadership. As much as any president in this century, Bush is by training and instinct at home in the world of foreign affairs and has a keen appreciation for a strong United States that acts vigorously abroad. He was successful in his intervention in Panama to remove General Manuel Noriega from office; in previously extending most favored nation status to China against the stiff opposition of the Senate majority leader; and in the most compelling issue faced by the United States at any time since perhaps the Vietnam War—the resolution of the Gulf crisis through deployment of U.S. forces, including a ground war against Iraq.

The Gulf crisis is perhaps the most instructive instance of the consequences of today's dilemma of governance. President Bush had before him the example of one state's naked aggression, which additionally threatened both U.S. allies in the region and the U.S. economic lifeline and set a precedent for future aggression by other dictators. This enabled him to assemble an unprecedented political and military international coalition against Saddam Hussein's Iraq, and to garner equally unprecedented support from the UN Security Council, which passed 12 resolutions, one of which took the step of authorizing the use of force by the coalition after January 15, 1991, if it were deemed necessary. Bush was supported by 82 percent of the American people. Yet despite a high-quality Senate debate and the eventual support he received from Congress after the vote, only 10 Democrats in the Senate voted to support the president to authorize the use of force, and then only after extensive lobbying by the White House. Such a margin was too close for comfort and failed to send a message of unmistakable unity to Saddam Hussein about U.S. policy resolve. It demonstrated that even on an issue on which the stakes were high and the president enjoyed near world support, he could still not be completely confident of marshaling the full support of a Congress controlled by the opposition.[11] Speaking for the majority of the Democrats during the final hours of the debate, Senator Paul Simon (D–Ill.) made this very point. He said the vote "shows a deeply divided Congress . . . and it is the smallest vote for the authorization of force in the history of this country since the war of 1812."[12] The lesson to be drawn is that the two parties remain almost irreconcilably far apart.

Two themes emerge from consideration of these issues. First, in the absence of consensus, presidential leadership is necessary and can enable the United States to act successfully in a crisis. Second, the two parties, controlling different branches of government, remain deeply divided over the role of the United States in the world, the use of force as a tool of statecraft, and the desirability of U.S. intervention abroad. This is hardly an optimal way for the United States to conduct foreign policy, nor does it augur well for the ability of the United States to lead in shaping the new world order.

The decay of the cold war consensus, the dispersion of congressional power, and the certainty that a Democrat-controlled Congress, whose view of the U.S. role in the world differs vastly from that of the administration, will continue to insist upon having a major role in foreign policy, suggest that more, not less, discord about U.S. interests will almost certainly be the norm. Simple exhortations that the two branches of government must respect each other's institutional sensitivities will solve nothing. At this crucial juncture in world affairs, the Bush administration's emphasis on greater interbranch coordination and cooperation is at best a palliative because the system underlying today's gridlock is too ingrained, too partisan, and too fragmented. For the new world order, what is needed is a new beginning.

A New Beginning: Lessons From the Period After World War II

There is a strength to the U.S. system of government that is all too frequently overlooked in discussions of restoring bipartisanship. This system forces the executive to build and secure a consensus for its policies, in short, to develop a mandate. In the long run, there is no substitute for a reinvigorated consensus—whatever that consensus may be. The only alternative would be to condemn the United States to a period of drift and disagreement. That consensus requires, first, that Americans define their vital interests and goals, and, second, that the United States as a nation create anew a sense of national purpose in the world. There is at least moderate reason to believe it can be done. To start, it is instructive to recall the unique circumstances under which bipartisanship was first created in this period.

The terrible destruction wrought by World War II, the horror of the holocaust, and the enslavement of half a continent by the Soviet Union brought home the folly of isolationism—the policy long preferred by the Republican party. The sense of the Soviet threat, shared by so many Americans, left little doubt that the United States had to be actively engaged in the world lest the painful experiences of the past be repeated. This made possible one of the most creative phases in U.S. foreign policy. It rallied both ends of the political spectrum and ended the period of "fortress America" that had dominated U.S. involvement in world affairs.

At that time, a Democratic administration and a Republican Senate overcame their differences and embarked upon a working partnership to create consensus in the aftermath of war. It was made possible in part by the personal relationship President Truman developed with the chairman of the Senate Foreign Relations Committee, Arthur Vandenberg, who put his prestige on the line to obtain the support of his colleagues for U.S. participation abroad. In a burst of creativity and with an acute sense of the historic moment, Truman had his secretary of state, George Marshall, and undersecretary of state, Robert Lovett, meet informally with Vandenberg to draft a general statement of

U.S. foreign policy principles. From these meetings emerged the Vandenberg Resolution 239, which laid the groundwork for the North Atlantic Alliance and the Marshall Plan and, in effect, served as a blueprint for U.S. participation in world affairs. This set of principles was buttressed by a practice that institutionalized congressional involvement in policy-making. It also included appointing leading policymakers from the opposition party to key positions—Lovett and John McCloy being two examples.[13] Finally, in contrast to the practice of the last two decades, this series of arrangements made Congress equally responsible—and culpable—for policy successes and mishaps. As such, both sides had a shared stake in success and the temptation to use foreign affairs to achieve partisan advantage was minimized. All of this made effective executive leadership possible and the acceptance of executive leadership legitimate. The result: in good measure guided by a shared blueprint shaping the U.S. role in the world, the two parties created at a historic moment what could properly be called "a U.S. foreign policy."

Toward a Bipartisan U.S. Foreign Policy

Now, at an equally defining point in world history, can a bipartisan U.S. foreign policy be recreated? There is little choice but to try, and the effort should be made first and foremost by the president. If President Bush truly wants the United States to have a successful hand in shaping the new world order and rejuvenating the old style of bipartisanship, then he should resurrect the initial arrangements and spirit that characterized Truman's administration. It will not be easy, nor will it be accomplished by calling on the opposition to support the administration blindly. But it can be done.

Reducing and explaining the problems of the world as a simple dichotomy of good and bad, democracy versus totalitarianism, has become increasingly difficult and with the end of the Cold War may no longer be possible. This dilemma is compounded by the complexity of the emerging international system. Sustaining support for an active foreign policy in the new world order will also prove to run counter to the cultural style of the United States, which is a nation of problem solvers. In international politics there are no permanent solutions, there is no such thing as enduring peace, and no such creature as complete peace. One solution often begets unforeseen problems. A prolonged engagement in the new world order, with no seeming end and no grand rationale to demonstrate conclusively the need for U.S. internationalism, will complicate this task further. The situation will be exacerbated by the almost ubiquitous presence of Cable News Network (CNN) and the other TV networks, with their instant but abbreviated coverage, and the soundbite analysis emanating from think tank experts. The American people will be given the impression that solutions, often absurdly simple, exist for deeply complex problems, or they may decide it is better to ignore these problems altogether.

In the face of all this, Americans may, in Averell Harriman's famous words, choose "to go to the movies and drink Coke"—to wit, opt for neo-isolationism.

Bush and his eventual successor will also face another truism. Even with bipartisanship and harmonious executive–legislative relations, there will always be limits to the ability of the United States to pursue a foreign policy with subtlety and nuance. The new era of multipolarity, marked by smoldering ethnic and nationalistic conflicts and the proliferation of weapons of mass destruction, will place bipartisanship at a premium. It may be true, however, that the circumstances of the changed world are insufficient to provide an easily articulated rationale or simple rallying cry to unite the country and the two political parties around a new bipartisan consensus.[14] It is also certainly the case that a new consensus would look different from the one that governed U.S. policy during the Cold War. But over the long term, the alternative to bipartisanship is neo-isolationism and drift. At stake is no less than the shape of the new world order.

A starting point for rekindling bipartisanship in a national debate about the U.S. role in the world can be found in the constellation of goals Americans almost uniformly share. These goals include the preservation and expansion of freedom, the promotion of democracy, a wish to discourage dictatorship, and the desire for a defense capable of protecting U.S. interests. Each of these issues is consistent with the nation's heritage and has the potential to provide a fixed sense of national purpose in the world for U.S. foreign policy. Americans also clearly have been moved by the events of the last two years: the democratic revolution in Eastern Europe and Latin America and the call of the Chinese student movement in Tiananmen Square for greater liberty. Americans almost overwhelmingly supported U.S. leadership to defeat Saddam Hussein's aggression. And in the wake of the Gulf War, they demonstrated concern for basic human rights in supporting humanitarian measures to alleviate the plight of the Kurds.

Thus, if there is an overarching theme to rally Americans in shaping the new world order, it is that having won the Cold War, they should now win the peace, and that the United States should continue to foster the global trend toward democracy and human rights. Many conservatives will bristle at this notion, saying that looking after security concerns and not the domestic organization of other societies should be the focus. They will be joined by many on the left of the political spectrum who argue that the United States cannot be the schoolmaster of domestic politics everywhere in the world. Both sides would add that budget realities at home must constrain U.S. efforts abroad. But on the other side of the ledger, the majority of Americans have an affinity for democratic societies and believe in the promotion of freedom. The idea is dawning on policymakers of both parties that Americans believe in Edmund Burke's injunction, that "the principles of true politics are those of morality enlarged," and that the nation should act abroad out of both self-interest and principle.

Moreover, history suggests that the more democratic a society is, the less prone it is to oppress its people at home or to be warlike abroad. This makes a powerful case that a more democratic world is a safer world, one that best serves U.S. security interests as well. Thus, there is reason to believe that both political parties would support this goal, not just with rhetoric but with action. Fostering democracy through support for the National Endowment for Democracy and the Agency for International Development (AID), for actions by private voluntary organizations and entrepreneurial business ventures, and by making effective use of such multilateral institutions as the new European Bank for Reconstruction and Development should be a priority.

At times, the use of force, directly or through some military assistance, will be necessary (as in the Gulf), or desirable (in helping an elected government make the successful transition to democracy in the face of insurgent movements, as in the Andean countries). There can be no pat prescription as to where, when, and exactly how U.S. force should be applied. But in a world where managing complex regional problems that could erupt on a larger scale will almost certainly be the norm, securing a bipartisan agreement that there will be some circumstances requiring some application of U.S. power will be called for. This is not to say that there should be an excessive reliance on military solutions to problems that often have a political or economic dimension. But it is a sober recognition of the realities of international life, where power politics often governs activities between states, and where force, therefore, cannot be ruled out as a means of statecraft.

Balance of power politics should be complemented by an increased commitment to the use of multilateral institutions, including the UN. President Bush has discovered that the UN and related organizations can serve as powerful diplomatic tools to augment U.S. policy goals and facilitate greater burden-sharing. This has been the case for international peacekeeping, monitoring elections, building a foundation for collective action against a rogue regime such as that of Saddam Hussein, mounting massive humanitarian relief efforts, or helping to solve seemingly intractable problems such as the one besetting Cambodia. In short, there should be a blend of balance of power politics with world order politics to enable U.S. policymakers to confront complex challenges.

As the new world order begins to take shape, the United States must debate the nature of its own participation. Think tanks, the media, and the great universities can and should all take part. But the debate must be led and initiated by the president.

This is a time of enormous opportunity. After 40 years of the cold war struggle, the United States is now in a position to help create a more democratic and peaceful world, marked by respect for human rights and self-determination. It is also a time of peril and challenge. The democratic revolution could fail, nationalistic and ethnic tensions could lead to war, the boundaries of the state system could come under relentless assault, and terrorists could acquire atomic devices or chemical and biological weapons. Instead of a world characterized by international law as envisaged by Hugo Grotius and a "zone of peace" between liberal democracies described by Emmanuel Kant, it could be a world where borders are redrawn, anarchy sets in, and states and ethnic groups use force as a commonplace instrument to resolve outstanding differences. It is, then, a historic juncture for the United States, and the country has a choice as to the nature of the role it wants to play and the kind of world Americans want to live in. No less than after World War II, this is, in Paul Nitze's words, a time to debate the issues and "get it right." But if Americans continue to be wracked by partisan bickering, they will not "get it right." Instead, the remarkable achievements of the last 40 years will be squandered, as will the precious opportunity to secure a freer, more decent, more stable, and less conflict-ridden world. The United States can be a force of positive change into the next century. This will only happen, however, if the conflict that divides Americans at home is put to rest, and bipartisan consensus is once again restored.

The opinions and conclusions expressed in this article are solely those of the author and do not necessarily reflect those of the National Defense University.

Notes

1. No less prominent a commentator than William Hyland, editor of *Foreign Affairs*, has already called for a reorientation of U.S. energies to "our domestic crisis." "Downgrade U.S. Foreign Policy," *New York Times*, May 20, 1991, op-ed, p. A–15.

2. Henry Kissinger and Cyrus Vance, "Bipartisan Objectives for American Foreign Policy," *Foreign Affairs* 66 (Summer 1988), p. 899.

3. Paul Kennedy, *The Rise and Fall of Great Powers: Economic Change and Military Conflict from 1500 to 2000* (New York: Random House, 1987).

4. See *Myers v. United States*, 272 U.S. 52, 293 (1926).

5. See the discussion in Eugene V. Rostow, *President, Prime Minister, or Constitutional Monarch?* McNair Papers, no. 3 (Washington, D.C.: National Defense University, 1989), p. 5.

6. James Madison, *The Federalist Papers*, Nos. 47–48 (New York: New American Library Books, 1961), p. 310.

7. David L. Boren and John C. Danforth, "Why This Country Can't Lead," *Washington Post*, December 1, 1987, op-ed.

8. One example alone is telling. At midnight, during the Panama/Nicaragua 1990 foreign aid supplemental, a senator slipped in an amendment dictating that up to $5 million in aid go to "the children of Cambodia." Only the two Senate floor managers were present on the floor at this late hour, disposing of what were supposed to be noncontroversial amendments. This particular provision was never openly debated or discussed in committee or on the floor, either with regard to its need, its potentially deleterious impact on the peace process, or the signal it would send to the warring Cambodian factions. In contrast, the equivalent amount of $5 million in nonlethal aid to the non-Communist resistance, under the long-standing "Solarz Program," was subject to extensive floor debate, as well as discussion in numerous hearings.

9. See the discussion in James M. McCormick and Eugene R. Wittkopf, "Bush and Bipartisanship: The Past as Prologue?" *The Washington Quarterly* 13 (Winter 1990), pp. 5–16.

10. See Alton Frye, "Congress: The Virtue of Its Vices," *Foreign Policy*, no. 3 (Summer 1971), pp. 108–121.

11. It is noteworthy that perceptive commentators repeatedly spoke (and rightly so) of the political courage and the isolation of Representatives Stephen Solarz (D–N.Y.) and Les Aspin (D–Wis.) in actively supporting U.S. use of force in the Gulf.

12. *Congressional Record* 137, no. 8 (January 12, 1991), p. S396.

13. As deputy director of then-Secretary of Defense Frank Carlucci's bipartisan commission on military base closure, the author witnessed firsthand how the commissioners and senior staff, dedicated to a common goal, could overcome any possible partisan differences and work in a nonpartisan, pragmatic fashion. Although a blue ribbon commission is by its nature different from the day-to-day workings of government, the work of the Carlucci commission demonstrated that the practice common in Truman's day of appointing able people to positions without regard to party affiliation can foster effective bipartisanship and sound policy-making. For discussion of this point, see Zbigniew Brzezinski, "The Three Requirements for a Bipartisan Foreign Policy," in *Forging Bipartisanship*, White Paper, *The Washington Quarterly* (Washington, D.C.: CSIS, Georgetown University, 1984), pp. 18–19.

14. Strongly asserting that foreign entanglements in the future "are a necessity," Charles Krauthammer highlights the challenge of creating the consensus necessary for continued U.S. internationalism. He writes: "Compared to the task of defeating fascism and communism, averting chaos is a rather subtle call to greatness." Charles Krauthammer, "The Unipolar Movement," *Foreign Affairs* 70 (America and the World: 1990/91), p. 33.

Congress and U.S. Foreign Policy: Comparative Advantage or Disadvantage?

Robert A. Pastor

IS CONGRESS AN asset or a liability to U.S. foreign policy? The question has a long and distinguished lineage as does the negative answer to it recently offered by Aaron Friedberg.[1] U.S. diplomats have often expressed an uneasiness that effective diplomacy is incompatible with democracy. This long-standing anxiety has been exacerbated by several modern trends, among them an increasingly divided government, an assertive Congress, and a complex new foreign policy agenda.

This article will argue that Congress is an asset that is appreciating in the modern world and that the nervousness over the ability of the United States to act strategically is unwarranted. The interaction between Congress and the executive branch in the making of foreign policy sometimes leads to conflict or stalemate, but this is neither inherent nor inevitable. A closer reading of the foreign policy process suggests that there are many more instances of cooperation leading to effective policy than of disagreements leading to conflict. Moreover, the changes that are remaking the world actually play to the comparative advantage of an interbranch political system. Let us first review the critique of Congress and the criteria for judging a foreign policy mechanism.

De Tocqueville's Criteria

Although a devotee of the new government in the United States, Alexis de Tocqueville acknowledged that its constitution made it "decidedly inferior to other governments" in the area of foreign policy. In de Tocqueville's view, the qualities needed for a good foreign policy—secrecy, perseverance, patience, unity, and quickness to act—were those in which the U.S. democracy was deficient and aristocracies were well endowed. De Tocqueville chided the congressional and popular propensity "to obey impulse rather than prudence, and to abandon a mature design for the gratification of a momentary passion." Only the restraint and intelligence of its president, George Washington, he argued, saved the young nation from certain failure. The defects of aristocracies were many, but in foreign relations, these defects were not harmful because it was "rare for the interest of

---

Robert A. Pastor is professor of political science at Emory University and director of the Latin American and Caribbean Program at Emory's Carter Center. He is author of *Condemned to Repetition: The United States and Nicaragua* (Princeton: Princeton University Press, 1987).

the aristocracy to be distinct from that of the people."[2]

Pessimism about the foreign policy making ability of the United States began with de Tocqueville and has continued among renowned diplomatic historians and students of U.S. government. For those who think of U.S. democracy as a modern form of government, George F. Kennan offered a scathing indictment of its competence in foreign affairs:

> I sometimes wonder whether . . . a democracy is not uncomfortably similar to one of those prehistoric monsters with a body as long as this room and a brain the size of a pin: he lies there in his comfortable primeval mud and pays little attention to his environment; he is slow to wrath—in fact, you practically have to whack his tail off to make him aware that his interests are being disturbed; but, once he grasps this, he lays about him with such blind determination that he not only destroys his adversary but largely wrecks his native habitat. You wonder whether it would not have been wise for him to have taken a little more interest in what was going on at an earlier date and to have seen whether he could not have prevented some of these situations from arising instead of proceeding from an undiscriminating indifference to a holy wrath equally undiscriminating.[3]

In the case of the United States, the concern about democracy's disadvantages in foreign policy has tended to focus on three inherent problems: the electoral system, particularly the use it makes of foreign affairs for crass political purposes; divided government and the swings in policies from one administration to the next;[4] and the proclivity of Congress for micromanagement. Increasingly, these problems have been viewed as related to and caused by congressional assertiveness. The implication is that Congress is an albatross around the president's neck, restraining him, "tying his hands," or embarrassing him with investigations. When the president needs to act boldly, Congress compels him to hesitate and look over his shoulder. It then embarrasses him by publicizing policies that should be kept secret. Few people articulated this view as forcefully as Lieutenant Colonel Oliver North in testimony before Congress during the Iran–contra hearings:

> The Congress is to blame because of the fickle, vacillating, unpredictable, on-again-off-again policy toward the Nicaraguan democratic resistance. . . . In my opinion, these hearings have caused serious damage to our national interests. Our adversaries laugh at us, and our friends recoil in horror.[5]

More often than not, Congress has served as a surrogate; critics denounce Congress for interference, but their real purpose is to criticize those who resist a presidential policy they support. Thus liberals scolded the Senate for inaction on the Strategic Arms Limitation Talks (SALT) II and more generally for restraining Democratic presidents,[6] and conservatives reproached Congress for impeding aid to the contras and more generally for blocking Republican presidents.[7]

In de Tocqueville's time, secrecy seemed an essential quality of a good foreign policy, and modern presidents, preoccupied by "leaks" from their subordinates or Congress, would probably agree, although they spend more time shaping public opinion than making private policy.

Secrecy is undoubtedly useful and

sometimes imperative as a government assesses options for dealing with crisis decisions. The prospects for an effective response to the Soviet installation of missiles in Cuba were improved because President John F. Kennedy had time to consider his options and then could disclose both the threat and his response in a manner of his own choosing.

In contrast, probably the most important reason why the issue of the Soviet brigade in Cuba proved a political debacle for President Jimmy Carter in September 1979 was that the information leaked before it could be assessed, and it was reported with a spin that put both the Carter administration and the Soviet Union in a hole from which it was virtually impossible to escape. Several senators led by Frank Church (D–Idaho) and Henry Jackson (D–Wash.) leaped at the initial report and insisted that SALT II could not be ratified unless the brigade was removed from Cuba, an outcome made less likely because of their announcement. If Carter had had time to assess the information before it was disclosed, the problem could probably have been resolved to Congress's satisfaction.

Secrecy is sometimes indispensable in foreign policy making, but premature leaks are not unique to the U.S. system; nor has anyone ever demonstrated that Congress is more culpable than the executive. During the Gulf War, both branches kept vital information secret. Nonetheless, most observers would conclude that the cost to democracy of plugging or precluding leaks exceeds the benefits. Thomas Jefferson understood this point intuitively; Richard Nixon learned it by experience.

On the other hand, treaties and international economic issues need to be debated publicly. The failure of the Johnson, Nixon, and Ford administrations to consult on Capitol Hill before and while they negotiated new Panama Canal treaties permitted opponents to sabotage negotiations. With the administration silent, Senator Strom Thurmond (R–S.C.) was able to assemble a blocking group of more than 34 senators, who cosponsored a resolution rejecting any treaties. In 1977, Sol Linowitz and Ellsworth Bunker, Carter's conegotiators for new Panama Canal treaties, were instructed to consult fully and frequently with the Senate, and the Republican leadership acknowledged that the consultations were unprecedented and of great importance in securing the two-thirds vote necessary for ratification.[8] In the case of Panama, secret diplomacy was a recipe for foreign policy failure, and congressional consultations were a formula for success.

Secrecy can also be a liability in policy-making when it precludes important information or alternative views from being heard. President Ronald Reagan's decision to sell arms to Iran is a recent example of a policy that was unlikely to have emerged from a wider circle of advisers. Keeping Congress in the loop can slow the process, but as one scholar of Congress recently wrote, "second-guessing by Congress can keep presidents from pursuing ill-conceived policies."[9] The inclusion of other views or interests not only increases the prospects of avoiding mistakes and forging a better policy, but it also gives groups a stake in the policy's success. Because of the increasing importance of public opinion, it is probably more important today for a government to secure a supportive political base for a policy than to conduct a policy secretly. To build a sustainable base, the policy needs to be considered and debated publicly. In seeking a vote in Congress on war in the Persian Gulf, George Bush profited from Lyndon Johnson's mistake.

Some security policies need to be made quickly, and when the president consults informally, and the issue clearly requires an immediate response, Congress rarely inhibits it. Recall the quick response to the bombing of Pearl Harbor or the blockade of Berlin.

De Tocqueville expected that U.S. impulsiveness would mean an erratic, impatient, inconstant foreign policy, and contemporary writers have criticized the swings in approach from one administration to the next, and the pushing and pulling of a divided government.[10] These scholars have viewed U.S. foreign policy as rootless, and yet as one looks at the broader sweep of that policy, the continuity is more impressive. In the nineteenth century, the United States deliberately chose to remain aloof from Europe's struggles; its principal foreign engagements came on the North American continent or in the Caribbean area. In the post–World War II era, U.S. objectives have demonstrated more continuity than discontinuity. The country has sought to maintain an alliance of industrialized democracies, contain Soviet and Communist expansionism, open the international economic system, decolonize and develop the Third World in a way that reduced the prospects of Soviet bloc influence there, and promote U.S. values in human rights and democracy. Even the collapse of the so-called postwar consensus as a result of Vietnam did not have a discernible effect on these objectives. Specific policies varied by individual presidents but, contrary to de Tocqueville's surmise, the major goals of U.S. foreign policy have remained remarkably stable. The continuity in U.S. foreign policy in the postwar period is clearer with distance from newspaper headlines or the speeches of politicians who are trying to displace incumbents.

In reviewing de Tocqueville's criteria and contemporary complaints about the U.S. government's foreign policy making capabilities, one should not judge the U.S. system solely on its own terms but also in comparison with other systems. As Winston Churchill noted in his famous quip, democracy is the worst form of government except for all the others. The advantages of dictatorships over democracies are more apparent than real, while the defects of the latter are more real than apparent. Dictatorships might be capable of quick, secret, and Machiavellian actions, but over the long term such regimes have weak foundations, and although their policies might appear consistent for a period, when the regimes fall the nation's policies often shift 180 degrees. "While democratic elections give the impression that the continuity of policy is in question," Kenneth Waltz writes, "the likelihood of discontinuity is higher in authoritarian states."[11] Compared to the shift in Soviet foreign policy between Leonid Brezhnev and Mikhail Gorbachev, the differences even between Carter and Reagan are trivial.

It is also worth comparing the U.S. interbranch model with parliamentary systems. Some Americans, Woodrow Wilson among them, have preferred the constancy, moderation, and unity of parliamentary governments, but the swing from Conservative to Labour governments in Great Britain in the postwar period has been much wider than the pendular swings in the United States between congressional assertiveness and executive predominance. More generally, the swings are more severe in a parliamentary system because the newly elected party takes full control of both the executive and the legislative branches at the same time. There is no Congress to serve as ballast to the new executive, as it often does in the United States.

Those preoccupied with interbranch deadlock in the United States should examine the multiparty parliamentary systems in Italy, Greece, Israel, or the Fourth Republic in France. These governments have been virtually paralyzed for long periods. Thus, even before one assesses the interbranch system on its merits, a simple comparison with dictatorships and even with parliamentary systems suggests that the recurring problems of inconsistency and paralysis are hardly unique to the United States, and may be worse in other systems.

The Comparative Advantage of the Interbranch System

Friedberg argues that the intensifying problems of a divided government make the United States less able to cope with changes in the way the world trades, defends, and negotiates. In effect, his argument is that the U.S. system is not flexible enough to deal with a rapidly changing world. I will argue the opposite—that the United States is better positioned to adapt its means and its goals to changes within and outside itself and is better able to negotiate because of an assertive Congress.

Although Congress is frequently criticized for undermining the president's foreign policies, a president who is sensitive to a public mood that stimulates congressional concern can turn Congress into an incomparable bargaining asset in international negotiations. The clearest use of Congress as a bargaining lever has been in trade negotiations, but the pattern has relevance for all economic and most diplomatic issues. Robert Hormats, who served in senior economic positions in four administrations, said that "the general attitude on Capitol Hill is to strengthen the hand of the executive to get tougher in negotiations."[12] John Connally, secretary of the Treasury during Nixon's first term, acknowledged that the administration frequently "used the Congress as our bargaining lever," particularly with Europe.[13]

The process by which the two branches make foreign policy is often confusing, particularly, although not exclusively, to foreign governments. At the initial stage of policy-making, both the president and Congress send signals to one another and abroad at the same time. A congressman introduces an amendment with 50 cosponsors that threatens Japanese products with tariffs if Japan does not remove its barriers to U.S. exports. A senator introduces an amendment that threatens to cut aid to Mexico if that government does not cooperate more in the pursuit of drug traffickers. The intent of both resolutions is to send signals in three directions, each with a different purpose: to the foreign government—Japan, Mexico—to open up its markets or cooperate on drugs; to constituents, to indicate that their congressman is acting on their concerns; and to the State Department, to push it to negotiate more forcefully.

It is difficult for a foreign government to distinguish between a congressional signal—say a resolution to limit textile imports—and a possible future policy, for example, textile quotas. An analogy in the security area is when one government has to judge whether a neighbor's defense buildup constitutes a security threat. The survival instinct embedded in most governments tends to lead them to take the warnings seriously and exaggerate the threat. Japan is so dependent on the U.S. market that the risk of closure constitutes a threat to its national security. Moreover, because the United States is less dependent on trade, particularly with Japan, its threat to close the U.S. market is credible. The threat affects the political debate in Japan, compelling the government to make a political choice it would prefer to avoid—between losing some exports or putting a protected industry at risk.

More often than not, the U.S. threat helps Japan to make the hard choice in favor of an open trading economy. This means that a congressional threat provides the State Department with additional leverage in its negotiations, and if it uses it well, the process works, the world economy opens, and there is no need for Congress to transform a signal into a policy, a resolution into law. The signaling process therefore strengthens the executive's negotiating hand, and congressional leverage helps to expand global markets. Those who cried doom—that the United States was going protectionist and the world trading system was closing—have repeatedly been proven wrong.[14]

In the 1980s, when the U.S. trade deficit began to grow, Congress deflected protectionist pressures by compelling the executive branch to use the leverage of the U.S. market. That was the intent of Section 301 of the 1988 Omnibus Trade Act, which threatened closure of the U.S. market if target countries did not reduce their own trade barriers. Up to now, the system has worked; the president and U.S. trading partners have responded sufficiently to keep the international trade regime opening or at least not closing. There are also signs that Section 301 is achieving its purpose.[15]

Those who think that Congress has been protectionist and the president has been for free trade have failed to realize that the public clashes concealed a more subtle—and more important—interaction between these two branches. Since 1934, although individual congressmen have introduced thousands of protectionist bills, none of these has become law. Congress has passed and the president has signed numerous trade laws, and all have aimed to reduce trade barriers. Both branches share U.S. trade goals, which combine a demand for fairness for domestic manufacturers and labor and a freer world economy. Congress has tended to show more concern about the first goal while encouraging the president to do more about the second. Although it sometimes appears to be undermining the president, Congress's insistence that the United States should close its market if its trading partners do not open theirs strengthens his ability to negotiate an open world trading system. And those who argue that this strategy can no longer succeed because of the relative decline of U.S. economic power miss the more important point, which is that Europe and Japan remain much more dependent on the U.S. market than the United States is on theirs. Paradoxically, the more the United States declines, the more leverage it has.

Friedberg's second concern is that congressional intrusions make it more difficult for the president to negotiate effectively in a multipolar world. Congress has sometimes embarrassed U.S. negotiators by forcing them to renegotiate agreements, but this has often benefited the nation. When the Senate refused to ratify the first Hay-Pauncefote Treaty in 1900—an agreement between the United States and Great Britain to build but not fortify a canal in Central America—the secretary of state was obliged to utilize leverage he was unaware he had. The second Hay-Pauncefote Treaty, signed and ratified two years later, granted the United States the additional and necessary right to fortify a canal.[16]

In the 1970s, the administration's perception of what the Senate would accept defined the parameters of the negotiation between the United States and Panama on new canal treaties. For new treaties to be ratified, the United States could not pay Panama and would have to retain a right to defend the canal permanently. The Carter administration incorporated these minimum conditions into its negotiating strategy, and although Panama wanted the exclusive right to defend the canal together with billions of dollars for its past use, it accepted the two conditions because it realized that the Senate's position was fixed and left it with no other choice. On the security issue, the treaties were a little vague on the issue of whether the United States could act unilaterally to defend the canal if Panama did not cooperate, and the Senate therefore clarified this point in the treaty. The threat of nonratification would not have been credible in a parliamentary system. If Carter had not needed to obtain Senate approval, he might have accepted a more ambiguous statement that would not have served U.S. interests as effectively as the amendment written by the Senate.

In El Salvador, Congress helped to compensate for the Reagan administration's less-than-grand strategy that stressed defeating the Farabundo Martí Liberation Front (FMLN) guerrillas to the exclusion of other interests. Congress attached stringent human rights conditions to aid to El Salvador in 1981. When the president resisted these conditions, Congress tightened the amendments. In late 1983, the administration finally decided to assert these conditions and threatened the Salvadoran military with a loss of aid if death squads continued to act with impunity. This finally got the attention of the Salvadoran military, and although human rights abuses by the military did not end, they were reduced. The policy became more effective when the Bush administration internalized congressional priorities. Congress now strengthens the executive's hand as it plays the bad cop to the president's good cop.

With regard to overall U.S. policy toward Central America during the last 15 years, the role of Congress has been that of a balancer. It compensated for each president's emphasis on a specific interest by identifying and supporting the other interests that were neglected. During the Carter administration, Congress strengthened the security provisions of the Panama Canal treaties and inserted conditions into the aid program to the Sandinista government that required the administration to certify to Congress that the Sandinistas were not supporting the FMLN insurgency before they could receive aid. Between July 1979 and early November 1980, this leverage proved to be effective in deterring the Sandinistas from giving such aid despite considerable pressures from both Cuba and the FMLN.[17]

Although the Republicans captured both the Senate and the presidency in 1980, Congress as an institution pivoted around the new conservative president and compensated for his one-sided approach to Central America by encouraging the administration to give a higher priority to human rights and negotiations. Congressional initiatives on human rights were not necessary during the Carter administration but were important again under Reagan. Conversely, amendments aimed to get the administration to give more attention to conventional security concerns in Central America were not needed during the Reagan administration, but were imposed on his predecessor. A similar interbranch pattern of compensating for presidential preferences is evident in U.S. policy toward the Soviet Union and defense expenditures.

An effective foreign policy requires that a government adapt to changes in the world. Congress often presses presidents to pursue new interests, like human rights or drug interdiction. Presidents assimilate and often respond to these new priorities, but the best device for adjusting U.S. foreign policy interests is the election of a new president. Congress pressed Secretary of State Henry Kissinger on human rights, but only the inauguration of Jimmy Carter assured that this issue became a high priority for the State Department. Similarly, Carter beefed up the defense budget in 1979 in response to Soviet expansionism and a decidedly conservative shift in the U.S. mood, but a militant assault on Soviet expansionism had to await the inauguration of Ronald Reagan. Slow to respond to Gorbachev's initiatives, Reagan finally felt the congressional winds blow from a different direction than they did during the Carter years. As a result, Reagan began to negotiate seriously with the "evil empire," meeting with his Soviet counterpart four times during his second term. But again, it took the election of George Bush before the United States would begin to negotiate wide-ranging nuclear and conventional arms agreements.

Between presidential elections, congressional pressure functions as the principal mechanism for the United States to adjust priorities. When a plague of repression descended on South America in the 1970s, it was Congress that pressed a reluctant Ford administration to give human rights a high priority. When cocaine exploded as a domestic and international issue in the 1980s, Congress pressed the Reagan administration to give it more attention.

The third concern raised by Friedberg is congressional "micromanagement," particularly of defense policy. As Louis Fisher has written, that is "a relatively new word to express a very old complaint: intervention by Congress in administrative details."[18] Although the growth of congressional staff has been criticized as the source of the problem, in fact, their numbers have hardly kept pace with the increasing complexity of the issues facing the federal government and the rise in the numbers of executive branch officials and consultants. The relationship between the two branches has not changed significantly since the Constitution was ratified.

Congressional amendments can affect the margins of policy, and, as Alton Frye has commented, "in complex questions of foreign policy, the margins are frequently the vital edges, and Congress's ability to shape them is of real importance."[19] Friedberg concludes that the United States is not capable of formulating and implementing a coherent military program,[20] but that is questionable. In a global strategic context, the question is not whether the U.S. process is supremely rational—whatever that may mean; the issue is whether the U.S. program is better than the alternatives. Here, it seems difficult to argue that the United States is less able to fashion a coherent military program than its rivals.

In the nineteenth century, when de Tocqueville wrote his treatise, the ability of a leader to deploy troops quickly and in secrecy was considered essential to a successful foreign policy. In a world in which the quick dispatch of troops may be a costly temptation, the restraint offered by Congress may be an asset, although no president will ever view it as such. As secret protocols have become an embarrassment at home and abroad, Congress's mission to compel the executive to defend its actions publicly may give the U.S. system an advantage over closed systems. Indeed, the openness of the U.S. political system combined with the growing importance of the media have given U.S. policymakers experience that other diplomats and government officials do not have.

The system also confers another special advantage on the United States. More than 20 years ago, Kenneth Waltz observed that the fragmentation of power and responsibility in the U.S. political system encouraged "competititive political habits and in the twentieth century [this has] more often than not produced governments of innovative zeal and vigorous leadership."[21] The Bush administration's lobbying success at the United Nations on the Persian Gulf crisis was partly due to skills acquired in a democratic system.

Congress, an eminently domestic institution, obliges the executive to give more attention to economic and domestic interests. To the extent that these issues of interdependence are on the cutting edge for the next generation of foreign policy makers, Congress's involvement ensures that the United States will be better equipped to deal with the future than others.

This idea, of course, runs counter to the theory that a decline of U.S. hegemonic leadership bodes ill for a freer world economy. In fact, Congress is quicker to adapt to the implications of the decline of U.S. global economic power than the executive branch and has imposed on a recalcitrant executive a strategy that could conceivably reverse the decline and maintain the open world economy. The president continues to request foreign aid in a manner that implies he has not understood that the United States is no longer a surplus nation, and the aid it gives abroad, in effect, represents additional debt owed to the Japanese. Executive trade negotiators are also inclined to play the traditional postwar role of world leader and make concessions rather than insist on them from others.

In the early postwar period, the United States needed to play the Kindlebergian role of hegemonic leader, making concessions and giving aid to open the world economy. Today, to keep the world economy open, the United States needs to play rougher, demanding more trade concessions, encouraging others to contribute aid. Ironically, the less flexibility the president has—or appears to have—the more leverage he has in international negotiations.[22] Congress makes this possible.

In the end, the interbranch process is more efficient and effective than the closed, narrow process of dictatorships because it allows for peaceful change of leadership and modification of priorities to take into account global changes and domestic concerns. The interbranch process also gives the president added leverage in international negotiations.

Interbranch Conflict, Abdication, and Delay

Needless to say, the interbranch process does not always work, and when the relationship between the two branches breaks down, U.S. foreign policy suffers. To argue that congressional assertiveness is the cause of conflict, however, is equivalent to arguing that today's high divorce rate is due to the new assertiveness of women. Sometimes, Congress and women are culpable; sometimes, the president and men are to blame.

Tension is built into the system. Conflict or stalemate occur when there is a difference of views on policy, both branches reject the democratic injunction to compromise, or one branch judges that the other has overstepped the constitutional boundary in pursuit of its policy preference. Like divorce, or war in the international system, interbranch conflict in U.S. politics can never be ruled out, although the statesman and the wise politician will find ways to pursue their interests short of having to pay the high price of war. The question is not how to silence the Congress or compel presidential responsiveness, but rather how to ensure a harmonious relationship and prevent interbranch conflict.

Disagreements between Congress and the president on aid to the contras in the 1980s only turned into conflict when it was disclosed that some officials in the executive branch were circumventing legislative prohibitions. There are many other examples of collisions between the branches on foreign policy—among them the ending of the war in Indochina, war powers, the Turkish arms embargo, the Jackson-Vanik amendment, and the sanctions against South Africa. In each of these cases, the president chose to confront Congress or circumvent the law rather than negotiate or execute the law. When this occurs, the congressional asset becomes a liability, but although Congress is often blamed, the responsibility must be shared by both ends of Pennsylvania Avenue.

The second kind of interbranch breakdown occurs as a result of abdication of mutual responsibilities. Although the Founding Fathers built a system of competitive institutions, Congress and the president sometimes decide not to compete; they defer to each other in a process of mutual abdication of responsibility that has a long-term, debilitating effect on the U.S. capacity to lead.

Two examples—tariffs and taxes—will suffice. On both issues, each branch has a particular role and comparative advantage. Congressmen as individuals defend particular interests. The president defends a broader conception of the national interest. In trade policy, this means that Congress tries to protect injured or influential industries and unions from unfair competition, and the president tries to lower trade barriers for the benefit of the whole nation. In tax policy, it means that Congress tries to lower taxes for particular groups, and the president tries to keep the government solvent, often by requesting a rise in taxes.

Robert Dahl described the individual roles of both branches neatly, the presidency being "the instrument of majorities; the Congress of minorities."[23] A problem with Dahl's characterization is that it overlooks the crucial *national* role played by Congress in ensuring that its particularistic concerns are grafted in some general form onto the national law and in supporting the president's bills.

Whenever each institution fails to play its assigned role, policy suffers. In 1929, President Herbert Hoover asked Congress to pass a protectionist trade bill, and he opened up the floodgates. The final bill included specific tariff increases on more than 20,000 items. "I might suggest that we have taxed everything in this bill except gall," said Senator Thaddeus Caraway (D–Ark.). "Yes," Senator Carter Glass (D–Va.) replied, "and a tax on that would bring in considerable revenue."[24] The absence of presidential leadership to lower tariff barriers was the single most important reason why the worst trade bill in U.S. history passed Congress. Fortunately, the lesson was learned. No president after Hoover would ever again request Congress to raise tariffs.

Similar roles are played by the president and Congress on tax policy. No politician ever likes to raise taxes; it is a responsibility, however, that most will accept if they are convinced that is the only way to maintain U.S. solvency. By and large, the process begins with the president working with the leaders of the House Ways and Means Committee and the Senate Finance Committee to negotiate a coalition in favor of higher taxes.

When President Kennedy requested a tax cut, he was able to keep the floodgates closed because of the discipline of these two committees. When President Reagan requested a tax cut, the two committees were much weaker, and Reagan did not attempt to keep the floodgates shut. The result, according to Catherine Rudder, was that "the process was out of control. Once the spigot was opened, there seemed to be no way to shut it off."[25]

Both Smoot-Hawley and the Reagan tax cuts had enduring economic consequences for the United States. The rise in U.S. tariffs under Smoot-Hawley provoked tariff retaliation by most U.S. trading partners, and from 1929 to 1933, U.S. exports fell from $5.2 billion to $1.7 billion; world trade, from $34 billion to $12 billion. Scholars have written that Smoot-Hawley significantly deepened and aggravated the world depression.[26]

The Reagan tax cuts combined with massive defense spending led to unprecedented budget deficits and a ballooning of the national and foreign debt. During Reagan's term, the debt of the United States increased threefold, to about $3 trillion, and the United States was transformed from the world's largest creditor into the world's largest debtor nation. As a military superpower facing a declining Soviet threat, and with other economic powers financing the U.S. deficit, the United States did not immediately feel the impact of the decline in real power represented by its increased debt. Nonetheless, like Smoot-Hawley, the long-term consequences of the Reagan tax cut will be very serious. The cause of both failures—in trade and taxes—was the abdication of responsibility by Congress and the president but particularly the latter, whose leadership role is crucial in these two areas.

The third dysfunction in interbranch relations is the length of time and the amount of presidential capital needed to gain approval of a major foreign policy law or treaty. When the president makes a compelling case that the national security of the United States demands the approval of a particular bill or treaty, Congress rarely rejects him. This was true for the Panama Canal treaties and the war in the Persian Gulf. But if the policy is unpopular, the president will almost certainly have to devote a much larger proportion of his time and political capital to gaining approval for it, and he will have less time for and influence on other foreign policy issues. Also, if he needs to ask Congress repeatedly to approve an unpopular policy—such as contra aid—he will deplete his political capital and is likely eventually to lose the votes, as Reagan did.

The increasing complexity of the world and its growing interdependence with the United States means that the agenda will grow, the trade-offs between domestic and international interests will become more delicate, and the role of Congress will increase proportionately. A few difficult issues—like the canal treaties or contra aid—can delay consideration of the entire foreign policy agenda for prolonged periods. Given a fixed amount of time and a limited number of decision makers, this systemic delay might be among the most important problems that stem from interbranch politics.

The president must be very conscious of his agenda and very selective in his approach. Carter filled his agenda with a host of controversial issues at the beginning of his administration. Although he succeeded in gaining approval of the new Panama Canal treaties and new energy legislation, both issues were costly, and ironically, his victories left him weaker politically. Reagan learned from Carter's experience and selected a smaller, more manageable agenda. His victories—the tax cut and the defense budget—came more easily in Congress, and he looked stronger as a result.

To a certain extent, one's judgment of congressional involvement is colored by one's assessment of the administration's policy. If one believes that an administration's policy on South Africa or the Middle East is correct, then congressional intrusions are viewed more negatively than if one views the administration's approach as flawed. The congressional style of foreign policy making is admittedly messy, public, and sometimes contradictory. But as Francis O. Wilcox, whose career spanned both branches, observed: "If Congress has frequently seemed to be going in one direction and then in another, that is partly because it is a collection of poorly coordinated, strong-minded individuals. But more importantly, it is because that is the way the White House and the Kremlin have moved as well."[27]

A New Engagement

For six years, Ronald Reagan persuaded, cajoled, and threatened Congress to support the Nicaraguan freedom fighters. George Bush decided to try a different approach, partly for reasons of personality and partly because the politics were different. In his inaugural address, he called for "a new engagement between the Executive and the Congress." The Republicans had controlled the Senate until 1986 and, with some arm-twisting, President Reagan could wrestle the House to comply on a key issue. But the Democratic control over both Houses in 1988 was firm, and Bush, ever the pragmatist, understood that he would have to reach out to accomplish his program. Appropriately, he described his term as the "age of the offered hand," and turning to the Democratic leadership on the podium during his inaugural address, he asked that "the old bipartisanship . . . be made new again."[28]

Bush and his secretary of state, James A. Baker III, were serious and passed the first test. On March 24, 1989, they signed a "Bipartisan Accord on Central America" with the congressional leadership, barring any military aid to the contras but permitting humanitarian aid so that the contras could remain as a force through the Nicaraguan elections on February 25,

1990. Preempting a divisive vote, this agreement effectively removed the contra issue from the U.S. political landscape while at the same time increasing the prospects for resolution of the crisis in Nicaragua.

The most recent but far more significant test occurred in the jousting between the branches on the question of declaring war in the Persian Gulf. In the end, Congress supported the president, and his efforts to, first, avoid war and, later, to win it were all the stronger because of that support.

Although the Bush administration has had disagreements with Congress on China, the defense budget, Panama, and the Persian Gulf, among other issues, these have been relatively minor and contained, particularly as compared to the titanic interbranch struggles during the previous eight years. This point should serve as a warning to those who would recommend structural changes to improve the way the two branches relate to each other.

The constitutional relationship between the two branches is not the problem; indeed, the interbranch model provides the best vehicle for U.S. leadership in a complex world. The essence of forging "a new engagement" between Congress and the president is attitudinal—to recognize that both branches are responsible for conflicts and that they occur as much because of presidential arrogance as of congressional assertiveness. If, for example, President Bush, flush with the success of a military victory, chooses either to ignore the Congress on an important issue or to bash the minority who voted for continuation of sanctions rather than war, he will rapidly transform interbranch comity into partisan conflict.

The way to make the United States a more effective global actor is for each branch to modify its approach to take account of the other's perspective. An assertive Congress can be a positive force, and a lever in international negotiations, as Thomas Mann has shown, when the two branches respect and maintain the delicate balance between them.[29] Interbranch politics is often viewed as a liability in foreign policy making, but with sensitivity to the distinct roles of each institution, the president and Congress can transform the process to the comparative advantage of the United States.

An earlier draft of this article was presented at a conference chaired by Robert Art and Seyom Brown on "American Foreign Policy Towards the Year 2000" at Brandeis University, Waltham, Massachusetts in April 1990. I am grateful to Jeffrey Herf, Robert Art, Michael Nacht, and Geoffrey Kemp for their comments on previous drafts.

Notes

1. Aaron L. Friedberg, "Is the United States Capable of Acting Strategically," *The Washington Quarterly* 14 (Winter 1991), pp. 5–23.

2. Alexis de Tocqueville, *Democracy in America*, vol. 1 (New York: Vintage Books, 1945), pp. 240–245.

3. George F. Kennan, *American Diplomacy, 1900–1950* (Chicago: University of Chicago Press, 1951), pp. 66–67.

4. See, for example, I. M. Destler, Leslie H. Gelb, and Anthony Lake, *Our Own Worst Enemy: The Unmaking of American Foreign Policy* (New York: Simon and Schuster, 1984).

5. Excerpts from North's testimony were reprinted in *New York Times*, July 10, 1987, pp. 4–7.

6. See James MacGregor Burns, *The Deadlock of Democracy* (Englewood Cliffs, N.J.: Prentice Hall, 1963). For a later statement, see Lloyd N. Cutler, "To Form a Government," *Foreign Affairs* 59 (Fall 1980).

7. See L. Gordon Crovitz and Jeremy A. Rabkin, eds., *The Fettered Presidency: Legal Constraints on the Executive Branch* (Wash-

ington, D.C.: American Enterprise Institute, 1989).

8. Howard Baker (R–Tenn.), then-Senate minority leader and member of the Committee on Foreign Relations, announced at the opening of the hearings that the U.S. negotiators "did much more [in consulting with the Senate] than anybody I have ever known has done." Senate Committee on Foreign Relations, *Hearings: Panama Canal Treaties, Part I*, 95th Cong., 1st sess., September–October 1977, pp. 87–88.

9. Thomas E. Mann, "Making Foreign Policy," in *A Question of Balance: The President, the Congress, and Foreign Policy*, Mann, ed. (Washington, D.C.: The Brookings Institution, 1989), p. 3.

10. Destler, Gelb, and Lake, *Our Own Worst Enemy*, and James L. Sundquist, "Needed: A Political Theory for the New Era of Coalition Government in the United States," *Political Science Quarterly* 103 (Winter 1988–89), pp. 613–635.

11. Kenneth Waltz, *Foreign Policy and Democratic Politics* (Boston, Mass.: Little, Brown, 1967), p. 309.

12. Robert Hormats, interview with author, Washington, D.C., October 10, 1982.

13. Cited in William Safire, *Before the Fall* (New York: Belmont Tower Books, 1975), p. 505.

14. An extended description of this interbranch and international process of negotiations and its results in trade issues over the last 50 years is developed in Robert A. Pastor, "The Cry-and-Sigh Syndrome: Congress and Trade Policy," in *Making Economic Policy in Congress*, Alan Schick, ed. (Washington, D.C.: American Enterprise Institute, 1983).

15. Clyde H. Farnsworth, "Efforts to Speed U.S.–Japan Trade Talks are Working," *New York Times*, April 2, 1990, p. C–2; and "Japanese Pledge to Lower Barriers to Trade with U.S.," *New York Times*, April 6, 1990, pp. A–1, C–5.

16. Samuel Flagg Bemis, *The Latin American Policy of the United States* (New York: Harcourt, Brace and Company, 1943), pp. 144–145.

17. See Robert Pastor, *Condemned to Repetition: The United States and Nicaragua* (Princeton, N.J.: Princeton University Press, 1987), pp. 208–212, 216–228. There are multiple reasons why the deterrent eroded and the Sandinistas decided to send arms to the FMLN after November 1980.

18. Louis Fisher, "Micromanagement by Congress: Reality and Mythology," in Crovitz and Rabkin, eds., *The Fettered Presidency*, p. 139.

19. Alton Frye, "Congress: The Virtue of Its Vices," *Foreign Policy*, no. 3 (Summer 1971), pp. 108–121.

20. Friedberg, "Is the United States Capable of Acting Strategically?" p. 17.

21. Waltz, *Foreign Policy and Democratic Politics*, p. 304.

22. For an excellent theoretical analysis of how this works, see Robert D. Putnam, "Diplomacy and Domestic Politics: The Logic of Two-Level Games," *International Organization* 42 (Summer 1988), pp. 427–458.

23. Robert Dahl, *Congress and Foreign Policy*, 2nd ed. (New York: W. W. Norton, 1964), p. 186.

24. Cited in Robert A. Pastor, *Congress and the Politics of U.S. Foreign Economic Policy* (Berkeley: University of California Press, 1980), p. 77. For an analysis of the policymaking process that gave rise to Smoot-Hawley, see pp. 77–84.

25. Catherine E. Rudder, "Tax Policy: Structure and Choice," in Schick, *Making Economic Policy in Congress*, p. 206.

26. Pastor, *Congress and the Politics of U.S. Foreign Economic Policy*, p. 79.

27. Francis O. Wilcox, *Congress, the Executive, and Foreign Policy* (New York: Harper and Row, 1971), p. 133.

28. Transcript of Bush's Inaugural Address, *New York Times*, January 21, 1989, p. 10.

29. Mann, *A Question of Balance*.

Exorcising Wilson's Ghost: Morality and Foreign Policy in America's Third Century

George Weigel

AS THE UNITED STATES goes about the making of the president, 1988, it seems certain that issues of morality and foreign policy will be argued with much heat, if not commensurate light, during the campaign.

What ought the United States do in Central America? Is strategic defense a more morally acceptable means of security than deterrence maintained by the threat of mutual assured destruction? What responsibilities does America have for the cause of human rights in the world? What is a human right, for that matter? Do the world's democrats have a moral claim on America's support? And what happens when those claims abut other grave national security interests?

There is something quintessentially American about these arguments. It is hard to imagine their equivalents arising on the Quai d'Orsay or in Whitehall—much less, one hardly needs to add, in Eduard Shevardnadze's staff meetings. They crop up with impressive regularity in our public discourse

George Weigel is president of the Ethics and Public Policy Center in Washington, D.C. A widely published commentator on questions of theology, ethics, politics, and peace, he is also a member of the board of directors of the Institute on Religion and Democracy.

for any number of reasons—among them, that Americans are an incorrigibly religious people who, since the days of John Winthrop and Roger Williams, have brought their religious convictions and the moral norms they derive therefrom into the public square. But the most important reason why the morality and foreign policy debate remains a hardy perennial in the garden of American political controversy has to do with the very nature of the American experiment itself.

Unlike other nations, which are based on the realities of tribe, race, ethnicity, or language, the United States is a country whose casements rest on an idea. Thomas Jefferson expressed it succinctly in the Declaration of Independence: "All men are created equal." At Gettysburg, Abraham Lincoln described Jefferson's claim as a "proposition" that would always be tested by our public life. Here, argued the great Jesuit theologian John Courtney Murray, Lincoln was speaking with "conceptual propriety," for in philosophy a proposition is "the statement of a truth to be demonstrated."[1] Jefferson's definition of the "American proposition" has had, and continues to have, a pronounced effect on the conduct of America's business with the world. In that sense, Murray's notion of a continually-tested proposition is validated by every morning's headlines.

Jefferson's claim was, of course, a moral claim. Its impact on U.S. foreign policy, for better and for worse and often for both, derives from its universality. The Founding Fathers did not pledge their "lives, fortunes, and sacred honor" to a narrow claim ("All English colonists living on the Eastern seaboard of North America between the Atlantic Ocean and the Mississippi River are created equal") but to a simple, flat, universal claim: All men are created equal. Moreover, the Declaration argued, this claim could be known by all men of good will. It did not derive from a sectarian religious tradition, but from human nature itself. "Nature, and Nature's God," had created all men equal.

Thus, from its inception, the American experiment was more than a matter of a new "is" in world affairs. The Founding Fathers asserted an "ought." Charles Krauthammer of *The New Republic* has made the connection between this "ought" and the distinctive character of American nationalism: "Our nationalism is unlike others, in that our very nationhood is bound up with and is meant to give expression to the idea of freedom."[2] That this morally based nationalism would have its effect on U.S. foreign policy was as certain a speculation as one could have made, even in the days of America's hemispheric isolation. Given the right historical circumstances, Americans would have to deal with the world. And they would, inevitably, cast that encounter in terms that reflected their originating experience and continuing experiment.

No small part of our present difficulties with the morality and foreign policy debate derives from the historical circumstances in which that encounter happened in World War I.

That it was Woodrow Wilson who first articulated the themes of America's entry as a great power onto the world stage has made an enormous difference. For Wilson embodied a specific form of American Protestant moral sensibility that has been the entry point for, as well as the chief defect of, the morality and foreign policy debate ever since April 1917.

Throughout the nineteenth century and well into the twentieth, the United States had a semi-established religion, what sociologist Peter Berger has described as *Kulturprotestantismus*.[3] This generalized Protestant religiosity carried with it a particular understanding of morality, traces of which can be found in artifacts ranging from the McGuffey readers to the League of Nations Charter and the Kellogg-Briand Treaty.

It was a morality that found the good in the will of God, rather than in human reason. As Murray once described it, Kulturprotestantismus taught that " . . . the good is good because God commands it; the evil is evil because God forbids it."[4] The notion that morality might have something to do with human reason and its capacity to discern moral norms from human nature and human history did not sit well.

The morality of Kulturprotestantismus likewise knew where one looked for the revelation of God's will: one looked to the Old and New Testaments. There was a fundamentalist current at play here. Scholarly biblical exegesis was not of much moment. One took the biblical texts as they stood, and applied them to the policy arena in a kind of one-to-one correspondence.

Wilson's morality also set great store by one's intentions. As Murray put it, "It set primary and controlling value on a sincerity of interior motives; what matters is not what you do but why you do it."⁵ This led rather easily to a form of extreme moral idealism, which taught that the motive of love which ought to inform one's dealings with one's fellows could be applied, forthwith, to relations between organized political communities. Thus individualism was a fourth distinctive element in the moral sensibility of Kulturprotestantismus: standards of Christian perfection applicable to the individual could also be applied to the behavior of states. Thus one could hope for, work for, and indeed expect the day when there would be no "moral problems" for domestic or international society, which blessed condition would automatically obtain if and when all men loved their neighbors.

This "older morality," as Murray was wont to call it, may have been marginally useful in providing rhetorical grease for America's sidestep into world politics. But it did little to illuminate those politics, and still less to provide moral standards for the formulation of policy. Its failure, though, should not be attributed to the fact that the world is an infinitely messy place, vastly plural in its religious, ethical, and ideological understandings and commitments, and thus constructed in a way that no moral norm could possibly be relevant to the design and conduct of U.S. foreign policy. Rather, the true fault lay in the concept of morality that was embedded in Kulturprotestantismus, and that can be aptly described as Wilsonian moralism. The deepest question to be addressed did not lie on the policy side of the morality and foreign policy dialectic. It lay on the first side of the equation. The priority question was, "What do we mean by 'morality'?"

A first and important cut at answering this question from outside boundaries of the liberal Protestant hegemony came in the work of Reinhold Niebuhr and other Christian realists. Niebuhr and colleagues such as John C. Bennett argued in the 1930s that Protestant moralism was utterly incapable of guiding the conduct of policy in the face of modern totalitarianism. Rather, the social ethicist had to recover a classic Christian understanding: that the Kingdom of God would not be a work of human hands. In this world as it is, Christian theology and social theory had to take account of the irreducible facts of tragedy, irony, and pathos in the human condition. To attempt blithely to transcend these facts of life in a fallen world, as Niebuhr believed Wilsonian moralism and Protestant liberalism did, was not only political folly; it was a corruption of Christian understandings of—in the classic images—the world, the flesh, and the devil. In the very first chapter of his seminal book, *Moral Man and Immoral Society*, Niebuhr stated flatly that "the dream of perpetual peace and brotherhood for human society will never be fully realized." That did not mean, as many have misinterpreted, that society and politics were somehow outside the boundaries within which moral reason could operate. It did mean that social ethics was a distinctive enterprise, which ought not be confused with the ethics of interpersonal relationships. One did not think morally about dealing with Hitler in precisely the same way that one reasoned morally about dealing with Aunt Mary.

Niebuhr's great accomplishment, which shaped and was shaped by his interaction with anti-Communist liberal internationalism of the early ADA sort, was to nail this point down for a generation: the voluntarism, fundamentalism, subjectivism, and individualism of the older morality made a chaos of both public policy and Christian doctrine. But Niebuhr did not venture very far beyond this essential contribution, and he never sketched a calculus by which moral reason could be applied, through the mediating virtue of prudence, to the design and conduct of foreign policy.

This was John Courtney Murray's critique of Niebuhr. Murray welcomed Niebuhr's insistence that complexity was the inescapable hallmark of policy choice; that historical circumstances had to be taken seriously; that the consequences of one's actions must be factored into the calculus of moral reason and policy choice; and that human tendencies toward evil were a built-in part of the human condition, not to be removed by therapy or baptism. In short, Niebuhr had dealt a serious blow to that sentimentalism which was a leitmotif of the older morality and a corrupting influence within it.

But Niebuhr had stopped too soon, Murray suggested. Niebuhr was correct to assert the distinctiveness of social ethics against the ethics of interpersonal relationships. But the problem posed by liberal Protestant individualism was, at bottom, a false problem, and Niebuhr's solution to it posed a new danger: to posit the distinction between social and interpersonal ethics without grounding both in the functions of human reason and its ability to apprehend moral norms through reflection on human nature and human history raised the prospect of social ethics simply dropping off the ledge of our public discourse.

Nor did the themes of irony, tragedy, and pathos, evocative as they were, provide much grist for a task that Murray deemed paramount: the creation of a public philosophy expressed in a mediating language that could cut across the pluralisms of Protestant/Catholic/Jewish and religious/secular in such a way that genuinely public moral argument, rather than public moral emoting, was made possible in American political culture.

What Reinhold Niebuhr offered, in short, was a sensibility that ought to furnish one corner of the intellect of anyone who dared to enter the minefield called morality-and-foreign-policy. But more than a Niebuhrian sensibility was needed, in Murray's judgment. One needed a natural law-based social ethic which recognized that society and the state had their own distinctive purposes, not to be confused with private purposes. One needed an ethic which acknowledged the centrality of national interest in the conduct of policy and was not embarrassed by it, but which related national interest to a larger scheme of national purpose by resolutely drawing the line at *raison d'etat* as a possible criterion for action. One needed a social ethic which knew that power—the ability to achieve a common purpose—was the central reality at the heart of any organized community. One needed a structure of moral reasoning which could distinguish, normatively, between power and sheer violence, and which could relate the proportionate and discriminate use of limited armed force to the pursuit of peace, security, and freedom. One needed, finally, a method of casuistry which could dialectically engage moral norms with messy human situations through the mediation of the central political virtue of prudence. One-to-one correspondences—between Scriptural texts or moral norms, and the exigencies of policy—should be held frankly suspect, and precisely on moral grounds. Moral reasoning was not a set of how-to-do-it instructions that might be followed by any dolt; it was a matter of endless argument, research, reflection, more argument, and empirical testing.

How does this question stand, as we enter America's third century, and, beyond the possible fascinations of intellectual history, why should those concerned with the day-to-day crises of power care anyway?

The second question is answered simply, if provocatively, by recognizing that the concept of value-free judgment in politics is an absurdity. There are no value-free judgments, no ethical free lunches. Every political judgement involves a calculus, usually inarticulate, involving questions of "ought" as well as "is." John F. Kennedy was simply in a rationalist Shangri-La when he told the graduates of Yale University in 1962 that the real problems of the modern world were not philosophical or ideological (and thus embroiled with issues of meaning and value) but technical and managerial. The central problem is not whether we shall apply what we understand to be moral norms and values to foreign policy, but how. The real issues have to do, as always, with the quality of moral reasoning that is brought to bear on a particular problem. And that must be of concern to anyone with a responsibility, in public or private life, for the business of America's encounter with the world.

As to the present quality of the argument, an exceedingly mixed picture presents itself, particularly as one surveys the American religious community, in which the morality and foreign policy debate is shaped to a considerable although not exclusive degree.

Intellectuals and activists in the great churches of mainline Protestantism—the various offshoots of Congregationalism, the Presbyterians, Methodists, and Episcopalians—seem to have reverted, in general, to a pre-Niebuhrian liberalism, now shaped by the personalist psychology of Carl Rogers, feminism, and the vulgarized Marxism that underlay some early forms of liberation theology. Mainline activist religious leaders show scant traces of a Niebuhrian sense of irony and ambiguity, and often seem more confident in their public policy judgments than in their theological convictions. The recent Methodist bishops' pastoral letter on nuclear weapons issues, "In Defense of Creation," was sharply criticized, for example by Duke Divinity School moral theologian Stanley Hauerwas, as one in which "the bishops feel more comfortable condemning SDI than they do in proclaiming God's sovereignty over our existence."[6] (That Hauerwas is a principled pacifist added even more piquancy to his devastating critique of his bishops' work.) Then there is the Presbyterian Church-USA, which has produced a study guide asking whether it is not time for American Presbyterians to think of themselves as a resistance church, on the model of the "Confessing Church" of the Barmen Declaration in Nazi Germany. Such pronouncements have raised important countercurrents; one might note the formation of groups like Presbyterians for Democracy and Religious Freedom, in which former Undersecretary of the Navy R. James Woolsey has taken a leading role. But the mainline church bureaucracies, their principal ecumenical agencies, and the mainline Protestant peace movement remain firmly in the hands of those who would argue for some form or another of the confessing church model. This seems a rather unlikely position from which to broker a wide-ranging civic conversation on morality and foreign policy.

Resurgent Protestant evangelicalism might contribute to such a conversation. The National Association of

Evangelicals, for example, has recently produced a "Guidelines" document for its new "Peace, Freedom, and Security Studies" program that challenges the mainline churches' theology and politics and calls on evangelical congregations and denominations to begin the kind of first-principles moral argument envisioned by Murray. That natural law forms of moral reasoning (even if identified by different terms, like "general revelation" or "two kingdoms") are not automatically ruled out of bounds in some evangelical intellectual circles suggests the possibility of an important new ecumenism.

This new ecumenism would engage, of course, Roman Catholic intellectuals, activists, and religious leaders. Here, one finds both good news and bad, from the point of view of the task identified by John Courtney Murray a generation ago. On the asset side of the ledger, there remains significant agreement among Catholic scholars in the United States that moralism remains an ever present danger, and that casuistry rooted in classic methods of moral reasoning is a moral imperative. Yet there is on the other hand a new Catholic moralism among activists and some bishops that occupies a considerable position in the American Catholic debate. Here, the traditional characteristics of Kulturprotestantismus—especially its fundamentalism and individualism—have been ecumenically transposed. Catholicism's rediscovery of its Scriptural heritage in the wake of the Second Vatican Council has been both a boon and a distraction on these questions. Murray used to tell of a distinguished journalist who was confused by the 1950s debate over morality and foreign policy because he could not understand what foreign policy had to do with the Sermon on the Mount; when asked by Murray why he deemed morality to be reducible to the Sermon on the Mount, he became even more confused and asked unhappily, "You mean it isn't?" That question is being regularly raised by Catholic activists today and suggests that one significant component of the American Catholic community will be of little help in constructing a public philosophy able to recreate public moral argument that is conducted without resort to biblical trump cards.

Some Jewish political intellectuals—one thinks immediately of Charles Krauthammer—are working hard at the problem of public moral argument on foreign policy issues.[7] Other Jewish scholars, like Rabbi David Novak of Jewish Theological Seminary in New York, are deeply interested in the natural law tradition as it bears on issues of public policy.

Thus there is good reason to think that a new morality and foreign policy debate, exorcising Wilson's ghost and scouting out new intellectual terrain ahead of today's right- and left-wing moralisms, may be aborning. It will be an interestingly diverse argument, involving as it will Roman Catholics, evangelical Protestants, Jews, mainline Protestants who refuse to concede the field to the resistance enthusiasms of their brethren, and secular scholars who appreciate the imperative public need for a movement beyond the rock of moralism and the hard place of relativism and/or Realpolitik.

What would the argument focus on? In the first instance, it would have to address, in a publicly accessible way, the question of the very meaning of "moral reasoning." Themes for such an address have been sketched above. But what about the application of moral reason to the policy agenda?

Where is there room for useful debate here? Two broad areas of concern suggest themselves to this observer.

First, assuming that the United States government is not filled with pacifists and/or radical neo-isolationsts, there is inevitably going to be a military component to America's encounter with a persistently hostile world. This suggests that the intellectual and cultural health of just war theory—that is, our ability to think through the ways in which the proportionate and discriminate use of armed force can (and cannot) contribute to peace, security and freedom in the world—is of crucial importance.

Where is just war theory alive in American political culture? Where has it died? It is alive in our military manuals, in the Uniform Code of Military Justice, in the service academies and the officer corps. It is alive among political philosophers, even if, like Stanley Hoffman and Michael Walzer, they feel compelled to reinvent it. It is alive in international law, although in a truncated form. And it is alive among Roman Catholic, mainline and evangelical Protestant, and Jewish theologians, ethicists, and religious leaders. It is dead or dying among many religious peace activist intellectuals and ecclesiastical leaders, and among Realists like Robert Tucker who continue to insist that just war theory is a matter of squaring the circle.[8]

A revival of just war theory in the argument over morality and foreign policy would address, among other things, the new pressures that modern forms of political violence—terrorism, guerilla warfare, low-intensity conflict—have put on the classic just war criteria. International law in its present form poses one set of problems, recognizing as it does that self-defense is the only legally legitimate reason to threaten or resort to force of arms. But what constitutes self-defense in a situation of chronic ideological and political conflict such as one finds in U.S.-Soviet relations? Can just war theory adequately ground the practice of deterrence, for example, and in what form? How does one discriminate between combatants and noncombatants in guerrilla warfare? What is proportional use of armed force in Third World conflicts? How does one determine that the last resort has been reached, and armed force thus justified, in revolutionary situations? What does just war theory do to illuminate decisions faced by U.S. policymakers in a situation like Grenada, where the immediate threat to U.S. security is minimal but the possibilities for supporting democrats and displacing tyrants are great? And how, if at all, can just war theory's classic *ad bellum* criterion of "punishment for evil" as a legitimate moral reason for the resort to armed force help guide policy in the face of international terrorism, particularly if it is state sponsored? Absent persuasive answers to, or at least persuasive argument on, these pressing issues, one important resource for considering the relationship between moral norms and foreign policy practice may well continue to die the death of a thousand intellectual cuts in our political culture.

Such a death is also possible because just war theorists, in the main, have done a less than satisfactory job in relating their theory to the pursuit of peace. Classic just war theorists speak of the *ius ad bellum* (what William V. O'Brien has called "war-decision law") and the *ius in bello* ("war-conduct law," in O'Brien's terminology).[9] But it can also be argued—and, in an American context, must be argued—that just war theory contains, in its interstices and its basic intellectual trajectory, an *ius ad pacem*, a concept of peace as rightly ordered political community. The resort to proportionate and discriminate armed force must be directed toward peace, which is to say toward the establishment of a minimum of public order in international affairs. How this can be done in a way that avoids the sentimentalities of much contemporary "world order" thinking is a large, although not impossible, task.[10] But given the pressures put on the classic theory by modern forms of political violence and, perhaps above all, by the fact of nuclear weapons, a just war theory that does not address the nature and pursuit of peace is unlikely to play the significant role it should in American political discourse.

Second, liberation theologies have contributed what seems likely to be an enduring phrase to our morality and foreign policy vocabulary: there should be, they insist, a "preferential option for the poor" in devising policy affecting the world's underclass. Thanks to the work of Peter Berger, Michael Novak, and others,[11] one can speculate and hope that the future debate on such questions of development economics will focus on means, rather than on whether such an option exists.

But there is another related issue remaining to be pressed here. Should there be a "preferential option for freedom" in U.S. foreign policy? Do the world's democrats, in other words, have a special moral claim on our attention and assistance?

Experienced theorists and policymakers are cautious, indeed even skeptical, about letting the American evangelical spirit loose in the world. There are surely cautions to be observed here, as the wreckage of the presidencies of Woodrow Wilson and, more recently, Jimmy Carter, attest. But one ought to draw and maintain a clear distinction between healthy realism and cynicism. The ghost of Woodrow Wilson is not going to be exorcised by the incantations of a Realpolitik that cuts straight across the grain of our national character.

Moreover, something that looks suspiciously like a democratic revolution is going on throughout the world. Fragile as the democratic achievements of recent Latin American and Philippine history may appear, they are genuine achievements. They reflect human aspirations that will not be ignored. Furthermore, there are strategic reasons supporting a "preferential option for freedom." Democratic ideology is the most persuasive answer the West can offer to the current Soviet public diplomacy barrage. Historically, democracies do not go to war with each other, and thus the democratic revolution serves the cause of peace. And, on Berger's and others' research, there would seem to be connections between democratic, or at least predemocratic, societies and economic development. Put the other way around, and as illustrated by the "four little dragons" of East Asia, economic achievement creates pressures for democratization which, if unaddressed, will eventually threaten economic achievement.

Therefore, one can make the case that a "preferential option for freedom" should occupy a central place in a post-Wilsonian consensus on morality and foreign policy. As Roman Catholic Archbishop J. Francis Stafford of Denver argued in a recent pastoral letter, America should "be a leader for ordered liberty, in and among nations."[12] The world will not become Connecticut in the twinkling of an eye, and foreign policy realists rightly warn against the perennial temptations of American universalism. But there are sufficient numbers of people, in transitional Third World societies in particular, who wish, if not to be in Connecticut, then at least to be ruled by something better than *caudillos*—peoples whose aspirations we ignore at our peril in the great contest with Soviet Leninism throughout the Third World.

One can also find, in the work of dissident intellectuals such as Czechoslovakia's Vaclav Havel, Poland's Adam Michnik, and Hungary's George Konrad, claims that Western policy should support the rebuilding of "the civil society" in Soviet-dominated Central Europe.[13] Havel, Michnik, and Konrad are not so naive as to think that democracy is about to break out in Stalin's empire; but they do argue that Western support for building some measure of predemocratic institutional and cultural distance between the individual and the Leninist state serves the causes of human freedom and, ultimately, peace. Aaron Wildavsky has made similar proposals for a U.S. policy of "containment plus pluralization" vis-à-vis the Soviet Union itself.[14]

The broad and bipartisan congressional support now enjoyed by the National Endowment for Democracy (NED) suggests that the democratic revolution has, in its various forms, struck a deep chord in the American conscience. Yet there are moral quandaries that deserve more public argument. On one hand, how should the claims of a country's democrats be weighed against the dangers of instability in the face of an aggressive Leninist enemy which, in the case of South Korea, is as close to Seoul as Dulles airport is to Capitol Hill? On the other hand, how do we determine when and if frustrated pressures for democratization will themselves lead to instabilities that threaten freedom? Then there is the question of where this dimension of the morality and foreign policy debate will be "located" in American political culture. For example, as many religious activists continue to beat a retreat from the bourgeois reformism of Corazon Aquino in the Philippines, who will make the moral case for democracy as the Philippines are caught between traditional authoritarian pressures and the New People's Army? Finally, there is the general question, by no means settled, of whether America has any business forcing change in other societies. By what authority do we conduct interventions for democracy around the world? A publicly persuasive answer to that question—an answer that cuts across partisan, denominational, and ideological grounds—is essential for the long-term stability of initiatives such as NED.

Americans like problems that can be solved with some finality. We have a cultural predisposition to avoid debates, like that involving morality and foreign policy, which by nature are open ended and perennial. But perennial need not mean "circular." It can mean, simply, perennial—and one can hope that such arguments lead, in time, to wisdom in policy-making as well as to shelves of scholarly books. The path beyond circularity in the American morality and foreign policy debate will be open, to return to the beginning, when we recover (or, in some cases, discover) that the key issue is the nature of moral reasoning itself.

Those committed to such a recovery or discovery can find inspiration (and perhaps chagrined comfort) in Jacques

Maritain's description of the plight of the social ethicist. In *Man and the State*, Maritain wrote:

> Moralists are unhappy people. When they insist on the immutability of moral principles, they are reproached for imposing unlivable requirements on us. When they explain the way in which those immutable principles are to be put into force, they are reproached for making morality relative. In both cases, however, they are only upholding the claims of reason to direct life.[15]

The Niebuhrian/realist rejection of moralism has been a necessary and cleansing exercise in this "nation with a soul of a church," as Chesterton once described the United States. But the realist tendency to identify morality exclusively with the moralism that characterized pre-Niebuhrian liberal Protestantism and that characterizes post-Niehbuhrian thinking on these issues in a depressingly large segment of the American religious community repeats the mistake it attempts to correct. There is another way to go at this, and that is to rediscover the tradition of moral reasoning as exemplified (but hardly exhausted) by the natural law tradition of Murray and Maritain. If, with Maritain, we believe that reason rather than unbridled passion ought to direct life (and even public policy), there is considerable work to be done in nailing down that claim by reconstructing the way in which we conduct public moral argument over America's right role in world affairs.

Notes

1. John Courtney Murray, *We Hold These Truths: Catholic Reflections on the American Proposition* (Garden City: Doubleday Image Books, 1964), p. 7.

2. Charles Krauthammer, "Isolationism: A Riposte," *The National Interest* 2 (Winter 1985-1986), p. 115.

3. Peter L. Berger, "The Social Sources of Apostasy," the 1987 Erasmus Lecture of the Center on Religion and Society, New York (unpublished manuscript).

4. Murray, op.cit., p. 263.

5. Ibid.

6. Stanley Hauerwas, unpublished manuscript, quoted in *American Purpose* 1:3 (March 1987), p. 23.

7. See, for example, Krauthammer's essay "Morality and the Reagan Doctrine," *The New Republic*, September 8, 1986, pp. 17-24.

8. See Tucker's commentary on the Second Vatican Council's Pastoral Constitution on the Church in the Modern World," in *Just War and Vatican Council II: A Critique* (New York: Council of Religion and International Affairs, 1966).

9. See William V. O'Brien, *The Conduct of Just and Limited Wars* (New York: Praeger, 1981).

10. See my probe toward such a reconstruction in *Tranguilitas Ordinis: The Present Failure and Future Promise of American Catholic Thought on War and Peace* (New York: Oxford University Press, 1987), chapter 13.

11. See Peter L. Berger, *The Capitalist Revolution: Fifty Propositions about Prosperity, Equality and Liberty* (New York: Basic Books, 1986); Peter L. Berger and Michael Novak, *Speaking to the Third World: Essays on Democracy and Development* (American Enterprise Institute, 1985); William Douglas, *Developing Democracy* (Washington: Heldref Publications, 1972).

12. J. Francis Stafford, "This Home of Freedom: A Pastoral Letter to the Archdiocese of Denver," p. 33 (pamphlet available from the Archdiocese of Denver).

13. See Timothy Garton Ash, "Does Central Europe Exist?" *New York Review of Books*, October 9, 1986, p. 45.

14. See Aaron Wildavsky, "Containment Plus Pluralization," in *Beyond Deterrence*, Aaron Wildavsky, ed. (San Francisco: Institute for Contemporary Studies Press, 1983).

15. Cited in Paul Ramsey, "Tucker's Bellum Contra Bellum Iustum," in *Just War and Vatican Council II: A Critique.*

The Comeback of Liberal Internationalism

Richard N. Gardner

THE COLLAPSE OF the Soviet empire in Eastern Europe and the dramatic changes now underway in the Soviet Union have opened up yet another debate on the basic philosophy that should guide U.S. foreign policy. For some, the answer will be a new isolationism—a "come home America" to focus on neglected economic and social problems. For others, it will be a new nationalism, a unilateral global exercise of U.S. power now that the Soviet Union seems too weak and self-preoccupied to stand in the way of the United States. The thesis of this essay, however, is that the extraordinary events of the last year should encourage Americans to return to the foreign policy philosophy that guided this country from the onset of World War II to the tragic involvement in Vietnam. It is the only foreign policy philosophy that will enable the United States to cope with the challenges and opportunities in the new era in which it suddenly finds itself. That philosophy is best described by a phrase that is now unfashionable and even repugnant in some quarters, but let us give

Richard N. Gardner is former U.S. ambassador to Italy and Professor of Law and International Organization at Columbia University. He cochairs with Vladimir Shustov of the Soviet Foreign Ministry an unofficial U.S.–Soviet working group on multilateral cooperation under the auspices of the United Nations Associations of the two countries.

it its proper name: liberal internationalism.

One should begin by defining the "*L* word." Liberal internationalism is the intellectual and political tradition that believes in the necessity of leadership by liberal democracies in the construction of a peaceful world order through multilateral cooperation and effective international organizations. In the period during and immediately after World War II, this meant first and foremost U.S. leadership. It still does, although now with a much greater sharing of costs and decision making with new power centers in Europe, Asia, and the developing world.

The historic point of reference for someone like myself is the era of Presidents Franklin D. Roosevelt and Harry S. Truman, when my generation came of age politically, and when this country led in the creation of a network of international organizations to promote collective security, economic welfare, and human rights. These organizations include, to mention only the most important, the United Nations (UN), the North Atlantic Treaty Organization (NATO), the Organization of American States (OAS), the World Bank, the International Monetary Fund (IMF), and the General Agreement on Tariffs and Trade (GATT). These organizations will be even more important in the future than they were in the past and will need to be supplemented by at

351

least one new organization—a pan-European institution built on the foundations of the Conference on Security and Cooperation in Europe (CSCE) that monitors progress under the Helsinki accords.

To someone of a centrist foreign policy persuasion, such as this writer, liberal internationalism always has been based on realism as well as idealism, on balance of power politics as well as world order politics. President Roosevelt had first to lead the United Nations to victory in the war against the Axis powers before he could found a global peace organization of the same name. President Truman found it necessary to create a NATO to contain Communist aggression even as he launched the Marshall Plan and the Point Four Program.

The L Word Myth

Contrary to what is often asserted by its critics, liberal internationalism has never meant utopian universalism. The early postwar presidents were willing to act regionally or unilaterally when global action was impractical. However, when acting outside the UN, they generally sought to act "inside the Charter," in Senator Arthur Vandenberg's felicitous phrase—that is, in conformity with Charter standards for regional action or individual and collective self-defense. Nor has liberal internationalism ever meant, as some have argued, an open-ended commitment to contain communism or fight for human rights in every part of the world, regardless of risks, and no such commitment was intended by the often-quoted "pay any price, bear any burden" rhetoric of the inaugural address of President John F. Kennedy. To make a commitment to the "survival and success of freedom" in the world, as Kennedy did, does not require mindless intervention everywhere. On the contrary, it requires the prudent and selective exercise of military and economic power where the benefits outweigh the costs. The Vietnam disaster was not the result of liberal ideology, but of a profound failure of judgment about Vietnamese realities and the futility, as Paul Nitze put it, of "trying to prop up a corpse."

The enemies of liberal internationalism have been those on the right who understand only balance of power politics and those on the left who understand only world order politics, when in fact both have been needed in the last 50 years in order to safeguard U.S. interests and defend freedom in the world. This will continue to be true in future years, even if, as this essay suggests will be the case, security threats from the Third World will take precedence over the threat from the Soviet Union. Still, it will be the world order side of liberal internationalism that will be required increasingly as the United States confronts the challenges and opportunities of the years ahead.

Let us be clear at the outset that a commitment to multilateralism should not be an excuse for isolationism or an abdication of U.S. responsibility. Where multilateral solutions cannot be found, other options must be considered. This is already done in trade policy, where the United States makes some agreements with all GATT members, some agreements with those members willing to undertake a higher level of obligation in new GATT codes, still other agreements in the form of free trade agreements with countries like Canada and Israel and, very exceptionally, where it uses the threat or application of unilateral trade restrictions to counter unfair trade practices, as under the "Super 301" authority of the 1988 Trade Act.

In the area of security, UN peacekeeping operations often will serve U.S. interests, but, for the foreseeable future, the United States will have to reserve the option of acting outside the UN together with its allies or even alone where UN action is impractical and freedom and security are at stake. Thus, the sending of U.S. and allied warships to the Persian Gulf was a justifiable action, as was the bombing of Tripoli in response to Libyan terrorism. When acting outside the UN, as noted earlier, the United States also should try to act "inside the Charter," conforming its behavior to internationally accepted principles interpreted in a way that the United States would be prepared to live with in future circumstances. The national foreign policy debate of the United States should not focus on the choice between balance of power politics and world order politics, but rather on how the two can be reconciled and harmonized in the complex circumstances that face policymakers in the real world.

How far the United States has strayed from this kind of discussion can be seen from the debates over two recent publishing events that have agitated the foreign policy community. Consider first Francis Fukuyama's article, "The End of History" and the debate it stimulated in the *National Interest*. Fukuyama began his article by equating the collapse of communism with "the universalization of Western liberal democracy as the final form of human government"—an outcome devoutly to be wished but hardly to be taken for granted in a world where repressive and authoritarian non-Communist regimes still hold sway over a large proportion of mankind. He claimed that the end of the ideological struggle between capitalism and communism would mean the "end of history" and usher in "a very sad time." The Cold War, he wrote with some nostalgia, had called forth "daring, courage, imagination and idealism." Now, with the death of communism, the United States faces only "centuries of boredom."[1]

That a senior official responsible for policy planning in the State Department could consider boring the prospect of a world of proliferating high tech weapons, smouldering ethnic and national conflicts, and population and environmental trends that call into question humanity's very capacity to survive on this planet, is, to say the least, disquieting. No less disquieting is the fact that neither Fukuyama nor any of the distinguished persons who commented on his article in the *National Interest* considered that the same "daring, courage, imagination, and idealism" that went into the Cold War might be needed in equal measure for the building of an effective system of international cooperation to keep the peace, defend freedom, and assure human survival in the post-Cold War era.

Another example of how far the intellectual climate has strayed from the postwar traditions of liberal internationalism may be found in the debate over Paul Kennedy's *The Rise and Fall of the Great Powers*.[2] Kennedy brilliantly described how dominant powers, such as Spain in the sixteenth century, France in the eighteenth century, and Great Britain in the nineteenth century, all lost preeminence because their political and military commitments outran their technological and economic capacities. The book can be read as a useful warning that the United States must not continue to neglect, as it clearly has in recent years, the technological and economic foundations of its national strength. Unfortunately, much of the debate on the book has centered on the sup-

353

posed inevitability of the decline of the United States as a result of so-called imperial overstretch and on the question of which power—Japan, a unifying Europe, or whoever—might now replace the United States as global number one.

As Joseph Nye has pointed out, however, the prospect that the United States faces in the real world is one of power diffusion rather than hegemonic transition.[3] The United States has the resources to play a world role and at the same time deal with its domestic problems. Moreover, there is no challenger around to supplant it as a world power when one looks at military, economic, and cultural factors in combination. Yet, the United States obviously will not be the hegemonic power in the twenty-first century that it was for much of the twentieth century. Therefore, the answer to the question of "who will be in charge of the twenty-first century" will be, as Harlan Cleveland once put it, that "nobody will be in charge." It is precisely because the United States faces a world in which nobody is in charge that it needs better international institutions for shared decision making and shared responsibility.

A New Soviet Union, A New Europe

How would a foreign policy guided by liberal internationalism respond to the opportunities and challenges that this country faces in the 1990s? Let us begin with relations with the new Soviet Union and the new Europe.

Mikhail Gorbachev's radical changes in the domestic political and economic order of the Soviet Union, if they can be carried through successfully, will make that country (or what is left of it after the possible secession of the Baltic states and other republics) a better place for the Russian people to live in and a less threatening and more cooperative country for free nations to work with. Perhaps less well understood are all the implications of his new thinking *(novoe myshlenie)* in the field of foreign affairs. He has set aside the Marxist–Leninist doctrine of international class warfare and replaced it with the Western and even bourgeois concept of the promotion of common interests and common human values. He has committed his country to respect the principle of free choice of political systems and nonintervention in the internal affairs of other countries. His willingness to stand aside and permit the collapse of Communist regimes in Eastern Europe should convince even the most skeptical that these expressions of new thinking are not just propaganda to lull gullible people in the West.

There is equal reason to take Gorbachev and his senior officials seriously when they call for the strengthening of the UN, the subordination of foreign policies to the international rule of law, and the entry of the Soviet Union into world economic organizations. Listening to Soviet speeches at the last two UN General Assemblies, in the words of one U.S. observer, has been like "hearing Adlai Stevenson in Russian translation." Does this mean that the concept of a cooperative world order launched by Roosevelt and embodied in the UN Charter is now, after 45 years of Soviet aggression and obstructionism, once again a realistic possibility? How should the United States respond?

To begin with, the United States should not lose the careful equilibrium between balance of power politics and world order politics that has brought it this far. Just as the Republican and Democratic Parties both can take credit for the policy of containment and the birth of NATO, so both can take credit for the modernization of the strategic deterrent, the deployment of the Pershing and cruise missiles in Europe, and the successful military aid to the Afghan resistance that forced Soviet withdrawal from Afghanistan. These three policies—courageously supported by both Presidents Jimmy Carter and Ronald Reagan—demonstrated to Gorbachev and the Soviet leadership that the West would resist Soviet aggression and intimidation and that the Soviet economy could not match Western military efforts.

As the United States fashions its policy toward the new Europe, the balance of power element in liberal internationalism will be needed in the future as it has in the past. Despite the demise of the Warsaw Pact, NATO and the presence of U.S. air, sea, and ground forces in Europe will be needed for the foreseeable future for at least three reasons. The first reason is to provide an insurance policy against a return of the Soviet Union to aggressive policies, a perhaps remote but still conceivable contingency if Gorbachev were succeeded by an orthodox Communist or a Russian nationalist-chauvinist. The second reason is to keep the formidable military potential of a united Germany locked into NATO's integrated military structure. The third reason is to provide a military capability against security threats to the NATO nations and their Middle East allies from countries such as Libya, Syria, Iraq, and Iran. The administration of George Bush has been right to emphasize the continued importance of NATO's military as well as political role, but it will have a formidable job of education to perform on this point with both U.S. and European public opinion in the months ahead.

If balance of power politics still will be necessary, it is in the new possibilities for world order politics that liberal internationalism finally can come into its own. Both the Soviet Union and the United States now perceive a common interest in working through the UN to avert or contain conflicts in the Third World that might otherwise provide occasions for their competitive intervention. A recent report by an unofficial group cochaired by Vladimir Shustov, director of the Research Coordination Center of the Soviet Foreign Ministry, and this author confirmed that there is now an unprecedented degree of consensus between our two countries on the need to strengthen the secretary general's role in preventive diplomacy and enhance the effectiveness of UN peacekeeping operations.[4] This broad measure of agreement in a private dialogue has been reflected in the UN, where the two countries worked together through the Security Council to end the Iran–Iraq War, to authorize the UN–OAS monitoring of Nicaragua's elections and the patrolling of Central American borders, and, perhaps most impressive, to make possible the successful transition of Namibia to nationhood through free elections. Looking ahead, it is clear that both countries are prepared to support an ambitious UN role in Cambodia and Western Sahara, once the parties to those conflicts are ready to compose their differences.

The potential for U.S.–Soviet collaboration on world order issues goes well beyond peacekeeping and peacemaking. The bilateral dialogue now includes regular discussion of transnational issues, such as drugs, terrorism, and the environment, and the common ground thus identified is reflected in Soviet–U.S. cooperation on these issues at the UN. It is increasingly clear that the main obstacles now to effective UN action are not differences between the United States and the Soviet Union, but between developed and developing countries.

This is not to say that there is a complete identity of views between the United States and the Soviet Union; of course not. The differences, however, are no longer ideological. Rather, they are based on different perceptions of national interest defined in pragmatic terms, in the same way that the United States often differs in the UN from allies such as France or Japan. What is particularly striking is the new Soviet emphasis on seeking consensus in UN bodies, particularly with the United States. It has abandoned its former policy of supporting the most extreme anti-Western resolutions sponsored by radical Third World regimes. There is no doubt that these beneficial changes are due to Gorbachev's personal leadership, but it is also true that the Soviet Foreign Ministry has played a critical role in the way it has implemented the new thinking and provided fresh ideas to give it content. For this, Foreign Minister Eduard Shevardnadze, Deputy Foreign Minister Vladimir Petrovsky, Deputy Legal Adviser Sergei Ordzhonikidze, and International Organizations Department head Andrei Kozyrev deserve much credit, as does the Soviet Union's able UN Ambassador Alexander Belonogov.

There are several factors in Soviet policy, however, that should dictate caution in assessing the prospects for future Soviet–U.S. collaboration on a world order agenda. To begin with, the Soviet approach to world order politics is much too UN-centered. Soviet rhetoric about the UN playing the central role in international politics is clearly unrealistic; the bulk of security and economic issues of importance must continue to be dealt with outside the world organization. Then again, as Soviet leaders will admit in private, their country only recently has moved from seeing the UN as a place for polemics to a place where serious business can be done; it is short of people with knowledge and experience in the way that UN political and economic programs actually function and it has had little to contribute thus far on the details of UN budget and administrative reform. Moreover, its financial contributions to UN voluntary programs, such as the United Nations Development Program (UNDP) and United Nations Children's Fund (UNICEF), are exceedingly modest. Finally, the political and public opinion basis for Gorbachev's and the Foreign Ministry's policies is fragile. One easily can imagine different UN policies coming from a future Soviet leader who was a chauvinistic Russian nationalist or a traditional Communist. Even with a Gorbachev, a Supreme Soviet with real powers over foreign affairs and budget might prove as skeptical toward spending money for international organizations as the U.S. Congress. Given its economic problems and its shortage of hard currency, moreover, the Soviet capacity to match its enthusiasm for greater UN activity with proportionately greater contributions will be limited severely for the next few years.

With all these qualifications, however, the new Soviet approach to world order issues should be encouraged by a positive response from the United States. U.S. policy toward the UN and other international agencies, as will be suggested later, is sometimes shortsighted and is handicapped by failure to meet its financial obligations. The U.S. must take a more positive approach to multilateral cooperation, and not just in the areas of UN peacekeeping and peacemaking or in the transnational agenda of drugs, terrorism, and the human environment. There are at least four other promising areas which Gorbachev's new policy has opened up.

Human Rights. The first is human rights. One of the most striking contributions of liberal internationalism was to make human rights a central concern of the UN, along with collective security and economic cooperation. There was thus established the revolutionary concept that how a nation treats its own citizens is no longer its own business alone, but also the business of the international community. Under Eleanor Roosevelt's leadership, the UN adopted the *Universal Declaration of Human Rights*, which stands to this day as the most comprehensive and widely recognized standard by which the human rights record of governments is judged. Despite initial opposition from conservatives in the United States, there is now a broad bipartisan consensus that human rights should be part of the U.S. foreign policy agenda and that this country's concern with human rights should apply to both right and left wing dictatorial regimes. Building on UN standards and benefiting from U.S. leadership, the CSCE process following up the Helsinki Final Act has been increasingly effective in monitoring human rights practices and it undoubtedly contributed to the dramatic transition of the East European countries to democracy.

Until the arrival of Gorbachev, the Soviet Union was in hard-line opposition on human rights issues, insisting that international discussion of its domestic human rights practices constituted illegal intervention in its internal affairs. Now the Soviet leadership is supporting international oversight of domestic human rights practices, suggesting that Gorbachev possibly may see in strengthened UN and CSCE human rights processes a way of reinforcing the reforms he is undertaking in his own country. Certainly it was striking to see the Soviet Minister of Justice Venyamin Yakovlev in Geneva in the fall of 1989 responding constructively to probing questions from the experts on the UN Human Rights Committee regarding the consistency of Soviet laws and practices with the UN *Covenant on Political and Civil Rights*.

There are a number of ways that the United States can seize the opportunity presented by the new Soviet human rights policy. The United States can work with the Soviet Union and the new democracies of Eastern Europe to make the UN human rights bodies more objective in examining human rights violations in every part of the world. The United States can encourage the work of the special UN rapporteurs investigating individual countries and those looking at specific problems such as torture, religious intolerance, and summary or arbitrary executions. The United States can mobilize the full resources of its government and private sector to make a success of the Human Rights Conference that will be held in Moscow in 1991 as part of the CSCE process. The United States can encourage private U.S. organizations to work with counterpart groups in Western Europe in providing assistance to the Soviet Union and East European governments in their efforts to promote democracy and the rule of law. Finally, the United States, at long last, could ratify the UN *Covenant on Civil and Political Rights*, thus enabling this country to participate in the Human Rights Committee's periodic reviews of compliance by the Soviets, East Europeans, and others of their obligations under that Instrument.

International Law. Another historic component of liberal internationalism has been its emphasis on the development of international law and on international adjudication and arbitration as a means of resolving international disputes. Here again, a changed Soviet approach is opening up new opportunities. For years, the Soviet Union insisted on contrasting Communist and Western approaches to international law and opposing the compulsory jurisdiction of the International Court of Justice (World Court). Now Soviet leaders are emphasizing that the foreign policies of nations should be subordinated to a common international rule of law. Moreover, they are asserting their willingness to accept the compulsory jurisdiction of the World Court in certain circumstances.

This new Soviet interest in international law and the World Court comes at an awkward time for the United States. In recent years, the executive branch and the Congress have been less than consistent, to say the least, in their commitment to international law. The unilateral reinterpretation by the United States of the Anti-ballistic Missile Treaty (ABM), the U.S. failure to pay legally binding UN assessments, the U.S. mining of Nicaragua's harbors, and the U.S. termination of its acceptance of the World Court's compulsory jurisdiction are just a few of the examples that could be cited. Yet, the observance and further development of international law is in the national interest of the United States, a democratic nation that believes in the rule of law at home, and a status quo power that seeks stability and order abroad. Those Americans who say that there is no such thing as international law really are asserting a profoundly un-American idea—that the United States should not honor its international commitments. The turnaround in Soviet attitudes could be the occasion to reexamine some current U.S. attitudes.

Moreover, the United States could initiate an intensive dialogue between officials and scholars in the Soviet Union and the United States on the content of international law in key areas, including controversial ones like the use of armed force. It is in the respective national interest of the two countries to provide clear limits on the use of armed force by both large and small nations, while at the same time permitting nations to resort to force for individual and collective self-defense and in other exceptional circumstances, as in defense of their citizens overseas. A dialogue on international law may not lead to full or early agreement, but it could narrow differences and enhance mutual understanding. Of course, the United States should also begin such discussions with its allies in Europe and Asia, to try to bring order out of the present disarray between the industrialized democracies on the use of force and other sensitive international law questions.

On the question of the International Court of Justice, the United States and the Soviet Union have begun official discussions on a common acceptance of a limited form of compulsory jurisdiction. It is not realistic to expect the two countries to accept such jurisdiction in controversies arising out of the use of armed force, where national security interests are too great, the facts often difficult to establish, and the international rules still insufficiently developed, especially where civil wars are concerned. Still, the two countries could accept the jurisdiction of the

Court for the interpretation of specific treaties to which they are parties, and perhaps also in certain carefully defined areas of international law, such as foreign investment or the law of the sea. To enhance their confidence in the Court, they could provide that cases between them would be decided by chambers of the Court, panels of 5 of the 15 judges selected by the Court after consultation with the parties. Once a Soviet–U.S. agreement is reached on a form of compulsory jurisdiction, it could be put to other UN members for consideration.

The Economy. Gorbachev's letter to the Paris economic summit of 1989 announced a new Soviet interest in participating in the management of the world economy. It is clear that the Soviet leadership sees advantages in ending the country's historic policy of autarky and in participating in the international division of labor and the transnational flow of investment, technology, and management skills. If the Soviet Union really moves toward a market economy and shifts resources from military production to consumption goods, it is in the Western interest to help reinforce these trends, not only through bilateral measures, such as trade agreements and joint ventures, but through enhanced multilateral cooperation. Observer status in GATT, the World Bank, and the IMF would be a good way to start. Full membership could be granted after a transitional period based on the achievement of specific reforms in the Soviet economy such as market pricing, enterprise autonomy, and ruble convertibility. During the transition period, teams from these international economic organizations could provide guidance and training to help the Soviet Union in its difficult transition from a command economy to a market economy. Membership in GATT, IMF, and the World Bank, however, should not give the Soviets a free ride. They should pay their full dues as a developed country by opening their market to Third World products and providing their fair share of multilateral development aid to poor nations in Asia, Africa, and Latin America.

Arms Control. The spread of advanced weaponry in the Third World represents a growing security problem and another priority for cooperation between the United States and the Soviet Union. There are now five acknowledged nuclear weapons countries: the United States, the Soviet Union, the United Kingdom, France, and China. Four other countries, India, Pakistan, Israel, and South Africa, are believed to have nuclear weapons capabilities. Iran, Iraq, Libya, and North Korea are seeking to acquire nuclear weapons. By the year 2000, there will be 40,000–50,000 kilograms of separated plutonium in international commerce as a result of peaceful nuclear activities, a target for theft by terrorists and radical governments. Many of the Third World countries that are now nuclear capable or that are seeking nuclear weapons are also busy developing medium-range and long-range missiles. There are 9 countries that have both missiles and chemical weapons, and that number could be as high as 15 or 20 by the year 2000.

Among the most important near-term goals for East–West cooperation should be the strengthening of the nonproliferation regime for nuclear weapons, the conclusion of a treaty banning chemical weapons, and a common missile control regime. With a world in prospect in which unstable Third World governments will be armed with long-range weapons of great destructiveness, U.S.–Soviet leadership in this kind of global cooperation is not utopian, it is *realpolitik*.

Eastern Europe. A final word in this review of East–West relations is needed on some implications for international cooperation of the emergence of independent democracies in Eastern Europe. First, UN work in peacekeeping, economic cooperation, and human rights will feel the benefit of the transformation of East European countries from satellites of the Soviet Union to truly independent actors. Second, the new European Bank for Reconstruction and Development should be supported as a vehicle to assist the transition of the East European countries to market economies. Third, the United States should begin negotiations on transforming the CSCE process into a permanent Organization for Security and Cooperation in Europe (OSCE), with a strong secretariat and four high-level councils to deal with political, economic, environmental, and human rights issues. The new OSCE could be headquartered in Berlin, if that city becomes the capital of a unified Germany. In addition to providing a more effective vehicle for pan-European cooperation, OSCE would give the new democracies of Eastern Europe a needed place for cooperation with one another and the rest of Europe, would provide an additional framework for reassurance about a unified Germany, and would reconfirm the presence of the United States as a European power. In supporting an OSCE, the United States should make very clear that it regards the proposed new organization as a supplement to NATO and the European Community, not as a substitute for them or as a means of diminishing their responsibilities.

Multilateralism and North–South Issues

If changes in East–West relations are providing new challenges and opportunities for liberal internationalism, the same is no less true of the trends in North–South relations. For most countries of Latin America and Africa, the decade of the 1980s was one of stagnant or even declining living standards. Now, as they enter the 1990s, the developing nations in these continents and the poor countries of Asia are rightly concerned that as large Western resources are mobilized for German reunification and aid to Eastern Europe there will be diminished attention to their own needs. Such a result would be particularly unfortunate at a time when many of these countries are moving away from the statist ideology, the poor economic management, and the widespread corruption that have been at the root of their failures in development. Although the principal responsibility for economic development will continue to rest with the developing countries themselves, the present $50 billion annual negative resource transfer from these countries to the developed world will have to be reversed if growth in the Third World is to be revived.

The idea of international assistance to help the less developed countries develop their human and material resources was launched in the Roosevelt and Truman period and accepted by all subsequent administrations, whether Republican or Democratic. This element of liberal internationalism, however, although accepted in principle, has received declining real financial support in recent years, except where immediate security interests have been predominant. Neither humanitarian considerations nor the clear economic interest of the United

States in Third World development have been sufficient to reverse the trend. Nevertheless, in the years ahead, liberal internationalism will find two new and powerful rationales for helping the developing countries: the threat of irreversible harm to the global environment and the peril of uncontrolled population growth coupled with massive South–North migration.

The people of the United States, like the citizens of other countries, are beginning to be concerned about global greenhouse warming, caused mainly by the burning of fossil fuels and tropical deforestation, phenomena that could cause catastrophic changes in the world's climate and sea level as early as the middle of the next century. They are also learning about the threat that the use of chlorofluorocarbons poses to the ozone layer, the global atmospheric shield against the ultraviolet radiation that causes cancer and other damage to life on earth. What has been less well understood is that these perils cannot be averted without the cooperation of developing as well as developed countries, and that for the Third World to take the necessary measures of self-restraint will require a huge amount of assistance in technology transfer, the training of people, and financial support. India may phase out the use of chlorofluorocarbons, China may moderate its burning of coal, Brazil may stop the destruction of its Amazon rainforest, but only at a price. That price will be new forms of multilateral assistance. Without it, Third World countries will have neither the economic means nor the political will to take their share of environmental responsibility. The United States and other developed countries would thus end up as environmental hostages to the Third World, as desperation born of poverty in poor countries accelerates the assault already underway on the world's fragile life support system.

Population growth could provide the second stimulus for a new interest in North–South economic cooperation. World population, which stood at only 1.5 billion at the beginning of this century and is 5 billion today, is predicted by the UN to reach 6.2 billion in the year 2000 and 8.5 billion in 2025. The world population will level off at 9 to 14 billion some time in the next century. Whether this planet's population stabilizes at the low or high end of that range will fundamentally determine the prospects for economic welfare and security, not only of developing countries, but of developed countries, including the United States. To understand the gravity of population trends, it is necessary only to consider that between now and the year 2025 Mexico is expected to grow from 85 to 150 million, Brazil from 144 to 246 million, Egypt from 51 to 94 million, Ethiopia from 45 to 112 million, Nigeria from 105 to 301 million, Bangladesh from 110 to 235 million, and India from 819 to 1,445 million. No government, no academic expert, has the faintest idea of how to provide adequate food, housing, health care, education, and gainful employment to such exploding numbers of people, particularly as they crowd into megacities such as Mexico City, Calcutta, and Cairo.

With such an explosive growth in numbers, there will be little hope of saving the rainforests, the topsoil, or the climate balance so essential to human life. Our descendants will witness human misery, political upheaval, and violence born of human desperation on a scale that one can scarcely imagine. They will also witness mass migrations from South to North on an unparalleled scale—a human tidal wave that is unlikely to be stopped by immigration laws and physical barriers. The rate of illegal immigration already being experienced in the United States and Europe is but a small augury of things to come.

There is no easy answer to the world population problem, but it surely has to begin with an international effort to make information and means of family planning available to all persons in the child-bearing years. Achieving this goal will require a substantial increase in the resources now devoted to family planning in developing countries. It will also require strengthened programs of health care and education and measures to enhance the rights of women in society. None of this is likely to happen without action through the UN system, and without leadership from the United States.

Although recent years have seen a growing understanding of the need for "sustainable development," there is still little appreciation of the magnitude of the investment sums that will have to be mobilized within the developing countries and from international aid in order to make this concept a reality in the Third World. A recent study by the former secretary general of the World Commission on Environment and Development, based on work done by the World Bank and the Worldwatch Institute, came up with some awesome figures for average annual financial requirements between 1990 and 2000: $19.3 billion for soil conservation, $5.3 billion for reafforestation, $27 billion for population control, $30 billion for enhancing energy efficiency, $15.6 billion for renewable forms of energy, plus $27.3 billion for reducing Third World indebtedness. This adds up to an average annual total of $124.6 billion or a total for the decade of $1,371 billion.[5] Even if these estimates are two, three, or even four times too high, they suggest that there is a large gap between the rhetoric of environmental protection in both developing and developed countries and the willingness of these countries to pay the price for it.

West–West Relations

Perhaps the greatest challenge to liberal internationalism will be in facing up to the economic and political adjustments needed in West–West relations. So much has been written about these issues that they need only be enumerated here: how to bring the Uruguay Round of trade negotiations to a successful conclusion, how to complete Europe's 1992 agenda in a manner that respects the interests of outsiders, how to strengthen the international monetary system, and how to achieve a fairer burden-sharing between the industrialized democracies on military and aid expenditures. All of these tasks will require greater progress in multilateral cooperation than has ever been witnessed before.

The most urgent requirement of all for the future of liberal internationalism is to get on with the reduction of the presently unsustainable West–West imbalances. In the last eight years, the United States has run cumulative current account deficits with the rest of the world of over $800 billion, transforming its position from that of a more than $100 billion net creditor to that of a more than $700 billion net debtor. Although the current account position of the United States has improved somewhat recently, the U.S. external deficit in 1990 will remain in excess of $100 billion and could start growing again as U.S. oil imports and the price of oil both rise. Meanwhile, the external surpluses of Germany and Japan are running at about $60 billion per year, with little diminution in prospect.

Unless corrected in the next few years, these large imbalances could one day trigger a financial crisis and a severe world recession. Even if such a dramatic outcome is avoided, the continuation of large U.S. deficits is likely to fuel U.S. protectionism, sour the U.S. foreign policy mood, and make it impossible for the United States to dedicate sufficient resources to the challenges and opportunities in East–West and North–South relations described earlier.

The measures needed to correct these imbalances are easy to recite and less easy to implement. From Japan, the need is for much greater efforts to open its domestic market, to increase its untied development aid, and to stimulate domestic demand. From Germany, the need is for similar actions and assurances that the understandable concentration on the economic tasks of German reunification does not come at the expense of Germany's global responsibilities. From the United States, serious action must be forthcoming in order to increase competitiveness and to reduce the U.S. budget deficit, which is still running at around $150 billion. That budget deficit would be in excess of $200 billion if the U.S. government did not employ the social security surplus for current spending, and if it included all the costs of the Savings and Loan bailout. The United States continues to pretend, through unrealistic forecasts and accounting gimmicks, that it is meeting the Gramm–Rudman–Hollings targets for deficit reduction but the truth is that without bold action the deficit will remain in the $100–150 billion range in the years ahead, and could increase substantially with a major recession.

The Gramm–Rudman–Hollings process has not actually reduced the deficit, but in combination with anti-internationalist political currents it has played havoc with the expenditures needed to sustain the international leadership of the United States. The U.S. overseas diplomatic establishment, educational exchanges, and bilateral development aid all have been savaged by harmful reductions. The United States is in arrears by $700 million in its contributions to the UN and its specialized agencies, which damages valuable UN operations in peacekeeping, development, human rights, and environmental protection and diminishes U.S. influence. The United States also lags behind in its payments to multilateral financial institutions, such as the World Bank, the International Finance Corporation, and the Asian Development Fund. As long as the U.S. budget deficit is not dealt with seriously, the United States is unlikely to face up to these financial obligations of world leadership, much less assume new ones. Urgent U.S. domestic needs also will go inadequately funded. From the problems of drugs, the homeless, education, and crumbling U.S. infrastructure, on the one side, to the problems of Central America, Eastern Europe, Third World development, and global warming on the other, the United States will be facing its responsibilities with empty pockets.

Although it has become commonplace to say it, it remains true that the problem of the United States is not a shortage of economic resources, but a shortage of political will. To reduce substantially the U.S. budget deficit and to support presently underfunded domestic and international programs of top priority would require $100 billion per year in the short run and $200 billion per year in the long run, which represents 2 percent and 4 percent respectively of the $5 trillion U.S. national income. If progress in U.S.–Soviet relations continues, the United States can fund much of this through cuts in the defense budget. Still, this country will also have to bite the bullet of finding additional revenue. The slogan of "no new taxes" is simply not compatible with the requirements of U.S. world leadership. The sooner the United States faces up to this reality, the better.

A Liberal Internationalist Future?

There are three provocative questions about the future of liberal internationalism that deserve attention before concluding this essay. Unfortunately, each requires more discussion than space allows, but they can at least be identified and some answers may be sketched.

First Question: Can multilateral diplomacy and multilateral institutions deal with the world order agenda in a manner that is acceptable to the United States? It is in the nature of any large organization that no single member can have its way all of the time. Reliance on international organizations does involve risks. It may lead to decisions to act over U.S. opposition, or the failure to act when the United States is prepared to do so. The deficiencies of the UN and many of its agencies are well known: uneven administration in the secretariats, inadequate influence for the major contributors over budgets and programs, poor coordination of sectoral activities, and often a paralyzing lack of political consensus. The situation is better in the international financial institutions, where weighted voting applies, and in the central trade forum known as GATT. Even in these institutions, however, the United States cannot have its way all of the time. The United States must balance the disadvantages of working through international organizations against the disadvantages of acting alone. Multilateral action usually serves the U.S. national interest, enlisting needed support from other countries, sharing economic burdens and political responsibility, and accomplishing tasks that the United States could not achieve as well, or at all, by unilateral action. The United States must, of course, have the common sense to be selective—putting, for example, its main emphasis for peacekeeping on the Security Council, where the United States can exercise the veto, and opposing General Assembly recommendations that work against U.S. interests.

If a policy based on greater use of multilateral institutions is to be credible, the United States will need to devote more high-level effort to making these institutions work more effectively. Multilateralism must not mean the tyranny of the small country majority or the lowest common denominator of recalcitrant members. Multilateralism should mean structured decision-making devices to provide "power steering" on budgets and programs and greater use of "coalitions of the willing" in which like-minded countries act together under a UN umbrella, through programs financed by voluntary contributions. More attention should also be given to finding outstanding persons to lead the international agencies. For example, the United States should start right now to identify first-rate candidates to replace UN Secretary General Javiér Perez de Cuellar when his term expires at the end of 1991.

Second Question: Can liberal internationalism coexist with domestic liberalism? To put it another way, is the ambitious multilateral agenda outlined in this essay sufficiently compelling to obtain the needed commitment of U.S. leadership and resources in the face of equally compelling domestic priorities? I believe the answer can be yes, but the case for a greater commitment of U.S. resources to international affairs has yet to be made effectively to the U.S. electorate, to the Congress, or even to the U.S. foreign policy establishment.

A little over 20 years ago, in 1969, UN Secretary General U Thant warned that mankind had

> perhaps 10 years left . . . to launch a global partnership to curb the arms race, to improve the human environment, to defuse the population explosion, and to supply the required momentum to world development efforts. If such a global partnership is not forged within the next decade, then I very much fear that the problems . . . will reach such staggering proportions that they will be beyond our capacity to control.[6]

I confess to having written those words for U Thant in 1969, and to having unduly foreshortened the timetable for remedial action in an effort to dramatize the issues. But looking in 1990 at those same problems—weapons proliferation, population, the environment, and the growth in the numbers of the world's desperate poor—it may no longer be an exaggeration to say that the next 10 years will be decisive. If the international community does not take effective action on these problems in the 1990s, what kind of world will today's children face in the next century? If a president were willing to put the question in this way to the people of the United States—governing as if the future mattered—liberal internationalism would have a chance of success in the face of the competing claims of domestic liberalism.

Third Question: Will the Democratic Party or the Republican Party be the best protagonist of liberal internationalism in the crucial decade that lies ahead? The answer is far from clear.

President Bush might not relish the designation, but he may wind up as one of the most liberal internationalist presidents of recent years. He has brought the United States back to the moderate Republicanism of the era of Gerald Ford. His broad experience in foreign affairs, including his brief service as U.N. ambassador, has given him a realistic appreciation of the international problems facing the country and the value of working through global organizations as well as through our alliances. Although he attacked Michael Dukakis for an excessive devotion to multilateralism during the 1988 presidential campaign and called the UN "an unreal place . . . torn by tensions," one of his first acts after inauguration was to invite Secretary General Perez de Cuellar to Washington for a private working dinner. He has pledged that his administration "will do its best to strengthen the UN and to reassert positive leadership there."[7] He has appointed as UN Ambassador one of the State Department's finest career diplomats, Thomas Pickering. He already has exercised strong leadership in NATO on East–West issues, particularly in the conventional arms negotiations. He has demonstrated a firm commitment to the multilateral trade and financial institutions and is pledged to multilateral action on the global environment.

It is too early to make an assessment

of the Bush presidency in foreign affairs, but from a liberal internationalist perspective there are at least two important areas that cause concern. One is the world population issue where, in deference to the "right to life" movement, the president is carrying forward the Reagan administration cutoff of aid to the UN Fund for Population Activities and to the International Planned Parenthood Federation. If the U.S. government is serious on world environment and development, it has to face up to the population question. The second area, as already suggested, is fiscal policy. The Bush administration's failure to deal realistically with the budget deficit and the need for new taxes is opening up a large gap between its proclaimed objectives and the means available for achieving them. This is as painfully obvious in international affairs as it is in domestic policy.

What of the Democrats? Many leaders of the Party still carry forward the Roosevelt–Truman legacy of liberal internationalism, but the longer the Party is locked out of the White House the harder it will be to exercise the leadership that does justice to that legacy. Congress is dominated increasingly by constituency politics, and it is difficult to reconcile constituency politics with U.S. leadership in a rule-based international system of cooperation. The temptation toward unilateralism and shortsighted nationalism is particularly evident in the negative attitudes of some congressional Democrats on trade policy and on appropriations for the State Department and the multilateral financial institutions. At the same time, some senators, such as Bill Bradley and Albert Gore, have been charting new and constructive directions on the global environment, Third World debt, and East–West relations.

This article closes as it began, with the "*L* word." If the Democrats refuse to give in to shortsighted constituency pressures, if they are not afraid to be known as liberals in foreign policy, and if they define their liberalism in a realistic way to encompass both world order politics and balance of power politics, then they may earn the chance to recapture the White House and once again direct the country's foreign policy. If they fail to do these things, it will be the Republican Party, exercising the powers of the executive in response to the new imperatives of interdependence, that will be the standard bearer of the liberal internationalist tradition of Roosevelt and Truman as the United States moves toward the twenty-first century. Still, the question of which political party carries forward the tradition of liberal internationalism is less important than the categorical imperative that one of them must do it. The successful pursuit of all U.S. foreign policy concerns—in security, economics, environment, and human rights—hangs in the balance.

Notes

1. Francis Fukuyama, "The End of History?" *National Interest* 16 (Summer 1989), pp. 4 and 18.

2. Paul Kennedy, *The Rise and Fall of the Great Powers* (New York: Random House, 1987).

3. Joseph Nye, *Bound to Lead: The Changing Nature of American Power* (New York: Basic Books, 1990).

4. Joint Statement issued by the United Nations Associations of the U.S. and Soviet Union on "The U.N.'s Role in Enhancing Peace and Security," Moscow, April 1989.

5. James MacNeill, "Strategies for Sustainable Economic Development," *Scientific American*, September 1989.

6. Statement to the Seminar on the Second UN Development Decade, May 9, 1969, reprinted in *Journal* of the Institute on Man and Science, No. 1, 1970.

7. Letter to United Nations Association Chairman John C. Whitehead, June 8, 1989.